THE GIRL WITH THE DUCK TATTOO

THE GIRL WITH THE DUCK TATTOO

A MEMOIR

SARMA MELNGAILIS

COPYRIGHT © 2025 SALAMANDER 72 LLC
All rights reserved.

THE GIRL WITH THE DUCK TATTOO
A Memoir

FIRST EDITION, REVISED 2026

ISBN   978-1-5445-4898-2 *Paperback*
       978-1-5445-4897-5 *Ebook*

Cover photographs © SALAMANDER 72 LLC.
Front cover photo by Jon Knautz, back cover photo by Chris Dempsey.

For Leon

CONTENTS

INTRODUCTION 13

PART ONE: BACK IN THE REAL WORLD 27

PART TWO: THE ASCENT 129

PART THREE: THE EVIDENCE 239

PART FOUR: MR. FOX 263

PART FIVE: THE DESCENT 449

PART SIX: LEAVING THE REAL WORLD 601

Photographs related to this memoir, arranged by chapter, can be found at **thegirlwiththeducktattoo.com**.

"I can think of no right more fundamental than the right to peacefully steward the contents of one's own consciousness."
—SAM HARRIS, *WAKING UP*

INTRODUCTION

I

Everything I'm writing is true. My recollection of some details might be imprecise—floating memories I can't quite place in a timeline, and stretches of time I can barely recall—but the basic facts of the story are correct and, for the most part, verifiable. Where I don't have exact wording, dialogue is recreated to convey the essence of what was said. In many cases, I do have the exact words—drawn from Gchats, text messages, emails, and my own journals. My intention is to portray others accurately and fairly. In some cases, I've changed names to protect people's privacy.

11

There are people who, if you let them into your life, are capable of targeted and elaborately thought-out cruelty—the kind we'd like to think happens only in psychological horror films. These people are real, and they are out there in droves. They will study you, figure out your worst-case scenario, and turn it into a plan for a nightmare specifically tailored to you. They will then go to great lengths to make this nightmare your reality.

In the end, it will often appear to have been your fault. The wreckage will be yours alone to repair, while they slip away to find their next target.

III

MAY 2016

PIGEON FORGE, TENNESSEE

"Baby, there's going to be one more gut shot. Just one more."

I kept thinking about this—what Mr. Fox had said to me only one day before. *One more gut shot.* Did he know this was going to happen?

I knew he'd meant *gut shot* metaphorically. As in, one more emotionally painful thing to endure. Of all the shit he'd put me through, there was, again, just *one more thing* I'd have to do before it was all over, before the *happily ever after*.

One more gut shot.

Except now, pain was literally shooting through my gut, as I squatted, dry heaving into a stainless steel toilet, under bright lights, in the corner of a gray, windowless room. My audience was a bunch of women—some lying on the floor, others sitting on the concrete bench that lined two of the walls—all looking bored.

Together we were the occupants of a holding cell in a rural county jail in Pigeon Forge, Tennessee—the surreal, carnivalesque, LSD-trippy tourist town at the base of the Smoky Mountains, also known as the home of Dollywood.

IV

The memoirist Mary Karr wrote, "For the more haunted among us, only looking back at the past can permit it to finally become the past."

I've never been in a war zone, seen people killed, or nearly been killed myself. I've never been beaten or tortured. Not physically, at least. But what happened—what this book is about—feels like a disturbing, deranged nightmare that I wish I could forget. Or better yet, undo. Thinking about it is uncomfortable, tormenting, and lonely. But dredging up this darkness seems to be the only way to get it out of me. I want it to *finally become the past.*

Late in 2011, a certain "Mr. Fox" appeared in my life—through my Twitter feed. What began as casual online banter with a stranger ultimately destroyed my life's work: my restaurant Pure Food and Wine and its associated brand One Lucky Duck. Others were hurt in the process. Furthermore, in a uniquely agonizing way, the damage appeared to have been done by my own hand, as if I'd murdered my own baby.

Generally, there's a framework within which people can understand major losses. Death of a loved one, a cancer diagnosis, a house burned to the ground, a disabling accident, a devastating breakup. These misfortunes people can fathom, and sympathy flows freely. There are often corresponding support groups, and someone will know someone—or know someone who knows someone—who has endured a similar loss. Or they've read about it in novels or seen it in films. Most adversity is explainable, and there are labels.

I don't know how to label my story.

There's no quick summary to describe what happened. Or what I *allowed* to happen. Or what I did. Was it something I did? Or something that someone *did to me*? Or something that *happened to me*? I struggle with these distinctions.

Please allow me to tell this story in the messy context of not quite knowing where my responsibility ended and his began. Did he *force* me to do things? Yes. Physically? No. Could I have run away? Yes. Was my brain—in a perplexing way—hijacked? Yes. Do I understand how that happened? Not really. Maybe in some abstract way I can read about the psychology of it and see how this could happen to someone. But to me? No. I can't look back and recall exactly when or how my brain was hijacked, which I guess is the whole point. But something like that happened. Something *truly fucked up* happened that left me broken, humiliated, ashamed, and very much wanting to die.

Instead, I'm writing this book.

I have to at least try to understand *how* it all happened.

I want my story to be useful. I want to help someone avoid walking into a similar mind-bending nightmare. And it *was* avoidable. Huge red flags waved furiously in front of my face from day one—I just didn't see them. By reading this, I hope you—if ever faced with your own Mr. (or Mrs.) Fox—will recognize the red flags and confidently back away from that person before their concealed, creeping malevolence takes root.

If, like me, you missed the warnings, then this story is also for you. Maybe the aftermath was heartache, confusion, and obliteration of your self-esteem. Maybe the damage ran deeper, inflicting painful financial losses, even leaving you broke or in debt. Perhaps people you care about were hurt too. Maybe your whole world was turned upside down, leaving you freaked out and alone, not knowing what to believe, unable to make sense of what happened or how you got there. Maybe, like me, you went through all that—and then *also* ended up locked in jail. I don't mean figuratively, as if trapped in a situation, but an actual jail with bars and barbed wire and surly, intimidating corrections officers. That's where I found myself.

If you have a story that bears even a remote resemblance to mine, then I hope this book makes you feel less alone, less ashamed, and maybe less stupid. That last one was a charge often lobbed at me. People would ask, "How could you have been so *stupid*?!" We shouldn't have to feel stupid, on top of everything else.

To those in my orbit who suffered collateral damage: *I want you to know what happened—all of it.* And there's no way to do that other than a full-length book. I am deeply, profoundly, painfully sorry that so many people were hurt—financially or otherwise—by the implosion of my life, caused by me. Or, *not prevented* by me. From my not having known better.

I'll try to answer questions I've been asked over and over, like: *Why didn't you ask for help? Why didn't you call the police? And... what in the world did you see in that guy?* These aren't easy to answer. Before I started writing—before going back to pore over details, conduct research, analyze, and hypothesize—I had no answers. This book is an exploration to find them. I'm pretty sure there will always be a degree of lingering, frustrating mystery. Some things I may never understand.

In *The Art of Memoir*, Mary Karr explores the motivations of memoirists, including Kathryn Harrison, who recounted the story of her incestuous relationship with her father. "It's through shame and silence that a perpetrator seeks to capture someone else's soul, sentencing her to a lifetime of collusion with him." For Harrison, publishing her book was "a way to reclaim what was left of me." It's hard to explain why and how that makes sense, but it does. I don't want to be silent or feel ashamed anymore. I want my soul back.

Also, I'm writing this story because I'm furious. At whom? I don't know. At Mr. Fox, and all those who seek to manipulate, control, and exploit for personal gratification. To him, and to other predators out there: I want to expose the tactics and weaponry you so cleverly disguise, so you might at least be somewhat disarmed in your quest to take down your next target.

I want this book to be useful. *Please let it be useful.*

* * *

I don't consider my story a tragedy, even if it felt that way. As I remind myself all the time, no one died. *No one died.* At least there's that. The tangible damages suffered—not just by me but others too—are significant, but also, theoretically, recoverable. Realistically, no. Miraculously, maybe.

Over the years that Mr. Fox was in my life—more than five in total—my reasoning detached from my emotions. What began as an intriguing fantasy quickly turned dark. Over time, I grew increasingly terrified and disgusted by him, eventually existing in a constant state of foreboding. And yet, for reasons I didn't understand, I remained oddly *attached* to him—as if only he could protect me. His grip on me was such that anytime I pulled away, he managed to drag me back into his alternate version of reality.

The bondage was psychological. I wasn't physically restrained from leaving him or from running to anyone for help. Yet, conditioned to fear those options, I saw no way out. I focused instead on the path he promised would relieve all the pain—and lead to a place where all my dreams would be realized.

Ultimately, it took getting arrested to set me free.

PART ONE

BACK IN THE REAL WORLD

"Sociopaths have both the power and the inclination to ruin lives, and this is just what they do to strangers on the Internet."
—M.E. THOMAS, *CONFESSIONS OF A SOCIOPATH*

CHAPTER ONE

MAY 2016
PIGEON FORGE, TENNESSEE

"You sure you ain't took nothin'?" a female voice asked.

I couldn't speak. Nausea and the intense throbbing in my head made forming words feel impossible. Still hovering over the toilet bowl, I gently shifted my head side to side to confirm, *No, nothing.*

Indeed, I'd not swallowed, injected, or smoked any kind of illicit drugs. That, among other things, set me apart from the twelve or so women in the room. Most of them had already gone through, or were still going through, withdrawal of some kind. I was coming down from something, too, but it wasn't illegal. It was just… coffee. Caffeine. My usual two to three cups a day had just been abruptly halted, and now the resulting migraine was another layer of punishment. *If and when I get out of here, I am never drinking coffee ever again. Not ever. Never, never, never.* That was what I told myself.

Dry heaves finally subsiding, I got up off my knees and wiped my mouth with toilet paper, careful to use only a few squares from the one dwindling roll we shared. I washed my hands under the trickle of water from the tiny stainless steel sink, tried to rinse out my mouth, and dried my hands on my jeans. I stepped carefully over or around supine bodies on the way back to my much-coveted spot on the concrete bench along the back wall of the drab gray room.

Pulling my allotted fake wool blanket over me, I lay down. As I did, it felt as if someone was gently placing a cinder block on my head. This was the worst migraine I'd had in years—the kind that forces periodic vomiting of whatever is left in one's stomach. On top of that, I felt generally *gross*. I had no way to brush my teeth. My T-shirt smelled ripe. My face was greasy, my socks funky.

* * *

It was the second day of what would turn out to be six full days—nearly a week—locked in this windowless, airless, chilly holding cell in Pigeon Forge, Tennessee. Except calling it a "cell" implies bars of some kind and a view of something beyond them: other people, rooms, guards, anything. No, this was just a solid concrete box—gray walls, gray floor, gray ceiling—with harsh fluorescent lighting that kept the room exceedingly bright twenty-four hours a day. No darkness at night, not even dimming. No telling what time it was. The door—also gray—had a tiny four-by-six-inch plexiglass rectangle at eye level, sometimes covered by a flap. That stupid little flap was a big deal. Never mind that when that flap was up, the only view it provided was of a wall on the other side of the hall. But when the flap was down, the room felt significantly more claustrophobic. Like the air was going to run out. Like we were in some kind of eternal purgatory—and would *never* get out.

There were no cameras in the room. If someone had a seizure and died, or a fight broke out, our only option would be to bang furiously on the door. Unfortunately, banging furiously on the door got precisely no one's attention. Or if it did, it was mostly ignored. We periodically engaged in such banging when our single roll of toilet paper ran out and we badly needed another. Usually no one came.

I learned that this room was known by its occupants as "the drunk tank," where females who'd been arrested were brought and stored. Some got out quickly on bail; some were transferred out to the "dorms," and some just remained, as I did. For six full days.

At times, up to twenty bodies were stuffed in this one room, lying like sardines on the floor, sitting against the walls, or lucky enough to get a spot on the benches. There was no separate bathroom—just a cold metal toilet bowl in the corner, the one in which I'd hurled three times. No partition, no wall, no nothing. Doing your business out in the open, with an audience to watch and hear it all, took some getting used to. This holding cell was basically a giant bathroom.

* * *

During the very strange year prior to my arrival in this cell, I'd watched a lot of Netflix, including the entire series *Breaking Bad*. On that show, the meth users were all haggard, with sallow faces, skin marked by sores, teeth blackened, or no teeth at all. Now, in jail, I was face to face with these same kinds of damaged faces.

Compounding this tragedy was learning that *all* of them had kids. Every single woman in the room, except me, had kids—even the ones young enough to be my daughters. *I could be a grandmother.* Ugh. That thought had never occurred to me before, but in here, I was the same age as women who *were* grandmothers. I'd never wanted kids of my own. My dog was the recipient of all my maternal instincts, and it was him I worried about. Meanwhile, the others seemed primarily preoccupied with whether the next person brought into the cell might have drugs on them to share.

With too much time to think, I'd look around and consider that maybe these women were not who they appeared to be. Perhaps this was a simulated reality, and these women were all actors staging this fucked-up nightmare just for me. Maybe it was all another of Mr. Fox's tests. And then I'd think that the casting department had gone a bit overboard. They'd raided the set of *Breaking Bad* for this production of *Sarma's Nightmare Stay in a Tennessee Jail*.

* * *

One night, three rowdy females were brought into the tank. Their familiarity with each other suggested they'd been arrested together—I assumed after some Pigeon Forge hijinks involving drugs or petty theft or who knows what. As usual when new detainees arrived, I felt uneasy. Would they get aggressive? Confront *me* in particular? What would I do? Would anyone else defend me?

I tried not to make eye contact. One of the newbies looked older than me, with brassy red-dyed hair and the smudged remnants of black eyeliner. She had less of a meth-face, more of just a generally *weathered* face—from years in the sun, smoking cigarettes, hard living, probably. The other two looked masculine—lesbians, I assumed. One was short and stocky, with roughly shorn hair and zero makeup. She looked aggressive. The other looked nicer somehow—softer. She also had choppy, short hair and no makeup, but her face was boyishly pretty. I liked her from afar. None of them appeared too distressed to have arrived in this place, casually chatting with others—as if we were all just hanging out, waiting for a bus.

Then, the stocky one called out, "Hey you!"

I looked up. *Oh shit. Moi?* She was staring right at me.

"You're from New York City?" she asked.

"Yeah," I said.

Now the whole room was paying attention.

"They're telling me here you're one of them… *vegans?*"

"Yeah, I am." I smiled, hoping I conveyed an appropriate mix of courtesy and confidence.

She squinted at me. "Huh. Well, you *know*, I heard if you're *vegan*… it makes your pussy taste sweet." Laughter broke out, some cackles, and a howl or two. My face started to feel hot, but I didn't mind the comment. I think she thought it would unnerve me.

"Actually, that's true," I volleyed back. "It really does."

"All righty then. Good to know." A few snickers.

The redhead meth-face chimed in. "You better be watchin' out when you sleep to*night!*"

The room exploded—more laughter, howling.

I kept the smile fixed on my face. A joke, I assumed. Hoped.

Henceforth, I was known in the tank as "Sweet Pussy." As in: "Hey, Sweet Pussy! Can I have yer sandwich if y'ain't gonna eat it?"

* * *

In any case, I was grateful for the distraction. With people coming in and out, there was always someone new to observe, or fear, or talk to. Pigeon Forge was a vacation destination—albeit a very strange one—so there were some out-oftowners too, usually arriving late at night, and drunk. I learned that the locals had a slogan for their town: "Pigeon Forge: Come on vacation, leave on probation!"

These diversions allowed me to avoid thinking about the discomfort of it all and the reasons I was there, which I didn't understand and was terrified to contemplate.

The officers and detectives who arrested me had explained that I was wanted in New York for grand larceny and fraud. *Grand larceny? Fraud?* It seemed surreal. I had the feeling one has when half asleep, unsure whether it's all a dream or not. I kept wishing, with every fiber of my being, that it *was* just a bad dream. The worst kind of nightmare, from which—any moment now—I'd wake up, exhale with relief, and then roll over and spoon my dog, Leon.

Instead, I could only keep wondering, *What's going to happen to me?*

* * *

Attempting to sleep was the worst. It helped when others were talking—to have something to listen to as I lay on the concrete floor, having lost my spot on the bench. During the check-in process, the officers take your shoes and anything like a belt, even the string of a sweatshirt hood. I had worn a hooded sweatshirt that I wished they'd let me keep. Instead of taking just the string, *they took my hoodie.* I was cold in my thin and increasingly stinky t-shirt. We were all issued a pair of worn-out Mario Batali-esque orange Crocs. With nothing else to lay one's head on, it was common practice to use these rubbery shoes as a makeshift pillow.

Actually falling asleep, losing consciousness, was a luxury in that brightly lit room. Only then was I free again, somewhere else. Waking up was harsh, reorienting to the reality of where I was. I had no idea what was going to happen or how long I would be there. I thought about my parents and people back home. I had no idea what was going on there either. I had been gone for almost a full year, entirely out of touch. All I knew was that, at some point, I would be transferred to New York. How that was going to happen, and when, I had no idea. What would happen when I got there? No clue. What had happened to my business? I didn't know.

* * *

My dog. When the detectives and police officers arrived in the hotel room where I'd been staying, Leon had greeted them with his tail wagging, jumping up, as if all these burly men had arrived for no other reason than to play with him.

The few times I'd let myself quietly cry in the holding cell, it was because of Leon. My boy. My heart ached at being separated from him, not knowing exactly where he was—praying he was okay. To my immense relief, the officers had not taken him to the local pound, which was what they first said they'd do when I'd asked, in tears, "What will happen to my dog?" Back in that hotel room filled with police officers, I'd sat on the bed, stunned and confused. They told me that my "husband" had been taken into custody. Mr. Fox had been staying in a separate room, adjacent to mine. There was one guy in a suit—a detective. The rest were uniformed officers, quietly going through my things—opening drawers, rifling through my bags.

Fortunately for Leon (and me), people tend to really like my dog, men especially. He's a guy's kind of dog: a seventy-pound pit bull mix with a red nose and blonde fur. Whatever other canine breeds are stirred into his gene pool give him slightly longer legs and a less stocky build than full-breed pits. His ears are especially big and floppy, and he loves people—all people. He charmed these police officers, as he tends to charm everyone.

But when they'd mentioned the pound, I panicked. "The pound? He can't go to a pound! He can't! *Please*. He's a rescue. I don't want him to go back in a cage!" I looked at them, tears now running down my face, eyes pleading, dying inside.

Then, to my immense relief, they relented. "Okay, okay ma'am. Don't worry. We love dogs. It's okay. Kevin here will take him. One of us will keep him until someone can come pick him up. It's okay. We'll make sure he's taken care of."

I was so relieved. "Oh god, thank you. *Thank you.* Thank you *so much*."

I was apparently being arrested and taken to jail myself, which hadn't quite registered yet, but the idea of Leon locked up in a pound had been too much. These officers agreeing to spare him that treatment made me want to hug them.

* * *

Considering the circumstances, they were very kind to me. I guess it was clear that I posed no immediate threat from the moment they arrested me. When

Leon initially started barking over a commotion in the hallway, I went to the door to see who was there. Looking through the peephole, I saw cops. I opened the door. "Is something wrong? Can I help you?" I asked. I was in a casual summer dress and a pair of faded Vans sneakers, my hair in a ponytail.

"No, ma'am. Go back in your room," one of them said. But before I could shut the door, another one said, "Hold on! It's her!"

What was going through my mind at this point, I don't know. I think I was numb and confused.

"We're going to need to come in, ma'am."

I pulled the door back and held onto Leon's collar as he tried to greet our new guests.

A big, strong-looking guy—the one in the suit—held up his phone. There was my picture, one of my promotional headshots from long ago. At the bottom of the photo was a white banner with the word "Wanted" on it. It looked fake, like some kind of joke.

"Yes, that's me." I felt numb. What was going on?

"Ma'am, we're going to need to take you in. You're being arrested. We just took your husband in. He's been arrested too."

"Arrested?" I was feeling sick to my stomach now.

One of the officers pointed to a very large Band-Aid on my shoulder. "What's this?"

"Oh," I said, and pulled it off. Underneath there was no wound, just a tattoo of a duck.

He looked at it, nodded. "Oh yeah, I see. Okay, that makes sense."

I wanted to explain that it was Mr. Fox who made me keep it covered, but I knew the explanation didn't matter. Mr. Fox had pushed me hard to get it permanently disguised—to get a bigger tattoo over it. But I didn't want to let go of my one and only tattoo—the logo for my brand—that had identified me in so many ways over the last ten years. I'm so grateful today that I at least didn't let him ruin that. Standing in front of the officers, however, the giant Band-Aid over my tattoo seemed like damning evidence that I'd knowingly avoided being identified and found.

* * *

After they had mercifully agreed not to take Leon to the pound, I started worrying. Panicking, really. What was I being charged with? How long would this take? When would I get Leon back? And what about all my stuff?

"Is this your phone, ma'am?"

"Uh-huh."

"Okay, we're going to take this. Any other electronics? Computer?"

"Just that iPad over there."

"Any firearms or weapons here, ma'am?"

Firearms? I shook my head. No.

"You probably want to change into something. Like, something more comfortable. You got pants and a sweatshirt? It can get cold where you're going."

"Where am I going?"

"The local jail. You'll be held there until you're taken back to New York."

So I was going back to New York, finally. I must have looked stunned and disoriented. I couldn't comprehend what was happening. I stood frozen. The detective in the suit stepped forward. Despite the circumstances, there was kindness in his eyes. His name, I learned, was Ray Brown.

"It's okay. It's all over now," he said.

It's over.

For a big man and an authority figure, he said those words softly. Delicately. As if they had just discovered me after a long search. Like they'd rescued me from a captor.

How did he know?

CHAPTER TWO

YEARS BEFORE
NEW YORK CITY

Rewind a couple of years from this rural Tennessee jail, and you'd find me in New York City—co-creator and owner of a unique, highly acclaimed Manhattan restaurant called Pure Food and Wine. I was thirty-three when we opened our doors in the summer of 2004. Despite the city's notoriously competitive and challenging restaurant market, with its sky-high rent and operating expenses, we'd always done well. We weathered the 2008 downturn that took down many New York restaurants, even long-established ones, and followed that with an upswing. We withstood the recession better than many other high-end restaurants because we were different. If you wanted aesthetically pleasing, organic, raw-vegan food paired with good wine and creative sake cocktails in a sexy restaurant setting (or a dreamy garden in the warmer months), we were your only option.

Our garden was big—more spacious than the interior—and was part of what made us special. Outdoor seating is an asset for Manhattan restaurants, and ours was further valuable in that the space was private—behind the restaurant, surrounded by other buildings. Compared to the more common sidewalk cafes with pedestrians and traffic whizzing by, our guests could relax in relative quiet under a canopy of trees, the branches strung with glowing white lights. Also, rather than cheap plastic or metal furniture, ours was wood—the tabletops in polished mahogany and the chairs in the folding Parisian sidewalk cafe style, with bright cherry-red seat and back cushions. We'd paneled the walls along the edge of the garden with slabs of dark ipe (pronounced "ee-pay") wood. We used the same wood for the banquet seating along that perimeter, which we covered with long burgundy cushions and pillows. Our cloth napkins were a farmhouse-style: off-white cotton with a burgundy stripe. Back then we'd had to specially request these from the linen company because no other restaurants used them. Nowadays, they're everywhere, and I still like to think we started that napkin trend.

During regular service, every table was set with place settings, wine glasses, and votive candles. The L-shaped outdoor bar, a thick slab of dark-stained wood, was surrounded by eight square wood stools. We had the same stools at our indoor bar, made for us by an old Estonian man in his woodshop all the way east on Avenue C. (I kind of loved that man; he reminded me of my Latvian father, with a similar accent and mannerisms.) The garden was peaceful yet vibrant. The bright greenery, rich-colored wood, burgundy banquets, cherry-red pillows, and golden candlelight created a naturally seductive atmosphere.

The vibe was similar on the inside: custom-made wood tables, chairs upholstered in bright cherry red. The same ipe wood covered part of the walls, while the rest was painted a fiery burnt orange. There was no artwork other than three photographs, hung together on one wall, of a very precocious-looking duck. Low ceilinged and candlelit, the inside felt warm and inviting, with a glossy wood-topped bar near the front. Four wood-framed glass doors opened up in the summer to face a small front patio with seating for eight to ten. This area was three steps down from the sidewalk and bordered with an iron fence. The semi-subterranean feel added to its coziness.

People sometimes had a hard time finding the restaurant. Our signage was a simple bronze metal "pure food and wine" lit from above to give it a subtle glow. Irving Place, the street on which it was located, was astonishingly quiet for being just one block from the very busy Union Square. Our next-door neighbor was the more brightly lit Mario Batali-owned Casa Mono, with illuminated colorful signage and a prominent corner location. Around the corner, Casa Mono connected to a small, casual bar called Bar Jamon, and then a few small storefronts beyond was our juice bar and takeaway spot, followed by a windowed kitchen with an entrance for staff or deliveries. Our spaces were all connected in the back, forming an L-shaped property that wrapped around those owned and operated by Mario Batali's restaurant group. It was convenient because I could come and go through the entrances on either street.

Batali's Spanish-themed restaurant and bar couldn't have been more different from us; they were known for organ meats, with a big grill up front at Casa Mono, and a giant cured pig's leg displayed prominently in the window of Bar Jamon. Meanwhile, our menu featured only plant food, nearly all of it *raw*. I realize this description hardly makes our menu sound appealing, but our food was good: vibrant, flavorful, beautiful, and, as a bonus, healthy. To this day, I've never tried a non-dairy ice cream as good as ours. It wasn't just good compared to other vegan ice creams—it was good compared to *all* ice creams. People couldn't reconcile how it was so rich and creamy yet contained no cream, milk, or eggs. At a food event during our first year, renowned chef Michael Lamonaco, having passed by our table to pick up a sample of our ice cream, came running back waving the tiny cup and spoon to tell me, "This is amazing! You are on to something *big* with this!"

And I think he was right.

Our ice cream sundaes were exceptionally good, and I take some comfort knowing they've at least been visually immortalized in photos on the Pure Food and Wine Instagram, along with our signature and seasonal dishes. Then there were the mini savory tarts we sent out with the tasting menus: pecan, black pepper, and pinot noir shells filled with herbed cashew cheese, caramelized shallots, marinated black trumpet mushrooms, and a drizzle of gooey apricot Riesling sauce. I can taste that combination of flavors and textures now in my mind. My insides ache when I think about all this, and about what it felt like sitting at the candlelit bar, marinating in the good vibes of that restaurant, safe and sound.

* * *

We frequently benefited from low expectations. It was common to hear of someone having been dragged to the restaurant by a friend, assuming they were going to hate it and expecting to have to dial for a pizza delivery as soon as they walked out, who was instead totally blown away. I loved it when this happened. Or when we got overflow from next door, since Casa Mono and Bar Jamon were both small spaces with limited seating and tended to be very busy.

The second summer Pure Food and Wine was open, a middle-aged couple introduced themselves, excitedly telling me that they'd first wandered into the restaurant about six months prior after intending to eat at Casa Mono but finding the wait too long. They'd figured, *Why not try this place next door?* They hadn't realized it was meat-free until already seated in the garden, but since the setting was so beautiful, they stayed to give it a try. *Why not?* That dinner, they explained, was revelatory; they'd loved the food and felt unusually good afterward, and they acknowledged that they could stand to lose a few pounds. From that day forward, they shifted their diet to incorporate more fruits and vegetables, cutting out most meat and dairy. They came back to the restaurant often. "I've dropped *thirty* pounds!" the man exclaimed, patting his belly. Moving his hand a couple of inches in front of his stomach, he added, "It used to come out to *here!*"

I loved stories like this. The accidental happy converts.

* * *

One Lucky Duck was the name of the brand I launched one year after Pure Food and Wine opened, at the same time that I began to formally split from my original collaborator in the restaurant—just as our cookbook, *Raw Food Real World,* was published.

Timed with the book's release, I launched an e-commerce site: oneluckyduck.com. It was an online store for our cookies, snacks, and other products, summarized by our tagline: "the best of everything for the ultimate raw and vegan lifestyle." We carried all the otherwise-hard-to-find ingredients to make the recipes in the book, plus skin care and supplements. The site also housed my blog, where I posted essays, often getting *very* personal about my aspirations and my struggles. My openness was a bit unusual, but it had a way of making my readers feel like they knew me.

I also renamed our juice bar One Lucky Duck Juice and Takeaway. It was a small and cozy spot offering fresh juices and shakes, a takeaway menu that mostly mirrored our lunch menu, and a rotating variety of desserts, cookies, and sweets displayed in a glassed-in pastry case. A freezer in the back housed pints of our popular dairy-free ice cream. A few small tables lined one wall, above which hung three photographs of baby ducks, sourced from the same photographer who'd supplied the big duck photos in the dining room. On the opposing wall, rows of shelving held various products, including our packaged cookies and snacks, made in our own kitchen, branded with the distinctive One Lucky Duck logo.

In the early years, we sold One Lucky Duck-branded snacks wholesale to other stores in and around New York City and then to the local Whole Foods stores, eventually expanding to over thirty Whole Foods locations, many in California.

By 2009, I'd published—this time on my own—a second colorful hardcover cookbook. Both books were sold in stores, on Amazon, and via our own locations. In 2010, we opened a second One Lucky Duck takeaway location across town in the Chelsea Market complex. Later, my younger half brother—who had worked at the restaurant for a while—opened a third One Lucky Duck outpost in Texas, where he lived. We were on a trajectory to keep growing.

* * *

The logo for the company was, of course, a duck—the one I got tattooed on my arm. I believed in the brand so much that I *branded* myself. We'd built a loyal following, and our tote bags, T-shirts, and other products emblazoned with the logo were popular. It thrilled me to see people carrying our One Lucky Duck bags around, effectively advertising for us. At the counters, we gave away colored One Lucky Duck stickers and included them in every online order. Customers would send photos of them stuck on laptops, kids' lunchboxes, bicycles, and so on. Again, more free advertising.

The response was encouraging. I felt with absolute certainty that we were building a movement, the aim of which was to make a healthy way of living—one that also benefited animals and the environment—appealing to the mainstream. We were stubbornly nonjudgmental in both our style and output and therefore attracted a diverse audience—not just hardcore vegans or vegetarians. Our customers were young and old, male and female, famous and anonymous, fashion plate and hippie—but usually they were *of means*. It always frustrated me that our food and products were so expensive, but our clean, unprocessed, all-organic ingredients, along with New York City rent prices, made that unavoidable.

※ ※ ※

Pure Food and Wine and One Lucky Duck were covered consistently in the press, nearly always favorably. Mainly this was because we were seen—especially at the beginning—as groundbreaking. No one had opened an upscale raw vegan restaurant in New York before. The only other like it had been in Marin County, California, and had closed by the time we opened.

I was particularly proud of how the media ranked us alongside other top-tier NYC restaurants. *Forbes* magazine featured annual lists of the city's best restaurants, and we were included four times in the three-star category—alongside names like Gotham Bar & Grill, Eleven Madison Park, The Modern, Veritas, wd-50, Blue Hill, and Babbo. Press mentions sometimes resulted from sightings of famous people at our tables. During interviews, I always felt squeamish when inevitably asked to name celebrities who had come in to dine. Wanting to respect their privacy, I disciplined myself to name only those who had already been publicly identified as having visited. Either way, it was fun seeing actors, musicians, politicians, athletes, and other celebrities at our tables or picking up an order from the takeaway.

Sometimes I learned that someone noteworthy had visited the restaurant without my having heard about it. I was having dinner one night at an Italian restaurant in the West Village with a friend who'd acted in a few films. Emma Stone was seated at another table with her then-boyfriend, Andrew Garfield. My friend had worked with her on a film, and on our way out, he introduced us. She shook my hand with a funny look on her face, as if something was registering in her brain. Then, having figured out what it was, she blurted out, "Oh my gosh, I *love* your restaurant!" I was flattered and reeled a bit from that encounter. When you're not used to being recognized, that kind of moment with someone famous feels funny, in a good way. Of course, I was probably carrying a One Lucky Duck tote bag, my regular stand-in for a purse, which might have given her a hint. But it struck me that I didn't know she'd ever visited the restaurant. Some people were in and out under the radar. New York City was kind of like that. You'd be standing in line at the grocery store and realize the frazzled woman ahead of you with no makeup on and a fussy toddler in the cart was Kate Winslet. No big deal.

* * *

There was always outside interest in expanding either Pure Food and Wine, One Lucky Duck, or both. Some of it wasn't serious, or else it was from a random person pleading to franchise in whatever random small town they were from, which made no sense. But most of the interest was incredibly flattering and sometimes intriguing. Rob Trujillo, bassist from Metallica (and a major crush of mine), told me he would be my investor if I would open a Pure Food and Wine in Northern California. Gisele Bundchen, at the time living in the West Village, repeatedly said she'd be my partner to open a One Lucky Duck near her townhouse. I don't know how serious these offers were, but they seemed reasonably so, and why I didn't take them up is another story.

There was interest internationally, too: a prominent group from Japan was eager to bring both Pure Food and Wine and One Lucky Duck to Tokyo, and after we met a few times in New York, I flew over to Tokyo for a few days to see their operations and tour the city. They took great care of me, treating me like a dignitary. A similar thing happened with a Turkish investor. I was flown first class to Istanbul, picked up in a fancy car, and installed in a low-key but very cool boutique hotel. It was one of the best short trips of my life. When discussing business, the investor and his colleagues treated me like a serious businesswoman. When showing me around the city, taking me to restaurants and bars, they treated me like a sister. When it snowed unexpectedly one morning, they called my hotel room inquiring about my shoe size so they could buy me boots (a heartwarming offer that I graciously declined—the snow wasn't that bad).

From the outside, it might have appeared as if I led a truly glamorous lifestyle. Traveling internationally in first class certainly made me feel like I did. On those trips, I most definitely *was* living glamorously. But the rest of the time, not so much. I returned home to unpack in my tiny, dusty, chaotically messy studio. The idea that I was frequenting the best organic spas, doing yoga every day, or regularly jetting off to fabulous vacations in Belize with a Louis Vuitton bag packed full of designer resort wear was just that: an idea. I was not doing those things. But I sometimes got the feeling people thought I was.

I *was* doing work I cared for deeply, surrounded by people I cared for deeply, and I could eat the most delicious healthy food all day long. I had so much to be grateful for. At the same time, I was working like crazy, often sleep deprived, and occasionally deeply unhappy—depressed, I realize now. I longed for things to be different. My normal state was to be outwardly upbeat and gracious, but inside I was overwhelmed—sometimes overcome with quiet desperation. Given what later transpired and what I know now, I would give anything to go back to that time of purity and opportunity, messy as it was. Back to the cozy, safe nest of my restaurant family. Back to my regular seat against the wall at the end of our candlelit bar or my table in the back corner of the dining room. Back to that good energy, soothed by the background music—always from a playlist compiled by me or my longtime bar manager, Joey.

* * *

Joey was nearly as much a part of that restaurant as I was. Hired in our first year, he was one of many staff who had been witness to, and part of, many changes and transitions, including some that involved my personal life. Like the acrimonious, tabloid-chronicled split between me and my original partner in the restaurant, Matthew—who had also been my live-in boyfriend for four years—or when my cat died. Together we weathered business challenges including the recession and two brutal hurricanes, one of which shut down lower Manhattan for over a week. We even survived a corrupt CFO and attempted coup. "Attempted coup" sounds dramatic, but I nearly lost the brand to the control of a couple of fat corporate guys who sensed the untapped value and thought they knew better than I did. Never, I vowed, would I take my eyes off the road again.

Meanwhile, with so many artists and musicians on the staff, I went to as many of their shows and performances as I could, trying to be a good mom. In the early years, I stayed late to drink wine with them after hours. When I didn't, it warmed my heart knowing they were hanging out late into the night even in my absence. One could have said I was naive, letting them take advantage of my lax ways, but I didn't see it that way. I was glad they wanted to stay in each other's company. If it cost me a few thousand dollars a year in extra wine, so be it.

For years I conveniently lived directly across the street. Sometimes, when the lines to the bathroom were too long, I ran across the street to my own. Or if I called in the morning and no one answered when a host should have been on duty, I ran over in my pajamas to answer the phones until they finally showed up. I remember going to sleep one cool summer night, my window open, hearing the distinctive loud laugh of Jeri, one of our longtime and best servers, hanging out with others on the front patio. This was among the best and most comforting sounds to fall asleep to. It reminded me of when I was little, sometimes going to sleep hearing the wine-fueled laughter of my parents and their dinner-party guests downstairs, easing me into my dreams.

Like many restaurant families, we were an incestuous lot. Relationships sparked between coworkers, and sometimes things got messy, but we weren't a dysfunctional family. Everyone genuinely cared for each another and for the business. From time to time there was a father figure of sorts in the picture, like Adam, a bookkeeper-turned-general manager who stood out for not socializing much with the staff. But he was well liked and ran a tight ship, keeping everyone accountable for costs and reining in my permissiveness by proposing sensible rules to which I grudgingly agreed. At the same time, he was supportive of our generosity in structured ways, like giving raises to hourly staff where and when we could, or the time we doled out $30,000 in holiday bonuses simply because we'd had a good year. I carried a ton of personal debt during these restaurant years (from a prior relationship), but I wanted our family to feel supported.

I was also—always—deeply and firmly optimistic. I knew we were headed for much bigger things and I'd eventually pay those debts. I knew the growth I privately envisioned would come about and I'd stay in the driver's seat. I knew I'd never sell out or let someone else dictate who we were or change our style and culture merely for the sake of inching up profits. It wasn't about money. As clichéd as it sounds, it was about changing the world. I wanted to be part of a meaningful shift, a global shift, toward the consumption of more plants and fewer animals, promoting healthy and compassionate living and abating destruction and suffering. I wanted our work and our brand to matter, to make a difference. And I wanted it to outlast me.

CHAPTER THREE

MAY 2016

PIGEON FORGE, TENNESSEE

It was my third day in the holding cell, my stomach empty from heaving out its contents. What passed for food in this jail was so wildly unappealing, and I was hungry. And thirsty. And cold. And increasingly stinky. My teeth felt fuzzy, like each tooth was wearing a little sweater. I longed for dental floss and a toothbrush, or anything minty. Also a cold glass of water. A pillow. Basically, I longed to get the fuck out of there.

A heavyset officer opened the door and looked right at me. "You," she barked. "There's someone here to see you."

Holy shit. My mind was spinning as I scrambled to my feet, slid into my oversized Crocs, and eagerly followed the woman out into the hall.

"Detective Brown is here to see you," she said.

Holy shit.

Ray Brown was the detective—the one who'd come into my hotel room and, in the kindest way possible, let me know that I was being arrested.

I didn't know what to think about him being there now, but I was glad he was. I hoped for good news. Like maybe he was going to tell me it was all just a huge misunderstanding and he was taking me out, back to Leon.

I was led into a small gray office—the same room where I'd been fingerprinted, questioned, told to throw a striped jail uniform top over my t-shirt, and photographed for my mug shot.

There he was. In other circumstances, he might have looked intimidating: a big brawny man with a bald head who looked as if he'd seen it all and didn't suffer fools gladly—like you could perform a whole comedy routine in front of him and his deadpan face wouldn't budge. If you were casting a TV show like *The Wire* and needed a burly white guy to play a hardened detective, Ray Brown would be your man.

His having spared Leon from the local dog pound was a kindness for which I badly wanted to hug him. But beyond that, there was something about his energy—something that made me feel like *he knew.* Or at least knew I wasn't a hardened criminal. I assumed my hotel room had been thoroughly searched after I was taken away. In contrast to the squalid condition of Mr. Fox's room, mine was neat and clean. Furthermore, there were no drugs to be found, just a bottle of Ambien (prescribed to me the year prior) that I'd been saving for emergencies. No syringes or empty liquor bottles. No guns, knives, or weaponry of any kind. No sex toys (just dog toys). No leather whips, ball gags, or stilettos. Just a tidy room filled with ordinary things: my clothes (mostly summer dresses and a few pairs of sneakers), lots of books, and a stuffed pig on the neatly made bed. Plus a mini fridge full of green juices from a nearby Walmart, bottled water, microwaved sweet potatoes, greens, and fruit—much of it for Leon.

Detective Brown sat in one of two chairs facing a gray desk. As I came in, he stood briefly and motioned for me to sit in the chair behind the desk. It felt a bit odd, me being the one behind the desk. I was the detainee, after all, and here I was, sitting behind the desk in an office in the jail, like I worked there.

Despite his intimidating looks, Detective Brown was soft-spoken and kind. He made it clear he wasn't there to question me; he simply wanted to explain what he knew about my situation and answer any questions I had. He also told me that his office had been inundated with press calls. He shifted a bit in his seat as he explained that most of the calls were inquiring about the pizza.

I'd had no idea there was a pizza involved in my story until another detainee told me about it. One morning (or afternoon, or evening—you could never tell in that brightly lit, windowless room), a youngish woman was brought in. She seemed familiar with the guards and a few of the others—a regular, apparently.

She had short blond hair, a pale, pock-marked face, and the blackest set of rotting teeth I'd ever seen. Yet it was easy to see she'd once been pretty and, theoretically, still could be again. She looked at me a bit more closely and then blurted, "I know you! Ain't you that girl from New York City?"

My eyes widened. I nodded, unsure how she already knew who I was.

"I seen you on TV!" she said. "Yeah, last night you were on the news! You're the one who got arrested 'cause of a pizza!"

"A pizza?" I asked.

"Yeah! They said you guys ordered Dominos and that's how you got busted! On the run and all!"

Dominos?

So that's how I found out. Apparently, Mr. Fox had ordered a pizza and paid with a credit card, which tipped off the authorities. I already knew what he'd likely ordered: extra cheese and a side of ranch dressing. Yes, he liked to put ranch dressing on pizza. *I know.* Disgusting. For the past couple of years, he'd regularly demanded that I fetch his food, so I knew his preferences—like his very specific Chipotle order, which I'd memorized, since getting it wrong would inspire his wrath, or the vile concoction he made me get from Subway. Every time, I felt compelled to tell the person behind the counter it wasn't for me. As if to say: *I'm not this gross. I'm not the person about to consume this tuna sub with extra mayo.* Yes, with *extra* mayo—because apparently the soup of mayo in which the tuna already swam wasn't enough—plus pickles and olives. Yuck. My only consolation was that maybe all that tuna was slowly poisoning his brain with mercury.

* * *

Detective Brown told me the delivery had only just arrived when they arrested Mr. Fox. To arrest him, they asked the front desk attendant to call Mr. Fox down, claiming there was some issue with the payment. Brown reassured me they were doing their best to tell the press that I was most definitely *not* the one who'd ordered or eaten the pizza. I thanked him for this, even though the whole issue seemed silly and far down the list of things I was worried about.

In the end, despite their efforts to clarify the situation, the pizza was still linked to me in story after story. "Former Vegan Restaurant Owner Who Allegedly Defrauded Investors and Stiffed Employees Tracked Down After Domino's Pizza Order," read one headline on *People* magazine's website. Or per the *New York Post*: "Vegan Restaurateur Orders Dominos Before $2M Bust." Even more than a year later, *Forbes* magazine's website blared: "The Vegan Fugitive, Done in By Domino's Pizza, Takes a Plea." That stupid pizza. Oh well. At least a couple of articles included the officers' diplomatic attempts at clarification. A *Daily Beast* article titled "The Hustler Who Hooked Up with and Brought Down New York's Vegan Queen" noted, "New York tabloids wasted no time gloating about the downfall of the vegan proprietress, who was reduced to the height of hypocrisy: ordering cheesy pies—an allegation one detective says is untrue. ('She did not order the pizza,' Sevierville detective Kevin Bush said. 'She was not consuming the pizza whatsoever')."

While this was only a teensy humiliation atop a mountain of humiliations, I still can't see a Domino's delivery person, storefront, or TV commercial without flashing back to my time in Tennessee jail.

I asked Detective Brown if he knew how Leon was doing—a much bigger concern than the pizza. He told me Leon was with the hotel manager, who had offered to take him home with her. He also said my father had called their office and was on his way to pick Leon up. *My father was coming to Tennessee.* I was relieved Leon would be safe, but then shut part of myself down to avoid considering what my father would be thinking.

I must have looked dazed.

"You doing okay?" Detective Brown asked.

"Yes," I said. "I mean, relatively speaking."

He went on to say he'd done some digging into my background. I was glad to hear this, given that prior to these events, my background was not only squeaky clean but also at least a little impressive: Ivy League graduate, early Wall Street career, businesswoman, cookbook author. My entire criminal history consisted of one speeding ticket years prior in Colorado. That was it.

Detective Brown said it seemed I'd gotten myself caught up in something and suggested I consider separating myself from my co-defendant, my husband. Hearing him say "your husband" made me cringe. I'd never gotten used to Mr. Fox being referred to that way. I never *wanted* to marry him.

I didn't even understand what the relevance of being co-defendants was or what separating from him meant in that context. I didn't want to understand. But I was glad Detective Brown seemed to have concluded I wasn't some criminal mastermind who had schemed to destroy my own business so I could vacation in Pigeon Forge with a scary fat guy I hated.

While Detective Brown didn't elaborate on what he knew about Mr. Fox, I'm guessing he'd researched him too (using his real name) and found his extensive record of arrests and criminal history. It was only years later that a cop I befriended in New York City told me he'd looked up Mr. Fox in their system and found an insane number of arrests—something like fifty—often under false IDs. None of that was ever revealed to me during my own criminal proceedings, but I know now that history exists. Maybe Detective Brown had seen it too.

He also told me that, along with a fake police badge, they'd found a fake gun among Mr. Fox's things. A very real-looking one, he said, with weight. I'd never seen the gun, but the thought of it felt eerie. I suppose less eerie than if it had been a real gun, but still. What was he doing with a *fake gun*? The badge I knew about. I explained to Detective Brown that Mr. Fox's father, who'd passed away, had been a Massachusetts cop. I assumed the badge had been his father's. Much later, my New York City cop friend told me that impersonating a police officer was among the things Mr. Fox had been charged with years earlier—I guess by pretending that badge was *his*.

Detective Brown then asked if I understood the charges I was facing. I told him I did not. I didn't want to. But I knew it would sound weird if I said I didn't want to know, so I let him explain. The twenty-four-count indictment included charges of second-degree larceny, second-degree criminal tax fraud, first-degree scheme to defraud, violation of labor laws, and more. If convicted on all counts, I could be sent to prison for fifteen years. *Fifteen years.*

Again, my brain did that out-of-body thing—like I was just an observer watching something that had nothing to do with me. And yet, hearing this information still made me queasy. It felt unreal. At this stage, I was confused as to why anyone would put me in prison. As soon as they learned what really happened, the charges would be dropped, right? They had to be. Or at worst, I'd be sentenced to probation for being negligent or just plain dumb. Never mind that *what really happened* was still something I didn't understand, let alone know how to explain. But what I did know for sure was that stealing from anyone, evading sales tax, and—most of all—destroying my own business and hurting my staff, were things I would never, in a million years, have done or intended.

There was a time once when I'd been interviewing a CPA about handling the restaurant's taxes. He asked me how many employees were on versus off the books. "They're all on," I told him.

"No, really," he said. "How many are off?"

"Really, they're all on," I reaffirmed.

He looked at me incredulously, clearly used to dealing with the common industry practice of paying at least some staff with cash under the table.

Likewise, every dollar of our cash sales was properly recorded. My general manager, Adam, and I once spent hours trying to figure out whether we'd been calculating "use tax" correctly to make sure we complied with New York State's complex tax laws. Bless Adam for always being so careful. It helped me sleep at night. We always did things by the book. Never mind that so many others didn't—I wasn't one to take those risks. Furthermore, I'm the sort that leans toward believing in karma. I also just generally feel like one doesn't get to break the rules and expect to live in a functioning society. What if everyone broke the rules? Nothing would work.

My point is, I'm no criminal. I'm afraid of getting in trouble. If I go into a store, look around, and don't buy anything, I worry they'll think I'm shoplifting.

And yet here I was, in jail, facing fifteen years behind bars.

* * *

I didn't know what to say. Mr. Fox's words—ones he'd repeated to me many times—now looped in my brain: *Whatever you do, if anything ever happens, the worst thing you could possibly do is throw me under the bus.* (Well, shit. What am I supposed to do? You *are* under the bus!) I'd never known what he meant by that—or what was coming. I suppose there's a lot I should have known. But Mr. Fox had told me so many crazy, ominous, and often entirely absurd things—how could I have known which, if any, to rely on?

Among the things he'd told me: that he'd pick me up in his private jet (he never did), that I was headed to Rome to finally meet his omnipotent brother

(I was not), that he was getting fatter and fatter *on purpose* because I was *supposed* to hate him (I did, but not because of his weight). He also implied that he wasn't really human.

My mind felt scrambled. Was Mr. Fox really completely full of shit? And if so, what the fuck now? I wanted to spill everything, to tell Detective Brown all of it, so then maybe he could tell me what to do and help me fix it. Make it all okay. I didn't want him to leave, and I didn't want to go back into the holding cell.

Mr. Fox had been in charge for so long that without him, I didn't know what to do. He'd always assured me everything would be okay. "You're doing good, kiddo. It's almost over," he'd say. (Never mind that he was eight years younger than me—I was *kiddo.*) He promised he would never leave me (if only he'd left me!). As long as he was there, he was in charge, protecting me, or so he made it seem. He also repeatedly reminded me that *nothing is real.*

Here I was, thinking, *Can I please go back to a place where nothing is real? Because it's feeling all too real now.*

Even though Mr. Fox mostly tortured me through the things he made me do, he always found a way to comfort me along the way. I wanted someone to comfort me now. He would critique me and berate me, but he also knew how to make me laugh. He could be incredibly funny. How does one make silly jokes while simultaneously destroying someone's life? It takes a special kind of person to do that. It made no sense to me. It made *more* sense to believe his version of things—his alternate reality—in which he was rescuing me, taking care of all my problems, and making me laugh all the while—because *Baby, don't worry; the happily ever after is almost here.*

I wanted to tell Detective Brown that Mr. Fox was either some kind of monster or a god—I wasn't sure which. And I meant that literally. I wanted to tell him about the vile things Mr. Fox had done to me, things I could only endure if he allowed me to first chug a few beers. I wanted to tell him *everything*—then crawl into his lap, burst into tears, and cry myself into a forever sleep.

Instead, I remained mostly numb, my mind still whispering that maybe this was all part of the test—*this moment* in particular. Would I stay strong and not throw Mr. Fox "under the bus"? I needed to know what I was supposed to do. But I didn't know what to do. So instead, I made conversation.

I asked Detective Brown if my social media accounts were still up. He said yes—he'd looked them up. Instagram, Twitter, Facebook, all still there. Somehow, that comforted me—that I hadn't been erased from the world. I didn't ask about my restaurant. I must have known it was probably closed, but I didn't want to hear those words. I couldn't let my brain consider everything that must have happened after we left New York. It was too much. I have a talent for shutting things out. I'm not sure if everyone does or if I'm just particularly good at it. When my father was going through treatment for prostate cancer years ago, I kept forgetting. I'd *forget*. I know that sounds awful, but dissociating was how I coped with scary circumstances.

Detective Brown told me I'd be extradited to New York. He didn't know how or when, just that it would happen within twenty-four days. If not, they'd have to let me go—but that wasn't likely. New York was coming for me, one way or the other.

After that, I didn't know what else to ask. So I did what I often do: I rambled about food and about changing the world with food. Maybe I was also stalling because I didn't want him to leave. And I *really* didn't want to go back into that holding cell. But of course, back I had to go. I asked him if he would come back, and he said he would. He pulled a business card from his pocket and handed it to me. I clung to that card like a winning lottery ticket.

CHAPTER FOUR

FALL 2011
NEW YORK CITY

When I first encountered Mr. Fox, I was starving for a certain kind of attention. Just a few months earlier, I'd broken up with my boyfriend, Tobyn. The nearly four years we lived together were blissfully free of fights or drama. Despite my being thirteen years older than him and our wildly different lives, it had been the best relationship I'd ever had.

Now, for the first time in my life, I was suffering serious heartache. More than just an ache—it felt like every day my heart was being put through a meat grinder. As the weeks passed, then months, I wasn't getting over it. Worn down by the near-constant sadness, I fixated on questions like why he didn't love me enough to stay or what was wrong with me. It reached the stage where I was angry with him for leaving me, even though I knew from the start that our relationship likely wasn't forever, given the age difference. Never mind that not too long before he left, I'd very seriously considered splitting up with him after I kind of *fell for* someone else, who happened to be a famous actor: Alec Baldwin. We met at my restaurant and became strangely close, talking on the phone, sharing thoughtful emails, and spending some time together, ostensibly as friends but with the awareness of a stronger connection—one I didn't feel I could explore since I was *living with my boyfriend.* I'd probably sensed the end was coming with

Tobyn, but the idea of leaving him felt too painful. I was still in love with him, even while part of me wished I could put him on ice and go date Alec for a while.

I didn't know what to do, so I did nothing. And Alec, respecting that I wasn't a single person, gradually moved on. Not long after, Tobyn came to his own conclusion—that it was time for *him* to move on. After some painful conversations, he packed up and moved out. Eventually, he left New York to head back to his hometown in Colorado. He took his best friends with him—also from Colorado—who had become my friends too. They were in a band together, so their leaving en masse made sense. Their departure from my life—his departure—left a gaping hole. By then, Alec had met someone new and seemed happy.

Now I was fully alone, which normally wasn't an issue—I always liked being single—but the heartbreak was new. I was approaching forty and suddenly felt vulnerable about my age.

At some point, I started writing angry letters to Tobyn. The kind you never intend to send but write just to purge the feelings. I wanted to convince myself he had faults—any justification to be outraged at his leaving or at his treatment of me when we were a couple. But the reality was that he'd always been good to me. I deeply admired who he was as a person, and I painfully missed his lanky, long limbs in the bed beside me. Still, it was easier to be mad than heartbroken, so I looked for reasons to be mad and spit them out in angrily worded letters, which I still have. *Dear Tobyn, Fuck you for leaving.* And so on.

I was busy as ever with the restaurant, but when I came home late at night, it was just my dog and me—no more Tobyn, no more of Tobyn's things lying around. I looked for ways to occupy my mind, maybe boost my shattered ego, maybe both. Social media was an alluring source for interaction, connection, and validation. I'd take selfies, pick the best one, apply the most flattering filter (usually the one that added a glowing tan where none existed), and add a caption—something to serve as a lame cover for posting it, maybe try to make it funny. Post. Then wait for the likes to roll in. In the meantime, I'd scroll. Read other people's amusing posts. Or click links to articles about the latest atrocities over which to be outraged, retweet them, add pithy comments, and see who responded, who retweeted. Rinse and repeat. Then back to my own post—check the likes; read the comments. It was the mental equivalent of eating a whole bag of Cheetos: junk you *know* isn't good for you, yet you can't seem to stop.

Alec had recently joined Twitter, and through this, we reconnected—briefly, and still just as friends. Now and then, we volleyed tweets back and forth. It was fun. With his sharp wit, it wasn't surprising that Alec was good at Twitter. After a while, I noticed him interacting with a user who called himself @DiscipleofTodd—whatever that meant. His avatar was a cartoon instead of a photo. I knew nothing about him, but I noticed he was very funny. His banter with Alec was entertaining.

Then he noticed me. He followed me, and I followed him back. He started commenting on my posts, and soon, our own back-and-forth ensued. It quickly moved to direct messages. He said his name was Shane Fox. I still didn't know much else about him, but since Alec followed him, I assumed they were friends, or at least acquaintances.

Shortly after he followed me, he changed his profile picture to an actual photo. But it only showed the lower half of his face. It was a grainy black-and-white image, both odd and intriguing. Normally, a cropped photo like that would seem suspect—like maybe he had tiny eyes too close together, a thick unibrow, a receding hairline, or a bulbous nose. Some reason to hide his full face. But in the photo, he had what looked like a week's worth of stubble, and his mouth caught my attention—full lips, but not *too* full. Just right.

After a while, I hesitantly asked about the photo. *Why the partial image?* I'm one of those people who's so overly sensitive to the feelings of others that I worried—what if he really *did* have some facial irregularity? What if asking made him feel bad? Still, I asked. He responded by sending me a full photo—though his eyes were obscured by sunglasses. *Okay, so his head is not deformed.* His features were well-proportioned. His hair was full and dark, cut short yet long enough to suggest that if grown out, it would be thick and wavy. His haircut, stubble, and aviator sunglasses gave him the look of someone with a military background. His neck was solid, making him look big and strong. He'd also said things to imply he was big and strong. He seemed capable and important, but details remained vague. I was intrigued and wanted to know more.

Feeling drawn to him was a gradual and steady process. Like the tide coming in, you know it's happening, but you can't *see it* happening. One steady wave after another, wetting just a little more sand, until before you know it, the water is ten feet farther up shore than before. Every comment, every new reveal, moved the tide a little more. He was clever and funny. He asked lots of questions, seeming genuinely interested in me—my goals, my hopes, and my dreams. He offered insights that felt oddly penetrating. I don't recall the exchanges, but I do remember that they made me feel admired, appreciated, and important. I was being pulled in. Like an undercurrent—when there's nothing to hold on to, you surrender to its force.

* * *

Words with Friends was a popular game at the time. It's basically Scrabble played on your iPhone. It was one of my escapes back then, and Mr. Fox and I started playing against each other. I'd considered myself pretty good at it, but he nearly always won, often with maddeningly obscure words. He was clearly smart, which made me feel oddly submissive. His ability to conjure up words I'd never heard of, deep knowledge of history, and almost encyclopedic recall of facts—it all hinted at something more. A kind of power.

I wasn't entirely oblivious to the fact that, by then, he had most likely read everything publicly available about me. My personal blog posts. My interviews. Press articles. Even the tabloid gossip about my breakup with my former partner. There was a lot to study if one took the time to look. My life was an open book, whereas I was left to puzzle over his. That alone gave him the upper hand—from the start, and always.

Mr. Fox had zero online presence—a search of his name yielded exactly nothing—but he had an excuse, albeit a totally lame one. He claimed his identity had once been stolen, so he'd wiped himself off the internet. That didn't make sense, but it left me to conclude—as I was supposed to—that there had to be another reason. As if I should assume his status as a secret operative in a world I didn't understand meant that *of course* he couldn't have any identifying online presence. These early confusions were never clarified, only layered over with further confusions. It was as if everything he said hinted at something else, which I was left to infer. He mentioned an *assistant* and referenced frequent business travel to the West Coast and abroad. Some of his comments implied he wasn't flying commercial. But when I asked specific questions, he deflected.

A more skeptical person might have doubted the veracity of his ambiguous claims or caught on to the inconsistencies. But I didn't. Instead, I found it flattering. *I must be special if this smart and mysterious guy is paying me attention.* I'd been feeling so low for months—rejected and sad. And now, finally, here was someone who seemed not only interested in me but also interested in who I was on the inside and what I wanted for my life.

* * *

What I knew about Mr. Fox came only in the form of crumbs he sprinkled out now and then, as if feeding me small doses of a drug, getting me addicted. When any detail disappointed me, I brushed it aside. For example, when I finally heard his voice, he had a Boston accent. He was, it turned out, from Massachusetts—but *still. Yuck.* Sorry Boston. You're my hometown, but I've never been a fan of the accent. And it was all wrong on Mr. Fox. It didn't fit the image of him I held in my mind. If he'd turned out to have a *British* accent, like James Bond? *That* would have been cool. But James Bond with a Boston accent? No. Just no. Anyway, I must have said something—made a joke about it, maybe—and right away he snuffed out the accent. From then on, his voice—deep and smooth—was much more appealing. I'd given him feedback, and he'd adjusted. He'd adjusted *who he was.* That's not normal. But at the time, I didn't think about it. I was just glad the accent was gone.

Eventually, Mr. Fox sent me a photo with his eyes visible. It was a selfie, taken lying down. His eyes were dark and huge. Everyone's eyes look bigger in a selfie than in real life—there's a little bit of what happens when you look into the back of a spoon. But my immediate reaction was a jolt of fear. His eyes were like two black holes. Maybe my subconscious interpreted them not as portals to a soul but as glimpses into hell. Before I could consider what that feeling meant, he sent more photos. I lulled myself into seeing his eyes as intoxicating. Strong and steady. Powerful. Any warning signals—like premonitions that this was the start of something dangerous—were overridden. My brain focused selectively on whatever bits of input soothed me back into the fantasy version of him.

That he wasn't rushing to New York to see me only made me more eager to see him. I started sending him more photos—the kind I'd not post online. Nothing explicit, just intriguingly sexy, I hoped. My stomach, maybe the top of pink underwear showing. He loved them, always wanting more. And I liked how that made me feel. It was a lot more fun than wallowing in heartache over Tobyn.

* * *

Mr. Fox was, in so many ways, the opposite of Tobyn—which, in the context of my heartbreak, added to his appeal. Tobyn was exceedingly boyish in appearance, and not just because of his age. His chestnut-brown hair flopped into his eyes (think early Justin Bieber), and I don't think he could have grown a beard if he tried. If he didn't shave for a week, the resulting growth was uneven and sparse. He had smooth, pale skin, expressive blue eyes, and a long, straight nose. His face, altogether, was beautiful. It reminded me of Uma Thurman. Like he could have declared himself to be her little brother, and you'd have thought, *Oh yeah, I totally see the resemblance.*

Tobyn was tall and lean. He biked or skateboarded everywhere and played ice hockey. His legs were strong, but he never set foot in a gym and was kind of lanky on top, which I liked. He had smooth, hairless arms and beautiful hands. I have a thing for hands, and his were gloriously perfect. He was a drummer, a truly talented musician. The band he played in—with his friends, the ones who also became my friends—was *really good*. It felt like what they were meant to do. When not at band practice, he worked at a craft beer store in Brooklyn.

Our relationship was one where I took care of most things, like the responsible adult. I helped him set up a new bank account, made all our travel arrangements, and, during the four years we lived together, paid the rent and household bills. It never bothered me. I never felt he was taking advantage of me, and I still don't. I was glad when he was out practicing with his band instead of at work, which, given his wage and part-time hours, didn't add up to much anyway. He was at a different time in his life, and I would have been paying the same bills whether he lived with me or not. His boyishness was one of the things I loved most about him. It came with a kind of purity. An innocence. He was pure good.

In contrast, Mr. Fox seemed worldly and successful. He seemed to have means. It sounded like he had accomplished a lot, though I could not have told you what. He carried himself with certainty, like someone used to being in control. He was also younger than me—by eight years—but came across as more experienced and wiser, secure in his himself. It felt like he would know what to do in any crisis. By then, I'd been running my business mostly on my own for nearly eight years. I had amazing managers and support, but I was still the one in charge. The one taking care of everyone else. And I was tired.

In the photos he sent me, Mr. Fox appeared big and strong, like he spent a lot of time at the gym. Normally that wasn't my type. But at this moment, the opposite of Tobyn was what appealed to me. Mr. Fox looked like a man. A *manly* man. He was sized like a football player. Not a quarterback—more like a linebacker. Or a bouncer. Someone who could kick your ass. And he talked tough. Once, he said he could see himself picking me up under one arm and Leon under the other. That visual appealed to me. *Someone pick us up. Take care of us. Please and thank you.*

Mr. Fox was aggressive and forceful. He exuded dominance. Tobyn, in contrast, was easygoing, sometimes to the point of being passive. Two years before we split, there was an incident involving one of Tobyn's friends. This friend was smart way beyond his years and extremely capable. The way he carried himself, spoke, and dressed, you'd think he was closer to forty than his early twenties. Sort of like Michael J. Fox's character on *Family Ties*. I'd hired him as CFO for my business. At first, he was great—accomplishing a lot—but later, he ended up betraying me (a long story in itself), and I nearly lost control of my brand. I fired him, of course, but I was stunned by what he'd done. I wanted Tobyn to be outraged and defend my honor, maybe go beat him up or at least yell at him. Something. Anything. But Tobyn was nonconfrontational. He was angry at the guy but never confronted him. *His* friend. Meanwhile, when I told Mr. Fox the story, he said that if he ever ran into that fucker, he'd pick him up, slam him against a wall, and make sure he never came near me or my company again. Hearing that—and imagining it—felt quietly thrilling.

Among the things I loved most about Tobyn, and what made our relationship work so well, was that he was so laid back. He never got jealous. I often came home late after long business dinners with men. I had a lot of male friends and was approached often by men at the restaurant—sometimes related to business, sometimes not. Tobyn never gave me a hard time or questioned me about any of it. Likewise, I never got bent out of shape if he was out late with his friends. If he was having fun, I was glad. We both felt secure in this way. Tobyn once wisely pointed out that he wouldn't be able to stop me from being with someone else if that's what I wanted, so what would be the point of getting paranoid about it? His reasonable approach to fidelity only reinforced my wanting to be faithful to him. We genuinely trusted each other.

In contrast, Mr. Fox seemed like the kind of guy more likely to get possessive, like I was *his* woman. That kind of behavior normally repelled me, but after four years of Tobyn's lax ways, I was drawn in by what I perceived as Mr. Fox's strong and protective nature. *Yes, please. Come pick me up under one arm and Leon up under the other. Carry us for a while.*

CHAPTER FIVE

MAY 2016
PIGEON FORGE, TENNESSEE

It was on my fourth day—at least I think it was the fourth day—in the brightly lit holding cell when I was finally, miraculously, able to shower. All of us were, in fact, *forced* to shower. Not because they wanted us to feel refreshed and clean but because one of the detainees in the room had lice. We were marched out into the hall, lined up, and sized up. Each of us was handed a top and a bottom—finally, we were getting out of our own stinky clothes and into jail-wear. The bottoms were baggy with an elastic waistband, and the top was short-sleeved and boxy. Both were made of a thick, burlap-like material with wide, horizontal gray and white stripes.

We stood in line, holding our new outfits, waiting our turn to step one by one into a small room with a shower. When it was my turn, I realized "shower" was a generous term. It was more of a *water assault.* I felt punched by a firehose of scalding water, while the needle-sharp peripheral spray stabbed at me from all sides. There was no temperature control—just a single button to turn the stream on or off. There was no soap, no liquid soap, shampoo, or conditioner. Instead, every fifteen seconds or so, the firehose released a burst of harsh, chemical-smelling detergent—for about three seconds. That was it. I had to time it just right, rinsing out the foamy chemicals before the next blast, or else starting the process all over again. It took me a few tries. When I finally pushed the button to stop the water, I stood there, dripping wet, like I'd just survived running naked through a car wash.

I did my best to dry off with what looked like a dishtowel—one that had been used and washed for over a decade. I still only had the same underwear, bra, and socks I'd arrived in—and worn for four days now. Fresh socks and underwear were not provided. I put my underwear back on inside out. I carefully picked up my bra (in which I'd wrapped Ray Brown's card to keep it dry) and put that on. I tucked the card back in my bra, the only place it would be remotely safe. I put on the boxy uniform, maneuvered my clammy, wet feet into my stinky socks, and slid on the Crocs. I could tell my skin was about to get insanely dry and itchy, and my wet, tangled hair would air dry into unruly clumps. I was a chemically sanitized mess in dirty underwear.

While we were getting cleaned, the holding cell had been treated to a chemical hose-down. On the way back, each detainee was handed a new wool blanket. By the time I got back in the room, bench seating was claimed. The only space left was the floor—still partially wet. I looked for a dry-enough patch and then folded my blanket into a small square and sat on it. At least until the floor dried completely and I could lie down. My hair, insufficiently towel-dried from the dishtowel, dripped onto the back of my uniform.

Shortly thereafter, "lunch" arrived. An officer stood at the door with a trolley, cheerlessly handing out trays. I accepted mine. It wasn't a flat tray with food placed on top, but more of a thick plastic platform—something that could likely keep you afloat in rough waters—molded in the most unappealing shade of brown imaginable, with indentations to hold various parts of our lunch. The edges were rounded, presumably to make them less damaging if used as weapons. Most of the "food" in these indentations was brown and unidentifiable, but there was a bright spot of orange-yellow syrupy cubes of canned peaches. I ate those first, licking the plastic spork clean. Next was the starch—reconstituted potatoes, bland and mushy. The center pile, which may or may not have been meat, I left untouched or offered to someone else. Breakfast and lunch arrived on those trays. Dinner, however, was tray-less—delivered in plastic baggies. An officer stood at the door and tossed them at us. Three baggies each. One containing a sandwich—two slices of white bread surrounding bologna, egg salad, or, when I was lucky, peanut butter. Another filled with broken potato chips. And the last, a small square of dense vanilla cake. Since that was the vanilla cake I'd tasted while throwing up on my second day, I no longer wanted any part of it. I usually gave away the sandwich, so dinner was often just the sad handful of broken potato chips. If you've been trying for years to lose that stubborn last ten pounds to no avail, head to Pigeon Forge and get yourself arrested.

* * *

The room got crowded that evening. New people arrived, sometimes in groups of two or three. The last one in that night was a girl—maybe eighteen or so—in a black T-shirt and jeans, with dark hair and heavy eye makeup. She was strikingly pretty. Her face and pale arms were covered in red scratches, some still bleeding. Her T-shirt was partially torn. She seemed amped up, wired, and definitely *not shy*. At least not in this moment. She moved through the space like she'd been there before—familiar with a few others in the room and probably with the space itself. We all heard her story. She'd been running from the cops and had nearly gotten away, through brush and over fences. We also learned that her father was a well-known local drug dealer. Notably, she seemed proud of that. She was angry and loud, commanding attention with her stories. Her name was Melanie.

A couple of hours later, she ended up on the floor next to me. Despite it being May and warm outside, it was cold in that concrete cell. Being close to someone, sharing blankets, helped for warmth. Though we hadn't said a word to each other, Melanie and I ended up nearly spooning under the same blanket. I was the big spoon. The room was mostly quiet now, everyone lying down. After a while, I felt Melanie's torso quiver slightly. I heard a sniffle and realized she was quietly crying. I wanted to whisper something to her, but I had no idea what. Instead, I scooted a little closer, tucking my knees behind hers. My arms were curled up in front of me, and I opened one hand and put my palm on her back, with just a tiny bit of pressure. It was meant to somehow tell this very tough girl, *Everything will be okay.*

* * *

Day five was another day of sitting or lying around, wondering what would happen and when. Another day of trying to think about anything other than the outside world, and what awaited me.

The only way to pass the time was focusing on other people—listening to their conversations, watching as much as I could without being rude. Sometimes I joined in. But whenever the conversation turned to me, I felt funny about what to say. They'd ask why I was there, and I'd say something about grand larceny—then immediately feel the need to explain that I wasn't *actually* a thief. But then I'd quickly realize that some of them likely *were* thieves, and I'd awkwardly find myself wanting to add, *Not that there's anything wrong with that!*

I didn't know how to explain my life and circumstances, so mostly, I stayed quiet. Or I commiserated with one of the women who'd been there as long as I had. Each time the guards came in, she'd beg for them to move us. Why they didn't I had no idea. I felt like there had to be some kind of law about how long people could be confined in temporary holding cells, but then again, it didn't seem like people's rights were much of a concern there. Weirdly, I was getting used to that room. Moving into a "dorm" would mean I'd have a bed, but it would also mean being dropped in with a whole new set of people, with new potential risks, new unknowns.

I thought back to my apartment in New York City—the one Mr. Fox had moved me out of, despite my objections. It was the last place I'd called home. It had been a full-floor unit, two bedrooms, two bathrooms. But it wasn't just mine. It doubled as our official One Lucky Duck corporate office and, before that, had also been the home of our e-commerce operations, from where we shipped online orders. Back then it was crowded. Less so after we moved e-commerce to a new space in Brooklyn, but still, by day my home had effectively been an office. It was only my private space at night and on weekends. The elevator opened directly into what should have been a living room but for us was the main workspace, with four or five desks for employees. Beyond that was the kitchen, a hallway, and a bathroom. In the back were the two bedrooms and another bathroom. One bedroom was my actual bedroom. The other, my office. I had fluffy shag rugs in both. The windows faced another building, and being only on the second floor, they let in zero sunlight. But the rooms were cozy, and right now, I longed to be in that office—sitting at my huge desk, with Leon stretched out on the fluffy carpeting by my feet.

Although, that apartment was also where I first met Mr. Fox.

CHAPTER SIX

LATE 2011
NEW YORK CITY

When he first told me his full name—Shane Anthony Fox—I thought, *What a cool name.* It never occurred to me that it wasn't real. I quickly started calling him Mr. Fox, and before we had even met in person, he started calling me Mrs. Fox. I liked the sound of it—Mr. and Mrs. Fox. As if we were characters in a movie, like *Mr. and Mrs. Smith.* He was always mysterious about his job. He said he worked in "commercial real estate" but also vaguely hinted that his *real* occupation was secret. As if he was, in fact, like Brad Pitt's Mr. Smith, working undercover.

I wouldn't mind being Angelina Jolie, I thought.

* * *

After nearly two months of texting and phone calls, Mr. Fox finally came to see me. It was late 2011. Looking back now, it makes sense that he waited so long. He let the anticipation build, along with my trust in him, so that by the time he *did* come, I let him straight into my home. Writing this now, I'm embarrassed by my own recklessness. But he'd made me feel safe. I had already invested so much of my time and emotional energy in this *relationship*—if that's what it was—that I was eager to be alone with him, all abuzz with pent-up yearning for him. For who *I thought* he was.

It had been over six months since Tobyn and I had split, and during that time I hadn't been intimate with anyone else. At first, I was too sad. But as time passed, I craved physical closeness with someone, *anyone*, if only to purge the pain from my system. So in my shy way, I tried to find someone I liked who would be interested in me. For whatever reason, nothing worked out. There was a waiter at my restaurant—Curtis—on whom I'd had a big crush. *(Hi, Curtis! If you're reading this, I had a massive crush on you!)* Like Tobyn, he was much younger than me. And technically, I was his boss, therefore I couldn't brazenly flirt with him. But I made subtle efforts, which went unnoticed or ignored, leaving me feeling like a creepy old cougar.

Another time, my very attractive dog walker, Justin—who had become a close friend—asked if he could crash at my place for the night because his brother wanted to bring a girl back to his apartment. We slept in my big queen-size bed with Leon. I wore a nightie. We cuddled. I waited for a sign. A hint. Some *movement*. But… nothing. We just slept. Nothing more. And no, he's not gay.

So it was in this state—feeling rejected, wondering, *What's wrong with me?*—that Mr. Fox arrived. Here was someone who was interested in me. This manly guy with a deep, sexy voice, who had only grown increasingly attractive in my mind, was finally coming to see me. With all that pent-up energy, I was *ready*.

I repeat, it was extremely reckless to allow someone about whom I'd verified nothing into my home. I was not, historically or by nature, a suspicious person. Nor was I very good at protecting myself in general. Boundaries? Not my thing.

It was a Friday night. I was nervous, running around my apartment tidying up, sorting out what to wear. By then, our conversations had progressed to the point of speaking graphically about sex—something I was *not remotely* used to doing—and partly because of that, I was already in a combustible state. I put on music and dimmed the lights. Despite it being winter, I chose a white summer dress. Clearly, we'd be staying indoors. I also started drinking beer—on an empty stomach. By the time he arrived, I was a little drunk.

My apartment was on the second floor. When Mr. Fox arrived, I buzzed him in, instructing him to walk to the back of the lobby and take the stairs. I went to the door, unbolted it, and cracked it open. I heard his steps, heavy and deliberate, on the staircase. Leon anxiously shoved his snout between the door and the frame, so I opened it wider to let him through.

"Hey, buddy. Nice to meet you," Mr. Fox said to Leon. Hearing his voice in person felt strange. Then he took the last few steps, and I opened the door to him fully.

"Hi."

"Hi."

Leon, being an excitable dog, demanded all the attention in those first moments, giving me a chance to look at Mr. Fox. He was wearing jeans and a blue hooded sweatshirt. Not quite as tall as I'd imagined, but still tall. He also appeared... *softer* than I'd expected. His face was rounder than in his photos, which made him look less intimidating—almost sweet. I knew he was big, but his bigness was more in the way NFL defensive ends are big—solid, with a layer of jiggle. Not solid and chiseled like the Rock. But there wasn't much time to process coherent thoughts. And again, I was kind of drunk. Before he even set his bag down, we kissed. To my relief, he was a good kisser. And he smelled good. He dropped his bag, and we inched our way to the couch, only a few feet from the door. He sat, and rather quickly, moving only the minimum amount of clothing needed out of the way, we had sex.

I cringe writing these paragraphs. Or, more accurately, I want to vomit on the keyboard. Because I find him so wildly repulsive now. But even if he were Prince Charming, I'd still feel embarrassed. This wasn't sex on the first date. It was sex *before* the first date. Maybe people do this all the time now with hookup apps, but it seems dangerous—both physically and emotionally.

It makes me sad for my younger self. For my lack of inherent confidence. For not knowing how to honor and protect myself better.

* * *

Afterward, it was still somewhat early, and we were both hungry. I changed into warmer clothes, and we went out to dinner in Midtown. It was a high-traffic Friday night, so we took the subway. As usual, I had my One Lucky Duck tote bag over my shoulder. We stood on the subway car, holding the rails, when a woman seated nearby glanced at the bag, then at me. She lit up. "Oh I love your place so much—I have your books too!" I thanked her, and we chatted. I remember feeling gratified that this happened, thinking maybe Mr. Fox was impressed.

By dinner, though, I was underwhelmed—fighting a deep sense of disappointment. He was just as funny in person and easy to talk to, but not as confident as he'd been on the phone. This could have been endearing—I don't like overconfident men—but it didn't match the image I'd built in my head. Furthermore, for someone who'd made himself out to be a world-traveler, he didn't seem comfortable in the upscale restaurant I'd chosen. His unease should have whispered, *He's not who he says he is.*

On top of all that, you'd think a worldly man of means would have booked himself a hotel, even if we ended up spending nights together. You'd think I would have insisted on it, but I didn't.

By the time he left the following day, I was relieved to be alone again—reasonably certain I wouldn't have him back. Something definitely didn't feel right. *Welp, there goes that fantasy,* I thought.

* * *

But reality is never that simple. In truth, I was confused and had no one to talk to about my feelings because I hadn't really told anyone about Mr. Fox. Unlike most people, I didn't have that one best friend who knew everything about my life. My employees didn't know about Mr. Fox. And notably, I *didn't* take him to my own restaurant that weekend. That was unusual. Normally, I would *want* to take someone to my restaurant, to show it off. I'd want someone I was dating to meet my staff, and for them to meet him. But with Mr. Fox, I didn't. That alone should have been an alarm bell.

I felt shitty that I'd let this guy into my apartment and had *sex* with him—right away. Had I met him in person at the start, I probably would have lost interest and walked away. If only I had walked away. Instead, he'd shrewdly allowed time for me to weave connections in my brain based only on what he told me—my imagination filling in the blanks to make him who I *wanted* him to be. In that way, I was already emotionally invested.

That attachment is probably why, despite my initial conviction to not see him again, I allowed him back in. It may have taken a few weeks, but he was back. He must have done some smooth talking on the phone. I've since learned how powerful voice alone can be in influencing an unsuspecting listener. And I certainly was unsuspecting.

I don't recall specifically what he said during our calls, but I'm pretty sure he'd already begun telling me, explicitly, that he could help me. I was overwhelmed with my business, encumbered with both personal and business debt, yet full of ambition to expand and grow. I'd felt stuck for so long, and because I was so open about myself, Mr. Fox knew all this. He would have known exactly what to say.

Beyond implying he could help me, he said things to further pique my curiosity, raising questions in my mind. And I have a hard time leaving questions unanswered. Mystery is alluring. It's why people stay up late reading detective novels. *I couldn't put it down*, they say. Well, Mr. Fox was a mystery. He was unlike anyone else I'd ever met—with something very powerful in his direct gaze—and I didn't understand who he really was. Even if I didn't think he was right for me, I wanted to know. It's hard to move on without answers.

Our second weekend started much like the first. I don't know why I let this happen again. He must have built up anticipation again. Maybe there was also an undercurrent of self-destruction in me—like when you already feel sick but you eat the other half of the pint of ice cream anyway. Again, I drank beer before he arrived, and again, we had couch sex. I vaguely remember telling him to be "careful." I'd been off birth control for over ten years. I should have insisted on proper protection, but I didn't. Tobyn and I had always just been *careful* in this way and never had an issue. I do know that I made it clear it was risky, that he should withdraw at the appropriate time. He did not.

My *immediate* gut reaction was that he'd done this intentionally. I was mad. And yet I mostly blamed myself for not having been clear enough. I didn't say much about it, but the feeling that he'd done it deliberately nagged at me.

Typing these words makes me queasy and embarrassed. I feel shitty about all the reckless things I did simply because I didn't have the confidence to put my own value above what someone else wanted.

If I could sit my younger self down, I would tell her that any guy who barrels into having sex without any prior conversation about protection is a guy who does *not* care about you. At least not in any meaningful way. And I would tell her that she's worth so much more to ever put up with that, *ever*. I'd also advise her to pay attention to this reflex to blame herself for the transgressions of others—even if she played a role too.

Still, I wasn't all that worried. I was thirty-nine years old and had never been pregnant. *What are the odds?* I thought. Probably very slim. Nothing to do but wait and see if my period came when it was supposed to. I was annoyed—confused, even—that I'd let him come back, that I'd allowed myself to be convinced. Still, I put it out of my mind. What could I do now other than get through the weekend? Telling him to leave early was the kind of self-protective move I wasn't bold enough to make.

* * *

Just over a week later, I was at the restaurant, sitting in the back with former supermodel Carol Alt on a Sunday evening. We were friendly, as Carol was a huge raw food advocate, and we bonded over that. But even more so, I felt connected to her because her longtime boyfriend was fifteen years younger. We sometimes talked about the inherent challenges of being the older woman in a relationship. She could understand my pain over Tobyn better than most. Even with Mr. Fox in and out of the picture—I was still heartbroken over Tobyn. Talking with Carol was therapeutic. She could empathize with the particulars of my heartache, the extra layer of *I'm too old* emotions.

I didn't tell her about Mr. Fox, at least not in any detail. But for some reason that night, a voice in my head kept chiming in, *You might be pregnant.* I don't know why. It was a feeling. I didn't want to wait to see if I'd miss my period. After leaving Carol, I practically ran to CVS to buy a pregnancy test.

At home, I went straight to the bathroom, tore the test from the package, and followed the instructions. And there it was—the purple plus sign appearing on the white strip. A welcome miracle for some and entirely dreaded for others. I was firmly in the latter category. *Fuck, fuck, fuck, fuck* was all I could think. The option of giving birth to his child never even crossed my mind. There was just one path. Practically tripping over myself as I pulled up my pants while bolting to my computer, I sat to quickly research options. It didn't take long to find the right place. The next morning, I made the call, took their soonest available appointment, and gave them my credit card number for the deposit. I felt incredibly grateful this solution was available to me and that—at the time—I could easily afford it. I was relieved the *situation* would soon be resolved.

But I was acutely aware of how differently this would have felt had it happened with Tobyn. First, if he'd gotten me pregnant, it would've been a genuine accident. Whereas with Mr. Fox, it had felt like a devious ploy. Second, with Tobyn, it would have been something we handled together. And it would've been a far more emotionally difficult experience. Tobyn is an amazing human being. I'd have felt horrifically conflicted about terminating a pregnancy with him. In contrast, a mini Mr. Fox felt like a hostile foreign object in my uterus that needed to be removed ASAP. Another sign I inexplicably disregarded. If I was so horrified over his impregnating me, shouldn't that have been a cruise-ship-sized red flag to stay away from him? Yes.

The day of my procedure couldn't have come fast enough. I arrived at the Midtown office alone for the midmorning appointment. It was an unseasonably warm, rainy day in early January 2012. Vacuum aspiration was the method to be used. *This thing is getting hoovered out of me*, I coldly thought. From my research, I knew it would hurt but was glad there was no need for general anesthesia—or any at all, really, beyond a couple of extra-strength Tylenols a half hour before. The method was apparently very safe.

In the procedure room, I put my One Lucky Duck tote bag on a chair, changed into my paper gown, and climbed up on the table—the kind equipped with stirrups. The doctor and a nurse came in. The doctor, an attractive and energetic blond woman, treated me with gentle kindness, walking me through what to expect. I lay back, scooted down, and put one socked foot in each stirrup. I was feeling that usual gynecological wildly awkward, fully exposed sensation—*nothing between my wide-open lady parts and this other person now; try not to think about it*—when the doctor, who had spotted my tote bag in the corner, said, "Oh, One Lucky Duck! I *love* that place so much! I go there all the time for takeout. You go there too?"

I propped up on my left elbow, pulling down my paper gown on that side to show her the matching tattoo on my shoulder. I gave her a crazed smile that I hoped conveyed, *This is sort of weird and funny, right??*

"Oh my god, that's *your* place! Oh wow, I love it so much. Such a great thing you're doing there!"

I thanked her, feeling awkward yet appreciative.

"Well, anyway, we definitely need to talk after this is over," she said, before shifting back to the task at hand. She was quick and efficient, talking me through the procedure. The nurse held my hand, and I squeezed hers back hard when it hurt the most, grateful for her presence. At first it felt like an intense punch in the uterus—like sharp, stabbing cramps. Then it just felt like regular cramps. When it was all over, I exhaled with relief. (And side note: the doctor and I did talk after, and are still in touch to this day.)

With my clothes back on and a giant maxi pad in my underwear, I walked home. I felt unusually hungry. It was a Thursday, which meant the Taïm falafel truck would be parked on Fifth Avenue, close to my apartment. When I reached Twenty-First Street, the truck was there, as expected. I ordered my all-time favorite comfort food. Not raw, but still vegan: a Mediterranean platter with a pile of silky hummus, pickled cabbage salad, tabouli, and the most delicious falafel with tahini sauce. I took it home to my cozy backroom office, sat at my desk, and scanned through new emails, while devouring the food. Almost as if I was trying to quickly fill the space that had just been otherwise occupied. *Baby out; falafel in*, I thought.

Then I got back to work.

I didn't tell Mr. Fox about any of this. I felt no reason, and certainly no obligation, to do so. I couldn't be sure, but it *felt* like he'd done what he did with intention. I was angry, and I resolved never to see him again.

However, I'd never been good at ghosting people—cutting off all contact. Even with my intention to pull away, I kept communicating with him. Part of me probably wanted an explanation. Something to make it all make sense. Closure, at least. I figured there was little harm in staying in touch. I didn't have to agree to see him.

Except eventually, of course, I did.

CHAPTER SEVEN

MAY 2016

PIGEON FORGE, TENNESSEE

Sitting in that Tennessee holding cell, I should have at least felt relief to be finally free of Mr. Fox, but I didn't. I was confused, still numb, and quietly freaking the fuck out. How could I not? I was incarcerated, facing a terrifyingly surreal list of ominous-sounding charges—ones that could, theoretically, lead to fifteen years in prison. Who would protect me? Who would explain what I had no clue how to explain? How would I know what was real and what wasn't? I had felt safer in the world of denial I'd inhabited for the past year.

Mr. Fox had kept me hiding under thick blankets of delusion, wrapping me in his reassurances—his insistence that *nothing is real,* that with him, I'd always be protected, and that the *happily ever after* he promised was just around the corner. He'd implanted in me the idea that he had some kind of special power. So as I sat in the holding cell, part of me imagined what could happen in that reality to get me out. At any moment, the doors might open and men in dark suits and sunglasses—like Will Smith and Tommy Lee Jones from *Men in Black*—would appear and wordlessly usher me through the county jail, out to a black SUV with darkened windows. From there? Who knew? A private plane to a private island, an Ayn Randian never-before-mapped island, where all the *real* leaders of the world convened. I'd have passed all the tests Mr. Fox had put me through. I'd be changed out of my striped jail jumper and into a silky steel-blue gown and formally inaugurated into this cabal.

This is seriously the kind of thing Mr. Fox made me think could, perhaps actually would, happen.

* * *

I was startled out of my daydream by the loud bang of the door outside our cell. Then the heavy thunk of the lock. Was it time to eat? Was someone being added? Would I finally be moved? Were the men in black suits actually here?

A guard came in, keys jangling, and looked at me. "You," she barked. "You have a video call."

For a few seconds, my mind scrambled—who would it be? Then I quickly realized it must be my father—who *else* would it be? But I didn't understand why it was a video call if he'd arrived in Tennessee, as he likely had by now. Turned out there were no in-person visits in this jail. My father was on-site, somewhere presumably not very far away, but we could only see each other via video. This seemed cruel. I was led out to the main room of the station. There, mounted on the wall, was a computer monitor and phone receiver. I was instructed on how to use it and informed that it cost money, which confused me.

"The cash you had in your wallet when you came in—that's in your account here," the officer explained.

I finally got the monitor working, and a grainy black-and-white image of my father appeared. I immediately burst into tears. My dad—my white-haired, seventy-seven-year-old father, who'd just driven who knew how long (seven hours, it turned out) in his silver Prius to get from his home in Washington, DC, to Pigeon Forge, Tennessee. I couldn't even imagine what he was thinking or what he'd thought all those hours of driving. We just sat there a while, holding the receivers while I cried and he watched me with a pained look on his face. Finally he asked, "Is it drugs?" And I thought, *If only*. At least if I'd been whacked out on drugs, that could have provided some sort of explanation for what no one could understand: why I had disappeared from my life as I'd known it nearly a year earlier. I didn't have an answer.

"No," I managed to spit out. "I wish it was," I added.

At any rate, it probably *looked* like I'd been on drugs. Five days in the holding cell, barely eating, and then my hair—which I usually dried with a blow dryer and carefully curled with a curling iron—looked insane. If left to dry naturally, my long and thick hair turns into an unruly, tangled mass that is not remotely attractive, except maybe to birds looking for a place to lay their eggs. I'm pretty sure my father had never seen me like this before.

"Did you get Leon?" I asked, wiping my running nose with my free hand.

He told me he was going to get him next. He'd already picked up my belongings from the hotel and was going to get Leon after this visit. The hotel staff had been kind, he said. They'd expressed concern for me. The women at the front desk had always been nice—when I passed through the lobby with Leon on our way back from a walk, they'd sometimes come out from behind the counter to play with him. Until we were arrested, they hadn't known anything about us, other than whatever vague lies Mr. Fox had told them.

My father said Leon was doing well. The hotel manager who had taken him home had young kids and other dogs, so he was in good hands. I was relieved—about Leon, at least. It hurt to be away from him, wondering what was going through his doggy brain—or what he was being fed.

"Thank you," I said, my breathing uneven, tears still flowing.

I don't remember much of what else we said, just how I *felt*. Mortified, awash in shame, and wishing I could die right then and there. The only other thing I recall is a discussion about a lawyer—my father telling me they would try to find one for me back in New York. I asked him if anyone had spoken to Big Dave.

I originally met Big Dave—who is, yes, quite tall—through my dog walker, and over time we became friends. Big Dave was the first person to whom I introduced Mr. Fox. Eventually, Mr. Fox had essentially co-opted Dave as *his* friend, to the point where it became awkward for Big Dave and me to communicate directly. Later, Mr. Fox led me to believe that Big Dave was in on "everything"—whatever *everything* was—and that he would always know what to do.

The last time I'd seen Mr. Fox, he'd told me only one thing. I was standing at the jail intake desk while the officer behind the window rummaged through my wallet and took my earrings and rings, inventorying it all. Mr. Fox was being escorted out of the booking room. As he passed by, the officer standing behind me sternly warned, "Do *not* look at him! Do. Not. Look at him!" But I couldn't help looking. I needed to look. I needed Mr. Fox to tell me what to do. He turned his head back toward me. "Call Big Dave!" he said. That was it.

I was allowed one phone call when I was brought in, but I didn't know Big Dave's number by heart. The only number I knew was my mother's. Fingers shaky, I dialed, relieved when she answered. My voice trembled as I'd quickly told her, "Mama, I've been arrested." I gave her the name of the town and assured her I was "okay." I didn't explain what had happened, since I wasn't even sure. I just asked her to call Big Dave right away and told her how to find his number.

Big Dave was, I'd assumed—hoped—the one who would have made *that call* to summon Will Smith and Tommy Lee Jones to come get me out, as I'd imagined. They just hadn't shown up yet. Now, sitting there, talking to my father, I wondered where the rescue party was. I was waiting for them.

"Yes, your mother spoke to him," my father told me. He then added that Big Dave had told my mother that Mr. Fox had asked if my parents could pay for an attorney for him, too—an outrageous request.

"What?"

This didn't make sense. Mr. Fox had apparently used his one call to contact Dave, so why weren't things being handled? Weren't they supposed to be *taking care of the situation—somehow?* Why did Mr. Fox want *my father* to handle things? This couldn't be happening. My heart sank into a dense pool of dread. My father, rightly, had zero intention of doing anything at all on behalf of Mr. Fox. It only got worse.

"I also had to pay the bill at the hotel," my father continued. "It was over two thousand dollars."

I felt ill. My father, a retired physicist, is a frugal person.

This was just one more clue seeping into my consciousness, dragging me closer to the harsh truth: Mr. Fox had, indeed, been *full of shit*. The unpaid hotel bill, combined with the bigger, more alarming fact of his asking that *my* father handle *his* lawyer? None of it made sense.

Mr. Fox's words came back to me—the ones he had said not long before the arrest: *Baby, there's going to be one more gut shot. Just one more.* He knew. It felt like he had known. Except instead of this being some final test, this was just *it*. The end. Had he just... run out of moves? Run out of money, and out of moves? Why he hadn't just driven off and left me there alone I couldn't figure out. And I'll probably never know.

* * *

After the call, I went back to the holding cell, picked up the wool blanket I'd left in the corner, wrapped it around myself, and lay down on the floor. I didn't know how to make sense of anything. I had no home. My business and brand—what had felt like my identity—were gone. A lot of people lost *a lot* of money because of *me*. Mr. Fox had made me humiliate myself and burn so many of the bridges I'd built over the years.

How could I have believed him? How did that happen? I so badly wanted everything—my life—to be over. Clearly, I had lost the game of life, the rules of which I never understood. I wanted to go to sleep for the rest of eternity, to hit the escape key. To *exit, stage left.*

Contemplating it all, my thoughts would inevitably wade into some variation of *If only he had just killed me.*

I considered various ways I might off myself once I got out of jail, yet none seemed viable or realistic. They were all too gruesome. And I didn't want to cause the people who cared about me more pain than I already had. But wouldn't it be amazing to just lay back in a car filling up with carbon monoxide and slip into a forever-nap? It would. But I'd probably fail at that, too, I thought. And end up only brain damaged. *Fuck.*

For anyone who has waded into the murky waters of suicidal ideation, I imagine a common fantasy is to avoid having to do the job oneself—to instead be tragically killed by another. That way, it wouldn't be our fault. Our loved ones wouldn't be mad at us for eternity. We wouldn't be thought of as weak, selfish, or cruel. In this fantasy, death would come quickly and painlessly. A shot to the back of the head. Or even better, drugged into unconsciousness, then snuffed out with a pillow. No pain, no mess.

Yet now my life was just that. Lots of pain. A big mess.

CHAPTER EIGHT

EARLY DAYS

MASSACHUSETTS

I was always a good girl, a quiet and obedient child. I didn't throw tantrums. I don't know if it was because I was so painfully shy that drawing attention to myself—screaming and crying in the supermarket—would have been more mortifying than the injustice of not getting what I wanted. Or did I, at some level, know that such tantrums likely wouldn't have been tolerated? I don't know.

My parents, my older sister, and I lived in Newton, Massachusetts, a suburb of Boston, in a middle-class neighborhood, in a standard brick house with a small yard and a one-car garage.

My father was a physicist at MIT, and most weekdays he rode his bike the seven or so miles from Newton to Cambridge and back. A couple of evenings a week he went to tae kwon do classes and eventually earned a black belt. Because of that, I know how to do a roundhouse kick, but that's about it. Most of what he taught me was of a practical nature. Like how to build or fix things in his musty, cluttered basement workshop. Or how to sharpen knives on a big spinning grindstone wheel powered by pumping an attached wooden pedal—sort of how I imagine Fred Flintstone sharpened his knives. My father also taught me how to play chess, how to build a proper fire, how to chop wood.

I was raised to be independent. I was not *daddy's little girl,* nor was I anyone's *princess.* But my childhood, compared to my father's—and even my mother's—was relatively trauma free.

My father was born in Latvia in 1939. When he was five years old, he and his parents, along with his older brother, fled their home ahead of the advancing Russian Army. They landed in Germany, where they lived in a displaced persons' camp until they were able to get to the US as refugees in 1949.

My grandmother, my father's mother, was born in Latvia in 1896. During World War I, her father, my great-grandfather, was killed in the streets by poison gas. Later, she gave up a career as an opera singer to become a pharmacist, opening her own pharmacy after realizing how vital medicine was in saving lives at that time.

My grandfather, my father's father, died when I was a baby. After that, my grandmother lived with us for a few years, helping care for my sister and me while my parents worked. We spoke Latvian with her and my father. On Saturdays, we went to Latvian school, and in the summers, we went to Latvian camp.

My mother grew up in Ohio with adopted parents, having spent her first six months in an orphanage. Many years later, she researched her birth parents and discovered they were both originally from Germany, having met—briefly—during World War II. By the time my mother learned this, my parents had long been divorced. But my father said it made sense that she came from German stock—he had always said she was "built like a brick shit house." This was his way of saying she was sturdy and solid, I guess. My mom's adoptive parents were strictly Catholic, and after high school, she joined a convent. But she didn't last long there and instead went off to college, leaving religion behind entirely and eventually moving to Boston. When she met my father, she was working as a research assistant in biology labs, first at the Harvard School of Public Health, then at Tufts Medical Center. Their honeymoon was her first time in Europe. What impressed her most on that trip was the food—how different it was from the industrialized supermarket fare of the 1950s and '60s. Later, while my sister and I were still young, my mom grew tired of laboratory research and decided to go to culinary school. She then took various kitchen jobs, eventually working her way up to sous chef in a highly regarded French restaurant. Working nights wasn't sustainable, however, so she left restaurants altogether and took a job running the executive dining room for a technology company—a position with daytime hours far more convenient for a mom with kids in school.

If my mother is ever asked what I was like as a child, she'll say I was a bit *odd*. As a toddler, she could keep me occupied for hours with a box of tissues. I'd sit in my crib, methodically pulling them out one by one, tearing each into thin strips while humming to myself, repeating the process until the box was empty. And apparently, I had a fondness for chewing on chicken bones, tried to eat eggshells, and insisted on eating whole sardines—never the broken ones—holding them in my fist with oil running down my forearm. No foreshadowing of a future in the vegan world there.

She'll also say I could be stubborn. In second grade, I refused to wear any shirt for most of the year except an increasingly worn-out KISS T-shirt. I was always particular about what I wore—usually dressing like a boy and often being mistaken for one.

* * *

I was nine years old when my parents separated. It was a Sunday afternoon, and I'd just been dropped off after a sleepover at a friend's house. When I walked through the front door, I found my parents seated in the living room with my sister, who was crying. I don't quite remember this, but my father says that after my mom explained they were getting a divorce, I looked at them coldly, then turned and went to my room. He came in a little later and found me lying on the lower half of my bunk bed, facing the wall. I wasn't crying—I never cried over it. He sat beside me for a while, wanting to hug me and talk, but decided to "respect my autonomy" and left without saying anything.

My parents separating came as a surprise. They'd never had dramatic fights, just occasional bickering over household stuff. Awkwardly, my father didn't leave right away, but eventually, he found an apartment nearby—a converted garage behind a big house, close enough that my sister and I could walk or ride our bikes there. A while later, he started dating the woman who would later become my stepmother. She was a writer from New York City, which made her seem glamorous to my sister and me. She was warm and funny and *fun*, and when my father announced one afternoon that they planned to marry, we were excited.

My mother dated here and there but no one memorable—until one day she brought home Bob, a man we'd met before. He was the CEO of the company where she worked, sixteen years older than her. My sister and I found him nice but a bit intimidating. He was around more and more until, eventually, he moved in. He hadn't yet formally divorced his first wife. They were separated, but the divorce was ongoing—messy and contentious. Then, one day, we learned that she'd had a stroke and was hospitalized. Bob had six kids, all older than I was. That night, many of them came to our house and stayed for many nights thereafter. Their mother remained in a coma for six months before she died, at which point the younger of his kids moved into our house too. There was a lot of crying, and generally a lot of chaos, which I wasn't used to.

My memories of those years are vague, as if my own internal experience was overshadowed by everything happening around me. At some point, when I was eleven or twelve, we all moved to a much bigger house in the same town. I can't recall the details—packing, unpacking, or anything from that time in general. Zero clue. Was it winter? Summer? No idea. The new house felt massive, with an in-ground pool in the back and an expansive front yard where my mom and Bob had their wedding.

Things calmed down after that. Bob owned property and a home in New Hampshire, where he and my mom eventually moved permanently, but back then it was where they spent most weekends. They also traveled abroad now and then. This left us kids with very little supervision. Sometimes my older stepsiblings were around, but mostly not. Either way, I liked that my mom and Bob were out of town a lot. Bob had a big personality—and with it a temper, something I wasn't used to. I felt far more at ease when he wasn't home.

Barely a teenager, I had unbridled freedom—at least on the weekends. No boundaries, no one watching. Somehow, I still got mostly straight A's in high school. But I might also have been sitting in an IHOP at 4:00 a.m. with older friends who'd been drinking, studying my French flash cards for a test in a few hours. I was fourteen when I lost my virginity, not intentionally. By fifteen, I had a twenty-three-year-old boyfriend. He was a graduate student at Harvard.

For some reason, none of this seemed odd to anyone at the time.

CHAPTER NINE

EARLY 2012

NEW YORK CITY AND NEW HAMPSHIRE

It was early 2012, and I hadn't seen Mr. Fox in many weeks, having resolved—again—to pull away and eventually cut things off. Yet we still texted and occasionally talked. Feeling no commitment to him, I went out now and then with other people. After one dinner, I came down with an odd case of what I assume was mild food poisoning. I couldn't eat without feeling nauseous and sometimes throwing up.

My mom offered to drive down to New York and bring Leon and me up to her house in New Hampshire. Getting out of my stuffy, dark apartment/office and escaping to the fresh country air was appealing. Leon could run off-leash, and I could work remotely from my laptop.

My mom's house is an incredibly relaxing place, with windows and French doors lining one side of the house, overlooking snowy fields and a hill that leads up to an apple orchard. My stepfather had passed away a few years earlier, so it was extra quiet. While there, I mostly lay on the couch by the fire with Leon. After a couple of days, my mom had to go out of town. Meanwhile, I was starting to get restless, feeling a bit better each day. I wanted to get back to the city but didn't want to wait until my mom returned. I'm also irrationally afraid of being alone out in the country. Put me in a densely populated, crime-infested city any day over solitude in the woods, where every crackle of leaves is a sure sign of an axe murderer creeping around the house.

Since I was still in contact with Mr. Fox, he knew my circumstances. He offered to drive up from Massachusetts—with his father, of all people—to pick up Leon and me and take us back to the city. I can't recall the excuse Mr. Fox gave for why he never drove himself. Whether he didn't have a driver's license or his own car, either should have been suspect. I also knew I shouldn't be opening this door again, but I really did want to get back home. And Mr. Fox was persistent, making it seem like no big deal. Just a ride. Finally, I agreed.

* * *

They arrived the next day. There was no doubt it was *really* his father—you could see the resemblance immediately. Mr. Fox Sr. was a gray-haired, spectacled version of Mr. Fox Jr., and they shared the same unusual build: an oddly wide torso. Like, even if they both got skinny, they'd still have super-wide torsos. His father had a strong handshake and seemed both pleased to meet me and impressed with my mother's house. It wasn't overly large or fancy, but the wide-open first floor—living room, large dining table, and kitchen all in one expansive space—made it feel grander than it was.

His father was also charming and funny. Goofy, even. On the way to New York, as we drove through a town called Athol, he pointed to the sign and said, "God, I feel like such an athol." They asked me questions about my mom and the apple orchard she now ran on her own. Not in a million years would it have occurred to me then that she was being sized up as a target.

Mr. Fox took a picture of me in the backseat of the car. I wore a pink sweatshirt and a green John Deere hat. I look less than happy in that photo. I remember feeling let down seeing him again after weeks had passed. As if, in the interim, I'd allowed my perception of him to shift back to the original fantasy version of Mr. Fox. I'm quite sure he'd originally made the offer as if they'd just drop me off and continue on somewhere. Yet, as would become routine with him, plans had somehow changed. Now it seemed Mr. Fox was staying with me? It was the weekend, so I didn't have the excuse of my employees being there. And after accepting the favor of a ride, it felt rude, especially in front of his father, to refuse to let him stay the night. What could be the harm?

This is where I'd tell my younger self, "Stop giving so many shits about what people think or about appearing rude. Stop. Embrace the awkward and stand up for whatever *you* want, for the outcome that makes *you* most comfortable. Being too nice can be dangerous."

I regretted accepting the ride, but I couldn't have imagined then how much I'd later regret having allowed him back in my home—back into my life.

CHAPTER TEN

MAY 2016

PIGEON FORGE, TENNESSEE

I'd spent six days in the Pigeon Forge holding cell. Finally, I was relocated to the dorms. The dorms were large cells, each with five bunk beds, housing ten people total. A big metal picnic-style table was bolted down in the middle of the room, and a TV was mounted high up on the wall. There was one bathroom—which had no door, but at least the toilet was mercifully around a corner—and a shower that was also semiprivate. A phone hung on the wall in the corner beside a computer kiosk.

The relocation was both a relief and a new kind of terror: I finally had a bed (relief), but I was now also surrounded by unfamiliar inmates (terrifying). I had no idea how long I'd be there, only that the state of New York had twenty-four days to come and get me. By this time, I'd already heard horror stories of grueling extraditions. People stuck on long, punishing transfers to faraway states, sitting for hours—handcuffed and shackled—in hot metal buses, stopping at various county jails along the way for overnight stays. The idea of making a days-long trip to New York this way—a jail crawl of sorts—sounded miserable.

I chose the only empty bed, a top bunk, carrying the bedding I'd been given. The lower bunk was occupied by a girl who appeared to be fast asleep, a long tube sock wrapped around her face covering her eyes. Across from us, another woman sat on her bed. "Hey, Mariah!" she called out loudly, kicking the bottom bunk. "You've got a new bunkie."

Mariah jolted awake, pulling the sock off her face. Squinting in the light, she looked up at me, clearly not pleased. I didn't know why the other woman had to wake her—this didn't seem like the way to start things off on the right foot.

"Hi," I managed.

"What's your name?" she asked, still looking pissed.

I introduced myself, going through the usual two or three rounds of spelling my first name. Mariah looked to be about twenty-five years old. I'd never heard of anyone named Mariah before, except for Mariah Carey, and I seriously wondered if that was who she'd been named after. Mariah turned out to be far more welcoming than this first impression conveyed. She even loaned me an extra pair of her own graying tube socks, since I was still wearing the same now-very-gross short socks I'd arrived in.

This new, larger cell was cold—I noticed immediately, probably because I get cold easily. Mariah was wearing a full set of long underwear. She explained how I could get my own set—as well as socks, snacks, and more—through their commissary system via the kiosk attached to the wall. Luckily, she said, delivery day was in two days, and I still had time to put in an order. She had a white long-sleeved thermal shirt that she said was too small for her.

"You can have it," she told me, "if you order me a medium."

"Okay," I agreed, grateful. Even though I wasn't sure if it was a suggestion or a directive.

I ordered long underwear and a few pairs of socks. I got Mariah her size-medium thermal top. I also ordered soap, shampoo, and conditioner, along with whatever snacks appeared the least *un*healthy, which included rectangular packets of square peanut butter cracker sandwiches. At this point, I'd have eaten nearly anything. The regular food they brought to us was so god-awful that I was hungry all the time. I also got a pad of paper, pens, and a few stamped envelopes. Then I noticed one could buy *coffee*—little bags of granulated instant coffee. Tempting as it was, I didn't order it, since I'd so recently suffered through the hell of sudden caffeine withdrawal.

Once I figured out how to use the phone, I called my mother and wrote down some phone numbers. Then I called my sister. These conversations were surreal.

I cried a lot and didn't know what to say. Mostly, the calls were practical, about the lawyer I'd need when I got back to New York. I gave my sister Ray Brown's contact information and asked her to reach out to him. I told her to ask him if he'd come see me again, if he had time.

* * *

It was on one of these calls with my sister that I learned my mother had given Mr. Fox money—*a lot* of money. I knew that a few times early on, Mr. Fox had asked my mom to *move* funds—to receive wires from me, then withdraw to hand over to him. I also knew he had occasionally borrowed from her. But I wasn't at all expecting what my sister told me, her voice laced with fury.

"Four hundred thousand dollars!" she practically yelled into the phone. "And she *borrowed* most of it!"

I closed my eyes, the sickening reality of what had happened breaking through my preoccupation with daily jail life. *Four hundred thousand dollars.* And it was my fault. I didn't know what to say or feel. Even now, writing this, my insides seize up, and I feel the creeping shame that makes me want to leap out the nearest window.

I should have known. I should have at least asked instead of assuming everything was okay. But I realize now I'd been in a massive state of denial. It seems he had both me *and* my mom under his thumb. Sadly, I don't think I'd have been shocked if my sister had told me our mom was out fifty thousand, even a hundred maybe—any amount would have felt *awful*, and massively upsetting, and I feel shitty even admitting that it wouldn't have surprised me so much. But *four hundred thousand*?

Mr. Fox had wedged himself between my mother and me. He always assured me she was fine. But then again, he also assured me I was fine. Not just us—he insisted that anyone who ever helped me would be more than fine, that they'd be taken care of after this was all over. *This* meaning the bizarre cosmic challenge through which he was, supposedly, ushering me. Not only would they be taken care of, he said, but even their kids would be. In some ethereal way, as if protected by angels. No harm would ever come to them. Their lives would be amazing. This was what I was told by Mr. Fox, who always implied that he himself was a celestial being with the power to protect people. Or, alternatively, to ensure their doom.

He also made it seem as if money would be unlimited. Whenever I'd ask what would happen to X or Y, this or that, he'd always say, "Don't worry about it, baby. Problem with a price tag." As in, anything that could be solved with money, he could easily solve. Not just small things but big things. There was a building for sale that I'd fantasized about turning into a hotel—a hotel version of Pure Food and Wine. It was more than a fantasy. I'd worked with a group from Hong Kong on real, tangible plans, with colorful, professionally bound presentation books. I visualized the hotel as a gut renovation of a building, just across from the restaurant. "What if someone else buys it?" I'd ask Mr. Fox. *Problem with a price tag!* Sure, just offer them $10 billion, an offer no one would refuse. Problem solved. He was always feeding me these tasty bits of delusion. I mean, that would be amazing, right? Just do, create, buy *anything* you want.

My sister also confirmed for me that the restaurant was, in fact, closed—having shut down not long after I'd disappeared nearly a year earlier. It wasn't shocking but was, nevertheless, crushing to know with certainty that my restaurant and business—my dreams—were gone. As if I'd been erased from the world, now banished to this strange purgatory jail.

Throughout all those months away with Mr. Fox, I'd had access to an iPad and an iPhone and could have easily googled it myself to see what had happened, but I didn't. It almost never even occurred to me. I didn't want to know. Self-imposed deliberate denial.

These calls were brutal, but they were also time limited and therefore usually rushed, which helped when I didn't know what to say or didn't want to hear any more. It was easier to be preoccupied only with my jail existence.

* * *

Mercifully, there were some old paperback books kicking around, so I was able to pass some of the time reading. Browsing through the selection, I noticed a theme: God. Most were young adult novels where the protagonist overcomes adversity through faith, and so on. I was just grateful for any story to keep my mind occupied. What surprised me was how many of the others managed to sleep most of the day, as if their bodies had adjusted to having nothing to do. After sleeping all night, they'd get up, have breakfast, and then go back to sleep. *All day.* I wished I could too.

I was relieved that none of the other detainees in the room looked particularly menacing. Especially when, from time to time, we heard the commotion of a fight breaking out in a nearby dorm. I was glad to not be in *that* dorm.

When the commissary orders arrived, everyone immediately dove in—ripping open packages and making ramen noodles with hot tap water, then slurping them up, followed by cookies and chips. I wondered if, for those who had been addicted to drugs before, getting deliveries of sugary and salty snacks was like getting a hit. It appeared that way.

A couple of the girls were huddled over something, almost like they were snorting it. Turned out, they were. "Do you want some?" one of them asked, noticing me watching.

They'd emptied clear plastic baggies of instant coffee granules onto the table, and forming it into lines, they *snorted* it. They were snorting *coarse granules of instant coffee.*

"Doesn't that hurt?" I asked.

"Nope! Sure you don't want some?"

I politely declined. Not only for the obvious reasons, but because the last thing I wanted was to be more alert than I already was, or risk not being able to sleep later.

I was fascinated by the lengths to which some went to procure things from the outside, and how they'd smuggle them in. One woman told me she'd once come in with a pack of cigarettes—up her vagina. *A whole pack.* She said they used a spork to get it out. *A spork.*

I was just excited to have long underwear and more socks.

* * *

My own life experience with drugs had been more of the experimental variety, and I'd gotten most of it out of my system early. *Very early.*

I'd been drunk more than once at age twelve, smoked pot, and taken LSD by thirteen. Looking back, it seems crazy I did those things so young, but it didn't seem crazy at the time. My siblings were older, as were most of my friends, and by the eighth grade I'd also gotten a part-time job.

I did well in school and never got in trouble with teachers or otherwise. I wasn't a classic rebellious teen, though people often assumed I was based on my appearance. I'd always had short hair, but when I turned twelve, I kept cutting it shorter and shorter, until the sides and back were barely a centimeter. Later, I buzzed the sides and back off completely and dyed the two or so inches on top a pale-orange shade. Then I went bolder—a bright Ronald McDonald shade of reddish orange, spiking my hair straight up (if you're old enough to remember the Muppets, think of the character Beaker). After that, I shifted to bright blue. Indigo blue. And blue it stayed for most of the following two to three years. In my town, I was known as "the girl with blue hair." Occasionally, I went bright green. It never felt rebellious. None of the four of my parents particularly liked it or the attention it attracted when I was out in public with them, but they didn't tell me not to do it. It's perhaps notable that at an age when most young people are desperate to fit in, I seemed to want the exact opposite—or at least that was the effect. I was naturally shy, so drawing attention to myself seemed incongruent. It was as if I needed my exterior to be consistent with how I felt on the inside—like an *outsider.*

I couldn't get the usual jobs young people had—scooping ice cream or working as a cashier—with the way I looked. Back then, I stood out far more than I would today. I was probably given a basic allowance, so I didn't *need* to get a job, but I'd wanted to earn my own money.

There was a frame shop in town run by a man named John, where my mother brought artwork or photos to be framed. It was also an art gallery—the walls, floors, and ceilings painted black, with artwork lining the walls. I went with her once, and we inquired if he needed help. He did. And hired me. The shop sat on a corner on the very busy Commonwealth Avenue. With my brightly colored hair, always visible through the big store windows, it was almost as if I was part of the artwork.

I had a lot of autonomy in that job. John, the owner, was more artist than businessperson, and over time—when I wasn't assembling frames—I set up systems to keep things organized. I kept track of my own hours, and at the end of each week, he wrote me a check.

I kept that job at the frame store on and off through high school and later worked a few others too. I opened a bank account and kept it reconciled to the penny. I was always careful with money, saving it rather than spending recklessly.

The idea that I'd one day find myself in debt by millions would have been unfathomable.

CHAPTER ELEVEN

EARLY 2012
NEW YORK CITY

Agreeing to get a ride back to New York with Mr. Fox was the mistake of a lifetime, and the beginning of the next phase—the one in which he started getting money from me.

    I'm not sure what he told me that weekend, how he managed to reel me back in. It must have been compelling because after that, he began coming back regularly, and I allowed it. Since I was hardly enamored with him, he must have relied on a different sort of emotional attachment. All hints of his initial discomfort in the big city were gone, and he projected unwavering confidence and strength. He probed deeper into my psyche with questions, like a therapist, and I readily gave him answers, probably feeling gratification at his interest in who I really was.

    I also can't recall the reason he gave me the first time he asked for money or how much he asked for. I'd guess it was roughly $5,000.

    I'm pretty sure it was on the phone. He was still in New York—he'd only just left me—but close enough to come and get it. What I do remember is the urgency, how he made it seem almost as if it were life or death. He framed it in a way that made it impossible to say no. If I turned him down, something really bad would happen. Would I want a bad thing on my conscience? To refuse him,

I would've been forced to say, "I don't believe you," and call him out right then and there for being a total fraud.

He also made it seem like the money was no big deal to him, just urgently needed at this very moment. As if he were a billionaire who happened to get caught without his wallet and needed me to spot him $20—*right now! Hurry!*—to buy a lifesaving EpiPen before he dropped dead on the spot. Or something like that. Would I risk letting him *die* over a few thousand dollars? Whatever his excuse was, it was vague. As if it was something he *couldn't* tell me; I just had to trust him. It's not my nature to assume someone would lie so boldly and brazenly. I can't imagine being capable of that myself, and maybe that's why it didn't occur to me that he was. Also—as you may have realized by now—I'm bad at saying no.

I gave him the money, and so it began. He kept borrowing. Sometimes he paid me back, but never in full. Just little bits here and there, enough to give me some degree of confidence that I'd get the rest. But from that first time onward, he *always* owed me money. His owing me money was a hook. A tether. A reason for me to *not* cut ties with him completely, because I wanted my money back. The balance kept growing over time, making it harder to walk away, even as things got weirder first and, later, more painful. Looking back, it's clear he did this to cultivate a state of dependency.

If I could go back and watch all this happening, like a movie, it would be like watching the girl in the horror film who is home alone and hears a noise in the basement. She has ample opportunity to run out of the house, jump in her car, and drive off to safety, but she doesn't. Instead, she heads down to the basement to investigate, while you yell at the screen about what a moron she is. Maybe that's what you're already thinking about me: *How could she be so clueless?* Well, yeah. *I'd* like to know too. Truly, I wish I could remember how he did all this, including the words he said to me, even how he said them. Not to relive it, but to at least understand what happened.

He never asked for money as if he were simply in need. It was always a short-term thing. Temporary. He implied he had huge sums of money stashed away somewhere—somewhere *far* enough away that it would take time to get to it. When I asked how he acquired it, he said things like "It's better you don't know." But then he assured me it wasn't *bad*. He wasn't a criminal. He would look at me and just slightly raise one eyebrow, as if communicating telepathically something like, *If I slayed a bunch of terrorists and in the process took their cash stash, so what?*

I was left to speculate about everything, since he told me nothing definitively. How was I to judge what I didn't know? He said things like, "It's people like me that make it possible for people like you to sleep safely at night." One time, he forwarded me a link to an article about "black ops" special forces. He didn't say anything, just sent the article. I'd never known anything like this existed, which I guess was the point. Of course he would imply he was part of an organization for which secrecy was the whole premise. How convenient.

I was clearly meant to conclude that he was part of this force. As if his sending me the article was his way of telling me without really telling me, since of course he couldn't *tell me*. This would also explain his random absences—sometimes lasting days, sometimes longer—when I'd barely hear from him, if at all. Before these trips, he'd tell me he would be "off comms" for a few days.

This should have been laughable. But I'd never known any military people, or black ops guys, or secret agents, and I figured they probably didn't all look like Matt Damon or Djimon Hounsou. They were just regular guys who could be goofy and ridiculous, and maybe a bit out of shape, like Mr. Fox. He did seem exceptionally intelligent. I'd witnessed him quickly come up with obscure words for maximum points in Words with Friends when he was right in front of me, not consulting any other app to cheat. It struck me as a little Rain Man-ish. He also had amazing recall. He could spout off facts from history, about which I didn't know much because, despite getting A's in school, my retention for historical facts was crap. Mr. Fox seemed to know a lot about a lot of things.

On his being—how do I put this—*not exactly in top physical form* when we first met, he claimed he'd been injured, that he'd gained weight in recovery, and that it made him feel bad. But he was on his way to being back in shape, he said. Naturally, I felt bad for him. Like I'd be an asshole to judge him for it. So I easily forgave him for misleading me about it before we met. But when I asked for specifics about his injuries, I got vague answers. If I pressed, he'd be vague again. By consistently dispensing only hazy bits of information, he kept my brain—the part trying to make sense of him—in a whirling state of disorientation.

On the underside of his right forearm, just above his wrist, he wore a big white bandage. The placement made me think of people who cover scars where they may have tried to slit their wrists. He wouldn't tell me what was under it.

On the backside of his other arm, near his triceps, something was lodged under the skin, a piece of metal, or something. I have zero clue what it was or why it was there. He claimed it was shrapnel, which would, I suppose, make sense since it was an irregular shape, in a seemingly random location. I still have no idea what it was, or why he didn't have it removed. It was about the size and shape of a broken Lego piece. Maybe it really was a Lego piece. Who the fuck knows.

* * *

Mr. Fox's seeming proximity to crime was unnerving, even if he claimed to be on the legit side of it—somehow tied to law enforcement or the government through whatever shadowy group he really worked for.

The closest I'd ever come to crime in my life was occasionally being the unwitting getaway driver for some guys in high school. I was sixteen—by then out of my brightly colored hair phase, with long dyed-brown waves—when I met Max and Leo, identical twins, four years older than me. With olive skin, hazel eyes, and wavy brown hair, they were good-looking and seemed to know it. They were also exceptionally smart but never went to college. Instead, they raced motocross, lived in their parents' basement, and led a bit of an outlaw lifestyle.

The town we grew up in was a mix of working-class neighborhoods and wealthier areas, the latter full of mansions with fancy cars parked out front. Max and Leo occasionally prowled those areas and stole car stereos. They had a unique technique whereby they gently and quietly popped out the back window to get in the cars.

I didn't question their behavior, still being in that adolescent stage of moral flexibility, and entirely enamored with them. Now and then, they called me needing to be picked up somewhere, usually in the middle of the night. There were no cell phones back then, just landlines. Our house had two—one for my mom and stepdad and one for my siblings and me. I kept a phone in my room so I could take calls without waking anyone. That I would get up out of bed on a weeknight and do this for them, regardless of whether I had a calculus test in a few hours, shows the lengths to which I'd go for whatever approval or connection I subconsciously sought from them. Or maybe I was just hardwired to want to help.

Once, returning from one of these nocturnal pickups—just before dawn, still in my PJs—I saw my stepdad in the driveway, headed out for a walk. Panicked, I grabbed an old paper bag from the floor of the car, awkwardly explaining that I'd had to make an emergency run for tampons. He didn't question me. It seemed that my mom and stepdad *preferred* not knowing what we were up to. I suppose they figured everything must be fine if I was getting A's and my limbs were all still attached.

Leo became my boyfriend. Despite his hardened motocross-racing exterior, he had a soft side. He was thoughtful, and he loved his cats. Eventually, he and his brother grew out of their phase of petty crime. Leo spent a lot of time at my house on weekends, and when I went away to college, we stayed together—at least during the start of my freshman year. Even as we morphed into being just friends, he was still the one—more than anyone—who made the six-hour drive to Philadelphia to pick me up or bring me back.

Once when Leo was driving me to or from school—I can't remember which—he wanted to stop at the Foxwoods Casino in Connecticut, only a short detour off our route. I was annoyed. I didn't want to go. He said it would be quick. *Okay, fine.* I'd never been to a casino before, so part of me was curious. It was around eleven o'clock on a weekday.

Stepping onto the dark, overly air-conditioned casino floor, I was struck by how many people were elderly. Gray-haired ladies perched at slot machines, some with oxygen tanks beside them, containers of quarters in their laps. Feeding the machines, pulling the handle over and over, as if in a trance. Leo played blackjack for a while until he lost $200, which felt sickening to me, like a completely stupid waste of money. I hated this place and everything about it. It reeked of stale cigarettes and tragedy. All these old people probably flushing away their Social Security checks in this tacky den of misery on an otherwise beautiful sunny day. It felt more than just unsavory. It felt predatory.

I resolved then that I hated gambling, and I always would.

Walking out, squinting to adjust to the bright daylight, I turned to Leo, "Yeah, what a hideously awful place. I'm never going back to a casino, like ever."

I could never have imagined then that, decades later, I'd be driven across the country—from casino to casino—by a man who would ensnare me in his lies and alternate reality. And furthermore, that I'd spend so much time back at this very same casino.

CHAPTER TWELVE

MAY 2016

PIGEON FORGE, TENNESSEE

Detective Brown came back to see me one more time. We sat in the same gray office. He told me my sister had been in touch—that she'd sent him photos of my recently born nephew. Pulling out his phone, he showed me the pictures. I stared at them. My heart twisted, tears filling my eyes. My nephew was ridiculously cute, and my sister—beaming in one of the photos—looked so happy. It was surreal. My one and only blood sister, who had wanted a baby for so long, finally had a baby, and I'd missed it. The pregnancy, the birth, all of it. Arguably, the most meaningful moment of her life, and I hadn't been there. It felt strange. Like waking up from a coma and, piece by piece, learning what had happened while I'd been unconscious for so long.

Detective Brown didn't know *when* New York would come for me but knew for sure they would. It was common, he said, for them to wait until closer to the end of the twenty-four-day period. I went back to the dorm, mentally prepared to settle in, figuring I'd be there at least another week. I wasn't expecting to be pulled out within twenty-four hours.

* * *

"MEL... MEN... MEG-NAY-LIS!" A woman's voice shouted. I jolted awake. It must have been early. The entire dorm was asleep. Unlike in the holding cell, here the lights were mercifully dimmed during sleeping hours. I sat up. One of the older guards, a big, stocky woman, stood in the doorway, glaring at me. I felt like they hated me even more for having an unpronounceable last name.

"Let's *go!*" she yelled. "C'mon. You're leaving." One of the things about jail is that no one cares when people are sleeping. They shout just as loud. Louder, even.

I felt seized with panic. *Already? At this hour? And no warning?* I quickly eased out of bed and hopped down from the top bunk. I didn't want the guard to keep yelling. But she did.

"Let's *go*. Take all your things. Hurry up!"

"Can I pee? And brush my teeth?" I whispered loudly.

"Do it *quick!*"

I rushed into the bathroom, a million things running through my brain. I wasn't ready. *Don't take me yet.*

I was already in my striped uniform—it was so cold in the room that I slept in my long underwear underneath it. I turned to look at the others, some now half awake, watching this scene. I lifted my hand to wave.

"Let's *go!*" the guard shouted. Had I gone to try to hug someone, she might have shot me—or that was how it felt.

I was led back to the main receiving area, then into a side room, where a guard gave me a bag containing my jeans and T-shirt from before, along with my hooded sweatshirt and sneakers. I quickly changed into my old clothes while the guard watched. At the front desk, they gave me back my wallet and earrings—and whatever else I'd had with me when I came in, which wasn't much—stuffed into a manila envelope.

I was handcuffed, then ordered to sit on a bench and wait. I was parched. Behind the officer at the desk, I spied a water cooler, the kind with a paper cup dispenser next to it. I stood and asked meekly if I might please have a drink of water, but before I'd even finished the question, I was loudly ordered to sit back down. *Really?* I knew I was about to travel, and being offered refreshments along the way wasn't likely. I tried once more—again asking with genuine politeness—pointing out that it was right there... yeah, no. Yelled at again. I sat back on the bench, irrationally feeling like I might die of dehydration right then and there. Aside from one or two kind jail employees with whom I'd interacted, most seemed needlessly cruel. Perhaps hardened by years of working there.

After another quarter hour or so, a police officer escorted me through the building and into a garage. I was put in the back of a police cruiser, one fitted with extra partitions. I asked the officer behind the wheel where we were headed.

"Men's jail," he said.

"And after that?"

"Airport."

Oh, thank you, lord. I'd been having visions of a days-long journey in one of those boxy prison buses, crawling across the country in the May heat, stopping off at various jails overnight along the way. When we arrived at the nearby men's facility, they brought him out. Mr. Fox. It felt so strange to see him. He was escorted to the front seat, to sit beside the driving officer. I guess they were told not to put us side by side. *I have so many questions!* I thought. But I wouldn't even have known where to begin. Or whether to believe him. As we drove off, he turned to look at me through the thick partitions. "You okay, baby?"

I just stared at him. Or, more accurately, glared. Then, he proceeded to casually chat with the officer. Chitchat. First about which airport we were headed to, then about Tennessee in general, the weather, and so on. As if the police officer was our Uber driver. I just sat there mutely.

Eventually we pulled up to the curb of a small airport. Four US Marshals were waiting. Two men, two women. All in plain clothes, except two had on windbreaker jackets that announced *US Marshal* in big white letters on the back. They all appeared to be in their thirties, give or take. One of the women was Black, the other Hispanic. One of the men was a white dude, the other of indecipherable ethnicity. So a reasonably representative cross-section of New York City, I thought. The white guy carried a medium-sized duffel bag, from which they began pulling out handcuffs and various metal paraphernalia. Mr. Fox and I were carefully released from the Tennessee handcuffs and put in the New York City handcuffs. A wide leather belt was fastened around my waist, the cuffs then secured to the belt in front of me. This was new. One of the marshals exchanged paperwork and signatures with the officer who had driven us there.

I watched the marshals' faces as they realized that even the extra-large leather belt they'd brought wasn't going to fit Mr. Fox. They looked at each other. *Oh well.* Just the handcuffs would have to suffice for him. I'd seen them pull ankle shackles out of the bag, but thankfully, they decided those wouldn't be necessary.

The two female marshals escorted me, one on each side, holding my arms. The two men escorted Mr. Fox. All I could think of, walking into the airport like that, my wrists cuffed to the wide leather belt around my waist, was Hannibal Lecter. All I needed was a muzzle over my face to complete the look.

* * *

Inside the airport, they offered to get us food while we waited for the flight. I thanked them profusely, asking for a very large water and any kind of fruit they could find. I had fantasies of fresh watermelon or a big fruit salad. They returned with just a banana, along with the water. They must have undone one side of my cuffs so I could eat the banana—I don't remember exactly. All I remember is the banana tasting like the most amazing banana ever. Like I'd never realized bananas were so fucking delicious. I chugged the water, relieved to finally hydrate. I caught my reflection in a window and saw that I looked, not surprisingly, like a crazy person. Frizzy hair, no makeup, wrinkled clothes. Mr. Fox wore jeans, a black T-shirt, and a plaid flannel shirt. I didn't want to think about how he probably smelled up close. I knew that smell all too well. Just thinking about it made me want to throw up the precious banana I'd just eaten.

I was surprised by how much freedom they gave Mr. Fox and me to talk. He kept asking how I was doing. It felt exceedingly weird to talk with him. *How the fuck do you think I'm doing?* was what I wanted to say. I told him about the six days in the holding cell. Mr. Fox seemed outraged, as if I'd had atrocious service at a five-star hotel. Meanwhile all I could think was, *How the fuck do you think I got here in the first place?*

I learned that he'd been spared an extended stay in the holding cell on the men's side and quickly transferred to a dorm. He told me I looked skinny. *Good. You look fat, you fat fuck.*

A couple of times, whichever marshal was closest to us got distracted enough that we could speak without being heard. I badly wanted answers, some hope. But I also I didn't know what I wanted, or what to say.

"Why don't you have a lawyer?" I finally asked. "What are you doing?"

He lowered his voice. "Don't worry. It's just gonna be a couple weeks of nonsense and this will all be over. Just remember—we gotta stay united. Okay?"

I didn't know what he meant by this, but—even knowing he was likely full of shit—I wanted to believe him. *Just a couple of weeks, and this will all be over.*

* * *

From this smaller airport, we flew to Atlanta, and from there, to LaGuardia, in New York City. In the massive Atlanta airport terminal, they let me take off my sweatshirt and wrap it around my handcuffed wrists, so the fact I was handcuffed wouldn't be so obvious as we maneuvered through crowds of travelers. A weekday. The airport was full of business travelers. I remember thinking, *What if I run into someone I know?* The odds were slim, but it had happened before—especially in a big hub like Atlanta. I imagined encountering some former managing director from a finance firm where I'd once worked—how comically awkward it would be, me in handcuffs, looking the way that I did. My brain does this: in tragic times I think of the most ridiculous possibilities. At funerals, I inevitably notice some absurdities to consider, or if there are none, I imagine them.

While most travelers were angling for overhead bin space, there wasn't much notice of their fellow handcuffed passengers. We'd boarded first—law enforcement was allowed to skip lines, apparently. Settled in our seats, I found it sort of amusing when the flight attendant tried to hand me a pack of peanuts, and I had to nod toward my restrained hands. Her face flushed as she quickly placed the peanuts down on my tray. Uncomfortable moments can be inexplicably gratifying.

When I needed to use the bathroom at the airport, the female marshals escorted me. They released my hands from the belted cuffs, then stood in the doorway of the stall while I peed, which was thankfully all I needed to do. The one closest to me seemed kind, almost apologetic for inconveniences like this. I kept telling her it was okay. Because she was the one most often nearest to me, she noticed the few times my eyes welled up with tears when no one else was looking. I wondered if she—like Detective Brown—could tell something was very *wrong*. It seemed like maybe she could.

As the plane descended, my heart hurt. I could see the New York City skyline—the skyline that had always thrilled and comforted me when returning, whether I'd been gone for a few days or a few weeks. This was the city I loved. This was home.

I'm home. Except I no longer had my own home here. And knew I wasn't going to any home just yet.

CHAPTER THIRTEEN

MAY 2016
NEW YORK CITY

One likely never forgets their first in-person view of the Rikers Island jail complex. Built on a four-hundred-acre island in the East River, between Queens and the Bronx, Rikers is New York City's main jail facility, with a capacity to house nearly ten thousand detainees, or inmates. The drive from the city feels like heading to LaGuardia Airport—until you take a different turn, cross a long, narrow bridge over water, and then it appears: a gray dystopian landscape. It looks like it could be the set of *Mad Max Beyond Thunderdome*. That's what I thought the first time I saw Rikers. The grim tapestry—concrete, menacing rows of barbed wire, scattered watchtowers, and layer upon layer of high metal fencing—conveyed a post-apocalyptic vibe.

Mr. Fox and I sat in the back of an unmarked car, driven by two of the Marshals who'd escorted us from Tennessee. As we approached the infamous facility, Mr. Fox continued making casual conversation with the Marshals, as if we were all headed to the beach for a picnic.

At times, the two up front talked among themselves, such that Mr. Fox and I could communicate without being overheard. I don't remember what I asked. I think I just repeatedly whispered variations of "What the fuck?" and hoped he would tell me something reassuring. He only repeated that it was critical he get out on bail—that was the most important thing. Implying that once he was out, he would get everything fixed and sorted. Of course he wouldn't explain *how* he would fix it all. He only repeated that we needed to remain united, that it would only be "a couple of weeks of nonsense." None of that reassured me.

As we wove through the sprawling jail complex, it started sinking in that I was at *Rikers*, a place I'd known only from news stories or episodes of *Law & Order*, yet never as somewhere I could end up myself. The Marshals explained that we'd be held there until a hearing date was set, likely within a few days, at which point we'd be transported back to the courthouse. We pulled up to the women's facility—the Rose M. Singer Center, or Rosie's, as it's more commonly known. Ladies first, I guess. I don't remember if I looked at Mr. Fox or not, or the last thing we said to each other. I didn't know it then, but it was the last time I'd ever see him.

* * *

One of the Marshals escorted me into a squat gray building—the intake center for the women's section of Rikers. She handed off some paperwork to the officer at the entrance and left. And just like that, I was alone. A detainee at Rikers, with no clue what to expect.

First, I was led to a cell next to the entrance, where a few other new detainees waited. After an hour or so, we were each given a uniform to change into, and a bag to put our clothes and shoes in, which was then tagged and stored away, who knows where. We were allowed to keep our underwear and socks—and bras, but only if there was no underwire. The uniforms were tan colored, a thick poly-cotton blend—short-sleeved tops with elastic-waisted pants. The shoes issued were black sneakers, brand new, like knockoff low-top Converse, but with Velcro straps instead of laces. They felt comfortable—a huge step up from the dirty old orange Crocs in Tennessee.

After that, we were moved to a room that looked like a giant sterile bathroom—three stalls but no toilets or doors. We were directed, three at a time, into a stall and told to remove everything. As in, get totally naked. "Squat!" came the order. I squatted. We were then ordered to turn, face the wall, squat again. When I turned back around, the officer told me to shake out my hair and open my mouth. All to make sure I hadn't stashed any drugs or weaponry in any of my orifices or elsewhere. I kept thinking how grateful I was to *not* have my period during all this.

Back in our uniforms, we were handed thin, salmon-colored booklets along with a few paper handouts, then herded into a larger cell to wait for whatever came next. At least there was plenty to look at. The layout was open, such that one could see what was going on at the admin desk and in the other cells. This at least provided distraction, and sometimes entertainment, as there was a lot of activity.

What stood out to me most was the pastel colors of the cells—one cell was painted pink, another lavender, another pale yellow, and so on. Like an Easter basket, except *jail*. I wondered who had decided to do this and silently thanked them. It made being there just a wee bit less gloomy, an iota less intimidating. More than that, it conveyed that someone, at some point, had made an effort. Someone cared. It was a small yet meaningful comfort.

Never mind that as I was contemplating this, a woman in an isolation cell nearby was screaming her head off. I wasn't sure the pastels were soothing to her.

* * *

After an hour or so—who knows—I was pulled from the holding cell and taken to the admin desk, where they photographed me and printed a photo ID card to clip onto my uniform top. Then, it was back into a different cell, in a new area, another stop along the conveyor belt of the intake process. Here, everything was painted dark blue. This cell had a separate door on a side wall, leading directly into the medical unit. Once through the door, I entered what looked a lot like a regular hospital, but with guards watching over everything. After more waiting, I was given a brief yet thorough checkup. Blood was drawn. I was told to pee in a cup—which I got to do in the luxury of a private bathroom, with a door.

I couldn't help feeling grateful. I hadn't had health insurance in a while, and here I was, getting a free medical exam. I was exceedingly polite to everyone—the nurses, officers, anyone I encountered. I wanted to tell them I wasn't a criminal—*I'm not a bad person.* But of course, I said nothing. Most were gruff, cold, and indifferent—but a few seemed to appreciate my good manners, offering me warm, sympathetic smiles.

From there, I was sent to another cell to wait some more. Then, sometime after 2:00 a.m., I was taken out and handed a bundle that included an itchy blanket, a couple of thin bed sheets, a small towel, a green plastic cup, and a small comb.

I followed an officer down a series of long hallways. Gone was the pastel color motif—now it was all cream-colored concrete walls and navy-blue doors. It felt like the halls of an elementary school. If only. After an elevator ride up one floor, then down another series of halls—pausing at every corner to pass through a metal detector—I was led through a series of heavy, electronically operated sliding metal doors. Finally, we entered a huge room lined with fifty beds, five rows of ten, each spaced maybe three feet apart. Most contained sleeping bodies. I found an available bed, which was basically a metal-rimmed platform bolted to the floor, topped with a thin plastic mat. I spread one sheet over the mat, then lay the other over it and the wool blanket on top of that. I kicked off my shoes and climbed in. There was no pillow.

I should have been exhausted and passed out quickly—but I wasn't, and I didn't. Instead, my mind drifted down the same *How did I get here?* path. I wanted to go back in time. If only I could rewind, do it all over. Maybe One Lucky Duck would have been big by now—even a household name, as I'd boldly dared to imagine it would be.

I lay in the semidarkness, wondering what it would be like to wake up there, with forty or so new roommates. Would I stand out? Would someone try to start a fight with me? After all, I wasn't covered in gang tattoos. I only had the one: my duck tattoo.

CHAPTER FOURTEEN

2012

NEW YORK CITY

The tattoo on my left bicep—the one I'd concealed under a Band-Aid before my arrest in Tennessee—was the logo for One Lucky Duck. I'd always assumed it would be my one and only tattoo. For a while, however, Mr. Fox had tried to convince me to get another. A fox, of course. An image of a fox head, with *Mrs. Fox* underneath it in cursive letters, just above my pelvic bone—the spot covered by bikini underwear. That I'd even contemplated this blows my mind. But then again, before I'd ever met Mr. Fox in person, he'd gotten me to a place where I felt like I loved him. He had a way of pulling me back there, even after I'd resolved never to see him again. My mind and heart were like a pinball. Every time I'd plonk my way down, just about to pass through the escape hatch—*pow!* Mr. Fox would bang the lever, propelling me back up into the chaos of the game, to be jostled around some more.

* * *

I'm grateful to report that I never got the fox tattoo. But I remained confused, not just about who he was but about my true feelings for him. It didn't help that I avoided telling anyone about the relationship, especially those closest to me. I was embarrassed about how I'd met Mr. Fox, unsure of his legitimacy, and generally uneasy about him. His claim of a secret job meant that if I were to introduce him, I'd have to lie, and I'm innately uncomfortable with lying. I'm also terrible at it. Furthermore, in those early days, when he came to see me, it was always on weekends, such that he didn't cross paths with my employees or anyone else in my life.

One person with whom I *did* discuss Mr. Fox was a new acquaintance I'd met through social media named Danny. It felt easy to talk him because we weren't close, and he didn't know any of my family or friends. (Why do I so often confide in near-strangers?)

Danny told me he was a pre-med student and a fan of my restaurant. When he first reached out, he expressed concern over my health and well-being, which was probably what endeared him to me—that he *cared*, or seemed to. I'm a sucker for that. He followed my Twitter account and had watched the back-and-forth with Mr. Fox develop. As Danny and I became more friendly, we communicated through email, Gchat, and text, but only saw each other a couple of times in person. Once, we had dinner at the restaurant—out on the front patio, with his small, fluffy dog, Pepe.

From the start, he told me Danny wasn't his real name. He was Indian and had a hard-to-pronounce-if-you're-not-Indian first name (just like I have a hard-to-pronounce-if-you're-not-Latvian last name). He showed me his driver's license, as if to demonstrate he wasn't hiding anything, unlike Mr. Fox. His long first name began with a D, just as he'd said.

Danny was *very* interested in what was going on with Mr. Fox. And, as I tend to do too easily, I opened up. Since these Gmail conversations still exist, I'm looking at them now—and I'm *floored*. I'm also alarmed, somewhat shamefully, at how open I was with this guy I didn't know very well. But mostly, I'm sickeningly fascinated by how accurate his warnings were. It makes me consider just how wildly different my life would be now if only I had listened.

I told him about Mr. Fox getting me pregnant. Again, why I trusted this random dude, I know not. Danny agreed it had to have been intentional. In our emails, he repeatedly pointed out all the obvious bullshit in Mr. Fox's Twitter timeline, which I'd kind of already known was bullshit, so it wasn't overly revelatory other than just shining a light on how ridiculous it was. In our written conversations, I sometimes sound annoyed, almost as if fending off yet *another* guy getting a bit obsessive. But I also agreed with Danny that Mr. Fox was likely a bullshitter. Some of the photos Mr. Fox posted, as if he'd taken them himself, were in fact pulled from the internet, as Danny discovered by doing reverse image searches on Google.

I told Danny he was probably right about Mr. Fox being a fraud—but to avoid any drama, I planned to back out of the relationship slowly. I don't know why I couldn't have just blocked Mr. Fox and been done with it. Maybe because I still wasn't sure about him. Or I didn't want to accept the loss of the money he'd borrowed. Or maybe I figured that since Mr. Fox lived in Massachusetts, a four-hour drive away, keeping him at arm's length as I let things fizzle out wouldn't be too hard. Clearly, something about him still had its hooks in me.

* * *

So much of what Danny pointed out turned out to be correct. In one email, he asked,

> Why allow a man to fuck with your mind, heart, and emotions like he did? Why would you sell yourself so short? Why even allow a man like that into your life in the first place? I mean, if you respected yourself more, had higher self-esteem, you would have screened him first. Rather than let him lie to you, pretend to be interested in the things you are, etc., you would have not even engaged in the first place. I mean, all the signs were there. You knew yourself something was amiss.

These conversations took place about three months after I first met Mr. Fox in person. Danny plainly saw what was happening. He continued:

> And you are worth way more than you are valuing yourself.
> It's like when Macy's puts an expensive item on the discount
> rack by accident. You are discounting yourself. The last time
> I saw you, you looked like a princess. You looked beautiful.
> Can't even picture you with this con artist. It's like
> picturing a vegan at a BBQ eating pork.

Danny was right that I undervalue myself. It seems to be my default. Anneli Rufus, in her book, *Unworthy: How to Stop Hating Yourself*, wrote, "Praise faintly sickens us, because we half-suspect it is the first part of practical jokes." Yes. Exactly. Compliments are uncomfortable. The terrified id in my core worries that someone will burst out, *Just kidding!* and I will be shamed for having had the audacity to think so highly of myself to have believed in their sincerity.

I told Danny about meeting Mr. Fox's father when they came to pick me up at my mom's house—how his father hadn't contradicted any of the stories Mr. Fox had told me. So yes, his father was in on it. Whatever *it* was. And now I was even more confused. Did that make Mr. Fox more legit, or less?

Danny pushed me to spend $175 on a background check, which I resisted. He wrote, *"I can't help but think the $175 is related to you being in denial and not wanting to know the truth."* Then he ended with *"HE IS PSYCHO. More worried now than before. Anyways, do the search and do the background check. I mean his dad is in on the con. That is fucking sick."*

Over the following weeks, Danny persisted in pressing me to investigate Mr. Fox. I'm not one to create drama where there is none (though it seems to find me anyway), so hiring a private investigator, as Danny urged, felt like going too far. I was reluctant even just to pay the fee to research Mr. Fox's phone number. Simply punching the number into Google didn't turn anything up. But why *wouldn't* I have gone farther? Mr. Fox had, sort of, already told me he used false names, implying he worked for a secret agency. What if that was true? What I did do, finally, was just give Danny Mr. Fox's cell phone number so he could go ahead and research it if he wanted.

One day, Danny sent me a text. No words, just an image. It was a mug shot that was clearly Mr. Fox—except younger, rounder-faced, in a suit—with a name under it: Anthony Patrick Strangis. This was jarring. It wasn't entirely shocking because by now, I'd more than suspected his real name wasn't Shane Fox, or at least that Fox wasn't his real last name. But *Strangis?* According to the mugshot, he'd been arrested in Florida years earlier—for, I think, grand larceny.

I felt epically stupid.

The guy I'd gotten myself involved with—the one who'd intentionally impregnated me, to whom I'd given thousands of dollars per his urgent requests, despite his unfulfilled promises to repay me—had an arrest record for theft. Most rational human beings would have immediately concluded he probably was *not* a member of a black ops force; he probably was not a government-backed secret agent of some kind. Probably he was a grifter—a conman targeting a woman with a big life in the big city and access to money.

So, naturally, I blocked all communication with him, relieved that I dodged a bullet—*phew!*—and moved on with my life, building my amazing brand and business.

Just kidding!

I did not do that. Instead, I let him explain.

* * *

I'm not sure how or when I confronted Mr. Fox about his real identity. Was it on the phone? In person? Text? It wasn't so surprising that Shane Fox wasn't his real name—he'd already implied, in his cryptic way, that he had multiple IDs, the way secret agents in movies have multiple passports with various identities. (Or the way criminals do?) But I hadn't expected an actual arrest record.

I'm guessing I texted him because it would have been hard to sit on that information. Maybe after he reached out, I texted him back something like, *Hello Mr. Strangis.* I don't know if that's what I did. I just know that at some point, I listened to what he had to say, and whatever artificially flavored explanation he offered up, I obviously drank it.

Probably, he acted nonchalant about it, like *of course* Shane Fox wasn't his real name—he'd planned to tell me eventually, *when the time was right.* Probably, he said he hadn't wanted me to know for my own safety.

I do remember later, standing in my kitchen as he explained to me in person—I'm not sure whether it was a week later, weeks later, or just days after I first learned his real identity—what that arrest was about: *Just some nonsense misunderstanding, really.* He told me a lot of things at once, including that he'd been married in Florida and had a son. And then, he told me they were both dead. Not in an accident but deliberately killed by some bad people. It was his fault, and therefore he lived with crushing guilt every day. He had a fake-pained look on his face. Clearly, he was lying. I knew this. His story about how they'd been killed made no sense. Why did I let him go on? Was I wanting to call bullshit but worried about the slim chance that it was at least partially legit, and how fucked up would I be to assume someone was lying about something so heavy? Still, I could have asked for their names and then looked it up—surely there would have been a news report, something. I could have demanded proof. But demanding proof seemed cold. I would have been justified—he'd already lied about his identity. But those lies he rationalized away, making it seem like I shouldn't have been at all surprised. Like I was the unreasonable one.

Later, that story changed. His ex and his son weren't *really* killed, but he claimed he'd needed to tell me that because, well, *She's crazy and probably even dangerous.* He didn't want me going and doing something dumb like trying to contact her. He finally pulled the white bandage off his inner forearm to reveal a big "Stacey" tattoo in cursive letters. He said it wasn't so much that he was hiding it from me but that he didn't like to look at it himself.

How is it that I knew he was bullshitting but didn't kick him out of my life? Why wasn't I running from him or barricading the door after he'd left and blocking his calls? Mr. Fox and all his stories—with all their twists, contradictions, and mystery—were exhausting. I could never keep up because he kept adding more and more to the existing tapestry of ambiguity, and I could never just step back and see it clearly. Instead, I kept allowing him back in my life. Unaware, of course, that he would ultimately destroy it.

* * *

Once my friend Danny started to realize that, rather than shutting Mr. Fox out, I was getting sucked back in, our back-and-forth came to an end. He wrote to me, "Hope you realize the isolation and his attempt to brainwash you are part of the continuing scam."

It's profoundly strange to read these communications now. They weren't just *hints* that Mr. Fox may not be legit. Danny was laying it all out: isolation and brainwashing, complete with his now-revealed criminal history. These were not just subtle red flags in my periphery that I could easily rationalize away. They were giant and waving furiously in my face, and for some reason, I shoved them aside, like a stubborn bull. All the evidence pointed in one direction, but after Mr. Fox spewed a jumble of words to explain himself, I ignored the evidence and dismissed Danny and his warnings, almost defiantly.

It was as if Danny was screaming at me that my house was on fire, and at first, I agreed. *Sure, maybe there's some smoke. Looks like some flames too.* But as his warnings escalated, I got angry at him for being so aggressive—and then told Danny he was clearly mistaken. As I turned, and strolled directly into the burning house.

CHAPTER FIFTEEN

MAY 2016
NEW YORK CITY: RIKERS

My first night at Rikers was not restful. It felt like I'd just barely fallen asleep, finally, when we were woken up for breakfast. The clock showed 5:30 a.m. People shuffled into the brightly lit adjoining room to line up at a window that opened into a compact kitchen. We were each handed a tray, and could sit anywhere at a dozen or so bolted-to-the-floor tables and stools.

Breakfast was a small box of Frosted Mini-Wheats cereal, which, after what I'd gotten used to in Tennessee, felt amazing and exciting. We were also given a small container of skim milk, two slices of soft wheat bread, a blob of grape jelly, a pat of butter, and—miraculously—an orange. A whole fresh orange. I felt like I'd just been served a glorious feast on a silver platter. The thin plastic trays had compartments, with one large one for the cereal. Yes, I ate mine with the milk. I was hungry.

I learned that I was in the "intake dorm," the first stop for detainees arriving at Rikers. Some only stay a day or two, or three or four, before getting released. Others are moved to semipermanent dorms after about a week. Either way, everyone in the dorm was fresh into Rikers. Still, it was easy to tell that for many, it wasn't their first time.

I quickly made friends with whomever appeared remotely friendly and willing to engage in conversation. One woman, about my age, mercifully let me use her account to make phone calls. I learned that one must have money on one's account to make calls. Then, on my second day, before I'd even had a chance to explain to my family how to deposit money for me, I punched in my ID and heard the automated voice tell me I had a credit of $25. I had no idea how it got there, but I was glad for it. Calls were expensive, and I felt bad using this woman's account. It wasn't until much later that I found out it was Joe, a guy who had, many years earlier, been my personal assistant. He'd seen the news about my being sent to Rikers and figured my family wouldn't know enough about the system to realize I'd need money right away. God bless Joe. The process for putting money on one's account isn't very straightforward (as Joe knew), and it took my sister a couple of days before she was able to do it for me. That initial $25 helped a lot. I thought about my fellow detainees who may not have had families, or families with any means. That jails charge detainees to make calls is, in itself, fucked up.

* * *

My family had been scrambling to find an attorney for me since my arrest in Tennessee, so by the time I got to Rikers, I had one. My uncle's girlfriend's daughter was a lawyer who knew another lawyer. And that's how I got the attorneys my father and stepmother hired for me: Sheila, who had her own practice in downtown Manhattan, and Cesar, her more junior associate.

On my third day, I was woken up earlier than most of the others, as a guard roughly tapped my shoulder and said, "Court." Every morning, various detainees were shipped out to the different New York City boroughs for court. Those of us with hearings that day were woken up before everyone else so we'd have time to shower and eat breakfast before being corralled downstairs. Then came the long, tedious process of clearing us to exit the building and board the buses heading to court.

The first stop was a large gymnasium on the first floor. Once again, I had the odd sensation of being in a high school rather than a jail. We stood in line to go, three at a time, into what looked like a bathroom but wasn't. It was just a tiled room with three empty stalls. *Here we go again: naked squats*, I realized. Having done this part of the routine before, it wasn't a surprise. I got naked. I squatted.

Next, we were sent down the hallway and back into the large cells—the Easter-egg-colored cells—in the intake area. Each borough was designated its own cell: Manhattan had one, Queens another, and so on. Because my company's corporate office address had been in Brooklyn—where we'd had a large production facility—that was where I'd been charged. I was put into the cell with others heading to Brooklyn. And then we waited. And waited. Buses arrived for each borough, and I watched as the other cells emptied, detainees organized into two rows and then handcuffed to the person beside them before being sent outside. I gazed around at the others in my own cell, considering who I hoped (and who I hoped not) to be cuffed to.

My seatmate for the bus ride into Brooklyn was an androgynous-looking girl, smaller than me, who looked like she had zero interest in conversation. I took the cue and kept quiet too.

I felt nervous and queasy over having to appear in front of a judge. I was still confused about the precise charges, why they had been brought, and what exactly had transpired in the wake of my sudden disappearance from the city nearly a year earlier. Some of the charges were related to "tax fraud," specifically sales tax. I knew we had gone a few months—perhaps more than a few months—without paying sales tax before I'd disappeared. At the time, this had made me queasy, but the intention had been to pay eventually, just late. For most of those months, we'd filed the proper paperwork indicating the correct amounts owed. Again, my plan had always been to pay once I was able—and according to Mr. Fox, being able to pay everything was always *just about* to happen, after *this one more thing* he'd tell me I had to do. In fact, in the month before disappearing, I had made two $10,000 payments toward sales tax. As I saw it, my company was just behind on payments, but not in outright avoidance. I had been in contact with the representative from the state about our past due balances. "Fraud" seemed to imply that I'd intentionally filed understated numbers, which I had not.

Grand larceny and "scheme to defraud investors" were also among the charges. These allegations were more complicated. Either way, there wasn't time to explain anything because I had only about three minutes to talk with the junior attorney, Cesar, with cell bars between us. This floored me. There was a lot I would've wanted him to communicate at that hearing if I'd had more time with him. Instead, it was a rushed exchange before I was handcuffed again and ushered into the brightly lit courtroom for the bail hearing. A guard kept repeating, "Keep your head forward. No looking back." The courtroom was crowded, but I didn't get to see who was there. Fortunately, Mr. Fox's bail hearing was separate, so I didn't have to see him.

I felt sick to my stomach as the assistant DA read the charges against me, making me sound like an awful person, a criminal. It was surreal to hear my name—and the name One Lucky Duck—repeated here, in this context. Like I was living a nightmare. The prosecution asked for a $1 million bail. Good lord. *A million dollars.*

When it was Cesar's turn to speak, he mostly read from a prepared statement, pointing out that I had no criminal history. He recited the bios of my parents, emphasizing that I came from a "good family." This seemed odd to me. How was the respectability of my family relevant to the amount of bail set? I was frustrated, knowing I could've prepared a much more compelling case for myself, on my own merits, had I understood the process or been given a chance.

The judge said a few words and set my bail at $350,000.

Bang went the gavel.

Cesar assured me this would be okay—my parents would figure it out. There wasn't much time to say anything more before I was ushered back through the side door and into a small cell. From there, I was taken upstairs to a room of cells and placed in an individual one to wait for the bus back to Rikers. The wait turned out to be seven hours.

Fortunately, I was given a mat—the same mats that were used as mattresses back at Rikers—so I could lie down. I had nothing to do but think. I was mortified at the amount of my bail—yet, at the same time, relieved it was only a fraction of what the DA had recommended. At some point, a male guard handed out sandwiches. Peanut butter or bologna and cheese. I asked for peanut butter and was handed a stack of four sandwiches. The peanut butter was cloyingly sweet, full of sugar, and there was a lot of it between the bread. Feeling full at least helped me fall asleep. The air conditioning was on high, making the holding cells feel refrigerated. I did what I saw others doing and pulled my arms inside my short-sleeved uniform top, crossing them over my chest to keep warm, and curled into a ball on the mat.

* * *

By the time I got back to my dorm at Rikers, it was way past dinner. One of the guards told me they'd saved a meal for me. Really? That wasn't something I'd expected. Any kindness at all in the context of incarceration can feel disproportionately meaningful.

On the tray was a pile of brown rice with a roast chicken leg and thigh, dark green beans, and cubes of what appeared to be canned pear. I was surprised at the chicken. Everything else I'd seen so far at lunch and dinner was suspect-looking patties of who-knows-what or thin sausages or hot dogs—all of which I'd given away to anyone who'd take it, usually in exchange for their vegetables, which they didn't want. But this—this was a clearly identifiable chicken thigh and leg. And it smelled really good.

I'm one of those vegans who (a) doesn't regularly call herself a vegan because who knows when I'll take a bite of something not vegan, (b) doesn't like labels, and (c) is principally opposed to adding to the demand for meat and animal products, versus specifically opposed to putting them in my body. While I did (and still do) think that a mostly vegan diet is optimal, if presented with something that would otherwise be thrown away, like chicken, I'll probably eat it. For an animal to suffer in a factory farm and be cruelly slaughtered for human consumption is tragic enough, but to then be thrown in the garbage? Wasting food is awful in general, but wasting food that involved pain and suffering? No. So I ate the chicken. And it was delicious. I picked and gnawed every last bit of meat off the bones and ate every last grain of rice. Between breakfast, the gooey peanut butter sandwiches, and this dinner, I probably consumed more calories in that day than I did in my entire ten days in the Tennessee jail.

* * *

My days at Rikers were now just occupied with going through the motions, talking with others in the dorm, and making calls. It's difficult to describe how this whole time felt—if I was feeling anything at all. I was in a state of limbo. Throughout the year on the road with Mr. Fox—and likely for long before that—I'd been in a kind of dissociated stupor. Now I was starting to wake up, but I had a way to go. It was more like that in-between state when you're still dreaming but are aware that it's just a dream—you're aware of your body lying in bed, waiting for full consciousness. I was an observer, watching myself move through one day after the next as a detainee, thinking how adaptable human beings are. Mr. Fox had taken me from one situation to another, and I kept adapting. Now I was at Rikers, getting used to that life. Soon I'd have to exit the strange world of jail, reenter the real world, and adapt again.

My family kept assuring me that they were working as fast as they could on the bail. They were panicked about each day I spent at Rikers. I kept telling them I was okay. Despite its reputation, and dangers aside, in some ways, I felt like I was at the Four Seasons compared to the small-town jail I'd come from. Also, as much as I was eager to get out, I was also afraid of leaving. Jail was its own alternate reality—a place in suspension, of being in limbo. But once I got out, I'd have to face what happened and try to explain what I knew I couldn't make sense of myself. I was also, I knew, creating havoc in my family—and as someone who can't stand feeling like a burden or having to rely on others, this was especially painful.

After one of these calls to my family left me reeling, I started to cry. I didn't know where to go since there wasn't anywhere to be alone. I didn't want to sit on my bed and be seen by those nearby, so I wandered into the common room and kept my head down. An older woman stood nearby. I'd noticed her before—quiet, never speaking to anyone. She looked to be about sixty-five or seventy, Black, missing more than half her teeth and most of her hair. I was surprised when she spoke, asking me what was wrong. I explained that I'd had a really special business, with a lot of employees, and how it was all gone. Everything was gone. Lots of people lost money, and I was the one being blamed. It appeared to be my fault.

She looked at me, right into my eyes. "You listen, child. Listen to me. If God seen to it to take all that away from you, that just means he got somethin' much bigger planned for you. Don't you cry now, honey. He got somethin' much bigger comin' to you."

I felt stunned. If I'd been allowed to collapse into her and sob, I would have. If I could have hugged her, I would have. But hugs weren't allowed. I sniffled, smiled through my tears, and thanked her, hoping she understood how much she had just helped me in that moment. I knew that it was precisely my tendency to believe fantastical things that got me into this mess in the first place, but I badly wanted to believe that she was right.

Once my family completed the financial gymnastics to arrange my bail, it was time for me to head back to court to be released. Before I left, still early in the morning, I took my bucket of snacks and Commissary items and quietly slid them under that woman's bed while she slept.

Wherever you are now, ma'am, thank you.

* * *

I was finally getting out—back to the real world, into the warmth of early summer in New York City. The place I'd called home for over two decades. Where I no longer had a home.

PART TWO

THE ASCENT

"Perhaps one did not want to be loved so much as understood."
—GEORGE ORWELL, *1984*

CHAPTER SIXTEEN

1994–1996
NEW YORK CITY

The first memory I have of being awed by the Manhattan skyline was a steamy summer day in 1994. Driving into the city in a big, rented U-Haul with my father, I was about to move into my first solo apartment after graduating from college. I'd been to New York City twice before, but this time, knowing I was here to stay, felt profound. There's no other skyline like it.

My apartment was on the eighth floor of a prewar doorman building on Second Avenue between Tenth and Eleventh Streets, in the downtown area known as the East Village. It was a one-room apartment with cream-colored walls and moldings—the kind you could tell had been painted over hundreds of times—and hardwood floors. The tiny kitchen occupied one corner, and the bathroom, with its prewar fixtures and classic black-and-white tile, had old-school charm. It was perfect, and, at $800 a month, fit my budget. Money was tight, but I was about to start a very well-paying job.

* * *

Somehow, my father and I managed to park and get all my things into the apartment, just the two of us—including my futon mattress, a compact old couch, a small table, two chairs, shelves, and so on. He had to leave to catch an Amtrak home, so I was left to return the U-Haul on my own. Driving that bulky box truck with no rearview mirror was my first driving-in-Manhattan experience, and I was relieved when I'd successfully unloaded it at the nearest U-Haul without incident.

I walked back to my new apartment, keys in hand, pleased with myself for moving to the city a full month before starting a training program at one of the big investment banking firms, Bear Stearns. I'd heard all the legends of investment banking's inhumanely long hours, so it seemed sensible to give myself a few weeks to settle in, get to know this massive new city, set up my apartment, shop for proper business suits, and otherwise prepare before starting my new job.

After basking in my quiet apartment for a while and opening a few boxes, I headed out to the nearest corner store for supplies—paper towels, dish soap, a few food staples. Even this errand felt thrilling. Checking out the corner store where I'd get to know the cashiers, passing restaurants with outdoor tables spilling out onto the sidewalk, packed with daytime diners—everything about being there made me feel high on a new kind of energy: the electricity of the city combined with my newfound complete independence.

* * *

You know when people ask, "When were you happiest?" or "What was the happiest time of your life?" I'm pretty sure this was it. Like Mary Tyler Moore in the opening of her 1970s sitcom, standing on the streets of Manhattan, gleefully tossing her beret up in the air—that's kind of how I felt. I was all alone, on my own in this very big city, feeling like I was exactly where I was supposed to be. My own apartment. No roommate. No one to answer to. I felt... *free.*

Finally having my own home, all to myself, was incredibly gratifying. The prospect of exploring my new town was exciting, and I quickly met new people. But in general, I really *liked* being alone. I still do, and always have. It wasn't until many years later that I figured out how this impacted my life overall, and, profoundly, that it was *okay*—it didn't mean there was something wrong with me.

In college, I lacked solitude during my freshman and sophomore years, jammed into tight quarters with roommates. In my junior and senior years, I shared an off-campus apartment with my college best friend, Marcus. I was generally more comfortable around guys. I spent most of my social time hanging out at a big, beat-up old house diagonally across the street from our apartment. It was the off-campus home to the Pi Kappa Alpha fraternity, which some of my guy friends had joined.

I've never really fit in among groups of women, and while I feel much more comfortable around men, I clearly didn't fit in as one of them either. Where do I fit? Maybe that's part of why I've always felt so *at home* in New York City, where loads of people don't fit into traditional norms and constructs. It's a city where one can—probably more than in any other city—be oneself, even if one hasn't yet figured out what that self is. That summer of 1994, I was about to step into the world of Wall Street, but for those first few weeks before my job started, I was completely free—able to do whatever I wanted, whenever I wanted. I wandered all over the city during the day and went out at night, sometimes with my sister's friends, who had also moved to New York and took me along to parties or events. Other times, I ended up out alone, meeting random people.

Many late nights, after drinking, I'd stop at the corner store—open twenty-four-hours, like so many places were in the city back then—and buy a quarter watermelon, my favorite summertime fruit. Back home, I'd get in my PJs, turn on the TV, and slice and eat the entire thing. Then, my distended belly and I would pass out, fully hydrated and therefore at least slightly less hungover the next morning.

I loved my new life. It was fun saying hello and chatting with the doormen—José on the day shift, Juan on the night shift. New York City doormen are their own species. They don't bounce from building to building or job to job; they tend to stay put. Even now, *thirty* years later, when I pass by, José or Juan will see me and call out, "Sarma!" And it always feels sweet that they're still there, and that they remember my name.

This city was where I finally fit, where I felt at home for the first time. It was just me, taking care of myself, living however I wanted—completely independent. I felt *free*. Or mostly free. I was about to become significantly *less* free once I stepped into the world of investment banking. But still, New York City—electrified with the energy of possibilities—was exactly where I wanted to be.

* * *

It had been a wise move to arrive in the city a full month before my first day on the job. By the time training began, I was ready. My apartment was set up. I'd walked the streets and learned my way around, and I'd stocked up on enough starter suits, plenty of pantyhose, and even a new briefcase (which turned out to be ridiculous—I stopped using it less than a month into the job).

Training was mostly a breeze. I sat in an overly air conditioned auditorium with forty-five or so other first-year analysts, hired right out of college, mostly male. I was surprised to learn that nearly everyone had just arrived in the city and was, unsurprisingly, stressed out trying to get their lives sorted. This only made me smugly congratulate myself for having arrived early. It's good to be prepared.

After a month of training, we were released into the wild. Each of us was assigned a desk, but due to the overall lack of space, a few conference rooms were converted into offices. I ended up in one of these—one room, five desks. It was like having roommates all over again.

I was immediately staffed on a deal involving a major aerospace and technology company. The vice president on the deal was a guy named Fred. He wasn't your typical Wall Street banker in a sharp suit and slick Ferragamo tie. Fred was a bit unkempt. His shirts were wrinkled, his ties creased, his desk perpetually messy. He was heavyset, with thinning blond hair that always looked like he'd been grabbing at it. He was like the Linus of our corporate finance department. But most importantly, and also unusually, he was genuinely kind. And very funny. He had a way of taking the work seriously without taking himself, or everything else, too seriously.

That he was kind and funny helped enormously because that week, I clocked 111 hours of work. Yes. *One hundred eleven.* Divided by seven days, that's an average of nearly sixteen hours each day. And yes, a seven-day workweek was the norm. The difference on weekends was that we could come in wearing whatever we wanted, and very few senior partners or managing directors were around. By the end of that first week, I also learned to ditch the dumb, impractical briefcase. Instead, I started bringing a duffel bag packed with sweatpants, socks, a T-shirt, sweatshirt, and sneakers—my late-night bag. After 8:00 p.m., it was a relief to kick off my heels, peel off my nylons, and get out of my suit. After so many hours, the waistband of my skirt—which had felt fine when I'd put it on that morning—felt like a bungee cord cutting through my midsection.

The hours were brutal, so it helped to be comfortable for as many of them as possible. I'd stay through the nights working on "comps"—pulling the stats of comparable companies and deal valuations to justify whatever valuation we were applying to a particular business—compiling all of it into "pitch books" that would be presented to the potential client. Later, I spent most of my time working on complex merger models. Basically, I lived and breathed Excel—modeling out the financials (income statement, cash flow statement, balance sheet) of each company individually, then combining them into one entity, making the proper adjustments, to see what the numbers looked like. Those three statements were linked in a continuous loop, and the way you knew you constructed your model correctly was if your balance sheet balanced: assets = liabilities. If it didn't balance, then you had to find and fix the error, and sometimes that was a maddening, frustrating process. Thus, when you finally found the error, when your balance sheet finally balanced, it could feel like God shining his grace down upon you—the relief of all relief. Praise Jesus.

For some reason, I quite liked working in Excel—figuring out the long equations needed to make the model display whatever scenarios were thrown at me. It was oddly gratifying. I'm not sure why. Math (and science) never particularly interested me, yet in high school, I surprised myself by scoring much higher on the math section of the SAT than the verbal. Heading into college, I had no idea in what I would major. By process of elimination, I chose economics. Then, after my second year, I decided to add a second degree from the Wharton School of Business.

* * *

How I ended up in investment banking after college wasn't so much a deliberate decision as something I slid into by following the herd. At Wharton, most soon-to-be graduates chased the same jobs for which there was a mostly unspoken hierarchy: investment banking was the top goal, and if not that, then you went for business consulting at one of the big-name firms. If that didn't work out, you took a job at one of the Big Six accounting firms (back then, there were six). So I followed the crowd and submitted my resume in all categories. Many firms conducted on-campus interviews. Once, when I showed up to a Goldman Sachs interview and introduced myself, the two guys I was meeting with looked at me funny. They looked at each other, then back at me.

"Is everything okay?" I asked.

"Um, yeah, it's just... well, your name—the name on your resume. We assumed you were an Indian *guy*."

"Oh! Well, sorry?" We all laughed. I realized there was nothing on my resume that indicated whether I was male or female. No women's hockey, no sorority, no Wharton Women's Association, etc. I didn't have a lot in the way of extracurriculars. Just a high GPA and my prior work history.

I was never truly comfortable in these interviews because I could already sense that I didn't fit in. I wasn't fascinated by the corporate world, or stocks and bonds, nor was I reading *The Wall Street Journal* every day as so many of my classmates did. I had subscriptions to *Food & Wine* and *Gourmet* magazines, which should have told me something. But for better or worse, I followed the path. I interviewed reasonably well and got hired.

* * *

Bear Stearns could be a brutal place. My first week was more of an outlier, but getting close to—or even surpassing—a hundred hours a week was normal. I once worked over eight weeks straight without taking a single full day away from the office. On two occasions, I worked more than fifty consecutive hours without sleeping, without even a nap. Yes, that's two all-nighters in a row. In this environment, a cheerful disposition would have stood out—like *What's up with Phil? Why does he look... happy?* It made more sense that everyone was bitter and exhausted, staggering up and down the halls like zombies.

I excelled in this job because, for some reason, I was capable of functioning well on little sleep. I wasn't the smartest analyst there by a long shot, and certainly not the most knowledgeable about Wall Street. But I was a hard worker, paid attention to detail, and was reasonably good at building complex financial models and sorting out long calculations while wildly sleep deprived. People noticed, so I tended to get staffed on the sorts of deals where this kind of intensity was required. After the first year, I was one of two analysts to receive the highest bonuses in our class. Shortly after bonuses were handed out, a bunch of analysts quit, so going into the second year, our class size had been cut in half.

Liar's Poker, Michael Lewis's legendary book about Wall Street, described the job I had as follows: "A few of the very best analysts, months into their new jobs, lost their will to live normal lives. They gave themselves entirely over to their employers and worked around the clock. They rarely slept and often looked ill; the better they became at their jobs, the nearer they appeared to death."

Lewis got it right. There was no *normal life*—or any life at all—outside the job. Being a people-pleaser, never wanting to let anyone down, propelled me to keep working, double-checking everything, never complaining, and never saying no. Now and then I'd break down, heading into the stairwell to cry, but I'd get it out of my system quickly, dry my face, and get back to my desk. I remember looking at some of the higher-ups and noticing that they *all* looked much older than they actually were.

The culture of investment banking seemed to value working freakishly long hours for the sake of... working freakishly long hours. If you were walking out the door at 6:00 p.m., usually because you'd pulled an all-nighter the night before, inevitably someone you passed on the way would snidely ask, "Half day?"

Among the analysts, there was an intense fear of being seen leaving early by a higher-up or, worse, the staffer (the person who assigned us to projects) who might conclude you clearly weren't staffed on enough deals and then yank you back in. The guys I worked with would sometimes do this neat trick: fold up your suit jacket and stuff it into a FedEx box, along with anything else you'd take home, roll up your shirtsleeves, grab the box, and literally *run* out of the office as if you were racing to get this incredibly urgent package mailed to a client.

* * *

My second year at Bear Stearns, I got a bit more comfortable, though I still generally lived in fear of people thinking I was stupid.

I was lucky to end up working mostly with the same people, staffed only on deals within the firm's technology sector group. One of the managing directors in the group, John, had previously worked at Salomon Brothers, the legendary Wall Street firm chronicled in the aforementioned book, *Liar's Poker*. We were a team, and John became my mentor. One day, I was standing by his desk, explaining some calculations in the model I was working on while he examined the printed-out version, and he kept stopping me. He finally said, "Sarms, you're a lot smarter than I am—you need to slow down and explain this to me." At this, all the motion in my world stopped. I thought, *What? He's a managing director. He's ten years older than I am. He does deals. How could I possibly be smarter? He must just be saying that.* This was how I thought, and usually still do.

The typical path for those who made it through the two-year analyst program was to return to business school for an MBA, stay at the firm, or go work elsewhere in finance—at a hedge fund or private equity firm if you were lucky. I got lucky. The last big deal I worked on involved the private equity firm Bain Capital. During the deal, an associate from Bain inquired about my future plans and suggested I apply to work for them. A move to private equity after investment banking was, I knew, an amazing opportunity. I was flattered. However, it would mean moving to Boston, and I *loved* New York City. Still, it was hard not to at least go through the interview process. I agreed, and they flew me to Boston for a full day of interviews.

The first thing that struck me about their offices was how many people looked *happy.* I kept pointing this out to the woman chaperoning me from one interview to the next. I felt like I'd entered an alternate dimension. My interviews went well, and shortly thereafter I was presented with a formal offer. The pay was better than the job I was leaving, and the hours, while still long, would be less. My coworkers at Bear were impressed. Bain Capital—then run by Mitt Romney—was known as one of the best private equity firms—so it was hard to justify doing anything other than accepting and moving to Boston, even though it pained me to leave New York.

After movers took my belongings and I boarded a shuttle for Boston, I looked out the window and cried as the plane ascended, watching Manhattan and all of New York City shrink beneath me. I knew I was leaving my home. But I also had a strong feeling that, one way or another, I'd be back.

CHAPTER SEVENTEEN

1996–1998
BOSTON AND NEW YORK CITY

In Boston, I rented a charming one-bedroom apartment in the South End, within walking distance of the Bain Capital offices. The firm was located in a medium-sized office tower above the high-end Copley Mall. Every morning, I walked to work and took an escalator up, cruising past the gleaming storefronts of Neiman Marcus and Chanel, the sound of a two-story waterfall echoing through the cavernous marble atrium. For the first couple months, I was again crammed together with other new hires in a big conference room. Bain was expanding onto another floor, but construction wasn't yet complete. We were called associates and existed at the bottom of the hierarchy. I was the only female among the ten new associates hired. I became fast friends with my coworkers, fully at ease working side by side all day and sometimes late into the night. Our bonding included laughing together at incredibly crude jokes—the kind that would probably get someone fired today—but none of us were ever uncomfortable.

When the new offices were finally ready, we were moved into our own individual spaces. For the first time, I had an *office*—not a cubicle but an office with a door I could close. I also had an executive assistant, Carla, whom I shared with a few others and absolutely adored. Some of my fellow associates had, like me, come from investment banking, but most had come from business consulting—

many from Bain & Co., the firm from which Bain Capital had been spun off by Mitt Romney. Back then he wasn't Governor Mitt or presidential candidate Mitt or Senator Mitt. Just Mitt—one of the nicest people there.

On the nights I stayed extra late, I noticed that the others who were also working late were from investment banking too. The consulting people didn't have much urgency, whereas we veterans of corporate finance assumed everything was urgent, martyrdom still hardwired in our systems.

At the end of my first year, we were given generous bonuses. In finance careers like this, salary is often significantly less than the bonus. So bonus time was a big deal. Many of my colleagues immediately went out and bought fancy things, like brand-new cars or expensive watches. I did no such thing. Instead I tucked my money away, saving it for coinvesting. But I did allow myself one splurge: a shiny chrome KitchenAid mixer. It was a thing of beauty, and I admired it the way some people admire a top-of-the-line sports car. I didn't have much time to cook or bake, but when I did, it was what I loved doing most.

With the rest of my bonus and any other money I could spare, I took advantage of the opportunity to coinvest in whatever companies Bain Capital was acquiring. With returns much higher than the industry average, I felt it made sense to invest as much as I could. And I was right, since those investments, over time, yielded many multiples of their original value.

* * *

Boston was familiar and beautiful, but it wasn't *home*. Only New York City was home, and I missed it. Bain Capital was a good place to work, and I could have stayed and likely earned a shitload of money—especially the way I'd been saving and reinvesting. But I didn't care for the work. I didn't care *about* the work. Nothing about it thrilled me. Furthermore, I'll never forget one of my colleagues telling me about a deal where he and another associate had to lay people off from a newly acquired company and how shitty it made him feel. It was jarring. I hadn't experienced that firsthand, at least not directly, but looking back, it's notable that those kinds of deals involving mass layoffs were business as usual. When Mitt Romney, my then-boss, ran as the Republican nominee in the 2012 presidential election, Bain Capital's deals came under scrutiny, particularly the practice of buying companies and laying off employees. It was a stark example of how easily things get normalized. I'm all for fair capitalism and market efficiencies, but there must be a more humane way to lay off workers—like offering larger severance packages. But that would cost more. It would shave a few basis points off a deal's eventual return on investment. And in the ruthlessly competitive world of private equity, returns are king.

The hours—while not as long as before—were still demanding. I was one of the lucky ones, getting to work on relatively fun deals. The one that took up most of my time was the acquisition of a division of a film company in Los Angeles. After our analysis, Bain decided to buy it, renaming it Artisan Entertainment. Years later, having coinvested, I made a hefty return on that deal—mainly thanks to *The Blair Witch Project*, which I never saw but heard was good (and *thank you*).

One of the perks of traveling to LA for this deal was staying in nice hotels. I've always loved hotels and restaurants—they're like art and theater to me. But fancy travels to LA and all, I wasn't happy in Boston, or in the world of finance. I wanted to be back in New York, so I decided to make it happen. Bain Capital has a Manhattan office now, but back then, leaving Boston meant I had to quit. When I gave notice, my coworkers were stunned. Who walks away from Bain Capital when a future of riches awaits those who stay? Me, apparently.

I also did what many, at the time, considered a big risk: I *bought* an apartment in Manhattan. I didn't even have a new job lined up yet, but with Bear Stearns and Bain Capital on my resume—and plenty of higher-ups who would give me strong references—I knew I wouldn't have much trouble landing a high-paying job at a hedge fund. Hedge fund hours were oriented around the stock market, meaning I'd have my nights and weekends mostly free. Surely, *then* I'd be happy?

In one of my exit meetings, a younger partner with whom I'd shared my plans asked, "But is that what you *really* want to do? I mean, do you really *like* this work?"

I paused, staring at him blankly, thinking, *Wait, you're saying YOU like this work?*

He continued, "I notice you're always talking about food—what you cooked over the weekend, what new restaurant you want to try—and your face lights up when you do."

I do? It does?

Then he said, "What if you took a job working for one of the big food magazines?"

Suddenly, I found myself trying not to cry. Why was I about to cry? I think because my gut knew he was right. I loved food. I loved restaurants. I loved the creativity and the hospitality. Even though my own mom had been a chef, I'd never considered working in the food world myself. Cooking was just my favorite hobby. Meanwhile, I clearly had so little genuine interest in finance. But I'd just taken on a mortgage and needed to cover the monthly payments, so the world of finance it would be. If I could have foreseen how much money I'd later make from my Bain investments, I might have had the freedom to take a lower-paying job I actually cared about. But there was no certainty in any of that. Finance job it was. At least I was headed back to New York.

The apartment I bought was at 50 Avenue A, between Third and Fourth Streets. *I owned an apartment! I had a mortgage!* It felt exciting and like such an adult thing to do. It was early 1998, and I was twenty-five years old. It was a two-bedroom, two-bathroom apartment with its own small washer and dryer—a luxury in Manhattan. The price was affordable because it was in Alphabet City, a neighborhood considered sketchy and dangerous back then. But I could see it was on the verge of changing. Also, the apartment looked awful. The seller hadn't even bothered with a fresh coat of paint. When my ex-boyfriend (now simply *friend*) Leo came to see it, his first words were, "Wow, what a dump!"

But I loved my dumpy new home, and it didn't stay dumpy for long. While I started putting feelers out for jobs, Leo helped me fix up the apartment. We ripped out the ugly florescent lighting and installed shiny, chrome recessed lights. We put on goggles and, with a sledgehammer, knocked out a dividing wall, opening up the kitchen-living space. I hired professionals to sand and re-stain the wood floors. Leo and I painted all the walls in soft, muted colors. When it was done, I was in love with it. No longer a dump, it was now cozy and cute. What mattered most was that it was *mine*—my own home. And I was building equity.

With the apartment finished, I adopted two tiny kittens—a sister and brother. I named them Sydney and Dallas. My first week with them, I barely left the apartment or changed out of my flannel pajamas. But eventually, I ventured out, heading to job interviews in one of my many suits.

One interview was at a major hedge fund whose offices were high up in the

GM building, overlooking Central Park South and the Plaza Hotel. From the conference room where I waited, I kept staring out the window. I'd never worked anywhere with a view like that before. First, I met the firm's founder. Afterward, he sent someone else in to meet me. A tall, dark-haired, handsome guy walked in. He was clearly more junior—probably ten years younger than the partner, but a few years older than me. He was funny and unusually kind. He didn't ask me any of the annoying try-to-stump-you finance questions or other typical interview questions I was used to. Instead, it was more of a conversation, during which he made me laugh, a lot. By the time I left, I was worried about what it would be like to work alongside him. I already had a crush.

I didn't need to worry because, not long after, I accepted a job elsewhere—at a newly formed high-yield fund. It was a small team, and the only other female was our sole executive assistant. My role? Analyzing high-yield bonds for purchase. *Fun!* I was hardly excited about the job, but it paid well. Then, shortly after I started, the bond market fell apart. There were very few deals to evaluate. Instead, my boss handed me a thick stack of research reports on the oil and gas industry, telling me to bone up on that industry so I could become their "oil and gas expert." *Oh great. How stimulating.* I was miserable. Feeling useless and bored (even while getting paid well) was painful. I found myself actually missing the insane adrenaline-fueled pace of Bear Stearns.

Meanwhile, the good-looking guy from the hedge fund interview—after learning I'd accepted another job—called and asked me to dinner. A few nights later, he took me to Raoul's in SoHo, a place known for its steak au poivre, and that was what we ate. Again, he made me laugh—a lot. He was six years older, further along in his career, and successful. But he didn't take it too seriously, and he wasn't full of himself the way so many finance and Wall Street types were.

Fast forward a few months, and it was becoming increasingly clear that we'd get engaged. Finally, about a year after we started dating, on a beach in Anguilla, he presented me with a very large, very beautiful diamond ring. I was incredibly happy. I was in love. And he was a ridiculously *good* person, the kind of guy any parent would adore. He'd been captain of the baseball, basketball, *and* football teams at his fancy private Manhattan high school. After that, he majored in English at Brown, then went on to get an MBA at Wharton (apparently, we'd overlapped for a year while I was there as an undergrad). And he made me laugh *all the time.* Even when I was cranky from horrible PMS, hating the world and myself, instead of getting irritated at my being cranky, he'd double down on being funny and make me laugh even more. People in my life—friends who'd known me for years—were shocked to hear of my engagement, that I was doing something so *normal*. But everyone who met him loved him.

Now, I was in yet another new world, spending most of my time at his place on the Upper West Side. It was definitely *not* my favorite part of Manhattan, but our plan was to eventually move downtown. I was also adjusting to the diamond on my finger. Knowing it was worth more than what some people earned in a year felt... awkward. And it was modest compared to what most of my fiancé's friend's wives wore. I loved the ring. But it also felt... *not me.*

* * *

After moving to the Upper West Side, I sold my beloved Avenue A apartment. I made a healthy profit—one and a half times what I'd paid after only a year and a half—but, looking back, I wish I'd never sold it. Next, with a new plan in mind, I left my job at the high-yield fund. It was exciting to give my notice, and kind of a thrill to tell them, "I'm going to culinary school!" I seemed to keep surprising people. I'd found a six-month program at the French Culinary Institute, downtown in SoHo. I didn't have a specific career in mind—just that I wanted to do something in food. I didn't then have ambitions about opening a restaurant or working my way up in fine-dining kitchens. I simply loved cooking and restaurants. I wanted to learn more, and my fiancé was supportive.

That spring and summer, I commuted downtown every weekday, sweating buckets in my school-issued polyester chef-wear, feeling gross from all the brioche, tarte aux pommes, and gratin dauphinois I was tasting. Sometimes, I walked all the way home—all ninety blocks—just to burn calories. In my free time, and after graduating in August, I planned our wedding scheduled for that coming November. Held at a penthouse loft space in the city, it turned out to be a great night—short on ceremony, long on party (it was 1999, after all). We paid for it ourselves, because we could. I had the profits from my apartment sale and Bain Capital returns rolling in periodically, and my future husband was about to get a huge year-end bonus.

After the honeymoon, it felt strange to have nowhere to be. No work, no school, and no plan. My husband was up and out the door early, leaving me with entire days to myself. After years of working brutally long hours, you'd think I would have been in heaven with so much leisure time. I had total freedom and no financial pressure. I could take my time figuring out what to do next. I should have been happy. But I wasn't, and I wasn't sure why. Maybe it was because I had no plan. And without a plan, I had no purpose. Instead of basking in the freedom and security, I felt... depressed.

I went to a therapist, who sent me to a psychiatrist, who prescribed Wellbutrin for depression and Ambien to help me sleep. The Wellbutrin helped, at least for a while. It was easier to get up and go about my days—days I now spent just being a *wife*. Something new. I took care of the household bills and bought my husband new clothes, socks, and underwear. I bought and wrapped baby gifts for all his friends who were popping out babies. I baked impressive cakes for birthdays. I was the good wife. I also shopped for myself, marveling at what it felt like to buy an expensive department store face cream if I wanted, or new clothes, without looking at the price tag.

My in-laws lived in the city, so we saw them fairly often. And my husband had a preexisting social circle—friends from high school, college, and business school—so we regularly went out to dinner with other couples. Our first summer as newlyweds, we shared a rental house in the Hamptons with two of my husband's friends—a professional couple, both in finance. It didn't take long to realize how much I didn't care for the Hamptons. It felt like the social extension of the investment banking and finance worlds. Getting a dinner reservation was a competition. People turned to look you up and down, assessing whether you were famous or important, or just judging your attire. At least my husband could laugh about it with me, even if his tolerance for this kind of vibe was higher than mine.

At social gatherings, I'd inevitably get asked, "So what do *you* do?" I hated not having an answer. Having no job was only temporary, but I was uncomfortable being just the blonde with a big diamond ring. *Wife* was my only designation, as if that was all I had to offer the world. I'd rush to explain that I *used* to work at Bain Capital and Bear Stearns, tripping over myself to prove I was smart. Why was I always so worried about people thinking I was dumb? Why was I worried about what people were thinking at all?

I felt out of place in this life. Everything was too normal. I didn't feel normal, and I wasn't at ease in this world. Probably, I wasn't fully at ease with myself. Without the crush of an all-consuming job, I was left alone to marinate in just being *me*—and I had no idea who I was, or who I wanted to be.

Living on the Upper West Side also didn't suit me. I missed the grit of downtown. Even our fancy gym felt wrong—with its four levels of carpeting (who carpets a gym?), floor-to-ceiling windows, spotlessly clean machines, and soothing music quietly piped in through hidden speakers. I missed my old spot: the grungy, basement-level Dolphin gym on Third Street, where heavy metal blasted, barely drowning out the grunts of heavily tattooed guys as they slammed down heavy weights. I felt more at home there.

But our location wouldn't be an issue for long. We were actively apartment-hunting downtown. We'd looked in Tribeca and SoHo, but the one I loved most was a 4,000-square-foot full-floor loft on Broadway between Twelfth and Thirteenth Streets—a block below the Union Square Greenmarket, not too far from my first East Village apartment. It was ideal. We submitted an offer.

Meanwhile, something unsettling was creeping in. I wasn't happy, but I couldn't quite name it. My husband was a truly good person, and fun to be with. I loved him. We spent more time with his family than I would have liked, but at least he made funny jokes the whole time, and it was hard not to admire his loyalty to them. Yet despite all his good qualities (and all of mine, ha ha), in some ways we weren't so compatible, and we started to fight more often. I had some kind of restless, wild-child energy in me.

I hadn't yet realized I might be one of those people who won't ever settle down.

CHAPTER EIGHTEEN

EARLY 2000
NEW YORK CITY

It was the start of a new century, and I was newly married. But I still hadn't sorted out a career, or what lay ahead for me. I wanted to work in food but wasn't sure in what capacity. Then I got a lead: an opening to be a recipe tester for a forthcoming cookbook by a chef I admired. When restaurant chefs write cookbooks, recipes need to be scaled down and adapted for home cooks. I'd be perfect for this, and it would keep me busy for a while at least.

When I called the chef's literary agent to inquire about the job, she told me it had just been filled. *Oh well.*

Then she asked, "Have you heard of Matthew Kenney?"

Um, yes. I certainly had. He was an up-and-coming chef whose eponymous Upper East Side restaurant, Matthew's, was my favorite in the city. Not just one of my favorites—but the one I always named when someone asked. The menu was Mediterranean, with a distinctive freshness that fit the breezy Casablanca-style decor. He'd opened other restaurants, but Matthew's remained his best-known. I had his first cookbook, *Matthew Kenney's Mediterranean Cooking*. I loved that book. The cover featured its best recipe: Moroccan Spiced Crab Cakes. In the upper left corner was a small headshot of Matthew, looking young and beautiful, almost femininely so.

I'd met him once. My sister had thrown me a surprise wedding shower, booking a large table for brunch at Matthew's. She'd told the restaurant I was a huge fan of the chef and so, in the middle of my wedding shower, Matthew stopped by our table to say hello. He was gracious, almost a bit shy.

The literary agent explained that Matthew was working on a second book and looking for a recipe tester. I couldn't believe it. What were the odds? I wanted this. She put me in touch with Matthew's assistant to set up an interview.

* * *

On the appointed day, I agonized over what to wear—something nice but not too formal. My mother-in-law had gifted me a sleek Calvin Klein black blazer at Christmas. It was fitted, with a straight collar and a bold silver zipper up the center. I wore it over narrow black pants and a white shirt, with simple black boots.

Matthew's office was a few doors down from his restaurant, on the fourth floor of a large brownstone on Sixty-First Street between Third and Lexington Avenues. I took the creaky elevator up and stepped through a small, closet-sized foyer into a reception area. A smartly dressed, attractive woman sat at the front desk. She welcomed me and told me to take a seat.

I sat on a narrow bench, facing a wall of bookshelves lined with cookbooks. I scanned the titles, mentally noting which ones I also had at home. Finally, a door beside the shelves opened, and Matthew greeted me with a smile.

"Sarma?"

I stood up and smiled back. "Hi."

"Matthew Kenney," he said. "Good to see you." His voice was soft and gentle, as was his handshake. "Come on in. Have a seat."

I followed him into his office. He wore slim charcoal-gray dress pants and a steel-blue dress shirt, perfectly tailored. The first thing I noticed was that there wasn't much on his desk, or on any surface. The room seemed bare. Which was why the lone cantaloupe sitting on top of a filing cabinet stood out.

"Do you always keep melons in your office?" I asked, hoping to break some ice as I sat down.

He picked up the melon, held it in both hands, then put it up to his nose. Closing his eyes, he took an audible whiff. "Lunch!" he declared.

Before I could fully process the thought, *Is he for real?* he extended the melon toward my face, "Smell that," he said.

I hesitated, then obeyed—because what else was I going to do? It smelled like… cantaloupe.

"Mmmmm," I replied, because what else was I going to say? And this is how our meeting started. Me wondering, *What kind of dude eats only a small melon for lunch? Is he gay?* He was married to a woman. *But maybe?*

I quickly forgot about the melon because it was hard not to be mesmerized by his features and how beautifully they fit together—his olive complexion, wavy brown hair, and deep-set dark eyes framed by prominent cheekbones and a sharp jawline. He even had a nice mouth. His attractiveness made me nervous.

We talked about cooking school, having both attended the French Culinary Institute—though ten years apart—and about how it was funny that we'd met at my wedding shower. For some reason, I became uncomfortably aware of my rather sizable engagement ring, which I wore alongside a plain wedding band. It often made me uncomfortable, feeling aware of what it said about me. *I have money.* Or at least, *I'm married to someone with money.* For some reason, I felt that he was aware of it too.

We discussed the concept of his new book, the style of recipes, and the particulars of the job. He would give me batches of recipes to test, and I would buy the ingredients and test the recipes. We'd meet periodically to go over my notes, rinse and repeat. By the end of the interview, he never said he'd get back to me. He never formally offered me the job, and I never formally accepted. It was as if I'd already had it before walking in. I could feel my insides twinge, excited to be working for this chef I admired. I'd be paid per recipe, though I don't remember how much it was. It doesn't matter, because he'd stop paying me anyway. Before the manuscript was finished, we'd be living together.

* * *

My new job pulled me, at least somewhat, out of my doldrums. It was fun to shop for ingredients, cook, tweak recipes, or, more often, work with nothing beyond a loose description of the dish he wanted. I was good at it. Over time, he even let me contribute some of my own recipes and ideas to his book.

I eagerly looked forward to my review meetings with Matthew. We typically met at one of his restaurants, but one day he suggested we meet for lunch at Il Cantinori—a cozy Tuscan restaurant on East Tenth Street known for celebrity sightings. It was a place more suitable for a date than a working lunch, but *okay*. We were seated at a small two-top, and when Matthew ordered a glass of white wine, he asked if I wanted one too. Wine at lunch? *Sure!* The conversation flowed, but it wasn't about the recipes. I kept awkwardly angling to pull out my stack of notes, but there was no room on the small table, and Matthew didn't seem interested in recipes. We talked about other things, and as we ate—and moved on to our second glasses of wine—it all started to feel less weird and more exciting. *Shit.*

Wrong as it felt, I found him alluring. At first, I dismissed it. Matthew was beautiful to look at, but he didn't seem like my type at all. When I got married, I was madly in love, thrilled that I'd never have to date again. My husband and I had been on the same page about kids—we didn't want any—and I'd found the idea of spending the rest of my life with him reassuring. And yet, only a year into marriage, here I was, drawn toward someone else. Someone so different. My husband had good values and a stellar character. He was kind, good-looking, safe, incredibly funny, and fun to be with. But we'd begun fighting more, and new issues were surfacing. Meanwhile, Matthew and I shared something fundamental: our passion for good food and restaurants.

In contrast to the finance-oriented crowd of newlyweds with whom my husband and I regularly socialized, Matthew existed within the more exotic and alluring universe of New York City restaurants and nightlife. He was surrounded by creative eccentrics: the gritty and industrious kitchen workers, the ambitious PR and fashion crowd, the chef entrepreneurs—sprinkled with an assortment of other oddball characters I was increasingly meeting or hearing about. Matthew had begun hinting that perhaps I could also help him with his restaurant projects, which was intriguing.

Meanwhile, my husband and I had put in a bid on the stunning 4,000-square-foot apartment downtown—the one I'd fallen in love with. My husband's bonus the year after we were married was more than four times the one he'd received the year before. And that earlier bonus had been nearly seven figures. He was now firmly a seven-figure earner, with a likely upward trajectory. Whatever our issues, I had a good husband and a safe future where I'd want for nothing. I could pursue whatever career I wanted without financial worry. But it was never my intent to rely on someone else, and I didn't quite feel like *myself* in the role of wife.

I was restless. And here was a shiny object.

* * *

I couldn't let us buy a multimillion-dollar home if I was having thoughts—however uncertain—of a different kind of life. So I abruptly ripped the Band-Aid off. In an incredibly sad and painful conversation, I told my husband that I thought we should get divorced. Hurting him sickened me. It felt like I wasn't just letting him down, but our families, our friends—every person who'd attended our wedding only a year and a half earlier. Throughout this gut-wrenching process, I repeatedly questioned whether I was doing the right thing—blowing up my perfect life. But I also felt propelled by some larger force.

I wasn't interested in any kind of fight. I didn't want alimony or to feel I was taking advantage of a situation. I just wanted what was fair. Through some tense conversations, we worked it out that I would essentially leave with what I'd brought into the marriage: my savings, the profits from my apartment sale, and my Bain Capital returns.

Once we'd hammered out this settlement, my husband said to me, almost as an afterthought, "Oh, and by the way, I only *said* I didn't want kids because *you* said you didn't want kids. I can't *wait* to have kids!"

What? I guess it's good we're getting divorced then? I thought. Ultimately, it *was* good, because my now ex-husband later became a father, and an excellent one.

* * *

After the divorce, I moved downtown into an apartment in the West Village. I probably should have spent more time on my own, but things with Matthew moved fast. By then, he'd not only begun involving me in his new restaurant projects but had also separated from his wife. Much like our first interview, where he never formally offered me the job, he and I became a couple without ever having an explicit conversation about it.

Since his separation, Matthew had been subletting an apartment from a friend, but he soon gave up the sublet and moved into my place. We were a team now. I worked on finishing his cookbook while also traveling with him to Atlanta and Portland, where he was opening new restaurants.

In the beginning, Matthew was consistently sweet, considerate, and loving. He made amazing food for us, regularly left sentimental notes in cards or on scraps of paper, and was attentive and supportive.

In those early days, our differences seemed superficial. Matthew's fastidious ways made me feel like a slob in comparison. Everything about him was stylish, curated, deliberate. His personal care products were top of the line, his grooming meticulous, and his bathroom always spotless. I appreciated nice products and an aesthetically pleasing environment but couldn't wrap my brain around spending $50 on a scented candle. I sometimes let blobs of toothpaste accumulate in the sink or left the mirror splattered from my flossing. I'm not a slob, but neither am I an obsessive perfectionist.

I teased him now and then about his metrosexual ways and fancy taste. It was easier to laugh about these things when everything between us was okay. But looking back, I can see the red flags. Once, he angrily snapped at a garage attendant in a way that shocked and mortified me. I told him so, and he was effusively apologetic, appearing genuinely remorseful. But now I see it for what it was: a moment where he'd accidentally let his guard down. Later, I overheard him on the phone—once with his ex-wife, another time with one of his operations managers, a smart, experienced guy older than him—and was shocked at how he spoke to them. Cruelly to his ex-wife and condescendingly to his manager. It was disturbing to hear, but I rationalized it away. Matthew had never spoken to *me* that way. At least not yet.

* * *

The project I spent the most time on—once the book was wrapping up—was the opening of a new restaurant to replace Matthew's after an electrical fire left it severely damaged. Rather than reopen the same concept, Matthew wanted to reinvent it entirely. The classic Mediterranean Matthew's would be replaced by a sleek, modern restaurant he planned to name Commissary.

Instead of focusing on the financials, I was drawn to the creative side—designing the menu, planning the interior, and so on. I trusted Matthew and figured he knew what he was doing. However, as the project and our lives progressed, I developed a creeping awareness of just how much I was paying for, in rent and living expenses, while Matthew was not. I knew things were probably tight for him, between rebuilding this restaurant and preparing to open another in Atlanta, so I didn't raise the issue. But it didn't feel good.

Then, the planned budgets were exceeded, and more money was needed to get Commissary open. Somehow, I agreed to put up $60,000 of my savings as an equity investment. The responsible thing to do before plonking down that much money would have been to conduct basic due diligence—to review the financials for *all* his restaurants, the budgets, cash on hand, etc. But we were rushing toward the opening date, and I simply trusted him. It seemed as if we were in this together now—both struggles and successes—for life.

Matthew's expensive personal tastes extended to his restaurants. The chairs he'd ordered for Commissary were modern, Italian-designed black leather, each one costing over $800. Yes, *$800 per chair*. A huge round bar was custom-built for the space, at a hefty cost. Whatever money he'd gotten from insurance clearly wasn't enough. On top of what I'd invested, he asked me for a $30,000 loan, promising I'd be paid back within a few weeks. I loaned him the money, but was never paid back. I was anxious but also wrapped up in the anticipation of it all. The restaurant was a few weeks from opening, and we were both working hard.

I told myself that once we opened, everything would turn around and fall into place. I was excited for the future, unaware that the world was about to change.

CHAPTER NINETEEN

2001–2003
NEW YORK CITY

On the night of September 10, 2001, Matthew and I took a rare night off to celebrate my birthday at a nice restaurant. The following morning, we stood outside our apartment on Greenwich Street, watching smoke rise from one of the Twin Towers, from what we assumed was a tragic accident. Then, what had appeared as merely a fluke suddenly became an entirely different story, as another plane approached, slicing into the second tower, right in front of our eyes.

The only word for how I felt is, logically, terrorized. This was no accident.

Speechless and numb, we went back inside to see if something on TV could help explain what was occurring just a mile south of us. I stared mutely at the screen while Matthew got right into business mode, calling his restaurant managers. I was taken aback at how calm he was, how unemotional. I noted that the focus of his calls wasn't so much to find out *Is everyone okay?* but more about whether they would stay open (*really?*) and how everything would be handled. I marveled at how he could function.

I sat in a stupor trying to understand what was happening, then clamped my hand over my mouth in disbelief as the TV screen showed one of the towers come tumbling down. And then, the other. It was surreal to watch this live footage, knowing how close we were.

At some point, we decided to go back outside. A slow and silent parade of human beings moved north up Greenwich Street. Everyone was covered in ash—men in suits, women in business attire without shoes, their faces ghostly white, hair stiff with dust. Some staggered, while others simply walked, staring straight ahead, like zombies, tears making wet streaks down their chalky faces. The only sound was the chorus of sirens. Whatever trauma I felt, their pain was unimaginable to me.

* * *

In the aftermath of 9/11, downtown restaurants in Manhattan were hit especially hard. Matthew's already fragile financial position—far worse than I realized at the time—slid from precariously sucking to seriously fucked.

I never saw his company's financials then, and I'm still not sure why I didn't insist on it. I continued going uptown to the newly opened restaurant early each morning—making huge batches of fennel and farro soup, prepping the desserts—all while funneling more of my money into the business. It pained me to see Matthew struggling. We were in this together, and I wanted to help.

By the time we celebrated my thirtieth birthday the following September, I was heavily in debt. When Matthew and I first started living together, I'd had a quarter of a million dollars to my name, money I'd earned, but I was now in debt by that amount. It was a half-million-dollar swing of the pendulum. How did that happen? It was *his* businesses that were collapsing, not mine. I'd just climbed aboard for the ride and got wiped out in the process.

I'd been operating as if Matthew and I were a team. I felt invested more than just financially. When I commit to something, I *commit*. I couldn't stand seeing the smaller vendors go unpaid, so when they called begging for money, I paid them out of my own pocket. When the cash flow from Matthew's restaurants hadn't been enough to cover payroll and checks were bouncing, I covered the difference. Staff came to me with their bad checks, and I either wrote them a personal check or handed them cash. I saved copies of every check I cashed, stuffed in a shoe box that I kept for years. They totaled more than $100,000.

Meanwhile, I didn't understand how Matthew could be so cold about it all. I figured he was in a state of denial.

More than once, I personally wired the rent for one of his restaurants straight from my own bank account. So when that landlord later sued Matthew and his company, I got sued too. The landlord and plaintiff in that suit? Donald J. Trump. Tina Brown once allegedly said, "You're not anyone in New York unless you've been sued by Donald Trump." So I guess I'd really made it?

I was exhausted, spent. *Literally* spent. When my money ran out, I swiped a credit card for a $20,000 "event fee" just to get money into the restaurant accounts. After my credit was maxed out, I looked for money anywhere I could. I took my beautiful engagement ring from my recent marriage down to the diamond district. (My ex hadn't wanted it back.) I sold it and used the money to pay staff. Before my credit rating declined, I agreed to get a no-income, no-asset mortgage and effectively bought a property in Maine from Matthew, taking on a nearly half-million-dollar mortgage so that his company could get needed funds.

Was I delusional? Or was I just riding Matthew's delusion, on the assumption that he'd never allow me to overextend myself like this unless he was certain of our future success. He was eight years older than me, after all, and had been successful before. I was new to the restaurant business; he was a veteran. I naively thought everything was going to be okay. But it never was.

Things got worse, and it became impossible to deny that there was no turnaround coming. The new restaurant wasn't suddenly going to start generating enough cash, nor would his places downtown stop bleeding money. Matthew's administrative staff—his assistant, CFO, and a few others—had long since left. Now it was just him and me in the office across the street, the one where I'd first interviewed for the cookbook job.

A debt collector named Randy regularly called Matthew, yelling so loudly I could hear his voice roaring through the phone receiver. One day, Randy showed up in person. Peeking out of my office, I saw an imposing man in a dark suit—pretty much what I'd imagined he'd look like. I crept back to my desk as he loudly pressured Matthew for money. Then it got quiet. On his way out, he saw me in my office and stopped. I looked up at him, wondering if he was going to yell at me too. He pointed his finger at me. "You!" he bellowed. "We're going to lunch. *Now.*"

I froze. *Lunch?* What was I supposed to do here? The best way to describe Randy is to imagine a Jewish version of Tony Soprano. I couldn't exactly say no to him.

I obediently stood up, grabbing my bag and my coat. As I followed Randy out the door, I looked over at Matthew. He only shrugged.

Really? I had no choice, apparently. And thus began my very odd friendship with Randy—for it turned out this was just the first of many lunch outings to come. To his credit, he never pressured me, at least not beyond what I could dismiss as good-natured flirting, to do anything untoward. After hearing about my background—how I'd worked hard in finance only to lose everything and more through Matthew's businesses—he was sympathetic.

Randy would, unexpectedly, resurface in my life many years later, genuinely and generously offering help after I got myself into yet another mess.

* * *

Around this time, I met Jeffrey Chodorow for the first time. A successful restaurateur with high-profile locations in multiple cities, he regularly partnered with well-known chefs. He'd begun a dialogue with Matthew, who—despite his business troubles—was undoubtedly a talented chef with the good looks to cultivate a celebrity persona. At the same time, Jeffrey was also in talks with another handsome, talented chef, Rocco DiSpirito, to collaborate on a restaurant that would be the focus of an NBC reality show. They needed a location, and one of Matthew's failing restaurants on Twenty-Second Street was an ideal space for it. Jeffrey ultimately took over that lease, and the Mark Burnett-produced show *The Restaurant* chronicled Rocco and Jeffrey as they launched Rocco's. As a result of Jeffrey taking over that lease, it was loosely agreed that he would, at some point, partner with Matthew (and me) on a new restaurant.

* * *

When Commissary finally closed, everything Matthew had launched—his restaurants, catering business, product line, all of it—was gone. In some way, it was probably a huge relief for him. I knew it was a relief for me, but I was also frustrated that he'd allowed it to bleed me out financially in the process, leaving me saddled with so much debt. You'd think Matthew would have been kinder to me than ever, but instead, it was the opposite. He began speaking to me the way

I'd heard him speak to others before—with ice-cold derision. As if he resented me. I didn't know how to deal with this.

After everything closed, we started consulting for Jeffrey—revamping the menu at his Hudson Hotel restaurant, creating new dishes for another—to cover rent on our new apartment on Eleventh Street and Fourth Avenue. After so many late payments at the West Village apartment, the landlord there wouldn't renew my lease. You'd think we'd have moved to a smaller, less expensive place, but somehow Matthew argued it made sense to upgrade. Never mind that he was being sued by a ton of vendors and several former employees. He insisted we needed a *nice* home, with an extra bedroom for a shared office, since we'd be working from home for a while. *Um, okay.* I'd always been obsessive about saving money, yet I foolishly—and inexplicably—agreed. I was also the only one on the apartment lease. Meanwhile, Matthew continued buying himself nice things and taking taxis instead of the subway.

Both our cell phones plans were also in my name, since my credit was still better than his. Once, when he was traveling, I reminded him to avoid using his phone too much—this was back when *roaming* charges could add up fast. Weeks later, a massive bill arrived. Shocked at the amount, I hit a last-straw moment and tipped over an edge. I sobbed, hard. Matthew didn't seem bothered, which only made me cry harder. I went into the bathroom, where I lay on the floor, letting the tears out. Finally, Matthew came in. I thought he was going to apologize or pull me up into a hug—*something*. Instead, he looked down at me, disdain in his eyes, and said, "Nothing ever gets accomplished from the bathroom floor." Then he walked out.

Eventually, Matthew filed for bankruptcy, wiping out all his debt—except for taxes. I continued to carry all of mine: loads of credit card debt and that stupid property mortgage with the brutal monthly payments—the servicing of which felt like flushing money down the toilet. Months later, I finally had someone appraise the property to see if I could sell it. I was advised I'd be lucky if I got half of what I owed. It wasn't just a little underwater; it was drowning. Finally, I stopped paying the mortgage. What was the point? My once-perfect credit rating had already been obliterated. Still, I was determined to eventually pay all my debts and be whole again. I didn't want to file for bankruptcy, like Matthew.

I resented him for my circumstances and was ashamed and angry at myself for having relied on a future with him. Finally, I could see that his character wasn't that of someone I wanted to spend my life with. But I was stuck. Where would I go? I had lost my independence. I couldn't afford to go anywhere.

A part of me still felt bad for him. I thought surely he *must* have felt bad for what I'd been put through and the debt I now carried—he just couldn't show it.

Unfortunately, it wouldn't be the last time I misjudged a man's feelings or intentions.

* * *

Alongside the consulting work, Matthew and I developed a concept for the promised restaurant collaboration with Jeffrey. Matthew had shifted from his Mediterranean culinary roots to embrace a new trend—high-end comfort food. He decided we should open an upscale burger place called Burger Bar, with a distinguishing focus on quality ingredients. This was still a novel idea in the early 2000s, as the "farm to table" movement—with menus citing the local farm that supplied the delicate greens for salads and the names of cheese mongers responsible for the crumbled blue cheese sprinkled on top—had only begun to emerge.

Burger Bar would take the classic greasy burger joint concept and apply those farm-to-table standards, using only the best grass-fed meat and artisanal cheeses, with an elegant atmosphere and prices to match. We developed a menu of creative burgers, weaving in truffles, fancy cheeses, heritage bacon, brioche buns, and heirloom tomatoes.

At that time, going vegan was something we'd never considered. *Raw vegan* was something we'd never even heard of. Back then, hardly anyone had.

That changed one night, with one dinner.

CHAPTER TWENTY

2003–2004
NEW YORK CITY

It was the summer of 2003. Matthew and I had plans to go out for dinner with his friend Robb Matzner. Robb was older but in ridiculously good shape, competing in the over-fifty category of bodybuilding competitions. We had reservations at the latest Jean-Georges restaurant in Tribeca, a place I'd been eager to try, especially with all the buzz surrounding it. So I was disappointed when Robb asked if we could change plans and go to a *raw food* restaurant in the East Village instead.

A *what?* I googled it and was overcome by disappointment and dread.

I had no idea that this dinner would change our lives.

We squeezed into our table in the tiny, packed restaurant on East Tenth Street. The place was hot and stuffy—the AC was probably broken—and it smelled faintly of wheatgrass, patchouli, and curry. Not exactly promising.

Robb ordered while explaining the benefits of eating raw vegan and how much better he felt since switching to it exclusively. I listened, skeptical, but once the food arrived, I was pleasantly surprised. It tasted *really* good. And despite eating a lot of it, I felt astonishingly light and energized. Not heavy and gross, the way I was used to feeling after a restaurant meal. While Robb talked, I noticed women who looked like models gliding in and out for to-go orders. We struck up a conversation with a young woman at the adjacent table, eating alone. She confirmed what Robb was telling us—she, too, felt like a new person since eating this way. But she added that none of her friends understood it or would join her. Glancing around the place, she sighed and said, "I wish someone would open a *cool* raw food restaurant."

And just like that, a metaphorical light bulb appeared above my head. The food was delicious but far from sophisticated. Could we marry a high-end restaurant vibe with an elevated version of this *raw vegan* food? Could it be the kind of place you could bring (and actually impress) a date?

* * *

That same night, Matthew and I decided to go raw vegan for what we thought would be a two-week experiment. *Just two weeks.* But after only a few days, it was hard to deny how dramatically different we felt, how much *better.* And our transition wasn't from a junk food diet; I'd already been used to eating a lot of salads, fresh fruit, and very little processed food.

The stark shift in how we felt fascinated me. I dove into researching the rationale, science, history, and logic of eating this way. The more I read, the more it made too much sense to ever turn back.

That summer, we'd been spending more time than usual at Matthew's Maine cottage rental—avoiding creditors and mapping out a way forward after the complete unraveling of Matthew's businesses. One afternoon, I sat alone on the porch in an old rocking chair, reading yet another book on raw veganism. I paused to look out at the ocean and realized I was having one of those *moments*—the kind you know you'll always remember.

It had suddenly hit me. This lifestyle was what the rest of my life would revolve around.

I didn't want to call myself a *vegan,* but that was effectively what I'd become. Not in the strict sense because I would always be flexible and open to tasting things. But this was no longer just about my diet; it was my future.

How could it be so controversial to eat in the most natural way possible? After only a couple of weeks eating this way exclusively, I felt like I was on a steady low dose of the drug ecstasy, full of energy and a borderline euphoria.

I stared out at the horizon. All my life I'd never been sure what I wanted. But now, a picture began to form in my mind: food as a way of living and healing, brought to the mainstream in a new way—an appealing way. *This* was what I was here to do. It was like finding something I didn't know I'd been looking for, and it felt *right*.

* * *

Matthew also felt like a new person eating this way. It seemed not just our bodies but our relationship began to heal with this new way of life. If nothing else, our excitement overshadowed our issues. We talked about the possibility—back then a crazy idea—of doing our own raw food restaurant. How could we go back to the burger bar concept? We discussed completely scrapping it and creating a raw vegan menu instead. It would be a bold and risky move, and we still had to convince Jeffrey. But it felt right.

Jeffrey Chodorow was an unusual partner for this raw vegan venture. He'd built a multiconcept restaurant empire, starting with his midtown flagship, China Grill, followed by Asia de Cuba and others—many of them anchored in the newest trendy boutique hotels. In the early 2000s, he had twenty-four restaurants across nine cities. They were mostly big, clubby, and high profile. Matthew and I worried what he'd think of this different and arguably high-risk raw vegan concept. But to his credit, Jeffrey was open-minded and fully supportive.

We were on our way to making our raw food restaurant a reality. And something told me this was just the beginning.

* * *

By the following summer, our new restaurant, Pure Food and Wine, had been conceived, fully developed, and brought to life. It opened in June of 2004.

Like bringing a child into a troubled relationship, it consumed all our attention, giving Matthew and me a shared purpose that allowed us to coexist. But our issues remained.

CHAPTER TWENTY-ONE

2004–2005
NEW YORK CITY

Pure Food and Wine was busy, consistently garnering press coverage. Noteworthy people came to dine, including world-renowned chefs like Alain Ducasse, who later sent us a lovely handwritten note. A few weeks after opening, the legendary New York City publisher Judith Regan had dinner in our garden. Matthew recognized her immediately. He followed the city's newsworthy figures and events, regularly reading the *New York Post's* Page Six—the prominent gossip column in which one usually did *not* want to see one's own name.

In addition to having her own imprint at HarperCollins (Regan Books), Judith had also hosted talk shows, spoken frequently in the media, and endured her own personal tabloid drama. She was known for being outspoken, ballsy, and powerful in the industry.

She asked to speak with us, so Matthew and I approached her table. Judith is classically beautiful, with strong features, ideally proportioned. Her face reminded me of Isabella Rossellini's. I found myself both admiring her and slightly afraid of her—why, I wasn't sure. In her husky, deep voice, she said, "I like what you're doing here. I love the food." Then, she added, "I want to publish your cookbook. And I want to do it in eight weeks."

What?

Having worked on Matthew's cookbook, I knew that an eight-week timeline was bananas. Moreover, we'd only just opened the restaurant and hardly had extra time. But this was Judith Regan. She wanted to do a hardcover book with beautiful full-color photography. I was humbled and excited.

Within a few days, I drafted a mini proposal, reviewed it with Matthew, and emailed it to HarperCollins. Shortly thereafter we signed a contract. Putting it together would take more like eight months than eight weeks, but even that time frame was fast.

To the wider public, co-authoring a book linked Matthew and I more closely. But behind the scenes, things were unraveling.

The book advance wasn't much—it usually isn't in the cookbook world unless you're on TV or world-famous. The monthly consulting fee we took from the restaurant barely covered our rent and basic expenses. I still had mortgage payments and credit card minimums to pay and therefore had to keep finding outside sources to make ends meet. It bothered me that we lived in a place we obviously couldn't afford. I was angry that Matthew seemed committed to living a comfortable lifestyle, buying himself cashmere socks while others were worse off because of him, including me. While I agonized, he seemed unbothered by it all.

There were employees from his former restaurants who, in the end, never got paid for their last two weeks of work. I know this because I kept a list of their names and the amounts they were owed. They'd been *his* employees, but since I had been involved, it still gnawed at me. One day, I received an unexpected check from a long-forgotten Bain Capital investment. Those investments had been illiquid until sold by Bain Capital, so I'd had no way to cash them in earlier. With some of that extra money, I went to a restaurant where I knew Gustavo, a former sous chef I had worked beside at one of Matthew's restaurants, was now employed. I gave him $500 cash—approximately what he'd been owed. A waiter named Matt, who'd also never been paid his last check, was working there as well, so I gave him a few hundred dollars. I tracked down another former line cook and gave him cash too. They were happily surprised that I had shown up, all this time later, to repay them what they'd likely long since written off. It made me feel happy too. When I told Matthew about it later that day, he was furious at me. Standing there in his cashmere socks, *he* was furious at *me*.

* * *

We had bitter, frustrating fights. Matthew seemed unable to comprehend the logic of my anger and only grew angrier at *me*. For what? Supporting him all those years? Sometimes, even in front of other people at the restaurant, he spoke to me with the same cold and condescending tone I'd been alarmed to hear him use with his ex-wife and manager years earlier. He was plainly checked out of our relationship. I wondered whether he even liked me as a person anymore—or ever had at all.

On more than a few occasions, I badly wanted to throw him out of our apartment—the one with *my* name on the lease, the payments for which I was responsible. But I knew if I made him leave, he'd most likely book himself a room at the latest trendy, high-end boutique hotel, using funds we were meant to share. That was the sort of thing he would do. We also had to run the restaurant together, and I was working hard to finish the cookbook that we "co-authored." How could we split? It wasn't just impractical; it felt impossible. By giving away so much early on, I'd trapped myself in this relationship.

Then, one day, Matthew accessed my private AOL email account (back when people still used AOL), read my Instant Messenger chat history, and found evidence of something going on between me and Barry, a manager at the restaurant. Personality-wise, Barry was the opposite of Matthew—sweet, easygoing, and funny. He noticed when Matthew had been especially cruel to me and used his goofy charm to cheer me up. He was genuinely kind to all the employees, the sort of guy who, if the dishwasher didn't show up, would roll up his sleeves and stay late to wash dishes, smiling and singing along to whatever music was blasting from the dish pit radio. He was also physically attractive.

Barry had been helping me develop the website that would later become OneLuckyDuck.com, so we spent a lot of time together alone. There was chemistry, and eventually, something happened. I didn't feel particularly guilty about it, because why would I? Matthew was being a ginormous dick to me, and we very obviously resented each other. We may have been sleeping in the same bed—there being only one in our apartment—but we hadn't had sex in ages. It was unspoken, yet seemed understood, that we'd split up once we had the means and the time.

Matthew was *livid*. Suddenly, I was the *bad* one. I had done something terribly *wrong*. I should be *ashamed* of myself. How could I have *betrayed* him like that? Somehow it was established that I had to move out, and I left to find a place to sublet—ending up in a room on the eighteenth floor of a building on Third Avenue, one block from the restaurant. The apartment belonged to a harmless-looking nerdy guy who worked as a bond trader at Goldman Sachs. When I'd responded to the ad on Craigslist and then showed up at his door, I'd had no idea it was to rent only a *room*, to be a housemate. I'd thought the ad was to sublet an entire apartment. Still, the room was clean, with a bed, a small desk, and, crucially, its own bathroom. I didn't care about the rust stains on the ceiling or the utter lack of charm. It felt safe and was conveniently located. I agreed to take it on the spot, awkwardly asking if I could move in that same day. Unfortunately, I had to leave my cats behind with Matthew. This was only temporary, I figured.

I got lucky that my new roommate was not only a really nice guy, but he was also nearly always at work or asleep by the time I got home late. In those days, I slept very little. There were nights when I lay on the bed in the dark, exhausted from work, while Matthew berated me on the phone, and I cried and cried and repeated *I'm sorry, I'm sorry, I'm sorry*. He'd keep me on the phone for hours, making me stay up most of the night. I could barely function, yet was now working more than ever. Matthew had immediately fired Barry, so who would take over Barry's managerial duties? Me, of course. I did something *bad*, so I had to suffer the consequences. I quickly learned how to do the payroll, sort out the schedules, and get the cash drawers set up each day. Like someone who deserved the punishment, I dutifully did all those things, going in at 7:00 a.m. and not leaving until after midnight, seven days a week.

As I worked more, Matthew worked less. He stayed in our large, comfortable apartment with my two cats while *I* moved out. On top of the restaurant work, I worked hard to edit the galleys for our soon-to-be-published cookbook. Matthew continued to blame me, at one point insisting that I had borderline personality disorder. I looked it up, bought books on it, dutifully reading them, thinking, *Do I? I mean, I do have a temper, I've yelled and gotten so angry at Matthew. But not for no reason? Am I crazy?* My mind was jumbled. I didn't know what to think other than, *I'm a fuck up.*

I much later discovered that Matthew had—*allegedly*—been with other women well before my own indiscretion. It had been an open secret among staff, who either assumed I knew or didn't want to be the ones to tell me. And maybe they were afraid of him, since it wasn't until after he was gone that they felt comfortable enough to tell me. Either way, looking back, it was hardly surprising.

* * *

Whereas I had no time to even consider a new relationship, Matthew started openly seeing other people. He began dating Natasha, his assistant—half his age. I didn't care about the relationship. What steamed me was that he could somehow afford to *pay* an assistant, keep up his membership at a fancy gym, and take care of himself while I worked nonstop and felt like an *izdirsta jāņoga* (which, loosely translated from Latvian, means *just-shat-out gooseberry*).

Matthew even found time to go away with Natasha for a long July Fourth weekend to the cottage in Maine—the cottage where I'd repainted the kitchen, where my KitchenAid sat, where the drawers were still full of my summer clothes.

During this weekend, I ran into Matthew's friend Robb at the restaurant. He asked how I was doing, but when I tried to tell him that I was fine, my face must have betrayed me. Robb told me to step outside with him. Because Robb had been the one to introduce us to raw food, which led to Pure Food and Wine, I felt an extra fondness for him.

Once out on street, Robb asked how I was *really* doing. I told him I was physically exhausted and emotionally—as well as financially—drained. Robb knew that Matthew had gone to Maine with Natasha because Matthew had borrowed Robb's BMW to drive there.

Robb then surprised me by telling me that, even though Matthew was his longtime friend, he couldn't watch what was going on any longer. He told me I was getting "fucked over." He was practically yelling at me. He told me things I needed to hear, things I needed to know, that finally opened my eyes. He repeated over and over, and with emphasis, that I was getting *fucked*. His message was a bucket of ice-cold water dumped on my head. He was right. Newly awakened, I had a whole new perspective.

Robb advised me to put numbers down on paper, document everything, and prepare for war. Before the end of the weekend, I'd made a spreadsheet outlining both Matthew's and my joint salary, our shared expenses, and the debt payments I believed should at least be partially his responsibility—since, in essence, they were *his* debts. The numbers made it clear: his living expenses far exceeded mine, and there was an overall deficit. When Matthew got back in town, I presented him with the spreadsheet. He was not happy. My numbers were correct. There was no disputing verifiable facts. Having backed him into a corner, I'd triggered something in him. Everything changed. Now it was war.

Robb had known this would happen. He'd warned me to be cautious, strategic, and, above all, an "ice queen." He correctly predicted that Matthew would use every piece of paper he could find against me. In the ensuing months, whenever I needed strength, I conjured an image of a mini Robb standing on my shoulder, whispering into my ear, "Remember… Ice Queen!"

* * *

Part of what kept me going in those dark months was a project that belonged entirely to me: One Lucky Duck.

CHAPTER TWENTY-TWO

2005

NEW YORK CITY

One Lucky Duck was mine—birthed from my mind as my very own child. Importantly, it was entirely separate from Matthew. While he and I shared credit for opening Pure Food and Wine, One Lucky Duck had been my side project—one he'd oddly opposed.

But this brand felt like my purpose, even my identity. It embodied hopeful change. I quietly visualized it having a lasting, meaningful impact in the world. A brand that could outlive me.

Why a duck? It's a question I was asked a lot.

Before I knew I needed a brand name, I'd had the idea of creating an e-commerce store—*our own* online shop carrying the otherwise-hard-to-find ingredients used in so many of the recipes in our new cookbook. By that time, we were also making and packaging cookies and snacks for wholesale. Selling them on our own website, along with supplements and skin care products, made sense. The tagline would be: *Everything for the ultimate raw and organic lifestyle.*

Now I just needed a name.

For the restaurant walls, I'd wanted something different—not the cliché images of fruits and vegetables. Instead, I'd found and fallen in love with photographs of a feisty looking duck in, of all places, *Gourmet* magazine. There was something about the image—*that particular duck*—that pulled me in. I had no choice but to track down the photographer and get copies of his prints.

Of course, because it was a vegan restaurant, no ducks were consumed. Thus, the name One Lucky Duck sprang forth in my mind. It was cute and unique. And, importantly, the URL was available. Next, I needed a logo. A duck, obviously.

The danger here was that it could easily end up looking like a children's brand, so I wanted it to be simple, sleek, and angular—a silhouette. I also wanted an air of a mystery. I liked the idea that people might see the logo on a T-shirt or bag and wonder what it represented.

With the help of a small investment from my friend Leo, I rented a two-room office space on Nineteenth Street, just two blocks north of the restaurant. One Lucky Duck had its own headquarters. It was easy enough to run back and forth, and it gave me a place from which I could work and think. My younger half brother, Noah, was my very first employee, spending his college summer helping me set up the office and set up our new e-commerce business. Oddly, I was also working with Matthew's much younger half brother Patrick on the web design.

We'd started putting the duck logo on packaging and stickers, and then one day the idea popped in my head that I needed the logo on *me*, permanently. I'd never gotten a tattoo before. I'd always wanted one but had never been attached enough to any image or words to want them emblazoned on my body for life. I didn't want a tattoo just for the sake of having a tattoo. It had to be special. Now I knew why I'd been waiting. I would brand myself with the brand.

Joey, our heavily tattooed bartender, recommended his tattoo artist in Brooklyn. The day of my appointment was sunny and perfect, early in June. I wore a black sleeveless summer dress and had my hair up in pigtails. With the logo printed out on paper in a few different sizes, I was ready, and I headed for the subway.

Early for my appointment, I entered the dark shop. Most of the people in it were large men with lots of tattoos and even more piercings. After checking in, I browsed through the albums of tattoo designs lying around. The images were mostly of skulls, serpents, bloody daggers, cartoonish women with huge boobs, fire-breathing dragons, cartoonish women with huge boobs riding fire-breathing dragons, and so on. Finally, the tattoo artist I'd booked came out from the back. I handed her the sheet of paper with my design. "Um, can I just get this duck on my arm?"

She smiled. "Sure." I didn't look like their typical customer, I figured.

I was nervous about the pain, but more nervous that somehow she'd fuck it up and I'd be permanently marked with a disfigured bird on my bicep. As it turned out, she did a perfect job, and the pain wasn't bad. Once it was all done, she applied clear goop and taped a square of clear Saran Wrap over it for protection.

I couldn't wait to get back to the restaurant and show the staff. Standing on the subway, my arm wrapped around a pole, I buzzed with energy. Somehow, this felt momentous. I knew I'd always remember this day. It felt like the beginning of something big—part of the future story of the brand. I imagined the logo everywhere—on packaging, shirts, bags, billboards, and more. My mind was already racing ahead, seeing it out in the world.

I was startled out of this dreamy state by a voice.

"Hey, what's that duck about?" A man nearby had noticed my fresh tattoo.

I looked at him and paused. A response flashed in my mind: *You're not going to have to ask me that question in a few years.* I kept that thought to myself. But I'll always remember it. There, on that train, I felt like I could see into the future. I saw a world in which—*one day*—everyone would recognize the duck logo, the way people recognize the Nike swoosh or the Apple apple. I know, those were wildly ambitious thoughts—ones I'm almost too embarrassed to admit I had. Still. I *felt* it.

He looked at me, waiting for a reply.

"It's my company logo," I explained. "I'm starting a brand called One Lucky Duck."

* * *

While it was hardly *widely* recognized, the logo *did* end up on packaging, shirts, tote bags, shopping bags, and more. And as the takeaway shop and our products gained popularity, the duck got more and more exposure. Within a couple of years, photos started popping up online—Katie Holmes, Anne Hathaway, and Gisele Bundchen carrying shopping bags with the duck logo on it. Miranda Kerr and Orlando Bloom were regulars for a while, and tabloids posted a photo of Miranda getting on the back of Orlando's motorcycle, our logoed bag prominently in hand. A picture surfaced of the singer Jason Mraz on stage wearing one of our One Lucky Duck t-shirts. It was a special edition we'd printed after I spied one of my employees doodling *One Lucky Duck* in the shape of the Metallica logo. "Oh my god, I love that!" I told him. "We need to put that on t-shirts!" And so we did.

Lena Dunham once posted a photo of her to-go order on Instagram, the duck logo front and center. We regularly filled large snack orders for Shailene Woodley, Shania Twain, and Tom Brady and Gisele Bundchen after they moved to Boston. Ann Curry told me she brought bags of One Lucky Duck granola with her on a visit to the Dalai Lama—who not only loved it but said he wanted more (yes, the *Dalai Lama!*). Even Oprah once had a huge to-go order for her flight back to Chicago. The thought of my One Lucky Duck logo flying alongside *Oprah* felt surreal.

That's a lot of name-dropping, I know—but it's only a fraction of the fascinating people who passed through both the restaurant and One Lucky Duck. Jimmy Fallon, Aida Turturro, and the elegant Cecily Tyson were regulars. Beyond the fun famous people sightings, what gratified me most were the emails and letters—especially ones from parents thrilled to finally have delicious, wholesome, gluten-free snacks for their kids on restricted diets. I regularly received photos of people's kids with One Lucky Duck stickers on their shirts or of babies wearing our pink organic cotton One Lucky Duck onesies. I had a surreal moment on the street in Toronto when a girl passed me, spotted the One Lucky Duck tote bag on my shoulder, and casually said to her friend, "One Lucky Duck—I love their stuff!" So, maybe it *was* starting to get widely known.

All of it felt like promise. And hope. What I'd envisioned on the subway that day no longer seemed so far-fetched. We were on our way. Even all those years later, with all that brand recognition, it still felt like just the beginning. Deep down, I knew the brand had the potential to grow into something massive—if only I could sort everything out.

CHAPTER TWENTY-THREE

SUMMER 2005
NEW YORK CITY

Finally, the release date arrived for Matthew's and my cookbook: *Raw Food Real World: 100 Recipes to Get the Glow.* Meanwhile—awkwardly—we were in the throes of our fiery, combative de-coupling. Most of the staff, Jeffrey, and the book's publisher knew about our split, but the public did not. For the sake of appearances, Matthew and I agreed to a temporary truce to get through the book's release party and its promotion. Neither of us knew then that within forty-eight hours, our breakup would be tabloid gossip.

* * *

It was a hot summer night in late July 2005, and the restaurant was closed to the public for our book release party.

The space looked beautiful. It always did, but this night—with half the tables removed, set up for a cocktail style party—it looked more *sexy lounge* than restaurant. Most of the guests had spilled out into the garden, where music played softly from outdoor speakers obscured by the bushes lining the perimeter.

I hoped the neighbors would give us a pass for noise, and fortunately they did. It was a special event, with a massive print of the book cover—probably ten feet tall—fastened to the brick wall facing our garden. It was funny to see our faces that big.

The cover photo was... odd. The two of us were seated at a dimly lit table with a small plate, partially obscured by a candle, and a full glass of white wine in front of me. Neither of us was looking at the camera. Matthew appeared to be smiling at some unseen person across the table, while I—also smiling—was looking *down into his lap.* My mouth was weirdly open, like I was about to say something, and my arm was positioned as if my hand was resting on... *probably* Matthew's knee under the table? Or... *yeah,* it just an all-around odd photo. Matthew looked devilishly handsome—and by that, I mean he kind of looked like a devil. But a devil with a healthy glow. That cover lasted only as long as the first printing. After that, at the publisher's suggestion, it was replaced with an image of just me.

Looking back at photos from that time, I kind of *did* glow. And I was skinny—probably way too thin, but as someone who'd struggled with weight in the past, I was of the mind that there was no such thing as *too thin.* People regularly told me, with a concerned look, that I looked skinny, which I took as a quietly thrilling compliment. I wasn't going to the gym, so my weight loss must have been from stress and anxiety. The stress and ongoing sleep deprivation aside, I did feel like I had "the glow" that our cookbook promised. I felt physically healthy and vibrant in a way I never had before. Moreover, finally breaking away from Matthew must have galvanized me. I had reclaimed myself, and my own power.

* * *

I dressed for the party in my eighteenth-floor sublet, trying hard not to sweat. The building's air conditioning had failed, and it was sweltering hot. Standing in front of a table fan, I carefully slid into a paper-thin, vintage-looking ivory slip dress with lace trim and a pattern of red roses—a dress I'd bought years ago. You'd think I'd have splurged on a new dress for this big night, but I had neither the time nor the extra funds. I paired the dress with a worn-out pair of green Pro-Keds I'd owned for over a decade. I was very tan, not from lying in the sun but from a tanning salon where I'd toasted my skin from fish-belly pale to golden caramel. My brand-new tattoo stood out on my bare, skinny arm.

As the party got underway, both my mother and sister tried to get me to eat something, but I was too anxious. Also, my hands were always full. I was never without a flute of prosecco, awkwardly clamping it between my left arm and side while my left hand held one copy after another of our heavy hardcover book, my right hand signing each one. This was all new to me—the attention, the photographs, being the star of the show. Or costar, anyway.

There were actual stars there too. I was photographed with Kyle MacLaughlan of *Twin Peaks* and with Elisabeth Rohm, known at the time for playing Serena Southerlyn on *Law & Order*. Daryl Hannah, an occasional diner at the restaurant and a vegan environmental activist, was there. So, too, were Ann Curry of the *Today Show* and her husband, Brian Ross. They lived in an apartment building diagonally across the street from the restaurant, and for the duration of the restaurant's existence were loyal regulars and good friends—especially Ann, who often came in for lunch alone after finishing her morning show.

Being the center of attention made me drink more and eat less than usual, and I got a little drunk. The evening was getting a bit weird. Matthew had invited his personal-assistant-turned-girlfriend, Natasha. I'd met her once before, awkwardly. I'd gone back to the apartment to get some of my things when I knew Matthew wouldn't be there, and walked in on her napping in the bedroom. *Oh, hello.* She was startled—afraid, at first—then surprised that I wasn't angry about finding her there. More than anything, I worried for her, almost maternally. I knew that she was exactly half Matthew's age. She struck me as sweet and intelligent. My eyes had been opened to the kind of person Matthew was, and she was clearly in the early stages of his attention.

I had told Matthew to invite her to the book party if he wanted. What I didn't expect was their getting all cozy in a banquette, in plain view of everyone, when our split wasn't yet public. It seemed unnecessary—deliberate, even—and in bad taste.

* * *

I don't recall too many more details from the rest of the night—only that after the bulk of the guests had left, including Matthew and his girlfriend, the staff and I moved indoors, turned the music up, and had a dance party that lasted into the wee hours. Late-night dance parties became a tradition in the years to come. Lost in the music, I forgot the stress and felt genuinely happy. I'd grown close to a lot of the people who worked at the restaurant. They'd watched what happened between Matthew and me—almost like kids watching their parents' marriage come apart—and their support made me feel both strong and safe.

A few days after the launch party, the following story appeared in the city's most widely read gossip column.

JULY 25, 2005

NEW YORK POST: PAGE SIX

"RAW FOOD" poster couple Matthew Kenney and Sarma Melngailis have split up on the eve of a big publicity push for their glossy new coffee table book.

Kenney and Melngailis—the Brad Pitt and Jennifer Aniston of the New York restaurant world—have lived together for four years. Last year they opened Pure Food & Wine, a health-oriented Irving Place eatery where the vegetarian victuals go uncooked, with backing from Jeffrey Chodorow.

The attractive couple have posed for countless magazine photo spreads and just published a book, "Raw Food/Real World," which features on its cover a giant photo of them having a romantic dinner.

The couple had a glam book bash at Pure Food last Monday, attended by Daryl Hannah, Kyle MacLachlan, Darren Star and Elisabeth Rohm. But we're told Melngailis hit the boiling point when Kenney, 40, showed up to the fete with his hot young assistant, Natasha, on his arm and proceeded to canoodle with her in front of the staff.

> Kenney calls the report exaggerated. "I have been dating [Natasha] for two or three weeks, but Sarma knows about that," Kenney told PAGE SIX. "Sarma's the one who told [Natasha] she should come to the party. [Natasha] might have had her arm around me, but we weren't making out or anything."
>
> As for the bust-up, "We tried to work things out, and we've been together off and on for several months, but we're not together now, and we're probably not going to be together," Kenney says. "But we are going to stay together as business partners… The business side has been great. We're doing incredibly well."
>
> Kenney continues, "It's a personal matter. She and I have been together for four years, and we went through a lot together. I didn't even tell my parents because we thought we might work it out. I only told the manager at the restaurant last week."
>
> Melngailis declined comment."

Thus read my Page Six debut. What I love about Page Six is how they manage to jam so many hilariously awful words into one short piece. "Eatery" is a word I can't stand—I'm not sure I can explain why. It just sounds silly—like if you called a library a "readery."

Also, "victuals"? Is there something wrong with just "food"? Then there's my favorite: "canoodle." Who says that? Anyway, I still have no idea who the quoted "friend of Melngailis" was. I hadn't been humiliated, just annoyed. And "Melngailis hit the boiling point"? Yeah, no. But that's how tabloids operate—exaggerating stories and distorting details. *It doesn't matter*, I thought.

Years later, when these same tabloids colorfully covered my supposed criminality with Mr. Fox, it mattered to me more.

CHAPTER TWENTY-FOUR

SUMMER 2005
NEW YORK CITY

Among the first things I needed to handle was getting Matthew out of the apartment we'd shared—since I was on the lease and liable for the rent, which, unsurprisingly, he had stopped paying. You'd think I could just change the locks and throw him and his stuff out. But no. Since Matthew had been living there, locking him out was illegal.

During an argument about this, he gave me one of his piercing looks and said, "I know the law. It'll take you a year to get me out of that place."

Oh great.

I didn't see any other option but to hire an attorney to start the process to evict him. The attorney filed a lawsuit, but of course Matthew first claimed he wasn't served properly and then used every tactic to delay the proceedings. Just as he'd warned me.

I needed to get the rest of my things and my furniture out of that apartment and into a storage space, along with my two cats. I'd also started to fear Matthew. Not physically, but in some deeper, instinctual way. I avoided being alone with him.

I arranged for a moving company to come to the apartment. I didn't tell Matthew ahead of time because I didn't want him to somehow sabotage it. But a few days before the move date, my contact at the moving company called to say he'd just received a call from a man trying to cancel my move. It had seemed off to him. He read aloud the number that had called (this being back in the days of landlines and caller ID). It was our apartment number. It was Matthew. I was shocked. How in the *world* had he found out about the move and which company I was using, out of all the movers in New York City? *How?*

I was wildly spooked. I'd made all the arrangements from my desk at my office on Nineteenth Street, jotting details on paper before transcribing them into my planner, which I kept with me at all times. Then I'd tossed my notes in the trash. Every Wednesday and Sunday night, I took the office trash to the curb for pickup the next morning. Could he have *gone through my trash?* Everything about this felt eerie. No one else knew the details of the move but me. It seemed paranoid to think he'd gone through my trash—or, more likely, had someone else do it—but how else could he have found out? I couldn't fathom any other explanation.

Other spooky things had been happening. One day, I was alone at the One Lucky Duck office—something I wasn't used to—after Matthew's brother (with whom I was still, somewhat awkwardly, working on website development) had left. Already feeling on edge, I nearly jumped out of my skin at the sudden loud banging on the door. This wasn't just aggressive knocking—it was fist pounding. Hard. My heart thumping, I looked toward the small glass window in the door and was confused to not see anyone there. The banging had stopped. I crept closer and shifted my gaze to the side. My heart nearly stopped. A big, dark-haired man stood flat against the wall, off to one side. *What the fuck?*

I bolted to the back room and called the restaurant, telling them to send over a couple of guys—whoever was up front—right away. As in, drop everything and *run.* Then I called the police.

As I sat in a panic wondering what to do, I faintly heard a woman's voice, "Sir, can I help you?" It was the landlady coming down the hallway stairs. The man didn't answer. He simply walked out, and was gone. He may have even passed Joey and the other employee who showed up, out of breath, followed by the cops, less than a minute after. While the whole thing was odd, everyone simply concluded that the man must have just had the wrong address, or something.

This seemed to make sense, yet I remained spooked. My gut told me it *had not* been the wrong address.

After all, a few years earlier Matthew had admitted to hiring a private detective to follow me. He'd suspected I might be having an affair with, of all people, Randy. I was *most definitely not*. But he told me he did that. I'm not sure why I wasn't angrier at that time, but either way, remembering this fact made the theory of his having someone dig through my trash—or even sending someone to scare me (or worse)—seem less far-fetched.

* * *

When moving day came, I had quite the entourage. My friend Leo was in town, having just delivered our new bright-yellow One Lucky Duck delivery van, its lime-green duck logo emblazoned on all sides. He drove us to the apartment along with my brother and his two friends, Jesse and Ethan, who I'd put in charge of getting my two cats safely into a cat carrier and out of there. Waiting for us outside the apartment at 8:00 a.m. were two bodyguards, ex-police officers who worked for Bo Dietl's private security company. If you live in NYC or watch Fox News, you might know of Bo Dietl. He happened to be a friend of someone helping me out, and they offered to send backup. Why not? This was all feeling so dramatic.

To add to the party, four big movers arrived in a truck, right on time. Meanwhile, Jesse and Ethan were filming everything with a small handheld video recorder. I was oblivious to the filming at the time, but watching it back now? Hilarious. Jesse narrated it like a field reporter covering the scene of a crime.

We all went into the building and piled into the elevator. When I unlocked and opened the door to the apartment, there was Matthew, dressed in a suit, sitting on the couch with his publicist friend John Mosley. It was eight in the morning. Why would he be in a suit and with a *publicist?*

What happened next turned out to be—the very next day—the lead story of the Page Six gossip column in the *New York Post*.

> **AUGUST 14, 2005**
>
> **NEW YORK POST: PAGE SIX**
>
> The bitter break-up of "raw food" poster couple Matthew Kenney and Sarma Melngailis has reached the stage where cops and private eyes have been called in.
>
> Last week, we reported the photogenic ex-lovers, who run Pure Food & Wine on Irving Place, were at each other's throats after breaking up on the eve of their new book's publication.
>
> While Melngailis claimed Kenney is in her debt to the tune of $500,000, Kenney countered that she had physically attacked him and bedded down with one of their restaurant's managers.
>
> Kenney, 40, has since started sleeping with his hot 20-year-old assistant, Natasha—leading one observer to quip, "Maybe there's something to this raw food after all."
>
> On Tuesday morning, after Kenney found out Melngailis would be moving furniture and her two cats out of the beautiful East Village apartment they used to share, Kenney, who still lives there, had NYPD detectives on hand to bust her for assault.

    Assault! It turned out Matthew had gone to the local precinct at 5:00 a.m. that same morning and filed a police report claiming I'd assaulted him. This was the post-OJ Simpson–Nicole Brown era, when any report of domestic violence was taken extremely seriously, and regardless of the veracity of the claim, an arrest was standard practice. A judge could later throw it out, but an arrest would happen. Matthew knew this.

    Having those two security guards there, courtesy of Bo Dietl—former cops—saved my ass. First, they explained what was happening and told me to stay calm. They made it clear I'd have to go to the precinct with the detectives who arrived shortly after we entered the apartment. This made me nervous. I'd never had a run-in with police before. But I listened and stayed calm. Given the messiness of the situation, it was resolved that *everyone* would leave the apartment until things were sorted out. The movers, bodyguards, detectives, Matthew, Matthew's publicist, Leo, my brother and his friends, and I—everyone but the cats—went out, down the elevator, and onto the street. The bodyguards had prepped me to be cool and cooperative. They'd also told the detectives there was no need for handcuffs, which was a good thing, because on the way out of the building I saw a man standing on the sidewalk, chatting with Matthew. It was Richard Johnson, editor of Page Six. I'd met him once before. He and Matthew knew each other—Richard had once stayed at Matthew's cottage in Maine.

"Richard?" I said.

"Oh, hi!" he cheerfully replied. "I was just on my way to the dentist, and here you are!"

Sure you were, Richard, I thought.

He smiled as if this was all some delightful coincidence.

I remembered that earlier that morning, before we'd gone inside, one of the bodyguards told me he'd spotted a car with press plates nearby. I'd dismissed the comment then, but it seemed relevant now.

I followed the detectives to their cruiser, relieved that I'd *not* been taken out in handcuffs. From the backseat, I tried to calmly explain the situation—that this had been set up. At the precinct I was taken into a room where the detectives asked more questions. They stepped out to take a call, returning after a few minutes to tell me I was free to go. I later learned that one of the bodyguards knew someone who knew someone at that precinct. I was lucky, and incredibly relieved. Matthew's claim had been bogus, but still. The whole thing was nerve-racking. Outside, the bodyguards picked me up in a big black SUV. It felt dramatic, like I was living in my own movie.

Back at the apartment, we all went up again, and the movers took out my furniture and whatever else was mine. My cats were herded into the carrier and loaded into the duck van. Matthew and I argued over some of the items, but the bodyguards gave me looks, wordlessly reminding me of their earlier warnings to stay unflappable. Under no circumstances was I to let Matthew provoke me. "It's what he's going to try to do," they'd said. "He *wants* you to get angry."

Remembering Robb's similar advice to be an ice queen, I stayed calm. Mission finally completed, we left.

The Page Six piece continued.

> Kenney's rep, John Mosley, said, "My client is just trying to clean this up as quickly as possible and move on with his life."
>
> Meanwhile, the pair are fighting over some of the pad's furnishings as well, and Melngailis, who moved out earlier last year although the lease is still in her name, says Kenney is an illegal squatter. Last week, he changed the locks and she changed them back, although she later had to give him a key.
>
> Melngailis says she's been trying to evict him since last month. Kenny counters that he and his ex have a written agreement allowing him to live in the apartment; she claims it's void.
>
> Perhaps strangest of all, we're told Kenney and Melngailis attend the daily 4p.m. management meeting at the restaurant and act like absolutely nothing is happening.

That last sentence was true. After that insane morning of drama, Matthew and I sat through our regular daily manager meeting *that very afternoon*, both acting as if nothing unusual was going on. At least in the presence of others.

I made a point to always be in the presence of others when Matthew was around. I didn't want to give him a chance to speak to me alone. But he did—once. I remember that moment vividly, including what I was wearing and the song that was playing. It was a warm, beautiful evening at the restaurant, and the garden was full. I stood against the wall near one of the entrances, taking it all in. I was in a black summer dress—the same one I'd worn when I got my tattoo—and the song "Dreams" by Gabrielle played softly from the speakers. Matthew strolled over and stood beside me. He didn't look at me—just out at the candlelit scene. Then, leaning toward me slightly, he said quietly, "I'll see to it this place burns to the ground before you get it."

I stood frozen for a few moments. I didn't reply to him—not out loud. But in my head, I said, *I'll be in it.* Then I walked away.

* * *

After Matthew eventually ran out of delay tactics, the date arrived for our appearance in landlord-tenant court. My attorney informed me that Matthew had no intention of backing down. I could keep fighting and ultimately win a judgment against him for the unpaid rent, by then totaling nearly $30,000. But it would take months, cost me more in attorney fees, and, importantly, Matthew was functionally "judgment proof." Even after his bankruptcy, he owed over $1 million in unpaid business sales taxes, all of which would legally take priority. I'd never be able to collect from him. Matthew knew this too. I felt I had no choice but to let it go. As a settlement, I agreed to take on the $30,000 debt myself, and Matthew agreed to simply vacate the apartment and surrender it to the landlord. I was relieved it was over. *What's another $30,000 on top of what I already owe?* I thought. *Pile it on.*

The final issue to be resolved was who would run the restaurant. Leaving Pure Food and Wine never even crossed my mind. I was emotionally attached to that restaurant. But it wasn't up to me. To the outside world, it may have appeared that Matthew and I had *owned* Pure Food and Wine, or that we were at least equity partners, but in fact it was 100 percent owned by Jeffrey. It wasn't for us to work out who would stay and who would go.

Jeffrey knew that I'd largely funded Matthew's company during its slide toward the edge of the cliff, leaving me in debt. He also seemed impressed by my finance background and Wharton education—where he'd gone to college too. Once, while introducing me to someone, Jeffrey blurted out that I'd graduated from Wharton, as if it was the most remarkable thing in the world, which was totally embarrassing in the way that it's embarrassing when your dad goes overboard bragging about you publicly (except my dad didn't do this). But, despite being mildly patronizing on top of embarrassing, it felt deeply gratifying, like he was proud of me. It made me feel like he might have thought of me, in some ways, as a daughter, which I liked.

Jeffrey could see how committed I was to Pure Food and Wine, and perhaps he also noticed that there was a closeness between the staff and me—a connection Matthew never had. Whatever his reasons, Jeffrey agreed that I should be the one to stay and run the restaurant. I'm not sure what I would have done otherwise, but I know I never would have left.

Matthew had already opened another wine bar on his own, as if he'd known he wouldn't stay. Either way, it was settled. Matthew finally walked out the doors of Pure Food and Wine, never to return.

That night, after closing, the staff and I had an after-hours celebration. They bought me a big bouquet of flowers with a card that read, *Here's to taking the co out of co-owner!* Just writing this now, I'm getting choked up. That time, and those people, were truly special. We took care of each other. Because I still had no home that allowed cats, Lani, a juice bar employee, had taken mine to live with her until I could figure something out.

I loved those employees, for whom I felt responsible. That place we ran together felt like our home, and that time felt like the beginning of a new era. I was relieved, but I was also scared, wildly unsure of how I would handle everything on my own.

CHAPTER TWENTY-FIVE

2005 ONWARD
NEW YORK CITY

The Matthew era behind me, I focused on taking the reins of the business. The head bookkeeper from Jeffrey's company came to train me in the restaurant's tiny basement office on how to reconcile the daily sales, process payroll, and keep all the various systems in place.

When not at the restaurant, I was at the One Lucky Duck office, working on the new online store and tending to our rapidly growing wholesale business. I tried to keep up with promotion of the brand, saying yes to most incoming interview requests. I also needed to be at the restaurant during dinner service to meet guests or help in the kitchen. It was a lot, and it was exhausting.

People kept telling me I needed to take a vacation, which was well intentioned but kind of annoying because (a) I couldn't afford one and (b) it felt... *impossible*. If I went away or even just lay in bed watching TV and eating bonbons for a week, the backlog of shit I'd need to address upon my return would be crushing.

I needed someone—a partner—to share my burden. Someone who shared my vision and goals, who'd be equally motivated by the long-term positive impact of the company, not just short-term profits. I was wary of certain types of investors—the ones who acquire brands in their nascent stages, fund a way-too-rapid expansion of the brand, and then flip it for a big payout. It wasn't uncommon for those businesses to eventually go under because, of course, they'd grown too quickly, having allowed the infusion of profit-driven capital to snuff out their unique *special something* that had initially inspired people to love the brand. I didn't want that to happen. Yet we needed to grow, at least the One Lucky Duck side of things. Unlike Pure Food and Wine, which was labor-intensive, with a limited number of seats to fill, One Lucky Duck had the branded product line and takeaway stores that could benefit from economies of scale.

The way I saw it, Pure Food and Wine would always be the flagship, where people could experience us in person—where it all started—and take food home from the One Lucky Duck takeaway. Meanwhile, people could order One Lucky Duck products online to be shipped anywhere in the world, making this part of the business ripe for expansion.

Each business segment promoted the others. Someone might stumble upon a package of One Lucky Duck cookies at Whole Foods, buy it, read the label, and then go online and discover that we had a restaurant, juice bar, e-commerce store, and cookbooks. Since healthy eating naturally spilled over into other areas of life, I envisioned one day adding a skin care line, or cosmetics, supplements, and even pet food and products. Those experiencing the positive changes from eating healthy would likely want the same for their pets. I'd created a logo and bought the URL for a brand I wanted to one day launch: Shiny Happy Pets.

I never liked the term *lifestyle brand* but that's essentially what I envisioned for One Lucky Duck and its sub-brands. I know. It was a *lot*.

People who listened to me explain my vision inevitably got excited. They could see that my concept made sense, that the timing was right and that I overflowed with what investors usually look for most: passion and conviction.

Most investors recognized the global potential of the One Lucky Duck brand, but some wanted nothing to do with the restaurant business. They advised me to fully separate the two businesses, whereas I wanted to combine them under one umbrella. I didn't want to be a key player on two or more different teams; I wanted everyone on the same team, interests aligned.

Furthermore, One Lucky Duck and Pure Food and Wine would be difficult to separate—they were fully intertwined and shared resources. Yet I was the sole owner of One Lucky Duck while Jeffrey still owned Pure Food and Wine. Jeffrey either had to be bought out or else become a partner in the entire operation.

One might reasonably ask why I didn't just partner with Jeffrey. There were a lot of reasons, among them that his other businesses were just so *different* from what we were about.

I was always optimistic that the right investor or partner would emerge. I was regularly approached not just by individual investors but also by a few major US food companies, and parties from overseas. As I saw it, any investor would need to essentially *buy* the restaurant at a cost of about $2 million (the amount Jeffrey had spent on the buildout and opening expenses). Occasionally, someone would suggest I walk away from Pure Food and Wine—let it go and focus only on expanding One Lucky Duck—which always rubbed me entirely the wrong way. The restaurant was the *heart and soul* of the whole operation. I didn't want to partner with someone who didn't see that. Yes, I took these things personally. It would be like someone proposing marriage and then adding, *But you gotta lose those kids of yours.* Yeah, *no.*

All this exploration was time consuming. Some investors met me for long dinners at my corner table at the restaurant or took me out offsite, until I realized they were so often wasting my time. Nearly all were men—ones who had approached *me*. Sometimes things got awkward. Occasionally I saw it coming, but too often I didn't. I wasn't great at deciphering people's intentions when they weren't clearly stated. I'd have loved to meet the right female partner. Or a gay partner. I just wanted someone I could rely on, who would always be straight with me. It all just wore me down.

I still carried the weight of debt from my time with Matthew, which included, among other things, credit card balances with absurdly high interest rates. Most stressful was the big fat mortgage for the Maine property I'd bought from Matthew's company, now deep underwater and heading into foreclosure. I'd only bought the property to bail him out and now was stuck with the obligation. On top of everything, I was drafting my second cookbook, this time authored just by me. I was on the verge of burnout. I needed help.

At least my living situation had improved. A one-bedroom apartment opened up in a residential building directly across the street from the restaurant. The only problem was that pets weren't allowed. Fortunately, I'd gotten to know the building owners, an old couple from Florida. I launched a determined campaign to convince them to make an exception for my cats. After making me jump through a vast array of flaming hoops, they finally agreed. I got my furniture out of storage and moved in. Most importantly, I had my cats with me again.

As exhausting as those first few years were, they were also exciting. The restaurant was getting tons of press, and building One Lucky Duck—with my young, creative, and talented employees—was genuinely fun. *They* were fun. Even though I was in charge, we were more like a group of friends working together on a cool project.

* * *

In those days, something interesting seemed to happen at the restaurant every week, if not every day. One evening, former President Bill Clinton came in for Father's Day dinner with his daughter Chelsea. At the time, Clinton had reportedly gone vegan—or at least mostly vegan—following heart surgery. At the end of the night, I gave him a bag full of One Lucky Duck snacks and a copy of my cookbook, into which I'd inscribed a note about my mission to help nudge the world toward consuming more plants and less animals. Or rather, I gave it to his Secret Service agents. Before leaving, the former president shook my hand, looked straight into my eyes, and—with his slight Southern drawl—said, "Thank you for what you're doing." This felt surreal, him thanking *me*. It was intoxicating to feel seen by someone so powerful.

Less than a week later, I was alone in my office, rushing through the mail. I almost threw one envelope in the trash that looked like junk mail—the kind designed to *look* official. I quickly tore it open to confirm it *was* junk mail, then nearly peed my pants as I discovered it was not. It was a handwritten note from the former president. In it, he thanked me for the book and One Lucky Duck snacks, calling himself a "lucky duck." He signed off with, *Hope to see you again. Sincerely, Bill Clinton.*

You would think that I'd have followed up—written back to establish a connection, maybe for some future brand-building opportunity, or something. But I never did because I'm an idiot. More than once I started typing a letter to him yet quickly felt intimidated, agonized over every word, decided he wouldn't read it anyway, and convinced myself that I was so busy I should do it later. I never wrote him back.

CHAPTER TWENTY-SIX

2006–2007
NEW YORK CITY

With so much going for us as a business, you'd think I could've leveraged all the attention and goodwill to take the brand to the next level. Except that I felt *stuck*—exhausted while not moving anywhere, on the hamster wheel of running multiple intertwined businesses. On top of the debts I carried, I was also now being sued by a major bank for the unpaid mortgage on the property in Maine. I'd never been foreclosed on before and didn't know what to expect. Didn't you just *walk away?* In this case, the bank took possession of the property and *still* sued me. It was scary and made me feel ashamed, as if I'd done something wrong.

Meanwhile, sitting for media interviews, I often found myself fielding questions about the designers in my closet, the name of my facialist, and where I traveled for vacations. I wondered if Old Navy counted as a designer. I never got facials, and vacations were something I only dreamed about. At one point, I was made an offer that might have given me that sort of lifestyle—if that was what I wanted. It came from the Turkish investor I'd gotten to know in Istanbul.

By then, Pure Food and Wine was a few years old, still receiving a lot of positive press, and known as *the* high-end raw food place—one of the reasons this investor had flown me across the ocean to discuss a potential collaboration. After retiring from an extremely lucrative career in telecom, he'd undergone a personal health transformation and immersed himself in the world of raw food and holistic living. Now he wanted to open a raw food restaurant in Istanbul, along with high-end, luxurious healing resorts, with plans to expand the concept to other cities around the world.

He proposed a structure whereby he would fund and oversee this expansion while I would run the food side of it all—as the creative director and spokesperson. I would have some stake in the business, but he would own and control it entirely. The idea of being well taken care of sounded appealing. But the idea of someone effectively owning me? Not as much.

Furthermore, he emphasized the *branding consultants* he planned to hire, implying that he didn't see One Lucky Duck as the right brand image, particularly for an international market. I explained what the brand meant to me, why I believed it worked, and how people seemed to genuinely love it. It was memorable, with an iconic logo.

He pushed back. "Yes, but you can't get *emotionally* attached to a brand."

That one line stuck with me. I thought, *Isn't that the whole point?* Brands are meant to connect with people emotionally.

He spoke with the kind of authority that comes from achieving immense financial success. But his success had been in *telecom*. I knew he was wrong about this. And I saw how stubborn he was.

As tempting as it was to have financial security, travel first class, live in style, and focus on my personal well-being—so I could be the polished, healthy-looking brand ambassador—I couldn't take this deal. I couldn't work for someone who believed hired consultants should dictate what makes a great brand. *No, thank you.* I would find another way.

While I declined the offer, we stayed in touch on good terms. Later, he launched his own brand—one developed by his consultants—and hired a chef to run the restaurants. The name they landed on for this enterprise was astonishingly generic and the logo was simply a circle swooshed around the words. I was quietly blown away by how bland and forgettable it was. It looked like it represented an insurance company. It was beyond uninspiring, as if the consultants had been aiming for maximum unremarkability. I wondered how much he'd paid them.

Under that brand umbrella, he opened a raw food restaurant in Istanbul, followed by another in London. I knew the chef he'd hired was talented, and I'm sure the food was quite good. But something must have been missing, because both restaurants closed not long after. I'm not sure what became of his healing resorts.

It was frustrating dealing with people—usually men—who assumed that their own history of business success translated to a universal all-knowing. At first, I'd feel flattered by their interest and confidence in my business. But then when our visions diverged, I'd grow defensive and protective of my brand. It also frustrated me that they held so many cards. They had the power to do what they wanted, while I felt like a total fuck-up—someone who didn't have her shit together, carried debt, and ran a company that had a complicated structure but no detailed growth plan or corresponding deck of financial projections with colorful charts and graphs.

* * *

I don't remember the connection, but one day I was made aware that the CEO of Hain Celestial—an enormous food company—wanted to meet with me. Hain Celestial was a conglomerate of health food brands. If you walked the aisles of Whole Foods back then, you'd have found that a huge portion—possibly the majority—of the shelved products were brands owned by Hain Celestial. The company's CEO, Irwin Simon, came to the restaurant early one morning to meet with me. The space was still dim—I hadn't yet turned on all the lights—but he made a memorable entrance, a big man barreling in wearing a shockingly bright-orange sweater. He looked like a human traffic cone.

From my online research, I'd learned that Simon had worked his butt off to build the company himself and had persevered through periods of doubt. That made him relatable, and he seemed like a good guy. We quickly became friends, and over the ensuing months, we tossed around various ideas for how we might work together. At one point, he said to me, "The future of food is *raw food* and that future is *you*." I believed him.

We discussed the possibilities. We talked food and the industry. One day, he took me to Hain Celestial's company headquarters to meet with some of his executives who'd been evaluating my products.

Our ingredients were, not surprisingly, costly. We used no grain flour, no processed sugar, no fillers, no preservatives—nothing but high-quality, nutritionally dense, healthy (but therefore expensive) ingredients. Hain Celestial's team had taken a bunch of my samples, along with the recipes (pursuant to a nondisclosure agreement) and run their own nutritional and cost analysis. Their conclusion was that selling through distributors, as they did, would make the prices prohibitively high.

His people gently questioned me about whether we could make ingredient substitutions, swapping out some of the expensive organic nuts for some less expensive filler. No, no we could not. Not without compromising the product, turning it into something fundamentally different from what it was.

There were more like Hain Celestial. Dole Foods was another that courted me for a while. (No big deal, just *Dole Foods*!) I got sidetracked by all this interest, by all the meetings. I even had lunch one day with the chairman of Dole Foods. It was all flattering, but nothing ever materialized into the right fit. For any potential investor, Jeffrey's ownership of Pure Food and Wine was an expensive hurdle—they'd need to buy out Jeffrey. Most of these large companies, like Hain Celestial, were only interested in One Lucky Duck and its growth potential. They had no desire to own a restaurant. Yet I stubbornly wanted to keep both Pure Food and Wine and One Lucky Duck under one umbrella.

* * *

In the meantime, I couldn't keep up with production of our snacks, which were being shipped to an increasing number of Whole Foods stores, especially out west. The shipping cost was expensive. For local store deliveries, one of my favorite employees drove around Manhattan and Brooklyn in our yellow duck van, blasting gangster rap, smoking cigarettes, and racking up expensive parking tickets. None of this was sustainable, nor was it the best use of our time and resources. Eventually, I made the decision to stop all our wholesale sales. All of it. People would have to buy our products directly from our shop or order through our website, where we could maintain our retail margins while also having far more flexibility to tweak recipes and introduce new products.

It was the right move. The pastry kitchen had been getting crushed by production, and the staff was so relieved. I'd proven the demand existed, and that there was more of it than we could handle. For now, that was enough. The right move was to find a co-packer to do the job for us at scale, but that could be sorted out in the future. I just wanted the right partner to help me do all of this.

By exiting the wholesale business entirely, I'd made my own life slightly more manageable. Meanwhile, I was flattered that our accounts were so upset that we pulled out. One day, I was buying groceries at the nearby Union Square Whole Foods when I heard someone yell down the aisle, "Hey, Duck Lady!"

I looked up. I didn't recognize the guy until he introduced himself as a buyer for the store. He practically begged me to sell to them again, at least just that one store. I wanted to accommodate him, but selling wholesale just didn't make sense, not until we could produce it at higher volumes and better margins. I tucked the encounter away as another empirical tidbit backing up my conviction that we were on to something big. Hain Celestial, Dole Foods, and others *coming to me* about selling my products. They came to *me*. We had something special.

* * *

Months went by, and I still hadn't restructured, but business was good, and somehow things felt just a bit less stressful. On a personal level, I still had to deal with the debt from my time with Matthew. And now Wells Fargo was suing me for a few hundred thousand dollars over the Maine mortgage I'd defaulted on, having already foreclosed and seized the property. I had to do *something*. A lawyer I knew practically yelled at me to file for personal bankruptcy. He said it was stupid not to. I'd resisted, but couldn't deny he was right. It was the only move, really. In fact, I should have done it much sooner instead of simply flushing money down the toilet making payments that weren't getting me anywhere.

The whole thing, unsurprisingly, felt really shitty. The bankruptcy attorney I worked with was nice but made it clear he thought I was nuts for taking on that mortgage in the first place. While I wasn't in debt from buying expensive clothes or reckless personal spending, I still felt ashamed and *guilty*. Like a bad person, or a deadbeat.

I couldn't have imagined then that years later, I'd be swallowed by a tsunami of financial disgrace—one that would make this bankruptcy process feel like no big deal in comparison.

CHAPTER TWENTY-SEVEN

2006–2007
NEW YORK CITY

I met Tobyn in November 2006, the year Ann Curry—then still co-anchor of the *Today Show*—turned fifty. It was Ann's birthday party that led me to him. I'd been reluctant to go. I was premenstrual, which meant I was even more tired than usual and feeling like a beached bloated whale, no matter what I wore. It didn't matter if my rational brain knew that, by most standards, I was objectively thin. I still wanted to lose five pounds. And my subconscious was good at convincing me that not having done so yet made me unworthy—of love, of attention, of attending Ann Curry's party full of interesting, accomplished, and presumably self-confident people.

I chugged a beer to dull the scream of my insecurities, pulling on the most tolerable outfit I could manage. Had it been anyone else, I would have skipped the event entirely, but I genuinely adored Ann, and she'd always been one of our biggest supporters.

Ann's party was held in a semiprivate room of a nearby Japanese restaurant. Walking in, I spotted her then-co-host, Matt Lauer, standing tall and lanky, drink in one hand, talking to no one. I'd met him once years before but knew he wouldn't remember, so approaching him would have been weird. Al Roker was there too. We'd done a cooking segment together once for his Food Network show, so I'd have felt okay saying hello, but he was midconversation with someone. I went straight to the bar and got myself a beer, then scanned the room for Ann.

When I found her, I gave her a hug and wished her a happy birthday, expressing genuine astonishment that she was actually fifty—she looked at least ten years younger.

"I want you to meet someone!" she said excitedly. "He lives in my building. He's great. His name is Bob… where's Bob?" She glanced around, then spotted him and pulled me over to introduce us. I sensed she was trying to set me up, which I was in no mood for—but at least I'd have someone to talk to.

Bob had a rugged and athletic-look—dressed casually in a plaid flannel shirt and jeans. He had a tan face, wavy light-brown hair, and bright-blue eyes. He was cute, with a mildly goofy, wide-eyed expression, as if everything were bewildering. He looked a few years older than me. Whoever he'd been talking to before wandered off, and we made our way through small talk. It turned out he'd co-founded an e-commerce site, which he'd sold at just the right time for hundreds of millions—an amount I estimated based on his self-described state of "not having to work again" and the fact that he was in the process of renovating a massive apartment. He looked more like a lumberjack than someone who'd made millions in online retail. He was originally from Colorado, he told me, which somewhat explained his look.

Neither of us knew many people at the party, so we kept talking. He mentioned a couple of young guys who'd just moved to New York from Colorado to attend music school, one of whom was the son of his good friend. They were crashing at his place and needed jobs. "They're great guys," he said, and suggested they might be a perfect fit for my juice bar or in the restaurant in some capacity. I gave him one of my business cards so we could stay in touch.

A day or two after the party, Bob emailed and asked me out to dinner. He wasn't really my type, but he seemed nice and fun, so I went. The dinner was… *nice and fun*. A few days later, he invited me to an ice skating party he was hosting at Chelsea Piers, mentioning that one of the guys he wanted me to meet about a job would be there. He also said Ann would be there.

At that party, Bob pointed toward a tall, lanky guy with chestnut-colored hair skating effortlessly around the rink.

"That's Tobyn," he said.

Tobyn clearly knew how to skate. Bob mentioned he'd played ice hockey back in Colorado, then waved him over to introduce us. Tobyn seemed a bit shy, looking down or away a lot, but I noticed he was cute. We briefly discussed the idea of him working for my business, and I told him to stop by the restaurant the following night. I knew I'd be having dinner and drinks with some of my One Lucky Duck staff, and I got the sense that Tobyn would fit in well with them. Since he was new to the city, I figured he could use some friends.

When Tobyn arrived, I motioned for him to take the empty chair I'd saved next to me. I'd had a cocktail or two by then and ordered a sake mojito for him. He wore a loose button-down blue shirt and army-green Carhartt pants. He seemed just the tiniest bit nervous, but in a good way. A healthy amount of reticence, sitting down at a table of new people, in a new city. But then he relaxed as I asked him about his background, music school, how he liked New York, and so on. I noticed that now he looked directly at me while we talked, as if tuning out the rest of the table. He kept flipping his floppy bangs from his face. I also noticed his eyes—hazel—that seemed to sparkle. His nose could've been modeled from a Roman statue—long and straight, with a skin-colored mole on one side.

After an hour or so, I had to remind myself that my intention had been to introduce Tobyn to the others at the table—people much closer to his age. They'd made plans to go out somewhere, and I encouraged him to go along. I was struck by the look he gave me—a mix of surprise and maybe even disappointment.

"You're not coming?" he asked.

I told him I had to get up early and needed to sleep but that he should have fun with them. After they left, I realized I was a little bummed at having sent him off. Oh well. Later that night, I wrote an email introducing Tobyn to my juice bar manager, leaving it to them to set up a time to meet and discuss a job. I knew he'd interview well, and we were looking to add people to the schedule.

* * *

It was early December, and we were overdue to put up holiday decorations at the restaurant. In my previous conversations with Bob, we'd arranged that I could borrow a tall ladder from his half-under-construction, high-ceilinged apartment. Bob had already left to spend the month in Colorado, so he told me to just ask Tobyn—who, by that time, had begun working shifts at the juice bar. One Sunday night, I went across the street and up to Bob's apartment, where Tobyn had the ladder waiting by the door. It was large and awkward to carry, so Tobyn suggested he bring it over to the restaurant for me. We rode the elevator down with Babs, Bob's friend who was also staying at the apartment. Many weeks later, she told me privately that she had felt an electric tension between Tobyn and me in that elevator. At the time, I wasn't quite conscious of it. But thinking back, I'm sure she was right.

I walked alongside Tobyn as he maneuvered the ladder out the building and down the block. We went in through the side entrance of the restaurant, which led into the pastry kitchen. He was careful getting the ladder in, to avoid smashing into the glass door, overhead lights, and people's heads.

"I guess over here is cool," I said, pointing to a spot where it could safely lean against the wall. Ladder deposited, he stood there and put his hands in his pockets.

"Do you want a drink? Something to eat?" I asked. "We can sit at the bar?" I tried to sound casual. Whether consciously or not, I very much did *not* want him to leave.

"Yeah, sure." He smiled.

I smiled back. "Okay, cool. Follow me."

I led him out of the pastry kitchen and through the narrow back hallway. He followed me through the kitchen and into the dining room. It was about half full—not bad for after 9:00 p.m. on a frigid Sunday night. We sat at the bar, and I ordered us mojitos and a few dishes from the menu, ones that were easiest to share.

I sucked down my first mojito faster than usual, faster than he drank his. It seemed I was the one feeling a bit nervous this time, though, again, he was easy to talk to. There was an odd, bubbly energy percolating inside me. Then one of the restaurant's regular oddball guests appeared at the bar and inserted himself into our conversation. He was someone I typically tried to avoid, and I shot Tobyn side glances that conveyed as much. Conveniently, I was able to use this guy's presence as a pretext to get Tobyn to stay longer, as in *Don't you dare leave me alone with this guy!* I ordered Tobyn a third drink. Or maybe it was a fourth by that time.

I drank enough mojitos that I don't recall exactly how it happened, but I must have suggested to Tobyn that he might, *perhaps*, want to come over to my apartment across the street to hang out more, and it turned out he did. It wasn't at all like me to be so forward, but I didn't want him to leave, or for the night to end.

Somehow, the next morning didn't feel awkward—even though it probably should have. He was, after all, only twenty-one. I was thirty-four, and also, technically, his boss. Instead, it felt easy and comfortable. Rather than getting up and leaving first thing, he stuck around, spending most of the day with me.

A couple of nights later, someone on the staff was having a Christmas get-together not too far away. I asked Tobyn if he wanted to come along with me. He did. We took care not to make it obvious that we arrived together, but later, we left together. And again, he stayed over at my place.

Then it was Christmas Eve. Tobyn was staying alone at Bob's house now, with Bob and Tobyn's best friend Jonathon both back in Colorado for the holidays. My own plan had been to spend Christmas alone with my cats. I know that sounds wildly depressing to most people, but Christmas Eve and Christmas Day were the only two days of the year that the restaurant closed. I found them supremely—almost spiritually—relaxing.

Naturally, Tobyn and I ended up spending Christmas Eve together. Then Christmas Day. Our situation was beginning to feel like… a *thing*. I wasn't sure how I felt about him being an employee now—about technically being his *boss*. But what was I going to do now, fire him? I couldn't do that.

One afternoon, I popped into the juice bar to get something. The space behind the counter was tight, and Tobyn was working a shift with Kate, a petite, naturally pretty nineteen-year-old. During the minute or so I was in there, I saw Kate look up at Tobyn with starry eyes. It was immediately obvious to me that she had a massive crush on him. After I walked out, I was struck by how much it *hurt*, almost physically. She may as well have just grabbed the big chef's knife off the counter and plunged it into my heart. I couldn't handle that. *If I'm hurting this much now, I can't do this*, I thought.

Later, I texted Tobyn and asked if he could stop by my apartment after his shift. We sat on my couch as I told him, gently, that I thought it was probably best if we didn't hang out anymore, doing whatever it was we were doing.

He looked down into his lap. "I figured this was coming," he said.

He looked genuinely bummed. I explained that I really liked being with him—*a lot*—but given our age difference, plus his working at my place, it just didn't make sense. Still he said nothing, just stared down at his lap. I explained further that, realistically, before long, he'd probably want to be with someone much younger than me—someone with more free time, less baggage, and that when that happened, it would hurt me. A lot. I wanted to avoid that.

"I'm just being realistic," I said.

He was quiet for a few beats, then asked if it wasn't just as likely that *he* could get hurt too. Wasn't it just as likely that some rich older guy in a tuxedo and a fancy car would come and sweep me off my feet, away from him?

"Someone with a lot more to offer," he added.

This was a valid point I'd not considered. Not that I wanted a rich guy with a fancy car, but that he could feel vulnerable too.

"Also," he continued, "there *could* be a meteor heading to the earth *right now* that'll take us all out next week. I mean, that could happen. So... " He shrugged. "If we want to hang out with each other, then shouldn't we just... hang out?"

He'd made a good point. Why was I pushing away something we both wanted just because of future worries?

I looked up at him and bit my lip. "I see your point," I said, slowly. "I mean, I guess... you're right?"

I smiled. Then he smiled.

And that was it. We resolved to keep hanging out. And we did, for the next four years.

* * *

Being Tobyn's boss was too awkward. We also agreed on that. To fix the situation, we decided that I would hire his friend Jonathon instead, and Tobyn would find a job somewhere else. I'd only briefly met Jonathon, but I could see he was a lot like Tobyn. If they were best friends, then he had to be a good guy.

A week or so later, Bob came back from his extended trip to Colorado—the Bob with whom I'd gone on a date, who now made it clear he was excited to see me and wanted to go out again. Tobyn and Jonathon were still living at his place while they looked for an apartment, but conveniently they'd just found one in Brooklyn and were about to move out. One of us—either Tobyn or me—had to tell Bob. I said I'd do it.

Bob stopped by the restaurant, and we sat in the private dining room in the back. After the obligatory *how was your trip* small talk, I told him that I'd started seeing someone over the holidays—who was now, well... *kinda sorta* my boyfriend. He looked surprised, and a little uncomfortable.

"Oh! Well, okay, no problem. I totally understand," he said graciously. "I hope he's a good guy!"

I looked at him sheepishly. I was dreading this moment. At the same time, I couldn't help thinking it would be kind of funny when I told him who it was, which I had to do, since he'd find out eventually anyway.

"It's Tobyn," I blurted out.

Bob's wide eyes got even wider. He looked stunned.

I shrugged. "It kinda just happened?"

I felt genuinely queasy. I don't like making people feel bad, and Bob was an incredibly nice guy. Yet nothing had ever happened between us beyond one proper date and a relatively chaste goodnight kiss. Still, this was awkward. Tobyn was Bob's friend's *son*, so Bob probably thought of Tobyn in a paternal way.

Maybe it was his relaxed Colorado vibe, but before long Bob turned out to be cool about it. A month or two later, Tobyn's parents came to visit from Colorado, and they, too, were incredibly easygoing. Warm and welcoming. I liked them immediately. By that time, I was also completely in love with Tobyn.

* * *

Tobyn stayed at my apartment a lot. Because I didn't work a set schedule and often worked late nights, we could lie around most mornings. One morning, tangled in sheets with the sun peeking through the window, we lay in bed lost in our own thoughts. Suddenly, Tobyn rolled toward me with a big smile. Holding on to the pillow beneath his chin with both hands, he looked like he had a thrilling idea he was about to share. I waited.

"Love!" he blurted (he sometimes called me *love*).

I waited. He smiled wide, his eyes sparkling.

"What's your favorite dinosaur?"

"My favorite... *dinosaur*?"

"Yeah, I mean, you've *gotta* have a favorite!" he insisted.

I didn't know what to say, because it's not something I'd ever considered. I also, in that moment, couldn't even remember the names of any dinosaurs. I hadn't thought about dinosaurs in at least two decades. Which is what I told him.

"Aw, come on. I mean, you saw *Jurassic Park*, right?" he asked.

I shook my head.

"You've *never* seen *Jurassic Park*? What about *The Land Before Time*?"

Again, I shook my head.

"YOU'VE NEVER SEEN *A LAND BEFORE TIME*?"

He was incredulous—shocked, even—and enthusiastically launched into a breakdown of various types of dinosaurs and their different shapes and attributes. While I lay there looking at him, I was feeling kind of *old*, yet *madly* in love with him. Tobyn was *who he was*—completely free. In this moment, he was silly. Generally, he was incredibly smart and thoughtful, sometimes saying astonishingly wise things. He could be quiet and reserved but was also observant and sensitive. Most of all, he was entirely comfortable in his own skin. And I envied that, because I wasn't entirely comfortable in mine.

* * *

Before long, Tobyn agreed to move in. Since he was already staying with me most nights, it was dumb for him to be paying rent in Brooklyn. I've always valued having my own space, privacy, and lots of alone time—but with him, it was different. His dirty socks on the floor weren't annoying; they were charming. He was comforting, even calming, to be around. And between his job and practicing with his band, I still had plenty of alone time.

After my dark and distant relationship with Matthew, Tobyn felt safe, pure, and *good*. I loved his friends—Jonathon plus his bandmates, all from Colorado—and grew close to them too. He fit in effortlessly with everyone at the restaurant and One Lucky Duck. My family and friends all liked him, probably in part because they could see how relaxed and happy I was when he was around. Even years into our relationship, I felt myself light up inside whenever he texted to say he was coming by the restaurant—whether I was sitting through a business dinner or just hanging out. I was always excited to introduce him to people. Those early relationship butterflies never went away.

CHAPTER TWENTY-EIGHT

2008

NEW YORK CITY

As any depressed person might confirm, being in love is a balm but not a cure. It casts everything in sunshine, but the underlying stresses and wounds remain. It helped that Tobyn was insightful and sensitive—wise beyond his years, what one might call an *old soul.* Being with him was comforting. He encouraged me, reminding me that what I was working toward was "righteous." He recognized what I was up against: the world's big, powerful food companies, determined to keep us eating whatever addictive, unhealthy "food" they were selling, and the pharmaceutical giants that would lose profits if more people discovered just how much could be healed through clean eating alone. He saw the big picture of what I was trying to do. And he never resented my busy schedule or if I had to miss one of his band's shows because of work.

Our thirteen-year age difference may have led outsiders to assume the relationship wasn't serious, but his understanding of me and my goals became a support I relied on. More than anyone, I felt like *he* truly saw me, and he was proud of me.

* * *

I wasn't quite sure what my parents really thought about what I was doing or if they understood. They generally didn't have much of a reaction to the press that I, the restaurant, or the brand received. Sometimes I forwarded them articles via email, but they never seemed particularly enthused. I learned that their response, or lack thereof, left me feeling worse than if I just kept it to myself—so over time, that was what I did. I also hated talking with them about *how things were going* because, more often than not, I was struggling and just wanted encouragement. I couldn't bear to hear my mother say, "Well, I hope you'll survive!" or "Good luck!" which are things she often said. I know she meant well, that it came from genuine concern, but every single time, I wanted to stab my eye with a pencil.

There's a scene in the documentary *Jim & Andy* in which Jim Carrey recalls telling his father about his first appearance on *The Tonight Show*, a huge, life-changing milestone for any comedian. His father only replied, "Well, I hope that pans out for you."

The look on Jim Carrey's face as he tells the story guts me because I know that feeling. It's as if the people who created us think we're aiming too high. Any success we have will come as a surprise, apparently.

Once while visiting my mom's house, I was rambling about the horrors of factory farming—and how if people learned about its destructive impact on the environment, along with how much better they could feel eating more fresh vegetables and fruit, then maybe, eventually, the cruel factory farming of animals could be eradicated. My mom listened patiently, as if waiting for me to finish, then smiled and said, "Oh *Sarma*, you're never going to change the world."

* * *

I was grateful for all the encouragement that came my way from customers and the validation from a steady stream of positive press. We didn't need a PR firm to land media placement—coverage found us on its own. Notably, much of it originated from outside the US, with a surprising amount from Japan. I always felt there was something there to pursue, given how often the Japanese media reached out for stories.

What felt particularly cool was when my father's native Latvia began taking notice, with articles appearing in Latvian publications. In the spring of 2008, a major Latvian magazine, *Sestdiena* ("Saturday"), reached out about profiling me and the restaurant. It was one of the country's more prominent publications, and they sent a reporter to New York to spend a day with me.

Weeks later, I heard—from my sister, who heard from my cousin in Riga—that the magazine had come out. Not only was I the cover story, but the cover itself was a closeup of my face. My sister sounded excited. She said it was like the equivalent of being on the cover of the Sunday *New York Times Magazine*. In short, a big deal. I'd not yet seen it and didn't have a copy in hand, but the journalist promised to send me a few copies.

My father and stepmom were visiting New York, and a family dinner had been arranged at Lombardi's—one of the city's famed old-school pizza places. I hadn't yet spoken to my father and was eager to tell him about the magazine cover. We sat at a big round table—Tobyn to my left, then my sister and her boyfriend, my stepmother, and finally my father seated just to my right. We got settled. Pizzas, salads, and two bottles of red wine were ordered, and conversation flowed. The waiter came by, pouring the wine. I sat quietly, full of giddy anticipation, waiting for the right moment to tell my father about the magazine feature.

While he'd never seemed particularly electrified by the domestic press I'd forwarded him in the past, I figured *this time* would be different. This was Latvia. My father is a proud Latvian, deeply connected to the Latvian American community. Surely, this was kind of a big deal?

The restaurant was loud. While the others talked across the table, I leaned in toward my father and told him about the magazine, the interview, and then, the finale:

"And… " I paused for emphasis. "Apparently, I'm on the cover! My face—big—on the cover. It's my face… on the cover!" I waited for this news to register, for his excitement to match mine. Or for any excitement at all. I waited.

"Huh," he said, looking down at the table.

I kept waiting, thinking, *He's… processing it?*

Then, he scrunched his face, as though someone had placed a severed rat's tail on his plate. I waited more. Finally, he leaned in and said, "I don't think raw food would do very well in Riga."

That was it. Maybe he figured raw food wouldn't be a great concept there—Latvia having a colder climate and, like most of Eastern Europe, more of a meat-and-potatoes vibe. Or boiled fucking cabbage. Whatever. That wasn't the fucking point. But that was all he had to say. I sat back, picked up my wine glass, and took a long sip. Everyone else was immersed in separate conversations, so they hadn't heard any of ours.

"I'm going to the bathroom," I said to no one in particular, pushing back from the table and walking off to find a sanctuary where I could be alone.

Thankfully the bathroom was a onesie, and there was no line. I went in, latched the door shut, and exhaled. I didn't want to cry and mess up my eye makeup. I took deep breaths as my eyes pooled with tears anyway. *Fuck.* I pulled down my pants and sat right down on the toilet to pee. Fuck hovering, or carefully making a paper nest, as one often does in public restrooms. I just plopped down. *Fuck it.* I looked up into the light on the ceiling, remembering that someone once told me looking into lights could snuff out a sneeze. Maybe it worked for crying? It didn't.

I washed my hands and checked the mirror to make sure my eye makeup hadn't run down my face. I didn't want to go back out and sit through this dinner. I just wanted to go home. Better yet, I wanted to go to Pure Food and Wine and sit at the bar, surrounded by Joey and whoever else was working, and our happy customers. I wanted to be… *among my people.*

It felt like an *I give up* moment. Like if that news didn't elicit an expression of pride from my father, nothing would. *I give up. I shall sustain myself off the feedback of our restaurant guests, customers, and other people out there who see me.*

Back at the table, I drank more wine, nodding affirmatively each time the waiter approached to refill my glass. I put salad in my mouth, chewed, and swallowed. I wasn't going to gamely eat a slice of pizza. Fuck that. Too often, I ate things I didn't really want to eat just so other people wouldn't be uncomfortable. Yeah, not this time. Under the table, I held Tobyn's hand and focused on him. He was having a good time. He got along with my family. They were all happy, that was something.

In the taxi home, finally alone with Tobyn, I told him what my father had said. By this point, I wasn't really sad. Just resigned, and somewhat pissed.

"I'm sorry, baby," he said. And then, as he was good at doing, he tried to make me feel better. He reminded me that my father just wasn't good at expressing himself, that of course he must be proud of me. My rational brain agreed. Surely, he must be proud of me. But why couldn't he say so?

Tobyn, wise as ever, said that my father probably *worried* about me more than anything. That, as a scientist, not an entrepreneur, he was probably inherently risk averse. And that what I regularly interpreted as lack of pride—from both my parents—was more likely just fear-based worry. I considered this. I knew, rationally at least, that Tobyn was probably right. I started to feel like a bratty crybaby. But still, it hurt.

* * *

Some people are raised by parents with excessively high expectations—the kind that can leave scars of resentment well into adulthood. My issue was different: I wasn't sure *what* my parents expected, if anything. The lack of overt pressure worked out early on because I put the pressure on myself—enough to succeed reasonably well academically and, after college, professionally. I think they were glad I was stable and taking care of myself. But the life of creativity and entrepreneurship is riskier than the straight corporate track I'd started on. I had no passion for the latter, but I did for the former.

If you'd asked me what my parents thought about my life and work while I was running Pure Food and Wine and growing One Lucky Duck, I would've had to guess. I sensed they didn't fully understand what I was trying to accomplish or why—and why it mattered so much to me. Or maybe they didn't think about it much. Or maybe they did and just didn't tell me. I don't know.

Sometimes I wondered if they thought I was trying to punch out of my weight class. *Why shoot for the stars when you can just stay down here?* Or worse, maybe they expected me to fail. Probably they didn't, but maybe they worried. Again, I don't know. Either way, I wanted them to be proud of me.

* * *

In 2007, I'd made progress toward restructuring and recapitalizing the business. I'd begun lining up investments to purchase Pure Food and Wine from Jeffrey, with the plan to merge it with One Lucky Duck under a single LLC, owned by me and my investors.

Then the 2008 financial crisis hit, and those plans were upended.

I already had papers drafted to take ownership of the restaurant, but with the downturn, my investors' capacity to fund the deal dwindled. Jeffrey agreed to sell me Pure Food and Wine for debt only. He took no money, but I now owed him roughly $2 million. I also took on a couple of smaller loans from investors to weather the downturn and keep growing. None of it was easy or comfortable. 2009 was particularly challenging, despite the successful release of my second book, *Living Raw Food*, which generated a commercially helpful new wave of favorable press.

By the summer of 2010, things were finally a bit more stable. I'd also decided to save time and cut costs by consolidating my residence with the One Lucky Duck office, moving both into a large space a few blocks north on Twenty-First Street. The rent for this space was lower than what I'd been paying for the two separate locations combined, making it a practical solution.

Tobyn—ever supportive—said he was fine with it. Still, living with me in a space that housed several of my employees five days a week had to be awkward for him, and it probably hastened the end of our relationship.

CHAPTER TWENTY-NINE

SUMMER 2010

NEW YORK CITY AND THE HAMPTONS

"Hey, Alec Baldwin just came in—he's seated in the garden," someone said, passing by the open door. I was in the restaurant's cramped basement office, catching up on work. It was midday on a Saturday, early in the summer. Upstairs, it was a perfect day for garden lunch service—neither too hot nor too cool, like being in a lukewarm bath.

"Okay, thanks," I called out.

Alec Baldwin had never been into the restaurant before, and I'd never met him. It was normal for the staff to let me know if someone interesting came in. A few minutes later, the floor manager called down to tell me that Alec's table had asked to speak to me. My first thought was, *Really?* Then, *Shit.* I was unshowered, wearing worn-out jeans and a loose tank top. I wasn't feeling my best. Oh well.

The garden was full. I felt the familiar pang of reticence at approaching any table, let alone Alec Baldwin's. I always worried I was interrupting. Even if they *did* ask for me.

Alec was gracious and, unlike some celebrities, looked exactly like he did on TV and in movies. He introduced me to his companion, a younger woman, probably about my age, with short brown hair. There was something very self-assured and regal about her, elegantly dressed, sitting with noticeably good posture. They seemed like friends—at ease and familiar with one another in a way that suggested this wasn't a romantic date. I learned that she was well versed in healthy eating and various types of cleansing—*cleanses* of all kinds were having a moment then—and that this lunch was part of her effort to introduce Alec to eating better, hence their calling me over to chat. I kept the conversation—about our food, the restaurant, the usual—brief, not wanting to linger or overstay.

After I left the table, I put together a bag of One Lucky Duck snacks and gave it to Alec as he and his companion were leaving.

I was still near the front door when, a few minutes after they'd walked out, Alec came back alone. He said he was waiting for a car to take him back to the Hamptons. I suggested we sit outside on the front patio. He had another bag—one his friend had given him—containing some kind of green-colored colon cleanse powder, which he showed me, making a joke about it. I don't remember what else we talked about before his ride appeared, but he asked for my business card.

After he left, I went back to the basement to finish my work. Later that day, I had to drive up to my mom's house in New Hampshire. I was also awaiting my travel companion, Bazooka—an older dog adopted by Abel, one of the servers at my restaurant—whom I'd agreed to dog-sit. Bazooka was a medium-sized mixed breed and probably the chillest dog I'd ever encountered. I'd met him a couple of times before when Abel brought him by the restaurant or to staff house parties. I was always falling in love with other people's dogs.

A few nights earlier, I'd been sitting at the restaurant bar, a few drinks in, while Abel told me about his upcoming trip to Spain. I asked who would be looking after Baz. He wasn't entirely sure yet. Probably one of his friends.

"I could take him!" I blurted out. "I'm going to my mom's house in New Hampshire next week. He can come with me! It'll be amazing for him, being out in the country, and fresh air!" Abel readily agreed.

You know how sometimes, after a few drinks, you agree to something that seems like a totally fantastic idea at the time, only to wake up the next morning and think, *Shiiiiiiit, why did I agree to that*? Well, this was the opposite. I woke up excited to remember that I'd soon be dog-sitting. Baz was mellow, well mannered, and as easygoing as a dog could be. I couldn't wait to have him for a week.

I'd rented a car, and Bazooka—ever the polite travel companion—lay quietly on a blanket on the backseat the whole way up to my mom's. When we arrived, I let him out onto the huge, freshly mowed yard, where he immediately rolled around on his back. I loved seeing him look happy in the peaceful, open space, gloriously free of traffic, concrete, and throngs of noisy humans.

* * *

Later that day, I sat at the big wooden table in my mom's open kitchen, laptop in front of me, when an email appeared from an address I didn't recognize. It was from Alec. In a series of witty, charming sentences, he asked if he might take me to dinner sometime. I smiled. *He wants to see me?* A buzzy sensation rose inside me—like bubbles in a glass of champagne, except happening in my body.

My mom was nearby, doing something in the kitchen—pitting cherries, I think. I told her, with some excitement, that I'd met Alec Baldwin at the restaurant, and now he'd just emailed me asking me out to dinner.

She paused her cherry-pitting, looking perplexed. "Oh, really? What for?"

What does she mean, what for?

"I mean, I don't know… we talked at the restaurant, and he was really nice, and… I guess he just wants to see me."

"Huh." She went back to the cherries, then added aloud, "I wonder what he wants to hang out with *you* for when he has all his Hollywood friends."

I looked at her. Then back at my laptop.

I decided to ignore what I assumed was a rhetorical question and crafted a short email reply to Alec, saying I'd be glad to get together when I was back in the city. (Never mind that I had a boyfriend—I left that detail out, figuring this was just a friendly get-together.) I mentioned where I was and attached a couple of photos I'd taken of Bazooka out on the lawn, rolling in the grass. His reply came quickly, asking why I wasn't in the photos. So I forwarded him a few my mother had taken the night before of Bazooka and me. Thus began our email exchange—and my time being friends with Alec, with all the conflicting feelings that would develop.

The day I got back to the city, an elegant square vase of white flowers arrived, addressed to me. They were from Alec. The host who'd accepted the delivery had seen the card and who they were from, and for the rest of the day, I was treated to sly smiles and light teasing from the staff. I was flattered he'd sent flowers. Also, I was clearly naive—or in denial or both—because this probably wasn't merely a let's-be-friends gesture.

* * *

I'd just rented the new apartment on Twenty-First Street, so Tobyn and I had to pack everything to move four blocks north—plus move the office. While I was preoccupied with all that, Alec was mostly in the Hamptons, performing in a play, so a few weeks passed with us emailing before we saw each other again. I told Tobyn about our correspondence, and as a big fan of *30 Rock*, he thought it was *cool*. He was always chill about these kinds of things. It wasn't in his nature to get jealous or make assumptions.

Eventually, Alec returned to the city, and we arranged to have lunch. He picked me up at Pure Food and Wine and took me a few blocks northwest to a Tuscan restaurant called Beppe. I was a little nervous seeing him again after all our back and forth, and wasn't I used to the attention—all the stares, double takes, and people so obviously trying to look, without looking like they were looking. It made me extra self-conscious. Alec, unfazed—clearly used to that kind of attention—ignored it. He was easygoing, funny, and full of questions. But I noticed that he never asked if I had a boyfriend. Meanwhile, I didn't know how to bring it up on my own—and part of me didn't want to.

This can be awkward with men in general—if they don't ask, do I just inject it into the conversation? What if I waited too long? Will they be mad, as if maybe I wasted their time? Should I have said it right away in our first emails? Probably yes. But also, I worried I was being presumptuous to assume he was interested in me romantically. Never mind that he sent me flowers. What if he was just exceedingly polite and all he wanted was some advice on eating better, or something? I didn't know. These things always get confusing. Particularly in a case like this, where I found myself really liking Alec as a person, regardless of any potential romantic context. But the longer I waited, the more dishonest it felt. What was I doing? It wasn't like I was in an unhappy relationship looking to get out—I loved my boyfriend.

* * *

Over the next few weeks, Alec and I kept volleying emails back and forth. His often ended with questions, which I liked. It ensured our communication would continue. He'd ask me how things were going, or what was stressing me out. I'm not someone who can easily respond to such questions concisely, so my replies tended to ramble. Yet in all that rambling, I never brought up the key detail of Tobyn—that I had a live-in boyfriend. The longer I waited, the weirder it got, especially as our conversations grew increasingly personal, even gently flirtatious.

Any opportunity to casually slip it in was long gone. *So my boyfriend and I were walking down the street the other day when...* No. That wouldn't work. I knew I had to come clean, honestly.

In a long email, I finally explained myself. First, I wrote about being overwhelmed, preoccupied with work and other drama, which I described in detail. Anything to delay my confession.

Stalling further, I mentioned how I was looking forward to dog-sitting Bazooka again over the coming weekend. Finally, I got around to acknowledging the minor detail of having a boyfriend—a much younger one with whom I'd been living for the past few years. Somehow, sharing Tobyn's age (he'd just turned twenty-four) felt like it softened the conflict. Alec, at fifty-two, was more than twice Tobyn's age. I was thirty-seven, right in the middle.

I was used to older (often powerful) men dismissing my younger boyfriend in a how-could-it-possibly-be-serious kind of way. Usually, this had zero effect on my unwavering commitment to and adoration of Tobyn. In fact, it only made me appreciate him that much more. I was still in love with him, despite knowing all along that our relationship likely had an expiration date, given his age. We were already more than three years in, and recently, I'd even debated breaking up with him. It had been maybe the only time I'd been truly furious with him. It was that classic scenario: boy is super messy, and girl—already overwhelmed and stressed—perceives the mess as screaming evidence that boy doesn't care about girl, that her needs don't matter. I was momentarily fed up, but I wasn't ready to give *him* up. I loved him.

Except there was Alec, someone I wanted to get to know.

I wanted both.

I confessed to Alec that I felt conflicted, that I was sorry for not bringing it up sooner. In an email I explained, honestly, that I hadn't said anything because "I was too busy working on being flirtatious, combined with concern that you may cease our interesting communication." I told him my relationship worked for me, in part because there was no drama, but also admitted, "A friend recently said I seem very lonely, which I think is probably true." (See what I did there? I have a boyfriend. But I'm clearly still missing something. I'm leaving the door wide open. I'm asking for us to leave it open.) I wrote that I hope I hadn't scared him off for good, then added that he had "the most intense energy of anyone I've ever met... it's at once intimidating, overwhelming, ridiculously attractive, energizing, dare I say intoxicating, inspiring... also hard to explain."

I was hardly pushing him away or putting up boundaries. But it was all honest. I may have left out the part about how deeply I loved Tobyn and that I had no plans to leave him anytime soon. This wasn't my way of suggesting an affair—that was not at all what I wanted. The truth was, I didn't know what I wanted. But everything I wrote to him was true.

* * *

I really liked Alec, a *lot*. Twice before, older and famous actors had asked me out, and both times I'd declined. In those cases, I got the impression they assumed *of course* I'd go out with them, because they were *famous actors*, or whatever. But Alec was different. He had none of that presumption. He was open and genuine, funny and kind, interesting and smart. We shared similar views on politics and animal rights. But more than that, it was his energy—maybe even pheromones—that pulled me in on a primal level. Our conversations flowed easily—sometimes about mundane things, sometimes about life in general, or what was stressing each of us out in our lives. We also eventually discovered a shared tendency toward something resembling depression. Or maybe just a midlife crisis for him, depression for me.

Alec's email reply to my confession was understanding and, like mine, left the door wide open. He barely mentioned my boyfriend at all. I replied again—this time even longer—further admitting my conflicted feelings. He was gracious, and told me if the relationship worked, then I should commit to it. I felt relieved that everything was in the open.

We continued talking on the phone, usually at night when Tobyn was working or at band practice. Sometimes I talked to Alec while painting the walls of the new apartment. Other times, while I lay on the purple shag rug in my office, staring at the ceiling. We emailed about life. He asked if I wanted kids, and I explained why I didn't. He pointed out how maternal I seemed with my staff and with Bazooka. Then he wrote—half joking—that it seemed it wasn't a girlfriend he needed, but a dog. *A dog.* This must have been what planted the idea in my head. And once I latched on to it, I couldn't let go; I was determined to help him find the perfect rescue dog to adopt.

* * *

In our conversations, I shared with Alec how drained and worn down I often felt by the pressures of running the business. By now, it was mid- to late summer, and he was spending nearly all his time at his home in the Hamptons. He suggested I come out for a day—or however long I wanted—to get some fresh air and relax. He assured me I'd have my own guestroom. Midweek in the Hamptons wouldn't be as annoyingly crowded as the weekends, and there wouldn't be much traffic there and back. Clearly, I needed something like this. And there was something soothing about Alec, a strange familiarity. No longer nervous, I'd grown more relaxed with him, more than I was with most people.

But what would Tobyn think?

No, I couldn't go. But... maybe?

Tobyn knew I was friends with Alec, knew that Alec sometimes called our landline, and seemed entirely chill about it. As always, his easygoing self-assurance was a thing to behold. Had he been a different kind of person—possessive, jealous, or suspicious—I'd have broken up with him. But he was *not* that kind of person. I honored and appreciated his trust in me. And yes, I loved him more for it.

Eventually, I worked out that I could get away for one night, midweek, to visit Alec. I'd take the bus out, stay over, then head back the following afternoon in time for Tobyn's band's show. I didn't go to all Tobyn's shows, but he'd somehow agreed that it was cool if I stayed overnight at Alec's. I reassured him we were just friends—which was true. For all Tobyn knew, it was a house full of people. (It was not.) I emphasized that I'd have my own room and just wanted to get out of the city for a day, that it would be fun.

That Tobyn was *so entirely okay* with it probably should have told me something, which I ought to have paid more attention to. Maybe he already had it in his head that we'd have to split up sooner or later, and I should've figured that out preemptively. But I didn't. I was still deeply attached to him, and to his overall purity and goodness. I was also attached to his bandmates, which included his best friend, who was also my valued juice bar manager.

Either way, I felt bad going to stay overnight at the home of another man, so I committed to making it back in time for Tobyn's show, as if to convey, *Don't worry. I'm still your girlfriend.*

* * *

On the bus to the Hamptons, Alec and I texted back and forth. At one point, I sent a silly text saying I'd packed a Vera Wang wedding dress. By then, we had an unspoken understanding that, despite a fondness for one another, a future together was, realistically, *not* realistic. Therefore, I did what I tend to do: I made jokes about what might have actually been painful.

Even if I'd ended things with Tobyn to try something serious with Alec, I knew it wouldn't have lasted. My life revolved around my all-consuming business, and Alec wanted kids. I also wasn't ready to let go of Tobyn. And even if I had been, I'd have had to kick him out of the apartment, which was his home too. I still loved him. I didn't want to be the bad guy. I hated the thought of his family and friends seeing me as the one who ditched Tobyn for an actor. And I'd miss them too.

When the bus pulled up to the stop, Alec was already there. He'd just come from playing tennis and was parked a short distance away, leaning against his antique-looking BMW. It was a perfect sunny day. Already I could breathe easier, away from the city. As we hugged, he apologized for being sweaty. I told him I didn't mind. We drove the short distance to his home, the tires crunching over the gravel driveway as we pulled up in front of a large, white-shingled house.

Off to one side, behind a row of neatly trimmed hedges, I spotted a pool. The yard was manicured—tidy but not overly perfect—and birds chirped from the trees overhead. As we walked toward the front door, a pair of small white rabbits darted out from under a bush, hopping across the lawn. I said to Alec, "I feel like we're on the set of a Disney movie."

He put his head down and spoke into the underside of his wrist. "Cue the rabbits. I repeat, cue the rabbits."

* * *

Inside, to the left of the front door, was a big wooden bench with a shit-ton of shoes under and in front of it. Upon closer inspection, they all appeared to be his—all men's shoes, at least. He kicked off his tennis sneakers, so I did the same with my old navy-blue Pumas. We padded across the wide-planked, gleaming hardwood floors in our socks as he gave me a tour. Sunlight streamed through windows. Books, papers, and personal things were scattered around, and photographs covered the walls. I loved how his home wasn't overly designed. It felt lived-in and comfortable.

Upstairs, he showed me where I'd be sleeping. As promised, a quaint guest room—bright and airy with a bed covered in plush white bedding and pillows perfectly fluffed, I presumed, by a housekeeper. For some reason, I felt unusually at ease around him, as if we'd known each other for years. As if he already knew me, and I was okay. As if everything about me was okay.

After the tour, he took me out to the pool. That morning, I'd had my hair expensively blown out, so I wasn't about to get in the pool myself. Not to mention, as comfortable as I felt around Alec, I still had irrationally persistent insecurities about my body. Meanwhile, Alec was perfectly comfortable peeling off his tennis shirt and socks and jumping into the pool. As some may know from the movies, he is a strikingly hairy man. I sat on the edge in my sundress, feet dangling in the cool water, watching him. Alec was quite big—a beast of a manly man—and so different from Tobyn, with his milky smooth, lean limbs. Tobyn was more *my type*, if I had one. But sitting there, I couldn't help feeling attracted to Alec, despite not wanting to.

* * *

Later that evening, we went to a reading Alec was scheduled to give at a local bookstore—a few chapters of *Moby Dick*. He was thoughtful, checking in about what I wanted. He told me I could stay at his house and relax if I preferred, and he'd come back afterward so we could go to dinner. But no, I was glad to be with him and wanted to go. Before leaving, I changed into a simple black sundress and a pair of brand-new red Pumas—my version of dressing up.

We drove to the bookstore and went in through a back entrance. The place was already packed. Alec was attentive, introducing me to the bookstore owners, always keeping his hand gently at the small of my back. The front of the store was jammed with folding chairs, most already occupied. When it was time for him to start, only a few minutes after we'd arrived, he handed me off to a store employee who had a seat saved for me near the front. I felt sort of special, being guided out at the last minute. Those already seated could easily deduce I'd arrived as Alec's companion, and therefore I attracted some curious stares.

The audience applauded as Alec approached the makeshift stage and took his seat on the stool set up for him. A young boy, also participating in the reading, was already perched on the stool beside his. Alec beamed at the boy, making small talk, clearly charmed. In his glasses and preppy outfit, this kid had that slightly nerdy, miniature-adult look.

Alec started to read. Since he was looking down into the book, I could freely study him, as others did too. I wasn't paying attention to the words, but as I listened to his voice, I felt myself drifting into a dreamy sort of daze. I started to feel some kind of pressure building inside me, as if my heart was swelling. Then I realized that a sizable knot of emotion was threatening to exit my body in the form of tears. *Oh fuck.* Why was this happening? It wasn't the story, because I wasn't listening to a word of *Moby Dick*. No, I was—quite suddenly—overcome by an emotion, a very *certain* feeling.

It hit me: *I love this man.*

I loved him? How could that be? But it was. I felt it. I sat there marinating in this epiphany. A mostly happy feeling, tinged with sadness. A perceptive person would've seen something happen on my face. In fact, someone *did*. Across the room, an elegant older woman was looking right at me. She was dressed in black, with styled white hair, dramatically made-up eyes, and red painted lips, and she looked at me with a kind and knowing smile. She'd been watching me. She knew. *She knows I love him,* I thought. I gave her a shy, uncertain smile and looked down. So there it was. Beyond my control. I loved this man. *Fuck.*

* * *

After the reading, we went to dinner, sitting on the front porch of an old-timey sort of restaurant. It was candlelit and cozy. I was relieved we didn't go to one of the trendy places where we'd be more exposed. At one point, Alec took a photo of me on his cell phone and showed it to me. It was dark and glowy—my elbows were on the table, hands folded under my chin, and I had an actual, genuine smile on my face. I looked happy in that photo. Genuinely happy.

Did we go back to his house and have hot sex? Romantic sex? Any sex? Nope. There was no pressure from him. Everything about that night felt easy and okay. Even if Tobyn hadn't existed, I might've wanted to hold out anyway. Too soon. It would have felt important to me that he didn't think I would sleep with someone so easily and quickly—even though so many times in my life I had. But this was different.

I remember wishing I could freeze time. Or, more specifically, freeze my boyfriend. Put him on ice for a while—six months maybe—so I could freely spend time with Alec. I had an almost overwhelming desire to take care of him in ways I knew I'd be good at, like making food for him. I wanted to *love him* for a while. I wanted to give him that. I wanted to see what it would be like. Would it feel right?

* * *

I'd gone to sleep in the guest room and woke in the morning to a text from Alec: *Awake yet? Come in here.* So I brushed my teeth and, still in my PJs, went over to his room. I climbed onto the bed next to him, and we kissed. His mouth was minty too. But he didn't push for more. Instead, we just lay there, comfortably tangled up, talking. I don't remember about what. I just remember it felt nice. I liked listening to him talk, hearing his stories. After a while I went back to my room to get dressed and pack.

We drove out for breakfast at a farmer's market with patio tables out front. Alec got a copy of the *New York Times,* and we sat outside, passing sections back and forth, occasionally trading comments about what we read. I ate cubed honeydew melon, he had a big muffin. I kept thinking how I'd get him eating healthier, how much better he'd feel without all that gluten. I couldn't help noticing how much I wanted to take care of him.

It was sunny and perfect out. Now and then, I peeked out over my paper and looked at him reading his section. Everything about being with him felt perfectly normal. As if we'd known each other for years, or decades.

After breakfast, he drove me around the area, pointing things out, telling me stories. We passed a friend of his in her driveway, and he pulled over to say hello, introducing us. We were out so long that eventually, it was time for lunch, and he drove us to a casual seaside restaurant. For midsummer, it was oddly cold by the water, and a light rain had started to fall. After we ordered, Alec quickly got up, saying he'd be right back. A few minutes later, he returned with a pale lemon-yellow hoodie that had *HAMPTONS* stitched across the front in white. It was a size small, which was cute because I tended to wear oversized, baggy clothes and wouldn't have thought to buy myself a small. But it fit nicely over my summer dress, and I rather enjoyed feeling petite, or delicate, even. He'd bought me a sweatshirt. *Sigh.* He was looking after me so well. I was completely relaxed, and I didn't want this trip to be over. I ate Manhattan clam chowder. Yes, people—I ate a few clams. Sorry. Hot soup is appealing on a chilly rainy day, and at least it was tomato-based, not cream. Finishing it quickly, I asked the waiter for a second bowl. All this energy buzzing through me made me hungry.

* * *

The night before, on our way back from dinner, we'd stopped at the ocean. I told Alec I hadn't been in the ocean in a long time, so he took me there. I told him I'd be right back and left him in the car to walk out to the water, taking off my sneakers and wading in to just below my knees. Then I thought about the opening scene in *Jaws,* when the girl wades into the water at night and gets eaten by a shark, so I backed out a bit.

Standing there with the waves rushing over my ankles, I thought about something Alec had said earlier, in our goofy half-serious fantasy talk, about how we could be good for one another. He'd come pick me up at the restaurant at night, he'd said. My life would be easier. I considered being taken care of in that way. He'd not outright said he'd pay my debts, but it was sort of implied. Looking out at the dark expanse of the ocean, I realized this was yet another reason it would never work. I couldn't let someone just wipe out my problems *for me*. The dynamics of the relationship would be forever tainted by my having cost a bunch of money, by needing to be rescued, and I didn't want that.

I liked being around Alec on even terms. It was soothing. He seemed to respect what I was doing and why I was doing it, and he treated me well. On the bus ride back to the city, it struck me that, around him, I liked *me*. I was comfortable with me. I wasn't used to that. I was more used to *not* liking myself, focused on my shortcomings or just feeling that there was something fundamentally wrong with me. But with Alec, I felt different, and I wasn't sure why.

Looking back now, that short Hamptons visit was like I'd been allowed to sample what a happily *relaxed* life could be, and how it could feel. To live without the weight of so much responsibility and debt.

* * *

Back in the city, I went straight to the bar where Tobyn's band was playing. As usual, the place was quiet—just a handful of people, including some friends, scattered around. Despite being really good, they hadn't built much of a following yet. Tobyn was setting up his drums. Jonathon, the bassist, greeted me with a hug, then Al, the lead singer. I adored Al. Still do. I loved that I was so close to Tobyn's friends. They were special people, and I loved them too. Do I love everyone? No. But I love easily, I guess. And I really did love my life with these guys in it.

Tobyn seemed mildly standoffish, but he was also focused on setting up his drums, and I was used to him getting lost in his own world when focused on something. Still, I'd have felt better if he'd looked up, smiled, gotten up to greet me with a hug and kiss. I *was* happy to see him, happy to be back. But his lack of excitement left me feeling… flat. Like something was off. Or maybe my heart was still in limbo, some part of me missing Alec.

CHAPTER THIRTY

FALL 2010

NEW YORK CITY

Alec and I continued emailing regularly, but the pace slowed as it became clear I wasn't leaving Tobyn, and we were stuck in the friend zone. Still, I wanted him to be happy. Seeing the kind of life Alec had, with all that yard space, it seemed a dog would fit perfectly. A dog, I rationalized, could expand his heart, maybe even help attract the right person. I began regularly trolling pet adoption websites, keeping an eye out for the right dog for him. It had to be a rescue, of course (over six million cats and dogs enter shelters each year, and nearly a million don't get adopted and end up euthanized). Never mind that Alec repeatedly told me he wasn't interested in getting a dog.

One day, while plowing through my inbox, rapidly scanning and deleting emails, I skimmed over a newsletter from wellness advocate Kris Carr, halting abruptly when a photo caught my attention. Her newsletter regularly featured two pets available for adoption. One of the photos hit me like a punch in the heart. A puppy whose cuteness overwhelmed me. Looking closer, I saw his name was Quinn.

Most puppy pictures tug at my heartstrings, but this one did something more. It yanked them hard, bringing my hurried email scanning to a screeching halt. According to the description, he was a five-month-old pit bull mix at a Brooklyn shelter. I'd seen loads of adoptable dogs, but there was something very different about Quinn. I felt drawn to him—to his tan colored face and big floppy ears. I clicked through to his profile on the shelter's website and immediately forwarded it to Alec, along with some kind of plea that he *must get this dog. This one! Hurry. This is the one!*

But Alec didn't want a dog.

And yet, there was something about *this* dog.

I tried to focus on my work, but I kept going back to the link and staring at Quinn's photo. Thus began my obsession. Eventually, to save myself the extra step, I copied the image onto my desktop for easier viewing, day and night.

At some point during my drooling over his photo, the idea of adopting him myself started to ever-so-slowly slide into my consciousness. At first, it was just a dreamy fantasy—Quinn and me, frolicking carefree through tall fields of flowers. But reality would snap me out of it. There were tons of reasons I shouldn't get a dog. Legitimate ones, such as being already overwhelmed with work and life. When I floated the idea to friends and family, they reasonably asked how I could possibly take care of a puppy when I was barely taking care of myself. *If you have to get a dog*, they said, *why not get an older mellow dog, like Bazooka?* Bazooka, the sweet dog who was so easy to care for. But I didn't *have* to get a dog, and this wasn't about just *any* dog. It was about Quinn. I stopped talking about it with others, since they only tried to talk me out of it.

My brain knew adopting a puppy wasn't rational, but this obsession gripped my heart. I Google-mapped the shelter to see exactly where in Brooklyn it was (and how to get there) just so I could feel connected to him. I couldn't let it go. According to his adoption description he'd been found with "severe demodectic mange." I googled that to find out what it was. The photos online were heartbreaking to look at. Apparently, however, it's a treatable condition, and Quinn's profile stated that he'd healed quite well on medication.

I emailed the shelter, casually asking if they still had him. I figured maybe I could still persuade Alec to get him, or that was what I told myself. The shelter emailed back. Yes, he was still there. They also attached an application for me. *For me?* Ruh-roh. I printed the form, but left it sitting in the printer.

* * *

Later that week, I woke up in the middle of the night, crying. Tobyn stirred next to me, and asked what was wrong. I whispered, "It's Quinn." For whatever reason, my heart ached for this dog, as if he were sitting in a cage at that shelter, waiting for me. There were tons of rescue dogs out there—why did I feel this way, about *this one?* Lying awake, I started doing the math. If he was five months old, as the shelter listed, that meant he'd been born in March. *March.* The same month I lost Dallas, my feline soulmate, after eleven years together. The thought sent a jolt through me. I'd never believed in reincarnation, never really *thought* about it. But there I was, wondering if it was more than a coincidence. A sign.

Maybe my mind was rationalizing a decision my heart had already made. Either way, I resolved, then and there, that I would go *see* him very soon. Just to visit, I told myself.

Tobyn left for a weeklong trip to Colorado. I had a feeling he didn't want me to get a dog—not because he didn't *like* dogs but because he knew how overwhelmed I already was. And he wasn't wrong. My home also doubled as the One Lucky Duck office, which meant I'd also be foisting a dog upon those who worked there on the weekdays. They'd have to deal with a giant puppy running around. What if he barked all day? Chewed through computer cords? Ate our inventory? How would I even manage walking a pit bull puppy several times a day?

Well, *I was just going to see him*, was what I told Tobyn, my officemates, and myself. Yet earlier that day, I'd stopped at Petco and bought a leash, a collar, and some dog treats. They were stuffed in my bag, along with the application I'd already filled out. *Just in case.*

I took the subway to Sean Casey Animal Rescue in Brooklyn late on a Thursday afternoon. I'd been calling daily to make sure Quinn was still there. At this point, I'd have been devastated if someone else had adopted him.

I was finally about to meet him. I felt anxious in both senses of the word—excited but nervous. In my head, I'd imagined a Lassie-type moment, something cinematic. But there was no slow-motion running to each other when they brought Quinn to me. He didn't gaze up at me with pleading eyes, silently begging to be taken home. Instead, he was distracted and hyper, as any caged puppy would be, full of frantic energy. His fur was still a little mangy, and he looked in need of a bath. But he was, just like in his photo, *very* cute. They let me take him for a walk around the block. He pulled hard on the leash, sniffing everything, peeing on this and that.

Back at the shelter, I spoke with founder Sean Casey, who told me about Quinn's history. He'd been found dumped on a Brooklyn street, suffering from severe mange. Sean showed me the photos they'd taken when he first arrived, and I couldn't believe it was the same dog. *Poor baby.* He was all scab, no fur. The mange was so bad that when they handled him, he bled. Quinn had spent his first month at the shelter in a cage, healing, on medication. Only after that did they take the super-cute photo they'd posted on their site—the one that ended up in that newsletter, the one I fell in love with.

I told Sean I needed to think about it, but left him my application anyway. One of the staffers put Quinn back in his cage, and I followed to say goodbye. The room, full of stacked cages, was a cacophony of frenzied barking, metal bars rattling as paws scratched at them. But Quinn flopped down in his cage, quiet. He looked up at me. I looked back into his puppy eyes, telepathically telling him, *Don't worry. I'm coming back to get you out.*

That was it. My decision was made. No list of pros and cons. No hesitation. In some way, it had already been decided for me. I had to come back and get him.

On the subway home, I made lists of everything I needed to get. I felt panicky, but in a good way. By the time I got home, my employees had left, and I ran around with frantic energy, shoving sneakers into closets, combing the floors for paper clips, binder clips, hair clips—anything a puppy could swallow. I kept thinking, *OMG, OMG, OMG, I'm getting a dog!*—not knowing what I was supposed to do, wishing I had two weeks to prepare, wishing I could speedread the canine version of *What to Expect When You're Expecting*, if one even existed.

* * *

I left early the next morning, hoping to arrive right when the shelter opened, but the trip took longer than I'd expected. As the train crossed the East River into Brooklyn, I started to cry. I couldn't hold it in. I didn't even know why—I just felt like my heart might explode. People on the subway probably thought I'd just been dumped by a boyfriend or lost a family member, a job, something. No, I was just about to adopt a puppy. Whatever was coming up and out of me, I knew I had to get it out of my system so I didn't cry at the shelter. I didn't want them to think I was a basket case and therefore an unfit mother.

I practically ran from the train station to the shelter, panicked I'd get there only to find a family loading Quinn into their car. But no, Quinn was still there, in his cage, as if waiting for me.

A trainer named Charlie spent a good two hours giving me a crash course in puppy training, for which I was endlessly grateful. Sean Casey Animal Rescue is an interesting place. They take in all kinds of animals, not just cats and dogs. At one point, I had to pee and was directed to a tiny bathroom. While peeing, I casually glanced over into the small sink beside me and found it occupied by a very large turtle. Oh, hello, turtle.

After about three hours, the staff at Sean Casey called me a car, and we loaded it up with the crate and everything else I'd bought from the pet store next door. Quinn stayed on the floor of the backseat, looking completely freaked the fuck out. I snapped a photo of his dirty, panicked face. Charlie had advised me to walk him around the block before taking him inside, so I called my office to have someone meet me downstairs. They took the crate and supplies up while Quinn and I circled the block, letting him sniff out his new neighborhood. That first afternoon was nerve-racking. I was a little afraid, not knowing his full background, if he'd ever been abused or mistreated beyond being dumped in the street, and if he might get aggressive. But after some cautious getting to know each other, he relaxed surprisingly quickly. He let me pet him, play with him, and eventually hold him. He was hyper yet incredibly sweet. He spent exactly one night in the crate I'd bought. After that, I left the crate door open, and he climbed up in the bed.

Though I knew him as Quinn, Charlie advised me to rename him. New life, new name. But what to call him? It was hard for me to think of him as anything other than Quinn. I considered my favorite movie, *The Professional*, with Natalie Portman and the French actor Jean Reno. Reno plays the lead character, Leon—a quiet, brooding hitman who I sort of fall in love with every time I watch it. Leon felt like the right name.

Miraculously, *Leon* didn't chew up any inventory, computer cords, or shoes. He somehow appeared to know the difference between his chew toys and everything else. Like a *very good boy.* Through a referral, I found someone to walk him on weekday afternoons: Justin, who I mentioned earlier in this story, and who gradually became a close friend (which is also how I met Big Dave). I walked

Leon in the mornings, and every afternoon, Justin came by to take him out with a pack of other dogs. Afterward, Leon passed out and snored on the couch for the rest of the day. That meant I could focus on work, go to meetings, or do whatever else I needed to do. Then Tobyn or I took him out before bed. Though Tobyn shared these duties with me, we both understood Leon was *my* dog.

Did my life turn upside down with Leon? No—and yes. It already felt upside down, so maybe he turned it right side up. Getting a dog seemed insane, but then also not at all. Like it was exactly what I was supposed to do.

For months I'd been trying to figure out what was wrong with me, why I felt so shitty and exhausted all the time. Did I have thyroid issues? Low iron? Candida? Parasites? Chronic fucking fatigue syndrome? My bloodwork always came back fine. I was simply overworked and overstressed—so much so that I was tired of people telling me to take better care of myself. Adding yet another "responsibility" to my life seemed crazy.

Had I subconsciously sensed that Tobyn and I were creeping toward Splitsville, and Leon would help me get through it?

Maybe I rescued Leon because I needed someone to rescue me.

CHAPTER THIRTY-ONE

2011

NEW YORK CITY

I only got to introduce Leon to Alec once. We met for a coffee at Irving Farm, just down the street from my restaurant. We sat at a small table out front so I could bring Leon. Alec didn't seem particularly enamored with Leon. Later, he wrote to me, "Is that the way to Sarma's heart? To come back as a dog?"

Yes. Yes, it is. My love for Leon was boundless. Overwhelming in the best way. When I was around him, I felt like I exuded more love. Loving a dog is pure and safe. This was why I'd wanted Alec to adopt one—so he would feel that way while he waited to find his human love. It turned out, however, he didn't have to wait long, and he didn't need a dog surrogate.

* * *

It was a freakishly warm February evening—so warm that we opened our front patio at Pure Food and Wine. I was home on the couch spooning Leon, in pajamas, watching the news, exhausted after a long week. With Tobyn out for the night and my staff gone until Monday, I reveled in the rare peace and quiet. Then my phone rang. It was Alec. "I'm sitting on the patio at your restaurant. Where are you?"

I told him I was home, in PJs. This wasn't one of those times I'd hop up, throw on real clothes, and speed-walk the six blocks to the restaurant—something I sometimes did when someone like Bill Clinton walked in or there was an emergency. Probably I was just wiped out, maybe PMSing. Our conversation was short. I texted the manager at the restaurant to make sure they looked after him.

A few minutes later, Justin texted, "Where are you? I'm at your restaurant. Alec Baldwin is here!"

"I know," I replied.

Sometimes, all I wanted was a break, a quiet night, but the constant action just a few blocks away was always there. Like being a doctor perpetually on call. Lives weren't on the line in my case, but it was *knowing* that something could be important enough to call me in at any moment, or else that I *should* be there. Or that I was letting someone down by *not* being there. This made it hard to ever fully relax, which was why I found Christmas Eve and Christmas Day—the only days of the year the restaurant closed—so blissful. Or my trips to Colorado with Tobyn, nearly two thousand miles away. Too far away to be expected to show up if a crisis occurred or someone important dropped by.

I explained to Justin that I wasn't feeling great and needed to rest. I felt a little bad about it, but oh well. I put my phone down and focused back on the TV, trying to snuff out that vague FOMO feeling. I really *did* want to see Alec. I would have loved to see him. I still had *feelings* of some kind that persisted. But I was exhausted and didn't want to move from Leon or the couch.

My phone pinged again. Justin texted, "Alec's talking to a super hot brunette."

"Cool," I texted back, while thinking, *Fuck off Justin, I didn't need to know that.* The hot brunette Alec met at my restaurant turned out to be Hilaria Thomas— later Hilaria Baldwin, and now mother of their [checks latest stats] seven kids.

* * *

Tobyn and I split up not long after Alec began dating Hilaria. Of course it happened that way. I became available as soon as Alec wasn't. Which, particularly in retrospect, was okay. He wanted a wife and kids, and if more had happened between us, it only would've delayed what he really wanted. Besides, I got the sense that we'd always have been better off as just close friends anyway.

Despite my emotional affair, Tobyn's departure was still wildly painful for me. We broke up amicably, but it wasn't fast and clean. Instead of ripping the Band-Aid off, it was peeled away at an agonizingly glacial pace.

First Tobyn moved out. His reasons for needing his own place made sense. Back in my prior apartment, when it was just the two of us, living together had worked. But now, with my staff ever present in the front room—sharing the kitchen, filling the space Monday through Friday—this wasn't really much of a home for him anymore. I hadn't really thought through how unsustainable it was. He needed his own place, to be on his own. I guess this was phase one of our breakup. To his credit, he was painfully honest in telling me that he wanted to see what it was like to be with other girls. I understood this rationally. He was in his midtwenties. I was an overworked thirty-eight-year-old.

He rented what was basically a large, windowless closet in an extremely sketchy-looking and most certainly illegal-to-be-renting-out warehouse building in Brooklyn. He shared the kitchen and bathroom with whoever else lived there. The bathroom made gas station facilities seem luxurious. I never saw the kitchen. I only visited once. What I remember more than anything was how incredibly dark the whole place was, which made me feel that much worse about his moving out. Like he must have *really* wanted to leave if this was where he preferred to be.

* * *

Tobyn still stayed over sometimes, usually on weekends when no one else was around. We woke late on Memorial Day—a day off for my office—and had late-morning, energetic, limbs-everywhere sex. It was exhausting and fun, and I felt happy, even though we were still technically broken up.

"Brunch?" Tobyn asked.

"Okay!" I said. This wasn't something we usually did but it sounded fun, and the day was stunning—sunny and warm but not too hot. Tobyn took Leon for a walk while I got dressed, putting on a dark pink sundress that, with the right bra, made my boobs look much bigger than they actually were. In this limbo stage with Tobyn, I paid a lot of attention to how I looked again, as if it was our first days together. I wanted him to *want* me again. I wanted him to not leave me.

We went to Barbounia, a busy Mediterranean restaurant around the corner.

I am not—never was, never will be—a big brunch person. Every weekend, I walked by this place, packed with lively, late-morning drinkers, and wondered who these people were, with so much leisure time to drink at midday. This weekend, we joined them.

We were seated at a high table near the bar. All around us people drank mimosas and Bellinis. We ordered our own pitcher of Bellinis. The white peach juice mixed with champagne tasted like the most delicious, sparkly sweet nectar, making it hard to leave my flute sitting on the table for long. By the time our food arrived, we'd nearly finished the first pitcher. The breezy, beautiful day, along with the buzz from the Bellinis, feeling somewhat attractive, and sitting there with Tobyn, all combined into a kind of perfect, fleeting happiness.

Our food arrived. We started in on the warm hummus, tabouli, cucumber salad, and crispy falafel while Tobyn started talking about the summer music festival in Colorado he planned to attend with his bandmates. I'd gone with him a summer before, during one of our trips out there. It had been fun.

"You should come, baby!" he said.

"What... really?"

He wants me to come along? My heart lifted. I started thinking that maybe he'd reconsidered our breakup, maybe he'd just needed some space. Maybe things would work out with us living apart, with more breathing room.

He smiled. "It'll be fun! We could drive and take Leon!"

Okay, *drive* to Colorado—*thirty hours*—for a music festival? So... was I supposed to be his roadie, hauling his drum equipment across the country? Probably his bandmates' gear too? I looked down at my plate, trying to steady a falafel ball with the side of my fork so I could cut it in half, wondering if I could rally for a cross-country drive—and whether it was the ride he wanted more than my company.

"I don't know," I said quietly, dunking half a falafel ball into smooth sesame tahini.

Then, Tobyn said this: "Aw, c'mon, baby. It'll be *fun*. Maybe you'll even meet someone there."

The falafel in my mouth turned to cement, heavy and impossible to swallow.

Meet someone there?

Did he really just say that, so casually? Hadn't we just had sex—really good sex—less than two hours ago? And now here we were, out for brunch, and he wanted me to drive him to fucking Colorado, where maybe I'd *meet someone?*

He might as well have reached across the table and plunged his fork into my heart. I couldn't look at him. My face went hot, and my eyes pooled. I lowered my head and turned to the side as tears spilled out. Hot, sticky, peachy champagne tears.

* * *

In the end, Tobyn and his band went to the music festival, and decided to move back there for good. So that was it. Band-Aid completely removed. Tobyn was gone.

I'd known all along we would break up. He was too young. I'd known, too—that day in the juice bar, in our first weeks together, when I watched the young, pretty girl in the juice bar look at him with starry eyes—that when the time came, it would hurt like fuck. And it did. On top of the heartbreak, our split made me feel *old*. Like I was past my prime, while he got to move on with the rest of his prime life.

It now seemed funny that I'd felt Alec was too old for me, a sixteen-year difference, just three years more than the thirteen between Tobyn and me. And yet Alec and Hilaria? Theirs was a twenty-six-year gap.

I was genuinely happy for Alec. Truly. But now, with Tobyn gone—presumably to also end up with a girlfriend much younger than me—my already shitty self-esteem was taking a beating. Being alone, feeling unwanted, with a bruised sense of self, I can see now, made me vulnerable. My weakened state combined with flimsy boundaries created the perfect conditions for someone like Mr. Fox to bulldoze into my life.

PART THREE

THE EVIDENCE

"Vegan Restaurateur, Wanted For Theft, Tax Fraud,
Brought Down By Cheesy Pizza Order"
—FORBES.COM, MAY 23, 2016

CHAPTER THIRTY-TWO

MAY 2016
NEW YORK CITY

I'd been at Rikers just over a week when I got word that I was getting out. My huge bail had been arranged through emergency third mortgages and other financial wrangling pulled off by my father and stepmother. I'd be bussed back to the Brooklyn court, where my attorneys would appear before the judge, my bail confirmed, and then I'd be free to go. No one had posted bail for Mr. Fox (not surprisingly), so he would stay put. *Good.*

The morning of my release, I went through the usual strip-and-squat routine, waited in a cell, got shackled to another inmate, and boarded the metal bus to Brooklyn. Once at the courthouse, I was led to a holding cell behind the courtrooms. Sheila, the attorney my father had hired, came to see me. It was our first meeting. She was polished and professional, maybe a bit older than me, with wavy brown hair in a sensible, medium-length style. She smiled warmly. She told me she'd been to my restaurant years earlier and loved it, especially the amazing the mallomars. Something about that—that she knew about and missed those special mallomars—made made me want to hug her, which I did once the hearing was over.

I was free to go, as soon as I got out of my jail uniform. Back at Rikers, I hadn't been allowed to retrieve the clothes I'd arrived in. Apparently, I'd have to make a special trip back later to pick them up. I'd have gladly abandoned those stale, stinky clothes, but my driver's license was there too, so I'd have to go. Cool. *Can't wait!*

Since walking out to the street in a jail uniform wasn't allowed, Sheila had brought me clothes—brand-new ones—in a bag from the Gap. What I'd asked for, and wanted, was just to borrow a pair of sweatpants and a T-shirt, and sunglasses to hide behind. *Oh well.*

I pulled on a pair of bright white jeans, which miraculously fit as if they'd been tailored for me. It registered in my thoughts that this was officially the first time as an adult—or perhaps my entire life—I'd ever worn white pants. Also in the bag was a small light-blue-and-white-striped sleeveless top. *Sleeveless!* I hadn't shaved my armpits in three weeks, not since before the arrest. *Sigh.* I wasn't looking forward to facing the photographers I'd been warned would be outside. And now, in this strange (albeit objectively *normal)* outfit, I felt even less like myself. More like I was heading to the US Open but forgot to do my hair and makeup. It made me feel like what I'd been accused of. A fraud. Could I put the plastic Gap bag over my head? Poke some eyeholes in it and pull the drawstring tight?

Sheila and I walked out of the courthouse and into a nearby garage as fast as we could, but I didn't escape the photographers' lenses. Somewhere out there exists a terrible photo of me from that day, arms clamped tightly to my sides like a toy soldier, hoping no fuzzies peeked out.

* * *

Safely inside her silver Mercedes, Sheila handed me a bottle of water, and something else. "I brought you some chocolate," she said. "I thought you might want some."

Only a female attorney would think of this. I took the beautifully wrapped, obscurely branded organic chocolate and wanted to cry at her thoughtfulness. I drank the entire bottle of water and then carefully unwrapped the chocolate bar and ate half of it as we made our way to my sister's brownstone in Bay Ridge.

On one hand, I felt immense relief to be out of jail. On the other, it was strangely disconcerting. At least while locked up, I didn't have to face everything.

Now I did. And I still wasn't clear about what "everything" even was. Having been yanked out of my bizarre existence with Mr. Fox, I was in a haze. It was like slowly coming out of a coma, while overhead, clouds of doom rolled in. Every reassurance he'd ever given me was, I was beginning to see, spectacularly delusional bullshit after all.

My life as I'd known it was now obliterated. In its place was a supersized pile of debt and other complications, under which I felt I might very well suffocate. I was horrified by the destruction and financial losses others had suffered. And my beautiful restaurant, along with One Lucky Duck, and the people who worked there, which had felt like my whole life... *gone*. It was a reality I still hadn't fully accepted.

I had no idea what would happen, but I never thought I'd be sentenced and sent back to jail. Doesn't a criminal need a motive? And criminal intent? Why would I obliterate my own life and destroy my life's work? After all, I'd lost more than anyone. I figured surely the prosecutors would see this once they got a chance to look into things.

* * *

It was weird being back in New York but without a home of my own—as if I was a visitor now. I was lucky to stay at my sister's in Brooklyn, and I had a new baby nephew to meet. I was also eager for a long, hot shower and to finally shave my armpits and legs.

I was apprehensive about facing everyone. My phone calls with my family from jail had been short, focused mainly on logistics. We hadn't discussed what had happened. How would I be able to explain something I didn't understand myself? Fortunately, no one asked too many questions during my first few days back.

My sister and I could just be together without having to talk about things, and being at her house was comforting. Her husband's teenage daughter had a bedroom in their brownstone, but she'd been living full time at his ex-wife's house, so her room became mine. I'd wake up in the incredibly comfortable bed and remember where I was and what had happened. I'd lie there, staring at the posters of Taylor Swift and Ed Sheeran, and wonder what it would be like to trade lives with them. Or my step-niece. Or anyone. I could have easily stayed in bed for days, but I got up and tried to be useful.

My new nephew—an objectively cute baby—was a near-constant distraction and a grounding presence. I've never been a baby person, but this child was a bundle of good energy, and a human who didn't judge me. I was glad to change his diapers, feed him bottles, pat his back until he burped, or just sit and watch him in his bouncy seat so my sister could go to a yoga class. I sometimes fantasized about changing places with him too.

I badly missed Leon, who was still with my father at his home in Washington, DC, but I'd see him as soon as my dad could get to New York.

The timing of all this had worked out oddly well. My sister was on maternity leave and had time to be there for me, taking care of me however she could. Like a second baby—an adult baby—she gave me whatever I needed, which was everything: a toothbrush, socks and underwear, clothes to wear, a new phone. I had nothing. Not even my wallet or personal effects, all of which had been transported from Tennessee to the district attorney's office in Brooklyn.

At least I was eating well. My sister already ate clean and healthy, but she'd gone out of her way to stock up on organic greens, fruit, almond milk—and a couple of bottles of New Zealand Sauvignon Blanc. The wine definitely helped. It was a strange, emotional time. We'd be folding laundry, discussing what to make for dinner, and I'd burst into tears with no warning. My baby nephew and I could relate to each other on this level. We both cried randomly, and no one really knew what to do to make us feel better. Alone in my temporary bedroom, I sometimes cried for so long I had to rehydrate just to be able to generate more tears.

* * *

After a couple of days, I headed into the city to meet with Sheila. She had her own law practice, with modest offices on a high floor of a building near Wall Street. Her corner office overlooked the Hudson River. We talked about what happened. I cried. I stared out the window. She asked questions, and I did my best to answer. My father had paid her retainer. Knowing how much my father had spent on me was painful. I hope one day to pay it all back, somehow.

Sheila introduced me to a concept called "coercive control." Later, when I read more about it, I wanted to palm-smack myself in the forehead. Or better yet, smash a cinderblock into my skull. I wondered if there was a handbook out there that the Mr. Foxes of the world followed. It seemed that way. While what happened to me was far more bizarre and darker than what coercive control generally entails, Mr. Fox had employed every single tactic.

I also learned from Sheila just how aggressive the Brooklyn DA's office was about my case. At this point, I still couldn't quite wrap my head around it. I continued thinking that surely once they *understood* what had happened, they'd not be gunning for me to go to prison or even go on trial. *It didn't make sense. Anyone would see that*, I thought.

I was wrong.

Because my mother was wrapped up in this—unfortunately having transferred significant sums to Mr. Fox—the DA's office had hinted that she might be indicted too, or at least investigated. My *mother*. My sweet, kind, amazing, seventy-something-year-old mom, who had been victimized by this destructive, demonic beast I had let into my life, and now *she* had to worry they'd be coming after her too? What. The. Fuck.

Since my mom no longer had any money—after losing all of it and more to Mr. Fox—her best friend paid the retainer for a reputable New York criminal defense attorney to represent her.

This was all surreal.

* * *

A few days later, my mother came to New York. A meeting was set up at Sheila's office with Cesar, me, my mom, and my mom's attorney, whom she'd only met once, briefly, before this meeting. His name was Patrick Brackley.

I arrived at Sheila's first and talked with her and Cesar. I really liked them both—the kind of people I'd love to sit around with, drinking wine, talking about life and politics. Then my mother and her attorney arrived. When Patrick Brackley walked in, my inner dialogue screeched to a halt and I thought, *That guy!?* He looked like a mafia lawyer. Dark charcoal-gray pin-striped suit. Glossy lavender tie. Thick, slicked-back salt-and-pepper hair. Tanned. Mid-fifties, probably. I was skeptical.

After some introductions, Brackley took over. It was clear he didn't care for small talk, which, given the circumstances, I appreciated. He asked questions that got right to the point and looked me directly in the eye. I looked back at him and answered as directly as I could—as weird as some of my answers may have seemed, as embarrassed and ashamed as I was by this entire mess. He could tell I was being forthright. By the end of the meeting I found myself thinking, *Wait, can't THAT guy be my attorney?*

I wanted someone to aggressively defend me, based on facts and logic, which, bizarre storyline notwithstanding, seemed to be mostly on my side. Especially logic—how would it make sense that I would destroy my own company and hurt those I loved? For what gain? Not to mention, when arrested, I wasn't even aware of my fugitive status—I was in a fugue state.

Psychological phenomena such as cognitive dissonance and trauma bonding were concepts I'd only discover later. I'd never heard of *narcissistic abuse* and had only just learned that *coercive control* was a thing, recently criminalized in some countries. I'd thought I understood sociopathy, or at least that kind of capacity for cruelty, after my time with Matthew, but clearly there was a lot more to learn. Cult mind control would turn out to be the most fascinating and relevant concept of all, at least to me.

But at the time, it was hard to even explain or understand much of anything. I was so relieved to be free from Mr. Fox because, among other reasons, his presence in my life was terrifying. But I noticed the strange paradox that parts of me were terrified *without him*. He'd trained me to fear any existence without him. He'd trained me to believe that he was the only one who could and would save me. That only he really *knew me*. So, here I was… still feeling foggy and unsure of my reality. It was like sliding out of one nightmare (living under the totalitarian rule of Mr. Fox) and into another (facing loss, destruction, humiliation, and scary criminal charges). It didn't help that one of the tabloids had started referring to me as the *Vegan Bernie Madoff*. As if Bernie Madoff and I were the same. As if I was a sociopath.

Those early meetings with attorneys felt so awkward because I was trying to explain things that I knew sounded extraordinarily *weird*. Or I knew my answers to questions often didn't make much sense. They'd ask me what happened, and I'd tell them what I remembered. It all seemed so ludicrous. Like I had to be making it up because it couldn't possibly be true.

Attorneys: "So, why is it you kept sending him all these money wires?"

Me: "He told me nothing was real, that everything would be *undone*. Like, *reversed*, sort of."

Attorneys: "You mean he said he'd give you back all the money?"

Me: "No, not that. More like... the money didn't matter. It wasn't real. He would just turn back time, rewind and redo. Or... *something*."

All this while they exchanged sideways glances and I fidgeted with a paperclip, twisting it in different ways until it finally broke apart in my hands.

* * *

Back at my sister's, I borrowed her laptop. On Sheila's advice, I set up a brand-new Gmail account. Better to start fresh and clean. I still didn't have access to my previous email account. After Mr. Fox and I disappeared from New York City, he had taken full control of my account, changed the password, and taken my phone.

At some point, I spent hours in back-and-forth with Google to verify my identity. Finally, I got back into my old Gmail. I was relieved to have access to it, but also afraid to look.

I looked.

At the top of my inbox were mostly spammy emails. I scrolled down and saw a few messages from people who'd heard about my arrest and reached out. Not as many as I'd have thought. Did everyone forget about me?

I typed Mr. Fox's email address into the search box to pull up our email history. We'd probably sent thousands of emails back and forth, and a bajillion Gchats. I hit *enter*, and... nothing. It was gone. All our years of email correspondence, not there. Of course he'd deleted it. Erased all the evidence, and emptied the trash.

But there was *one*. One email, from him to me. One I'd never seen before. It was dated July 26, 2015, just over a month after he'd taken me away and locked me out of my account. A single, short email.

It was mind-bendingly shitty, and a revelation of his true intent. By this point, nothing was surprising, and everything was painful—but this was still hard to see. What he wrote will make more sense *after* I've told the rest of my story, so I'll circle back to it then. Either way, I didn't dwell on it for long, because what I found next was worse.

I wondered if he'd *sent* emails, and if those messages would still be there, so I looked in the Sent folder. Yes. Fuck. Yes. There was one after another. Emails written as if authored by me. He wrote to people *as me*. To Jeffrey, Alec, my family, and others. Again, the specifics will make more sense later. But the way I felt reading these—it was like a layer of humiliation frosting on the many-tiered cake of my shame.

* * *

If anyone was to believe me—if any of this was ever going to make sense—I needed evidence. Some proof that yes, all of this really happened. Everything I'm saying is true. You may be wondering why no one just subpoenaed Google. Surely my emails still existed somewhere, buried in distant archives. I kept asking my attorneys if there was a way to get them. I never got any good answers. I admit I was not at the top of my game in terms of asserting myself, generally feeling demoralized and still in a haze. Also, I've never been good at *demanding* things. I tend to operate as if everyone in the world is doing me a favor, even when they're being paid. That tendency would naturally only be amplified in a weakened emotional state. My already lacking self-confidence was now mostly incinerated by the past few years, and by my current circumstances.

No one ever subpoenaed Google for my emails.

* * *

In the meantime, I had to figure out what had happened to all my stuff—the things from my life before Mr. Fox took me away. What had happened to it all?

For now, I'll just say that most of it was gone. I did manage to get back some of the things from just before we left, but most of my life's history—furniture, books, records, clothes, keepsakes, non-digital photos—nearly all of it was gone. Another gut shot.

At least over time, bit by bit, I was able to track down and recover parts of my digital correspondence with Mr. Fox, despite his efforts to erase so much of it. Luckily, what I found only corroborated what I'd already told my lawyers. I was so grateful for it. Because there it was, in writing. Him saying a lot of fucked-up shit.

CHAPTER THIRTY-THREE

SUMMER 2016
NEW YORK CITY
COLLECTING EVIDENCE: THE PHONE

Three crucial pieces of evidence helped me piece together what happened: an old phone, my journal, and my Gchat correspondences with Mr. Fox. Each discovery felt like a wildly lucky find, almost like a gift from above.

* * *

When my father arrived at my sister's house, I was finally reunited with Leon. I wondered what he'd been feeling all those weeks, first in Tennessee, then with my dad. Who knows, but being back with Leon was a comfort. Looking into his eyes always made me feel like everything would be okay. My father had also brought whatever of my belongings had been packed up by the hotel staff in Tennessee. I'd been told the police had taken all our "electronics," including my iPad and the phone I'd been using. But as I rummaged through my clothes, I found something they'd missed. It was an old phone, stuffed inside a sock, tucked into a tampon box.

During my years with Mr. Fox, he regularly erased his texts from my phone. Once he had me in a mostly submissive mode, he'd take my phone—sometimes just picking it up, other times demanding I hand it over—and delete our text history. He'd also scan through the rest of my conversations. This was something that, especially at first, stirred up a tornado-like rage in me. But over time, he got me desensitized to it. If I upgraded or replaced my phone, he took the old one rather than letting me trade it in. When I switched from a BlackBerry to an iPhone, he took my BlackBerry. And toward the very end—when we left New York, "on the run," as the press characterized it—he took that iPhone too.

There was, however, one phone he didn't get to take. Early in 2015, for some unexpected reason, I had to get a new phone when he wasn't around. I don't remember if I just didn't tell him or he forgot, but I kept the old one hidden. I must have felt, on some level, that it was important to keep, which might have been why I had it with me the entire year before our arrest—stuffed inside a sock, jammed inside a small tampon box, shoved deep in a pocket compartment of my suitcase.

And now, here it was. I pulled it out and regarded it—in its beat-up old waterproof case with a pink One Lucky Duck sticker on the back—like the Holy Grail.

I quickly plugged the phone into a charger and, once powered up, connected it to my sister's Wi-Fi and opened the email app. As expected, it kept telling me it couldn't refresh—couldn't download new emails—since the password had been changed. But the emails that had already been downloaded the last time the phone was powered on, over a year earlier, were still there. I knew that if I updated the password, I'd lose them. So I left it.

I was able to see a handful of Mr. Fox's emails from the week or so before I'd stopped using that phone. I took screenshots of every one. Then I checked my text messages. Whatever hadn't been deleted was still there. I took more screenshots. Scrolling through the saved photos, I also found screenshots that I'd taken much earlier of texts or emails from Mr. Fox—ones I must have instinctively known were important to save. Now I was getting somewhere. Some of these emails clearly showed him giving me orders, trying to scare me, and saying weird shit. *This should help me so much,* I thought.

* * *

Later, I found even more correspondence. Some because Mr. Fox had occasionally emailed me from within my own account. I'm not sure if he did this on purpose or by accident, but either way he hadn't deleted those.

Each new bit of communication I recovered was another layer of validation. There he was, in writing, referencing the precise things that had elicited weird looks when I'd tried to explain them to my attorneys. For example, I'd told them how Mr. Fox convinced me we were always being watched, always monitored, and that the only time we weren't—the only time he could really be straight with me, he said—was when we were "in the box." To get *in the box* he had to do something out of my sight. Then he'd return and say, *Okay we're in the box now.* He claimed that whatever he had to do to get us in this supposed box depleted his energy. One time, he went into the bathroom for a few minutes, then came out, declared us to be in the box, and told me a bunch of things—lies, certainly. Later, I went into the bathroom, and there was blood in the sink.

I was so grateful to have found evidence of Mr. Fox writing about so many nutty things, including our talks "in the box." I also came across a few oblique references to another kind of abuse, one I tried not to think about. Over time, I'd grown so repulsed by Mr. Fox that I avoided physical contact. But he found ways to get what he wanted anyway. This was something I didn't want to remember. Yet at the same time, I wanted people to know, especially the people who seemed to think I'd *run off* with him. As if I'd *wanted* to be with him. As if I hadn't, in so many ways, been his prisoner.

Once I found our Gchats, it became even clearer.

CHAPTER THIRTY-FOUR

FALL 2016
NEW YORK CITY
COLLECTING EVIDENCE: GCHATS

I discovered the Gchats quite by accident, more than two months after my release on bail. By then, I'd managed to get an apartment of my own back in Manhattan.

During those early weeks at my sister's, I had no idea how to start a normal life. I couldn't stay with her forever. But where would I live? And how would I pay for anything? I needed some kind of job ASAP. Preferably a flexible one that didn't involve a lot of other humans.

Back in the city, back in the *real world*, there were people I thought I'd hear from but didn't, while at the same time a few unexpected past acquaintances came out of the woodwork offering help, sometimes people I'd not spoken to in many years. One friend from years back, someone I knew through Matthew Kenney, oddly, resurfaced and helped me. He asked his son to drive me to Rikers the day I had to go back to retrieve my driver's license and old clothes so I wouldn't have to go alone. And then, in an act of generosity that nearly made me cry, he bought me a brand-new MacBook. It was something I badly needed if I was going to rebuild and begin sorting out my life.

Another person who reached out to help me was, oddly enough, also someone I'd known through Matthew: Randy, the debt collector whom I'd befriended all those years back. He'd read about my arrest in the tabloids, found out how to contact me, and wanted to help.

We met for a drink one evening at Tao, a big, nightclubby restaurant in Midtown. Still mostly in the business of debt collecting, Randy offered me a part-time job consulting for his company—writing articles about the restaurant industry, conducting in-depth research for his clients, and handling other random projects. Yes, the irony that I was working for someone whose business included *debt collecting* was not lost on me. But the job was flexible. I could work mostly from home—wherever that might be—and with hours that allowed me time for my court appearances, to work on my case, and, crucially, it provided income I badly needed. I quickly agreed.

Maybe because these people had seen what had happened between Matthew and me, they could recognize more easily than most that I'd once again been royally screwed over by a man.

Another friend who reached out was Porochista—a journalist I'd met many years before, shortly after my split with Matthew. At the time, she was writing for *New York* magazine and had come to Pure Food and Wine to interview me for an article about our healthy sake cocktails. We sat at the bar and sampled the entire menu of sake cocktails. By the end of the interview, we were not only drunk but also good friends.

Porochista was now an acclaimed novelist and teacher. Around the time I took the job with Randy, she told me she'd be traveling to LA for the month of August and asked if I wanted to stay at her apartment in Harlem with Leon while she was away. She insisted Leon and I would love it there. My arm needed zero twisting. *Yes, please.*

* * *

When the time came, my father once again came to town to help—driving Leon, me, and our stuff from Brooklyn up to Harlem. Porochista's apartment was on 120th Street, on the first floor of a prewar building. The living room windows faced north, overlooking the south side of Marcus Garvey Park, which runs from 120th to 124th Streets, about two avenue blocks wide. As she'd mentioned, there was a dog park right there on the south side where I could take Leon.

The apartment was small, and the clutter made me a bit anxious, but it was quiet and cozy. Best of all were the living room walls—lined with row after row of books I looked forward to browsing and reading, especially since she had no TV. My father, ever practical, insisted we go food shopping. No matter what else was going on, he always made sure I had enough to eat. He also left me with a few loaves of his dark rye bread. After he left, I sat back on Porochista's red couch with Leon, closed my eyes, and exhaled.

I quickly fell in love with Harlem's uniquely relaxed vibe, palpably different from anywhere south in the city. People of all ages hung out on stoops, everyone seeming to know one another. Absent was the intolerable density and chaos of Midtown or the pretentiousness of other neighborhoods. Importantly, there was a vibe of not giving a fuck who you were, or what you did, or what you wore, or who you knew. No judgment. It felt welcoming and comfortable.

I worked at my job for Randy, occasionally trekking out to his office in New Jersey. I got to know people at the dog park. I felt at ease here and didn't want to think about having to leave.

One day, about midway through the month, I was out walking Leon and chatting on the phone with my sister when she asked, "So where do you think you'll go after Porochista's?"

Um, what? I thought I was going back to your house? is what I didn't say. I quickly processed the fact that I had no home and that my sister wasn't exactly inviting me back. Swallowing the sudden urge to cry, I said, "I don't know yet, I guess."

It's not that she wouldn't have taken me back, of course. But in not immediately offering it, I assumed it would be best if I found someplace else to go. I didn't want to go back to Bay Ridge, but still felt hurt—even while, rationally, I was aware I'd probably interpreted the conversation more hurtfully than it was intended. Pushing my feelings down, I hurried back to Porochista's.

For a long time, I'd daydreamed about getting *my own* place. Never mind that I had no savings, millions of dollars of debt, and only this random job. But now it felt crucial that I somehow figure it out.

I looked for studios and small one-bedrooms in the area. When I mentioned it to Randy, he agreed to help me out—offering to advance me funds, let me work more hours, whatever it took. By the end of the month, I'd found a place and jumped through the necessary hoops to secure it. Since my credit was ruined and I had no recent income history, my sister cosigned for me. And—boom—I had my own apartment. It had all come together fast. I was *so* happy to have my own place.

I'd decided I wanted something and, obstacles and all, figured out how to get it. It was refreshing to feel even a little proud of myself for a change. The apartment was almost a mirror image of Porochista's—ground floor, two living room windows facing the same park, a tiny kitchen in the middle, and a dark bedroom in the back—except mine was on 124th Street, on the north side of the park facing south.

One pesky issue: I had zero furniture. But I didn't care. Leon and I slept on the floor for the first few nights. Then my mother came down from New Hampshire with a truckload of old furniture, dishes, and pretty much everything I'd need. Her massive basement, packed with years' worth of accumulated stuff, essentially outfitted my entire place. My mom being a borderline hoarder came in handy. I don't judge—I'm the same way. I have a hard time getting rid of things too.

One thing she didn't have was an extra mattress, so my dad bought me one for my upcoming birthday. I filled out the rest of the place with random finds—a coffee table, a tiny kitchen table, a rug—sourced from Let Go, an app where people in your area sell or give away things for free.

I loved my new place. My life was still a shitshow, but at least I had my own home, my own space. Just Leon and me. That was progress.

And, importantly, I had space to think.

* * *

Having searched my email account using Mr. Fox's email, I knew our email history was gone. I'd assumed our Gchat history was, too, since chats usually appeared in search results. But for some reason, it had never occurred to me to check the actual chat box off to the side.

If you remember Gchat from back then, you might recall that Gmail had a chat box on the left side of the screen, listing your most recent conversations. Mr. Fox wasn't visible on my list, since a lot of people had tried reaching me that year, pushing old chats down the queue.

I was spending most of my time in my new email account, only dipping into the old one now and then for research. One weekend, I sat at my desk, news on the TV, Leon curled up on the couch, poking around the inbox of my former account, probably looking for something. Absent-mindedly, I scrolled down the chat list to see who else was there. And then I saw it. Mr. Fox's name—and his cartoonish fox icon. I clicked. The chat box popped up. And there they were—our actual conversations. My heart started pounding. I scrolled down and saw more. *Holy. Shit.* I had no idea how far back it went, but I felt like I'd just tapped into a geyser, liquid gold spraying everywhere, and I had to frantically secure it all before it might disappear.

I carefully enlarged the chat box, took a screenshot, scrolled back a little more, took another screenshot, and repeated this process for the next four hours. I wanted to preserve it all, and I didn't see a more efficient way to do it. Maybe there was a way to download the chats, but I didn't dare risk somehow clicking the wrong button and losing it all forever. I went through at least two more marathon sessions—scroll, screenshot, scroll, screenshot—each lasting six to eight hours. The problem was, the further back I scrolled, the slower it got, the pages taking longer and longer to load. Eventually, I reached as far back as 2013, but I finally stopped because it was crawling—each new page taking a few minutes to appear. Later, when I printed everything page by page, it used more than three full reams of paper.

I was bleary-eyed and zombie-like after this, but what I'd found felt crucial, not just for my criminal case but also for the book I knew I'd eventually write. More than that, it was important for me personally, in my attempt to understand this mess. There was so much I didn't remember, and now I had reams of conversations staring back at me. Just skimming through them was both helpful and disturbing. Reading my own words to Mr. Fox, I kept wondering what the fuck I'd been thinking at the time. My memory of it all was so fuzzy.

As if on cue, a few days later, a bunch of what I was thinking at that time in fact appeared. And it was in my own words, in my own handwriting: my journal.

CHAPTER THIRTY-FIVE

FALL 2016
NEW YORK CITY
COLLECTING EVIDENCE: MY JOURNAL

It was September 9, 2016—nearly four months after my arrest. I was walking Leon along Marcus Garvey Park when my attorney called. She'd just learned from the assistant DA that they had a copy of my journal from 2014. *My journal? What?*

Among the things recovered from Mr. Fox's belongings in Tennessee, they'd found an old journal of mine spanning 2014 into early 2015. This seemed weird because I had assumed it was long gone and had pretty much forgotten about it. Back in early 2015, while still in New York, Mr. Fox had walked into my bedroom one night and seen me writing in it. He'd grabbed it away, reprimanding me that I "shouldn't be writing any of this stuff down." I therefore assumed he tossed it down the garbage chute, burned it, or something. Why he didn't, I have no idea. Why it was among his things in the car, I also have no idea.

Finding out that the prosecutors had it was strange. Who knew what embarrassing stuff was in there? Sheila told me she hadn't read it yet but would forward me a PDF once it was scanned and delivered to her. Hearing someone say "I haven't read it yet" about your journal feels weird. I'm not a famous person, political figure, or groundbreaking scientist journaling my day-to-day musings for the benefit of future historians. My journals aren't full of pithy observations or articulately worded reflections on life, destined to be quoted and attributed to me for eternity. No. They're pages of scribbled rants, complaints, goofy reflections, angst over the stubborn three pounds I can't lose, and, in this case, expressions of hurt and confusion, along with sad efforts to keep my own spirits high.

The following day, I checked my email and saw one from Sheila with the PDF attachment: 149 pages of my journal. I opened it and immediately started scrolling. Since it was my own handwriting, it was quick work. I could fly through the abbreviations and nonsense dribble, slowing only for the parts that felt significant.

Tears started falling. So much of it felt important. I continued reading through a watery blur, waves of gratitude washing over me. It was September 10—my forty-fourth birthday—and, with my tendency toward mystical thinking apparently still intact, I felt like the timing was significant. Like I'd just been given the best birthday gift I could possibly imagine under the circumstances: my freedom.

It seemed to me that this journal proved I had zero criminal intent. Reading my own words, I felt waves of empathy for the *me* back then who had written them, and sad for what I'd gone through. I also felt immense relief, certain that now, *finally*, the prosecutors would rethink the charges. Or at least offer me just probation and focus their efforts on Mr. Fox instead.

The journal only reinforced what I'd told my attorneys. It was validation. There wasn't a hint of malicious intent. It showed that I was afraid, angry, and confused by Mr. Fox. That I was worried about my business and employees. That I had ambitions to expand and grow. Notably absent was any excitement over fancy things, or longing for a new Rolex. There were no grand plans about conning people. And no kind words about Mr. Fox, other than occasionally writing that he'd been nice to me, which stood out among the more frequent laments about his being awful to me.

The journal starts on January 1, 2014, and ends three months into 2015. I wrote in spurts, sometimes abandoning it for weeks at a time. So much happened during 2014 that writing in a journal wasn't something I always had time for. But I felt wildly grateful for its existence. I figured there was simply no way anyone could read its contents and conclude that I had nefarious intentions. That I was, in any way, a criminal.

I had told Sheila—in a moment where I was particularly glad to have a female attorney—about the unwanted sexual things Mr. Fox had subjected me to. I had no doubt that she believed me, and I'd found some corroboration in texts and Gchats. But I found more in the journal, in the final entry, where I obliquely referred to what Mr. Fox had been doing. Reading it makes me feel an out-of-body sympathy for myself, something I'm not used to feeling.

On March 30, 2015, I wrote:

> The day to day here. It's what I can't take. Asshole torture non-stop at "home" will be what would kill me. Don't know what to do except keep going. Can't talk w/ anyone. Like no one. Ever. So. How to deal. It is a nightmare. Makes me feel for people who are kidnapped like that girl in the shed, or the ones in Ohio. Different kind of locked in. But the gross stuff. How does it not kill your spirit?

Did the assistant DA prosecuting my case read all this and conclude that perhaps I was not a depraved criminal and that they should instead focus their prosecutorial efforts on Mr. Fox? No. I'd been wrong. My journal didn't move the needle at all. The prosecution continued to pursue the same sentences for Mr. Fox and me, as if we should be punished alike for all that happened. The offer put forth by them in exchange for a guilty plea was one to three years in jail. For *both* of us. At least they agreed to drop the threats of charging my mother.

I also eventually recovered a recording of a call with Mr. Fox—another miracle gift. If nothing else, all this source material was crucial in helping me piece together what happened—to the best of my ability—for my own understanding, and for this book.

Sometimes I wonder what this would all be like if I'd been unable to access any of this correspondence. That's not a hypothetical I like to think about for long because it scares me.

I also wonder what this would be like if I'd been able to access *all* our correspondence. Or better yet, if every in-person conversation had somehow been recorded and preserved—if a fly on the wall happened to be a stenographer, its tiny fly limbs typing away furiously—since those were the times he said the weirdest things. I can only remember what he told me generally, if at all. Or else tiny snippets. Sometimes entire conversations and episodes are gone from my memory, only to peek through the surface after stumbling on a new clue.

But here is what I have—here is my story.

PART FOUR

MR. FOX

"Psychopaths tend to make exceptionally good eye contact. Whatever the motive behind it, there can be tremendous power in an unwavering gaze."
—SAM HARRIS, *WAKING UP*

CHAPTER THIRTY-SIX

ON BELIEVING

The story that follows may seem strange—or at times, absurd. It felt that way to me, even as I was living it. You may feel frustrated that I didn't see what now seems so obvious in hindsight: that I was being fed a delusion. I hope that by my sharing what I can remember—through journal entries, Gchats, and my own reflections—you'll better understand how it *could* happen. How the presence of someone like Mr. Fox in my life could, over time, lead to its complete unraveling.

***

I've been struggling, a *lot*, in trying to answer for myself—and for you, and for anyone who asks—the question of *how the fuck did I believe him?*

Mr. Fox didn't come at me with the loony tunes stories right out of the gate. The weirder ones only surfaced once I was financially tethered to him—after I had "loaned" him money and wanted it back. Early on, he'd hinted at his vast resources, planting the expectation and letting it take root. From there, the lies grew in scale and audacity. By the time the crazier ones came, I was already ensnared, my leg tangled in the creeping, sinister vines of his fiction.

But still. His lies were so absurd, so patently bullshit.

Derren Brown is a successful "psychological illusionist" who started out as a hypnotist and magician. I suppose he's now a combination of all those things, with Netflix specials, books, and a ton of content on YouTube. He's been interviewed on the podcasts of Sam Harris, Tim Ferriss, and Joe Rogan. I've listened to them all because I'm fascinated by how he's able to create illusions and impact people's behavior. In a 2018 conversation with Joe Rogan on *The Joe Rogan Experience* podcast, Brown offers one explanation for people's gullibility in situations where, to some, the lie might be obvious. He said, "The lie is so ugly that it's so much easier to believe something amazing must be going on there than just... is it just *that* ugly and pathetic a lie?"[1]

I'm aware of concepts like denial and dissociation. I've studied *coercive control* and have consumed a lot of material on cults and cult psychology. But there's something still so batshit crazy about how I went along with Mr. Fox for so long, until I was yanked away from him in handcuffs. I'm pretty sure I'm not batshit crazy, so what was it?

When he wasn't around, it was easier for me to resist him or push back—something you'll likely notice in the forthcoming Gchats. But everything was different in his presence. As if his physical proximity emitted some fucked-up radio signal that jammed my radar for bullshit. It stopped working when he was around, or he could override it. How did he do this? Did Mr. Fox have some hypnotic power over me?

It seemed like he did, because when I think of the things he told me to do (and how awful some of them were), I can't think of why else I would have done them. Every time, I told myself I'd never do it again. Yet every time, I did.

I don't have the time, space, or qualifications to attempt to parse out the mechanics of what may have been happening, from a mind-games perspective, or the psychology of it all. But I had a history of avoiding confrontation, plus a lifelong capacity for denial, which likely made Mr. Fox's work easier.

"You suppress all of the things that don't compute with the narrative and the ideal of what you want to believe," cult expert Steve Hassan said in a 2019 interview on *The Jordan Harbinger Show*.[2] I must have been doing exactly that:

---

1   Joe Rogan, host, *The Joe Rogan Experience*, podcast, "1198—Derren Brown," Spotify Studios, November 9, 2018, https://open.spotify.com/episode/4WelHDHIWoOx7fObfvroQZ.

2   Jordan Harbinger, *The Jordan Harbinger Show*, "237: Steven Hassan | Combating Cult Mind Control Part One," produced by Bob Fogarty, August 13, 2019, https://podcasts.apple.com/ca/podcast/237-steven-hassan-combating-cult-mind-control-part-one/id1344999619?i=1000446779255.

shoving away each new piece of evidence that corroborated the very real fact that I was being massively hoodwinked.

Part of how magicians succeed in amazing us involves this same unconscious tendency—to edit out the parts that contradict what we're being asked to believe. We *want* to be amazed. Another tactic that aids in successful mindfuckery (whether for entertainment or malice) is jumbling the mind with too much information, especially when loaded with contradictions. It leaves the target confused and, as a result, more suggestible. Mr. Fox did this to me a lot. Arguing with him was nearly impossible, because when I called out something he'd done or said before, he confidently denied it—and then I questioned myself, since I was disoriented and couldn't be sure.

* * *

But the lies early on? The truly ridiculous ones? Why did I allow them? Was I just unable to fathom that someone would actually tell such lies?

Part of Mr. Fox's game was to craft a facade of legitimacy. With me, he used Alec, via Twitter, to legitimize himself. I assume he later used being my husband to do the same to whoever else he was conning. They'd look at my public bio and think, *Well, she wouldn't have married him if he wasn't really this uber-wealthy and powerful guy like he says, so… I guess he's legit.*

Another factor was confidence. For the illusionist or magician to be successful, they need to exude absolute confidence. (The terms "con" and "con man" are abbreviated from "confidence game" and "confidence man.") Magicians practice for years and years to get good at what they do. Their deception is rehearsed, tweaked, perfected. The most successful lies are the ones the liars truly believe—or if they don't, they make it seem as if they do.

Mr. Fox had no shortage of confidence. He was always so sure of himself. I, on the other hand, was often full of self-doubt. Mr. Fox could be impressively charming and had a formidable presence—a sort of magnetic energy—which likely attracted some while repelling others. Despite being eight years younger than me, he carried himself as if he were older and wiser, as if he knew the secrets of the world. He acted like he was here to teach me—as if he was the authority and I was his subject. He even used expressions that only older people used or referred to simpler times—decades or even centuries earlier—implying he'd lived through them himself.

In fact, later, that was what he outright claimed.

He behaved as though he had everything figured out—including life itself. It wasn't just with me; he did it on Twitter, too, posting declarative judgments that subtly (or not so subtly) implied he possessed some kind of worldly insider knowledge. He never expressed worry about anything. He acted as if he *knew* that everything would be fine, that he had it all under control. And not just figuratively under control but as if he were *literally* controlling things.

Which made me feel as if he was.

Mr. Fox was skilled at deflection, and he always had an excuse—for everything. If I pointed out his previous lies, like those around his identity, he would lock eyes with me, pause for a few beats, and then, with a theatrical level of gravitas, say, "Sarm, there are times when the ends really do justify the means." He'd remind me that everything he was doing was *for me*—to give me what I'd always wanted. And since what I wanted involved improving the world for animals, humans, the environment... well, that just made the "ends" he was justifying that much nobler.

Later, when I ran out of money and he began pushing me to solicit money from others—again, no gun to my head, so yes, I did it, and I'm responsible—he repeated some variation of *the ends justify the means*. He assured me that the people who came through with money would get it all back and then some. If they were good people, he said, he would ensure that their lives would be safe and happy ever after, their children protected, and so on. Once this was all over, none of my current discomfort would matter. He reminded me that none of this was *real* anyway, yet at the same time insist that I was put on this earth to do great things—to save people and animals. All the pain was just part of the journey. I was being tested, and *then* I would be empowered. That was what he said.

All of that sounds ridiculous. I know.

Yet I could never figure out an alternative narrative that made sense.

Over time, I rationalized his lies. Consciously or subconsciously, I made them part of who he was. I knew his stories—at least many of them—were lies, but somehow it became a given that his identity included his *knowing that I knew that he knew that I knew he was lying* (follow that?). As if it was part of the overall game he played, in which I was his chosen participant. He relied on my belief in him overall, in the greater purpose he insisted was his ultimate goal. This greater purpose involved my being *special* and led to a forthcoming fabulous future—so yes, I wanted to believe that.

Mr. Fox strung me along by promising to take away all my grief and angst and frustrations and give me everything I could ever want, including everlasting youth. He acted so sure of himself, making me feel like I was destined to do big things. If these were all lies, they weren't just ugly—they were grotesquely and elaborately cruel. It felt like too much. He couldn't possibly be lying about *everything*. No one could be that deliberately and methodically evil, right?

As Derren Brown said, "It's so much easier to believe something amazing must be going on."

CHAPTER THIRTY-SEVEN

2012

NEW YORK CITY

The summer of 2012 was a good one for the restaurant, with cash flow higher than it had ever been. Revenue was massively season dependent, as the outdoor seating nearly doubled our capacity.

On a day when our balances were at their peak, I took a screenshot from my laptop showing the combined total across all the company bank accounts—over $600,000. I was astonished. We had never been so flush with cash.

My scheduled repayments on the debt I owed Jeffrey Chodorow after purchasing the restaurant were relatively informal, with the first few years being mostly interest free. Since he'd let me fall behind on monthly payments (at $10,000–$20,000 per month) during harder times, I now wrote him a check for $100,000 toward the balance. I was so excited to make this payment that I delivered it to his office in person. Soon thereafter, I wrote him another check for $50,000. I felt proud of myself, and I wanted him to be proud of me too. I didn't want to disappoint him.

* * *

With extra capital on hand, I finally set about finding a proper space for the growing e-commerce side of the business and, critically, the production of the packaged snacks. We had more than outgrown the restaurant's pastry kitchen, which was bursting at the seams with product we had no room to store. I found a 4,000-square-foot space in an industrial building in Brooklyn and started lease negotiations. By the end of the summer, we were moved in and producing our line of packaged goods there.

We had figured out ways to transport products and ingredients between Brooklyn and the Manhattan locations, but not having a car was inconvenient—especially for bigger runs or just to get to Brooklyn myself, since I liked taking Leon with me. So I bought a car: a pre-owned 2004 silver Honda CR-V.

A friend had asked, "Why not buy a nice car?" suggesting I spend some money on myself. But I didn't want a fancy car—I wanted it to be practical. Also, I planned to park it in the garage directly across the street from my Twenty-First Street home and office, and that was expensive. My used Honda was by far the crappiest car in that garage, but I loved it. More and more I thought of it as Leon's car, as it quickly filled up with his toys and cast-off dog hairs.

Looking back now, I can see that so many things were going my way that summer. If only Mr. Fox had not been there. This would have been the summer when I'd *maybe, finally,* have felt confident enough to really tackle the issue of finding the right partner/investor. Strong sales, combined with having just funded a significant expansion from existing cash flow, put me in a position to be discerning. I could have met prospective partners while projecting a vibe of confidence.

Had I done this, had Mr. Fox not been in the picture and I'd kept growing and expanding, would there today be a Pure Food and Wine in Tokyo, Moscow, and Los Angeles? Would One Lucky Duck Juice and Takeaway locations be spread across the country, our snacks made in vast quantities, delivered across the globe? One Lucky Duck might have, by now, become a widely known brand. Would we be sponsoring snowboarders at the winter X Games? Would I have achieved all the other things I wanted to accomplish, including being listed as one of *Fortune* magazine's top 100 companies to work for and assigning equity in the company to those who'd worked there for many years? Would they be getting rich the way original employees of Apple who held onto their shares did?

Would Eloy, the porter, have been able to retire? Would Chelsey, the bookkeeper, have paid off all her NYU student debt?

These were my dreams and aspirations. I wanted to grow at the right pace and in the right way so that the brand—a righteous and cool brand that people loved and loved working for—would last forever. Or at least outlast me.

Yet there was Mr. Fox.

And there I was: a plump and distracted duck, no protective fences around.

* * *

Since that first time Mr. Fox borrowed money from me, he only ever broke his promises to repay it, while somehow *borrowing* still more. With the business thriving and growing, and everything I had going for me, why didn't I cut my losses and finally kick this fat grifter to the curb? Shouldn't I have realized I was kind of a badass, having steered the company through a recession and into growth, without a partner or much extra capital? Why didn't I have the confidence to see that, despite being exhausted, I could keep going on my own—and be discerning, selective, and careful about who I let into my life and business? Was I just too overwhelmed?

I still longed for relief and freedom. I still carried personal debts, even after the Chapter 7 bankruptcy I filed after separating from Matthew (the settlement of which required me to pay $1,000 per month for five years), and I had old interest-collecting tax bills. I never took more than my usual salary—even with the company's strong cash flow—to pay off my personal debts. Growing the company was my priority, and I was full of ambition to do that, feeling in my gut just how impactful it could be.

Around 2010, I'd also begun working on a hotel project. Yes, on top of everything else. All the things I was juggling felt like full-time jobs in themselves. Fantasies of cloning myself regularly filled my mind. One Sarma clone would take a *very* long spa vacation, then go to the gym daily, get facials, do Pilates, and get my hair done so that I could properly represent our healthy living brand. That clone would do nothing but interact with customers, pose for press photos, and give interviews. Another clone would focus on business strategy, including evaluating potential partners or deals and creating financial projection models.

A third would manage the existing business with its never-ending employee issues and operational challenges. And a fourth would focus on the creative side: the branding, new product development, website content, and new cookbooks. Maybe one more to clean my apartment, do my laundry, and keep me organized. If only I had the resources to get all this done, and expand the business on my own terms.

But I had no clones, only myself. And these fantasies made me vulnerable.

* * *

One weekend, Mr. Fox told me he needed to come see me—he had something important to tell me. Probably he also claimed he was bringing some money to repay me. Well, okay. Fine.

We sat on my couch. It was daytime, but the apartment was dark. He took a bunch of deep breaths. Then he told me—just as he had before—that he could fix everything. But now, there was more. Things had changed. He said he could wipe out all my old debts, and then some. A windfall was what he meant. I wouldn't just be free; I'd have more money than I could imagine. I could expand my business, build anything I wanted, exactly how I wanted. I'd never have to grovel, never have to carry the shame of debt. I'd be empowered to build and create on my own terms. I'd be independent.

He knew this was what I'd long fantasized.

The only catch was, once it was complete, he'd have to disappear and never see me again, and he couldn't tell me why. He said all this with determined seriousness, looking distressed.

Part of me thought, *What? You can give me a fortune, but then you have to disappear? Are we in a movie or something?* But he was so serious about it, staring at me so intensely, it was hard to believe he could be lying. Meanwhile, I imagined what he described and what it would feel like.

It all felt very strange. Like a *fantasy*. I got emotional. If indeed he was serious, then the fact that someone would do this *for me* was rather heavy. It made me feel humbled, and special. Contemplating the wave of relief that would wash over me if he was serious, I started to cry. How could he not be serious?

Every problem in my life, including the one of Mr. Fox himself, would be solved.

His eyes told me he was serious. Yet who makes that kind of offer? Other than *in the movies.*

My insecurities questioned it. Was I really worthy? I rarely felt entitled to anything. I was the kind of person who hesitated to push the crosswalk button, fearing I'd inconvenience the drivers, making them thirty seconds later to wherever they were going. As if they'd look at me and think, *Who does she think she is? Making us all stop just so she can leisurely cross?* I never wanted to seem selfish or like I deserved special treatment. Which is why, more often than not, I just waited for the lull and darted across when I could.

But now, I felt special. I allowed myself to picture how it would feel to never have to rely on anyone else ever again. No men would treat me disrespectfully again. If they did, I could walk away. I wouldn't even have to bother with any wrath because they'd not be worth it. Lawyers, landlords, potential business partners—I'd been on the receiving end of a lot of creepy behavior, all of which I'd mostly had to tolerate because I didn't feel empowered. I visualized how, with ample resources, I could be the benevolent leader. I could steer the ship comfortably and confidently. I could overpay my good staff who deserved it and take excellent care of them. I could do so many good things.

Mr. Fox understood what I wanted, which was probably why he emphasized this freedom and empowerment as coming with no apparent strings. No obligation, no commitment to him, or anyone. His offer seemed so implausible and yet... *how* could he be lying? I mean, who would do that to someone? Knowing what I'd been through before, with Matthew and otherwise, what my business meant to me, how hard I'd worked for so long? The level of twisted cruelty required to fake an offer like that was simply unfathomable.

Mr. Fox left shortly after this discussion, and as usual, I didn't know where he was going. But he must have known that leaving me to marinate in this fantasy ensured I'd now easily allow him to return.

CHAPTER THIRTY-EIGHT

2012
NEW YORK CITY

One day I received an email from someone named Will Richards. Mr. Fox had told me to expect an email from an associate of his—an IT expert and computer genius, someone he'd worked with for a long time who was in an undisclosed location somewhere far away, on the other side of the globe. This man, Will Richards, I was told, would help secure my email and digital accounts from hackers. He would also *keep me safe.* From what? Apparently from the nebulous danger to which Mr. Fox alluded with increasing frequency.

I engaged with Will Richards. His emails tended to be formally worded and always contained a random six-digit number at the end, which I was to repeat at the start of my replies—an added layer of security. All of this had an air of spy-world mystery to it, as if I was now under the protection of a secret agency, of which Mr. Fox was an operative. Because Mr. Fox had somehow convinced me I'd been hacked, I dutifully gave Will my passwords.

* * *

Around this time, Mr. Fox had begun ramping up the covert agent theme of his narrative, which also conveniently explained his real vs. fake identity. He continued the story of his vast wealth, somewhere overseas, which, for some reason, he could never access. He was always *working on it.* At one point he asked me to look into the potential tax consequences of his transferring $5 million to me—just as a start, he casually said. I called my then-accountant about it. I remember my accountant saying jokingly, "Well, maybe you could just marry him?"

Meanwhile, Mr. Fox needed another $10,000 or so now and then. But I'm also pretty sure there was a stretch of weeks or more when he didn't ask me for money, and during that time, his air of legitimacy grew.

Late during the summer of 2012, he instructed me to look for a new home, to get me out of my dark office-apartment and into my own huge place that he/we would buy. The price didn't matter, he said. So I started looking. I got the Sunday *New York Times* with its color real estate inserts advertising expensive Manhattan homes and looked online. While browsing, I imagined living in these amazing spaces. Unless you already live in your dream home, it can be intoxicating to slide into fantasyland, visualizing yourself in a fabulous multimillion-dollar home. Imagine someone telling you that you *can* and *will* live in one of these homes—all you need to do is pick out the one you want. As if you knew you were about to win the lottery. That's how it felt.

I found a five-story townhouse on Fifteenth Street, just off Irving Place, two blocks from the restaurant. Having undergone a gut renovation, it was stunning. Importantly, it fit my main criteria of being as close as possible to the restaurant. At 8,500 square feet, it was far grander than anything I'd ever before imagined as a home for myself. And apparently, it could be mine. If you'd stopped me in that moment and pressed me on whether I believed Mr. Fox, what would I have said? I must have *wanted* to believe him, so I did, while also figuring that he wouldn't have us take these steps if we weren't going to actually buy it. Who would do that?

We got to know the broker representing the Fifteenth Street home, a genuinely nice guy. Almost instantly, Mr. Fox seemed to cast a spell on him—this seasoned real estate agent accustomed to working with high-net-worth individuals. He convinced the broker we would be his biggest clients of all time. Mr. Fox positioned himself as every broker's dream: a multibillionaire who'd rain down commissions as we bought building after building. The broker would never have to hustle and grind again with this whale of a client. (In hindsight, it was like a fast-tracked version of the spell cast on me.)

Mr. Fox was so successful at this charade that, in the following weeks, the broker behaved like a puppy, one who cheerfully came running to us the moment Mr. Fox called or texted. I can't blame him. Mr. Fox could be very charming when he wanted to be.

In another odd twist, the broker happened to have also represented Alec Baldwin when Alec bought his downtown apartment just one year earlier. Was this another sign? More than just a coincidence?

Mr. Fox told me that he showed the broker something on his computer, an account or other records, to verify his wealth—that he was legit. Why couldn't he show the same to me? *Don't worry, baby. It's better you don't know. It doesn't matter.* Um, okay. I must have figured if this fancy broker was cool with it, and was now spending loads of his valuable time with us, then we must have been *actually* about to get this amazing townhouse.

* * *

The stories kept building. Once Mr. Fox's mysterious overseas billions came into the country, we'd need a place to park it. The broker set up a meeting for us with private bankers at Barclays. *Barclays!* Mr. Fox concocted a story that somehow legitimized his imminent access to vast wealth yet also excused his lack of general financial prowess. As if he was inheriting the money. I'm not sure what he told the broker. Who knows. Anyway, for the Barclays meeting, Mr. Fox wore a fancy Rolex (whether real or fake I don't know), expensive shoes and jeans, and an XXL button-down in a slimming navy blue—one he wore more often than not. At the very least, he somewhat looked the part.

When we arrived at Barclays, if there wasn't an actual red carpet, it felt as if there was. We were received like VIPs and escorted to a large and elegant conference room, where we were met by two representatives of the bank. Mr. Fox charmed them, too, while we discussed things like asset allocation, risk management, estate planning, and so on. I was nervous, but then it wasn't like there was anything wrong, was there? It all just felt so... *weird*. And surreal.

After this meeting, we were set up to meet with Barbara Corcoran's personal accountant, which somehow went well enough that we were later told Barbara Corcoran herself wanted to meet us. *Barbara Corcoran!* The short-haired blond lady who was a regular shark on early versions of *Shark Tank*. Everyone wanted to meet the fabulous Mr. Fox, it seemed. The Barbara Corcoran meeting never happened, but I found it validating that the broker had spoken to her about Mr. Fox. Again, more legitimacy to bolster my fantasy.

Of course, Mr. Fox leveraged this validation to get more money from me. After all, he implied, it was no big deal, since all this wealth was about to come through.

* * *

I had a good experience with the real estate attorney I'd used for my Brooklyn space, and I hired him to begin contract negotiations for the Fifteenth Street townhouse. Things were moving along smoothly, and the broker was getting ready to introduce us to an interior design consultant. Then, the seller wanted to verify funds before accepting the offer, and—surprise, surprise—this slowed and then halted the process. At first, Mr. Fox claimed delays. Then another week passed. And another. I grew increasingly embarrassed, then queasy, having to make excuses that I didn't even understand. Of course, the deal never moved forward. I paid the three-thousand-dollar bill for the legal services for the townhouse we never bought.

What was Mr. Fox's excuse? I don't know. Just that it was delayed. He was working on it. "Don't worry," he said. "We just have to wait." Again, a rational person would assume that this purchase falling through would have been proof enough. That I'd have stopped believing Mr. Fox. I was upset and angry at him, but for some reason, I didn't back away.

* * *

Keeping me focused on what I *wanted* was part of his manipulation. Having me repeatedly tour the Fifteenth Street townhouse, making me believe we were going to buy it, put me in a dreamy sort of state.

He also told me to list out all my business goals, big and small. I found one such list in a recovered computer file. It included repaying company loans, expanding the juice bar, leasing additional space in Brooklyn, and hiring more people, as well as more ambitious goals like purchasing the building that housed the restaurant, along with my mother's property in New Hampshire so she'd no longer have to worry about having to sell it to an outsider.

The list went on, with even bigger business-expansion ideas. He made me believe that anything and everything I wanted to do was within reach.

The more time I spent in that dreamland, the more I detached from reality.

* * *

It made no sense to me that someone would have me map out my biggest dreams and tell me I could achieve them all, yet be bullshitting. Why would anyone do that?

CHAPTER THIRTY-NINE

LATE 2012
NEW YORK CITY

The dynamic that Mr. Fox cultivated between us was as though he'd arrived in my life to guide me. Like he was my Obi-Wan. He acted as though he knew everything, that he'd lived many lifetimes and could channel them all. He engaged with me as a therapist would, analyzing my past and addressing what he claimed were old wounds. He offered me life advice—the way a grandparent, teacher, or coach might—sometimes specific to me and sometimes generalized aphorisms.

He lectured me about seeking outside validation. He said things like, "When you finally wake up, you won't care what anyone else thinks of you." And I'd think, *What does that mean... wake up?* If I asked him, he just told me I'd know when it happened.

He criticized my tendency to share way too much with people, to trust too quickly. I mean, this was true—I've always trusted too easily, assuming people are generally good, and I'd been repeatedly burned for it. He pointed out, with some bitterness, that I had a dysfunctional need for attention and admiration, specifically from men. That was also probably true, and not that uncommon. Yet these were the very psychological hangups he was exploiting—ones that left me unequipped to protect myself from someone *exactly like him.* The weaknesses he pointed out helped pave the way for him to burrow himself into my life, to make me dependent on him, and oddly attached.

Other times he bolstered my confidence, and not superficially but in ways that in fact meant a lot to me. One day as I worked on my laptop and he sat idly nearby, he said, out of the blue, "Hey, let me ask you something."

I looked up at him.

"Is there any raw vegan restaurant better than yours in the country?"

I thought for a few seconds. "Well, *no*," I told him. "I mean, I think we're considered the best."

This was, I believe, true. There'd been an upscale raw vegan restaurant in Northern California opened by a formally trained chef, but that had closed before Pure Food and Wine opened. There were no other places like us at the time.

He then asked, "What other raw vegan restaurants are out there? I mean, in other countries? Are there any that are *better* than, or even as good as, your restaurant?"

I thought about it. At the time there were plenty of small raw vegan cafes around the world, but if there was another restaurant like ours, I'd have known about it. So I told him no, I didn't think there were any as good or better anywhere in the world.

"Well, you see," he said, "that's pretty interesting. There's *no* other place as good as or better than yours in the world. You get what that means? *YOU* are the best in the world at something. Like a champion."

I considered this.

He continued, "How many people out there can say they're the best in the world at something?"

This thought had never occurred to me. I mean, obviously it wasn't as straightforward or measurable as being an undefeated boxing champion, or a chess champion beaten by no one ever, or the fastest sprinter, swimmer, or highest jumper, or whatever. But still. It was interesting to consider.

"You see, that's rare," he said. "Think about that. Think about how special that is. You're the very best in the world at something. You got a lot to be proud of there, kid."

Proud of myself? I knew I could hardly take all the credit, but sitting there thinking about it actually felt pretty good. I never thought of the restaurant as something I created alone; Matthew was there at the start, so at first it was our collaboration, and I always pushed the credit for what we did, particularly the food, to the indispensable staff. Yet I *could* claim as my own accomplishment my skills as a curator—recognizing, bringing in, and grooming the right talent, along with enabling creativity, directing output, and keeping our standards high—serving as the orchestra conductor rather than playing any of the instruments.

Wherever the credit was due, I liked this new feeling of being the best in the world at something. It made me feel accomplished and important.

He also knew I didn't like to rely on others, which was why he'd offered me that particular fantasy of his bestowing a fortune upon me and then disappearing. And making me feel like he was doing it because I was worthy, not because he wanted something from me, or to be with me. With that fantasy implanted in my brain, he then managed a way to get me even more tightly strapped in on this strange ride:

He persuaded me to get married.

* * *

He didn't get down on one knee or present me with an engagement ring. Rather, he just convinced me.

He claimed that marrying him would make everything easier *for me*—transferring money to me, keeping me "protected," somehow conferring upon me the extra-important status as the wife of whatever he was. I protested at first, but as usual, he wore me down, badgering me that it was just part of the process, almost necessary. My acceptance also wasn't the way it usually happens. It wasn't a teary-eyed jubilant "Yes!" Instead it was an angry, "Fine! Fine, we'll get married. What*ever.* Ugh."

The actual marriage happened quickly; he must have figured we'd better do it fast before I came to my senses. We went to City Hall and got a marriage license. I was embarrassed. I remember seeing other couples looking excited, exhilarated, happy. Here I was, queasy and embarrassed.

License in hand, I managed to find someone who would officiate on very short notice. For some reason, during the short ceremony, I started feeling like this might be kind of momentous after all—even a bit romantic. Some part of me must have believed Mr. Fox, that somehow this was all destined. Maybe I also wondered if fairy tales were true and that, by the end of this ceremony, he might magically turn from frog to prince.

I wore a white knit sweater dress—it was all I had in my closet that was white and appropriate for November. It came to just above my knees, with a deep V-neck, form fitting but not tight. I wore black opaque tights and black boots. And, because it was raining that day, a raincoat. We were married standing under umbrellas in Tompkins Square Park in Manhattan's East Village, which I chose because it was near where the officiant lived and not that far away from us.

She read something I'd not heard before. I'd told her to read or say whatever she wanted because *who cares*. Turns out it was beautiful, and it made me feel sappy. I was also overwhelmed that we were actually doing this. Mr. Fox and I held hands. He wore his dark-blue button-down shirt under a black raincoat. There was no witness. The officiant agreed to just forge an additional signature. How appropriate.

It all happened so fast. It was done. I was married to Mr. Fox.

We then did what every couple does immediately after getting married: went to the movies. It was the afternoon, and we were close to a theater on Twelfth Street. We saw *Argo*, starring Ben Affleck. Then we went to an early dinner at a small nearby farm-to-table restaurant called Northern Spy, which I really liked and sadly no longer exists. I remember that the dish I ordered was made with farro, a grain not typical on menus.

It's not lost on me that I can recall small inconsequential details yet have forgotten huge swaths of important information from this period. I have zero clue what we talked about but remember that, as we sat there having dinner, "Marry Song" by Band of Horses began playing. It's a beautiful song and I pointed it out to Mr. Fox. It was just a random coincidence, though became yet another incident that Mr. Fox then leveraged to bolster his consistent posture of *See? This is all destined.* As if he'd somehow magically made the song play.

Although we were now officially married, not a whole lot changed right away. He didn't move in with me—that was still off the table. It was just business as usual afterward, and he continued to come and go sporadically. After all, love and companionship were not the point. There must have been some other point, but exactly what it was I'd be hard pressed to explain.

We'd agreed to not tell anyone. I certainly *didn't want* to tell anyone. How would I explain why I'd married him? Because I was so happy with him? No. Because he twisted my arm? Yes! How romantic.

I can't recall ever feeling physically attracted to Mr. Fox, except before I met him, when I'd mentally built him up into who I *wanted* him to be. But the actual in-person Mr. Fox? Not so much. His physicality was tolerable, at first. But over time I was increasingly turned off by him. He had stubby fingers and bitten-down nails, and a protruding brown mole on the back of his neck repulsed me. And he was (let's just face it) *fat*. And kept getting fatter.

In the early days, Mr. Fox was more like a defensive football player—big and solid, albeit with extra padding. Over time, though, he kept adding to the padding. He never once took his shirt off in front of me. We didn't discuss it. Later, I pointed to his increasing fatness when hurling vitriolic insults at him, but he genuinely didn't care. He'd claim he was getting fatter *on purpose*.

He also always maintained that he would become someone different one day—someone appealing. I would finally see the real him. He liked to remind me that he was getting his abs back (as if he'd once had washboard abs). He actually made it seem like he'd just show up one day looking *totally* different, maybe like Chris Hemsworth, with whom he seemed oddly obsessed.

Still, he carried himself with authority and self-importance. Somehow this made his praise of me feel more meaningful than it should have. As if the approval he bestowed on me was a validation of my worth. He told me I was beautiful in sweats and a T-shirt, with no makeup on. He told me I'd be beautiful "rolled in shit and dipped in breadcrumbs."

Normally, I felt insecure about my own physicality. I worried my stomach wasn't flat enough, I was too pale. My boobs were too small. And who knows what else was wrong with me. I was never comfortable prancing around in public in a bikini, much less getting naked in front of someone. But around Mr. Fox, I didn't care about these things. I didn't care what he thought about the particulars of my body, which was kind of a relief.

He must have sensed this and used subtle means to cut me down, even while giving me compliments. He regularly brought up my age, as if to remind me that however good he told me I looked, it wouldn't last. Tick tock.

On the flip side of all his seriousness, Mr. Fox could be very funny. He had a way of disarming me when I got anxious, by making me laugh. If I was annoyed or angry at him, he made jokes. Somehow things seemed less scary if he was acting goofy.

Meanwhile, he never seemed anxious. Normal people would likely exude some degree of perceptible anxiety if they were pulling off a massive con. But he was mostly relaxed, as if he knew everything would be fine. And he could be incredibly charming—the way he charmed my mother the first time they met.

* * *

I decided to finally introduce Mr. Fox to part of my family (though I wasn't ready to reveal that we'd just gotten married). It was Thanksgiving, and I brought him to dinner at the loft in Brooklyn where my sister lived with her then-boyfriend (now husband). My mother was there, so it was just the five of us, plus Leon.

More than likely I had something to drink before we went—I was nervous to introduce him to everyone. Mr. Fox was not nearly as heavy as he eventually became, but still large. I knew they'd be surprised by this. He was practically the polar opposite of Tobyn, whom they'd adored.

Anyway, it hardly mattered—Mr. Fox was totally charming. The lights were very dim at my sister's, with candles everywhere, and—as we tend to do at my family's gatherings—we drank *a lot* of wine. I don't remember the conversation, but I do remember my mom laughing—a lot. Mr. Fox was *on* that night, telling stories, being quick-witted and funny. He was laying it on thick with my mom. At one point, I remember her turning to him and saying, "I love you already!"

After dinner, Mr. Fox and I Ubered back to my restaurant for the staff late-night Thanksgiving. This was an annual tradition at the restaurant since opening; after Thanksgiving service for customers, we shoved all the tables in the dining room together to make one big family table, and the staff brought various homemade vegan dishes.

Our staff Thanksgiving dinners had always been incredibly special, but this one wasn't right. It felt off for me because Mr. Fox was there. I'm sure everyone else felt it too. I think most of the employees, especially the ones who knew me best, didn't like Mr. Fox and saw through his bullshit. Or at the very least, they noticed the contrast with Tobyn, who'd so easily felt like a natural part of the family. Around Tobyn, I was always relaxed, happy, and openly in love. I was very different with Mr. Fox.

A month later, I brought him to my mother's for Christmas. This also didn't feel right. This time, there was palpable tension between Mr. Fox and my sister's husband-to-be, who seemed intuitively suspicious of this new man in my life with an overbearing personality. Christmas was different from the one-night, candlelit, wine-fueled Thanksgiving dinner. It was a couple of days with lots of daylight to allow my sister and her husband to get a clear and sober look at Mr. Fox. Like my employee family, they also saw the contrast between how I appeared now with this big, brash lug (uneasy) and how I was with Tobyn (at ease).

I still hadn't told anyone that Mr. Fox and I had married—I don't know how I would have explained it when I wasn't even able to understand it myself. And I wasn't happy.

CHAPTER FORTY

2013

NEW YORK CITY

Eventually I realized that Will Richards—the mysterious associate of Mr. Fox's with whom I'd been corresponding—did not really exist. It was just an email account made by Mr. Fox from which he wrote to me, as Will. But in the beginning, I didn't question it because... *who does that?* I assumed Will was real. Until, slowly, doubt crept in. I repeatedly asked to speak to Will or get some kind of proof, but, predictably, none ever materialized. Still, I couldn't outright disprove Will's existence or Mr. Fox's stories. After all, just because I haven't seen proof of aliens doesn't mean they aren't out there. So what does one do in the face of uncertainty? Maybe you just hold on and wait.

In the meantime, Mr. Fox *did* get himself an actual assistant, flesh and bone, who I would get to know in person. A few doors down from my apartment on Twenty-First Street was an upscale Lebanese-Armenian restaurant called Almayass. Sometimes Mr. Fox would sit at their bar while waiting for me or when I didn't want him in my home-office—usually because my employees worked until at least 5:00 p.m. on weekdays, and I didn't want him around when they were.

At Almayass, there was a good-looking young Russian guy who bartended most nights, and Mr. Fox, with his flashy fake-or-real Rolex watches and wads of cash (probably *my* cash), made an impression on him. The guy's name was

Nazim, and he was twenty-two or twenty-three years old. Mr. Fox recruited him—likely with promises of future riches and a high life—to be his assistant. Nazim was new to the US without any family around and spoke English imperfectly, with an accent. He wasn't tall or particularly big, but he had the body of an MMA fighter, lean and chiseled, which I later learned made sense, as he'd been a competitive boxer in Russia. Nazim was sweet, with an eager, almost innocent energy about him. While I found this endearing, Mr. Fox clearly saw another vulnerable target.

* * *

I still wasn't used to being Mr. Fox's *wife* despite being married to him now for a few months. Rather than happy about it, I was sickly mortified. I didn't want people to know and hardly told anyone. How could I explain why I'd married him when I didn't even understand it myself? I couldn't exactly tell people I'd married him because he'd *insisted.* I couldn't admit—or even see clearly at the time—that he had a way of always getting me to do what he wanted.

And now, he began directing my behavior with respect to my company and employees, sometimes telling me specifically what to say. I existed in a state of nervous discomfort because of all the money I'd withdrawn from the company, which I'd then given to Mr. Fox. I didn't know how to explain these withdrawals to Adam, my very responsible general manager, who was rightfully growing increasingly alarmed.

On January 27, 2013, Mr. Fox texted me:

Email Adam. Tell him that you know the money situation has been hectic but you are leaving tomorrow for London and finalizing a deal this week with a new investor. That you expect a seven-figure transfer to go through later this week. Then forward his reply, if any.

Mr. Fox expected me to brazenly lie. When I objected, he claimed it wasn't a lie. Of course, I wasn't going to London. Or... was I? I didn't think so. But I never knew. Mr. Fox spoke vaguely of upcoming travel and of how soon we'd be *finishing* everything. I was confused about what was going on but knew one thing for sure: *he owed me a lot of money.* I needed the relief he kept promising, or some other way out.

Around the same time, Mr. Fox instructed me to go to Citibank to open a "gold" account. This level account required a certain high minimum balance, which I didn't yet have. The implication was that *of course* I'd need a gold account since any day now Mr. Fox would be dumping a lot of cash into it. Or a wire. Whatever. He always said he'd be *dumping* money there. I opened the account as instructed, behaving with the bank associate as if I would shortly be depositing *much* more and the fees they'd charge in the meantime were no big deal.

My logical mind assumed he wouldn't have me waste time and money to open the account for no reason, so it gave me hope. Over and over, Mr. Fox told me he was sending back at least *some* money, but later he inevitably had excuses as to why it was less, or was late, or didn't come at all.

* * *

Up until this point, Mr. Fox's stories had been mostly plausible only to the extent that, however unlikely, they were at least *physically* possible—in the generally agreed-upon version of reality we inhabit. Could he have been part of an extra-governmental black ops special force elite group as he implied? Theoretically, that would have been at least possible—however unlikely (or, laughable). But now he began weaving in kookier threads to his already implausible narrative.

He hinted that he was not a *regular* human, or not human at all. At first I wasn't sure if he was joking or serious when he'd say things like, "I'm so tired of walking around in this meat suit." I wasn't sure what to think when I asked for clarity and he said, "Don't worry, baby. It'll make sense when you're one of us."

Who is "us"?

Once, when I asked, "But who are you *really*?" he told me he was a "CA." He wouldn't tell me what the letters stood for. He said he couldn't tell me *yet*, but soon I'd know. "Soon, baby. Soon," he'd say. I wondered if I was supposed to be able to figure this out. What could C and A stand for? Naturally, I started making ridiculous guesses. I asked him, "So you're a clown assassin? A camel attorney? A chowder afficionado?"

That I did this feels like more evidence of my skills at denial. Stupid jokes! It's all funny! Ha *ha!* If I didn't laugh at this insanity, my only other options were rage and despair.

I still have no idea what he meant, if he meant anything at all. I feel like there's something I was *supposed* to guess, but I don't know what he wanted me to assume. Celestial angel? Cosmic alien? Who the fuck knows?

He alluded to a family of some kind, but not his actual mother and father and sister, whom I'd met. He spoke most often of a brother, unnamed, who seemed to always be around in some way, yet not in a way I could see him. Mr. Fox said things from which I was meant to conclude that this brother was powerful—in ways beyond mere mortal money or physical strength—and over time it felt like this mysterious omnipotent *brother* of his was watching me. Mr. Fox spoke of this brother as if they were at odds, fighting over power that perhaps they once shared and Mr. Fox needed to reclaim. Questions I asked were met with mind-numbingly vague answers, leaving me only more annoyed—and spooked—than before.

If only I'd watched the movie *Thor*, I might have then noticed the parallels.

* * *

Mr. Fox told me I should *not ever* take off my wedding ring. He said that as long as I wore it, I'd be "protected." It was just a regular silver band, but apparently it had special powers. He implied that I was more than just the wife of an important person, protected perhaps in the way the First Lady would be protected. Everything about Mr. Fox had morphed into something more… *ethereal. Cosmic?* I don't know how to describe it. He referred to me as his "TBH"—his *tiny blond human* (as if he was, in contrast, *not* human) and to the coming "HEA," the *happily ever after* future he'd arrived in my life to deliver, one in which my life's problems would evaporate and I'd be empowered, with Leon by my side for eternity.

Yes, Mr. Fox implanted the idea in my head that this future was one in which Leon and I could be together forever—as in, we'd live forever. He knew how attached I was to Leon and he knew the story of how, when I adopted him, it had felt like a force beyond me had made it happen. Even if we allow ourselves to think that our pets were *meant* for us, we know they'll likely leave us before we leave them; it's a feared yet expected future pain we usually avoid thinking about. Mr. Fox played on that fear.

In his book *The Cult of Trump*, Dr. Steve Hassan wrote, "Put a person in a situation where his senses are overloaded with contradictory incoherent information and the mind will typically go numb as a protective reaction. It gets confused and overwhelmed—critical faculties no longer properly work. In this overloaded state, people can become vulnerable to hypnotic suggestion and trance." This makes sense to me as at least a partial explanation for how Mr. Fox was able to drive me out of the reality I knew and into a place where grasping onto fantasy felt like the only option, and for how he was able to get me to comply with his demands. I was, in fact, confused and overwhelmed by his elaborate lies and his constant badgering.

Mr. Fox also did strange things that, at the time, seemed like evidence of his otherworldly power, like making it seem as if he knew what I was thinking. For example, he'd sit down across from my desk while I was typing on my computer and say, "Emailing your mom?" And in that precise moment, I *was* emailing my mom. Not like I emailed her every day or there was any reason he'd have known that I was emailing her. It seemed eerie that he knew.

Another time he said something like, "So-and-so is going to call you in the next few minutes." And *pow*, my phone rang, and it was that person. How did he know?

Looking back, I realize he must have been accessing my email, since I'd given my passwords to "Will." It didn't occur to me in those moments that he'd be accessing my email on his phone, where he'd have seen the email to my mother autosaved in the drafts folder. As for knowing who was about to call, that person must have emailed me saying, "I'll call you in a few minutes," and Mr. Fox then quickly deleted it, so I didn't see it.

These explanations are, of course, far more plausible than his having clairvoyant vision. But I wasn't thinking about the plausible explanations at the time, since I wasn't operating under the assumption that I might be involved with a conniving manipulator.

On top of examples like these, it sometimes seemed as if he just intuitively knew what I was thinking. More and more I felt like there was nothing I could hide from him.

I can see now that my fundamental error was preferring to believe that the world might be a magical sort of place than to believe someone could be so diabolical and malicious a fraud. Regardless of what tabloids and a segment of the public would later conclude, I know myself to be an honest and authentic person. I erroneously assumed others are, at their core, the same. It was as if I couldn't conceive someone would be so wildly, deliberately opposite.

Maybe I was just so exhausted and depressed—broken down enough—that I let myself believe in the possibility of a magical rescue.

After all, police departments have involved psychics to help solve murders, and there have been sixteen seasons of the paranormal reality TV series *Ghost Hunters*. People believe in alien abductions, the Loch Ness monster, QAnon, and, of course, the foundational claims of Judeo-Christian religions. My point is that I'm not the first person to consider improbable or scientifically questionable ideas. I just happened to pay a very high price for doing it.

CHAPTER FORTY-ONE

2013

EMAILING MY MOM

Throughout much of 2013, I was in limbo with Mr. Fox, giving him money but not so much that he drained me. It's hard for me to remember what happened that year or the things he said, since I don't have much correspondence between Mr. Fox and me, just bits and pieces, until September—when my records of our Gchats begin. I traveled more than usual that year. From iCloud photos and my own Instagram account I can at least tell where I was most of the time.

More and more, Mr. Fox devised ways to get me away from the restaurant and business. Now that I had a car, it was relatively easy to get to my mother's, a four-hour drive from Manhattan. I normally didn't go very often since I was always so busy. But Mr. Fox encouraged me to go frequently, and occasionally he came along. Later in 2013, I happened to do some business traveling, and while I was away, Mr. Fox spent time with my mother. At times, he went to see her without my knowledge.

I only learned the full extent of what happened between Mr. Fox and my mom after reading a bunch of emails she'd saved, despite Mr. Fox's explicit instructions to her to delete all the emails between them. In 2016, about a week or so after I'd been bailed out from Rikers, I was given a stack of these emails, a copy of which my mom had also provided to her attorney and mine. I read through the pages while sitting on the back porch of my sister's brownstone, wishing that the ground would crack open and swallow me down, to relieve me of this nauseating reality. Some of the emails contained bits almost comical in their absurdity, such that I wanted to laugh momentarily before stabbing myself in the face out of overwhelming fury and shame. I was the conduit through which this monster was unleashed on my mother. *This is all my fault.* The emails only got worse as he continued to string her along, convincing her to give him more money. Her desperation and agony, with which I could relate all too well, came through in her typed words, increasingly written in all caps, with many exclamation points.

In his exchanges with her, he still called himself Shane Fox. Even after he eventually told her his real name wasn't Shane but, in fact, Anthony, she continued calling him Shane. Even now, if he comes up in our conversations, she refers to him as Shane.

```
Sent: February 14, 2013

From: Shane Fox

To: My mom

I would happily give my life to protect Sarma. She is
everything to me. I will protect her and care for her always.
You need not worry about that.

I am back in NYC but I'm getting ready to possibly leave
today for another work related trip. It's been hectic lately.
My job and what I do is very difficult on Sarma. I had to
lie so much in the beginning about who I was and what I do. I
just couldn't tell her the truth. Not until I knew she could
handle it and this was more than just a simple relationship.
The problem is that a normal person would recognize that and
recognize the sacrifices I am making and accept it. But she
is so depressed and angry at life that it's tough for her.
```

She has admitted to me that she hates herself and has a hard time accepting how much I love her because she doesn't think she is worth that kind of love, so I must be 'toying with her' and that I 'couldn't really love her that much.' So it's extremely hard for her to form a true connection with another human being. Especially someone she loves. So she puts a big wall up and keeps the world out. I'm trying to break that wall down. I love her so much. She is everything to me and I want to love her forever. I want to bring her peace and freedom from stress and pain. For her to see that she has worth and value and that just because a few people have hurt her that she is better than to accept just being hurt. That she is beautiful inside and out and a great person. That she has a family and friends that love her. That I love her. But that's tough. But I'm working on it. But juggling my career and the intensity and stress of people wanting to kill me and then coming home and dealing with a depressed person and trying to constantly reassure them and let them know that it's all going to be ok. It just wears on me. But I love her so it's worth it.

Anyway, sorry for rambling on there.

I really do hope to see you soon. I would love to come up and have dinner with you and talk. Even if I just came up alone (it's tough convincing her to travel anywhere) so I could explain more to you and tell you more about me and what I do.

It's always nice to hear from you. See you soon I hope.

XO

-Shane

P.S. Please keep our talks between us. I find myself venting a little, but it's only because I trust you. I just don't want Sarma to feel like I was speaking ill of her. I will tell her eventually that I talk to you. But not yet. She will just scream at me about how "I embarrassed her" by telling you about my real job and about her and my relationship.

He wrote that to my mother—that whatever he was doing was for *me*, that I was depressed, that I didn't think I was worthy of *his* love? I may have had issues with self-worth but not to the degree that he described, certainly not in relation to him.

Among the emails my mom saved was one between her and me from weeks later. She'd emailed me saying she was worried about me and wanted to know how I was doing. My reply:

Sent: March 6, 2013

From: Sarma

To: My mom

Mama, I'm having a hard time. I don't really want to talk b/c it doesn't help, talking just makes me feel worse. The gym helped. I will try to go more often now. I stopped going to the gym for a long time b/c Shane had me running all over the place and he always said we are going to be traveling, so I would never schedule going to the gym. I can't handle him and I can't handle someone messing with my head like that. I've never been so exhausted and I'm having a hard time getting any work done. Anyway, Leon is taking care of me. Will be okay. XOXO I hope everything's okay up there.

Going to the gym had been something that kept me feeling okay, and Mr. Fox clearly didn't want that. I'd been working out with a trainer, also something he didn't like. He consumed more and more of my time and energy, making me do confusing, seemingly nonsensical errands or telling me to prepare for some important trip that never materialized.

* * *

In March, I drove to Washington, DC, with Leon to my father's house for my half brother's engagement party. While I was gone, Mr. Fox went to see my mother.

He told her we'd gotten married. He also told her that I'd been pregnant the year before and had an abortion. I'm not sure why he told her, but I'm assuming he likely framed it as if I'd been distraught and emotionally damaged by it. He portrayed me as unstable and having emotional issues.

Never mind that it was Mr. Fox's *provoking* that upset me and led me to behave in ways that confirmed what he was telling my mom. He deliberately created the very problems he claimed he was trying to help fix.

Once he told me something about my mom's past, something very personal that she'd told him, that I'd not known. Mr. Fox was getting close to her. My mom and I shared the quality of vulnerability—trusting people too easily. It sickens me when I think about him spending so much time at her house.

He also told my mother lies about his "career" and what he *really* did for a living, leading her to believe that he had huge sums of money coming to him that needed to be sorted out via complicated international doings.

```
Sent: March 20, 2013

From: Shane Fox

To: My mom

Everything is pretty much done and ready to go. Sarma has
fought me every step of the way. She has made this insanely
```

difficult with her outbursts and threats. Anyway, I would
like to come see you this weekend and give you all the
details of everything that is about to happen as well as
give you some documents in case anything goes wrong. I can't
trust anyone else with these things. I was hoping to see you
Saturday night? Maybe we could go to dinner? Then stay Sunday
at your place and have all the dominoes fall on Monday. If
you are around and that's all ok then that would be great
and very helpful. I will not be telling Sarma that I will go
there to your place. That would make it a liability as she
has done everything possible to ruin this so far. Please let
me know if it's okay to come up Saturday afternoon and stay
through Monday. I can have a car from work bring me up.

Thanks for everything.

Xo

Shane

When he referred to "dominoes falling on Monday," he probably led my mother to believe that he'd finally be getting access to this promised fortune, and by then he had "borrowed" money from her too, telling her she couldn't tell me, of course. So now he had both of us financially tethered to him.

* * *

Months later, he claimed to my mom that he was still waiting for *things to come together*. By this point, who knows how much money he'd siphoned out of both me and my mom. Neither of us can remember, as if it's too painful to even think about. When I have, on occasion, asked her questions about specifics, which I feel bad doing, I realize her memories are just like mine: blurry and full of blank spots.

```
Sent: August 3, 2013

From: Shane Fox

To: My mom

Hey you :)

Just checking in. It's been insane here the last few weeks.
Lots to inform you of. Lots happening. Mostly all Good stuff.
I have been able to come up with and implement a plan B.
Things are going nicely and I've maintained a 6 week window
for things to come together. It's been hard at times with
her, but I keep trying my best. Some days better than others.
I hope to come up and see you sometime early-mid September
and give you a run down on everything (I don't wanna write
anything in email). I miss you and Jack terribly. I hope you
are doing great.

Big big hugs and lots of love

-Shane
```

Big big hugs? Lots of love? He missed my mom and her dog terribly? What the fuck? And when he wrote, *It's been hard at times with her,* he obviously meant me. Probably because I'd been getting increasingly peevish (or desperately angry) about how he kept making promises, borrowing more money, and then breaking those promises.

* * *

I was nearly always angry with Mr. Fox, exasperated by what I didn't understand. While I never fully believed his stories, I also didn't entirely *not* believe them. He seemed so sure of himself. He repeatedly insisted that he would, finally, explain everything to me. Yet his stories never made sense—always shifting, details changing, wading more and more into the paranormal—making me only more confused and paranoid.

I once wrote to Mr. Fox that I was starting to feel sick, with a slightly sore throat, which was unusual since I rarely get sick. He replied, *You never should have taken that ring off,* as if taking my wedding ring off for a day or two made me sick. Then he told me not to tweet about being sick; I replied that I wasn't planning to but asked why. He wrote, *Because it's an advertisement that you're in a weakened state.* When I asked to whom I risked making this advertisement, he didn't answer. I *never* got any straight answers. Instead, I was consistently barraged with hazy, ominous accusations and suspicions... all meant to make me feel unsure of myself, or vulnerable. He wanted me to be afraid and to feel that only he could protect me from all these nebulous threats.

Mr. Fox also claimed to have a bullet lodged in his back, wanting me to think he'd been shot by bad guys while parachuting into a war zone to rescue a world leader, or something. Really it was probably just that he had a bad back from being a lazy fuck, playing video games all day (which he did) or sitting at a poker table all day (which he also did) or whatever it was he was really doing while making me think he was doing important things "for us," as he repeatedly asserted. About this supposed injury, he wrote, "*That bullet in my back has shifted. That happens sometimes and I just have to wait for it to pass. The pain is excruciating. Happening now. :-/ It's literally like someone scraping a knife across bone. It's just intense searing pain. Sometimes lasts 3-4 days.*" When I asked why he couldn't just take it out, he wrote, "*Yes but not now or in the next few years. If I have it done it will sideline me for 6-8 months. I have had too much going on to give up for that. So I just take the bouts of pain. I need a fixed up meat suit. And green juice.*" His "meat suit" is how he referred to his body, acknowledging that he was fat but also implying he was, in some way, other than human.

* * *

Meanwhile, the "six-week window for things to come together" he'd emailed my mother about in August came and went. Months later he emailed her the following:

Sent: October 1, 2013

From: Shane Fox

To: My mom

Hello. Sorry to have been so busy lately. Sarma has been increasingly difficult to deal with. All the paperwork has been sent to the IRS. I am waiting to hear back. I am trying to balance her shit with all this business stuff and also some final wrap up stuff from work. Loose ends and such. I have lots of paperwork and account stuff from the bank that I would like to come up and go over with you at some point. Remember, she still thinks that she will have control of the money, she doesn't know that won't be the case. I could come up in about a week to go over everything to wrap this all up. Like around the 8th or the 9th. Would that work for you?

Xo

Shane

Just a few days before he wrote that email to my mom, I expressed my frustration at yet another of his broken promises in our Gchats (which I assume is what he meant by *Sarma has been increasingly difficult to deal with*). Mr. Fox had asked me about brand licensing rights and various agreements and told me to be ready for an important meeting, which then (surprise!) didn't happen, after having assured me that by September 22, everything he'd been putting me through would be over, all promises delivered. It was now September 26.

September 26, 2013, Gchat

Me: Not sure why this is all being done now. I was set for a meeting. I got all dressed up for a meeting today. Not happening. I don't understand any of this.

Mr. Fox: What?

Me: You said by end of summer, by September 22nd, everything would be done and over.

Mr. Fox: STOP being like this please. Just please stop being a downer about everything. I don't have time for drama. I AM DOING THIS FOR YOU SO MAYBE DON'T ACT LIKE AN ASSHOLE and break my balls about every little thing. I am trying to pull this off and deal with serious work stuff THAT I WILL EXPLAIN SOON. So maybe just be cool and be my badass wife. No drama. NO DRAMA. Just be fucking cool please. PLEASE.

So that was me being difficult, apparently.

Regarding my mother, it seems as if he told her that, for some reason, he had to put funds in her name as opposed to giving them to me. He made my mom think that this was all to help me (as if he must *deal* with shepherding me through my bouts of mania, apparently). Meanwhile he claimed he was about to wrap this all up, *any day now!* And we'd have loads of money; all our issues could be easily solved henceforth. Yippee!

※ ※ ※

If only things had ended here, in 2013.

If only we'd discovered he was a fraud, cut our losses, and gotten free of him.

We could've been okay. But things didn't end here. We didn't cut our losses. We didn't get free.

Things only got *much* worse.

CHAPTER FORTY-TWO

LATE 2013
NEW YORK CITY

I don't know what Mr. Fox told my mother about what he did for a living or the source of all the promised forthcoming money, but I know the stories were—like those he fed me—intentionally vague and confusing.

I get that you may now also be thinking of my mother, *How could she be so gullible?* Please give her a break, and me too. Amid the aftermath of this entire debacle is a strange bond, however unfortunately generated, between my mother and me; we are bonded in feeling not only stupid and gullible but also judged by others who can't understand how we both could have been so *stupid* and *gullible.*

The problem for me is that this doesn't mean my mother and I are now blissfully close. It's overshadowed by the crushing guilt I feel that the suffering she endured *is all my fault.* For this reason, I sometimes find it agonizing to be around my mom too much because I want to run and dive headfirst into a lake, to be cleansed of this shame and guilt.

* * *

It's hard to make sense of how, on some level, I knew he was full of shit yet allowed it all to continue. His relentless pressure was exhausting.

September 30, 2013, Gchat

Me: Please just leave me alone this week.

Mr. Fox: I love you. I'm not the bad guy. I really believe in you. One of the things I love about you is your passion. You and I work much better as a team. As a team we can conquer the entire world. That is a FACT.

Me: You are an idiot. That is a FACT.

A friend reading early drafts of this book suggested I remove most of my combative and sarcastic replies. He said they don't fit the narrative of my being psychologically abused and make it seem as if I had more agency and awareness of what was happening. But these were my replies, and I find them only *more* important to include because I *was,* in fact, defiant much of the time, yet *still,* he overpowered me—or I was weak in his actual presence, or weak in the face of whatever tactics he used to get me to do what he wanted me to do.

I don't quite get it, and as you read these pages, you may not either.

* * *

As I mentioned earlier, Mr. Fox initially implied he worked for black ops organizations. I wasn't sure what to believe, or not. He sent me a link to an article from the *New York Post* with the headline: "Ex-Soldiers plotted to kill DEA agent, traffic coke," and then wrote via Gchat, "*Read this. Africa. Asia. Dirty Special Forces guys. Feds. This just culminated after a lengthy investigation. Sound like anything you have heard in the past year?*" I remembered that Mr. Fox had, a while back, rambled on vaguely about some dirty drug deals overseas, as if he were part of the elite forces foiling this plot, even referencing Africa, Asia, and South America. He continued, "*Just read the article. We can talk about it later in person. But I am sure reading it, that it sounded awful familiar.*"

The article at least made his claims more plausible. He claimed he was constantly working hard to protect me from danger, to make everything right for *us,* and that I was being ungrateful. In one Gchat exchange, we'd just gotten off the phone, and I was angry. Mr. Fox wrote that he'd been *"going through hell"* for me, under *"insane amounts of stress"* and had *"risked so much to protect"* me and my future. He wanted me back on *"his side."*

```
Me: I want to do good things. I want to be free. That's all.
Free to make my own decisions.

Mr. Fox: I love you. Please be on my side again. Please. Like
when we got married. Please. I won't let you down this time. I
love you.

Me: I'm TIRED. I don't want this relationship.

Mr. Fox: So you quitting on me.

Me: I don't want one noose around my neck to be taken off only
to be replaced by another. I can't live like that, with someone
controlling me.

Mr. Fox: I love you Sarma. <3
```

I find it interesting that I was aware enough to point out his controlling behavior. I was also already at the point of being mostly repulsed by him. Sometimes in the midst of serious conversations like the one above, he changed course to veer into casual sexy talk. He wrote that he'd been thinking about me all day and asked what I was wearing. I didn't want him thinking about me that way, or to encourage him. I responded, *"High-waisted mom jeans, ski boots, and a parka."*

He ignored my sarcasm and replied, *"I want you to send me pics of your legs, with your pants half pulled down your tan thighs. This is what I want. Make that happen."*

This kind of instruction only pissed me off. I replied, *"Gross, I'm taking Leon out."* It was rather unambiguous that I was repelled by him.

Yet still, he kept me afraid. As if I needed his protection. From what dangers? He always claimed there was something. Once, he claimed that someone who'd reached out to me was dangerous. He was referring to an older woman from California who had called me at my office number and rambled for over two hours—I'd been unable to get her off the phone. She'd sounded a bit insane, going on about how I should open up a restaurant where she lived in LA and telling me all about her life. Afterward, she sent me an email, which Mr. Fox must have read via his access to my inbox.

In reality, she was just a cuckoo lady, maybe one who indulged in martinis every day at lunch, and then talked and talked and *talked*, as she did to me that one afternoon. Meanwhile, Mr. Fox acted as if she was a dangerous assassin.

```
November 11, 2013, Gchat

Mr. Fox: I will destroy anyone that tries to harm you. And that
is a potential long list. There is another man that works with
Will and myself. You do not know him. His name is Gabriel. He is
looking into the situation, so I will tell you more in a day or
so. The likelihood that she is just a random whacko is slim to
none.

Me: And her motivation is to do what?

Mr. Fox: Bad things.

Me: Like what?

Mr. Fox: I will explain when I get home.

Me: NO. I'm sure you won't. You'll tell me some vague shit that
doesn't make any sense. And stop referring to this place as your
'home' because it's not.

Mr. Fox: Stop breaking balls. Check the emotions.
```

Me: I'm not getting emotional.

Mr. Fox: We need some Q and A. First up. Are you being totally straight with me. About everything. Is there anything you have kept from me for any reason at all. I won't get mad. And I'm not fishing. So be honest.

Me: a) No. b) You would get mad c) You are most likely wasting my time right now.

Mr. Fox: You know what, I will just let Will handle this. He told me that he tried to talk to you earlier and you bit his head off too. He doesn't need that shit. Neither do I. I got enough on my plate. Sorry for looking out for you.

Me: You are wasting my time. If there's something important, just get to the point. Tell me. You don't. Instead you're all cagey and weird. But I don't have time for this crap. And I still think there is no Will. As any rational person in my place would.

* * *

Obviously, I never actually spoke to this Will Richards on the phone, or met him in person, since he didn't exist—something I already suspected. The only conversations I had with Will Richards were digital and never when Mr. Fox was right in front of me. I was nearly sure Will wasn't real, but couldn't prove it.

Either way, I should have been screaming and running away.

Mr. Fox only ignored my resistance and my rage and continued bombarding me.

He also continually analyzed me and my past, as if I had emotional issues to work out—as if he was helping me. In one conversation he referred to abuse in my childhood, yet I don't know what abuse he was referring to. I'd once told him about a creepy pediatrician I'd had, but he implied there was something else.

I think he took advantage of the fact that my childhood memories are not just hazy but full of blank spots—large swathes of time I can't recall—which I think isn't all that uncommon. He made it seem as if he *knew* things, yet, as always, wouldn't give me any specifics.

```
November 14, 2013, Gchat
```

```
Mr. Fox: You like to embrace the role of victim. Why? Because
what does the victim not have? Power. What did you lose as a
kid. Power. And you can't deal with that yet. You repressed
it. You embrace the role of the victim. Because for you this is
all some epic chess match between you and the idea of being a
complete person. About give and take and power and control. And
that's ok. Typical amongst abuse victims. Plenty of people have
been abused and go through depression and mental illness. Lots
of brilliant people suffer from that stuff. So it's okay that
you play the victim because right now you need that.
```

```
Me: WHAT?
```

```
Mr. Fox: Deep down you want to feel bad. Because you were never
allowed to feel bad about what happened as a kid. So you act out
the role of the victim in other scenarios and then try and feel
bad about that.
```

```
Me: I'm the victim of your overbearing nature.
```

```
Mr. Fox: What I am saying makes sense. You were never allowed to
feel bad as a kid, and thus never allowed to heal, so you spent
your life setting yourself up for hurt and to be the victim so
you could then try and heal as you were never allowed to heal
from the original abuse. It's a cycle. And you have been doing
it your whole life.
```

Me: So I guess I'm just paying my shrink for pills and to watch him eat pudding.

Mr. Fox: Stay with me here. This is huge. You have spent your entire life subconsciously setting yourself up to be hurt so that you can be that victim that you never got to be as a child. That is where all the original pain stems from. You repressed it as another defense mechanism, but its been eating away slowly your whole life. And you set yourself up to be hurt so that you can then get the feeling of trying to heal. And being the victim. All just trying to recreate that hurt from childhood. Trying to get the power that was taken from you. So you give it up again and again. In hopes of being able to then take it back. Or heal. Or deal. Or all of the above. Wow.

Me: "Wow"?

Mr. Fox: Yes wow. So much makes sense now. This is also why you relate so well to people that you either consciously or subconsciously see as a victim. Gays. Animals. Look at your recent tweets about Obama. You now see him hurting. And what do you want to do? Hug him. Because no one ever hugged you. After you were hurt as a kid. It's all a cycle. And will repeat forever. Unless dealt with. That's what I been trying to help you do. Because I see all this. And know exactly what you are going through. I see the you that you hide from the world. The you that you hide from even yourself. It's going to be ok. I know that you don't think so now. But it will. You will have the courage to break the cycle one day. To accept how much damage you have done to yourself for so long. It would make anyone depressed.

Me: OK. Enough for now.

CHAPTER FORTY-THREE

CHRISTMAS 2013
NEW YORK CITY

I planned to spend Christmas of 2013 alone.

Mr. Fox wanted to spend it with me, writing to me in a Gchat on December 15, "*I want Christmas with my wife*" to which I replied, "*I want a husband that doesn't steal from me and lie to me.*"

Again, it's remarkable that I referred to his having stolen from me and lied yet somehow didn't put a stop to it. He kept promising it was all coming back and so much more. I at least wanted some of it back.

By now, he'd gotten an alarming amount of money from me. I'm not sure the precise amount, but it had to be well over a couple hundred thousand. I know that in a story like this, you might want to know specifics, such as where I gave him money, how much, and in what form. Cash? Check? Wire? And what was I thinking? The problem is that it's all fuzzy in my memory—worse than fuzzy. It's mostly not there. Just vague memories of feeling afraid at the bank, hoping they didn't ask me my reasons for withdrawing lots of cash or sending big wires. Only later where I have copies of our Gchats to read, along with some records I found, can I see references to specific wire amounts.

All I know is it was a lot. And it made me feel sick.

This financial tether made it hard to completely shut him out. In hindsight, it was kind of like getting carjacked by a psycho with a gun pointed at your head and then forgoing multiple opportunities to jump out of the car and escape because he was still holding onto your wallet and you wanted your wallet back, dammit. It makes no sense. Or it may make a bit of sense, but it's really dangerous and stupid. Get out of the damn car! Save yourself! Who cares about the money in your wallet?

But I didn't leave. And because of whatever sorcery Mr. Fox subjected me to, I still held out hope that he wasn't full of shit and that this whole ordeal would, as he so assuredly promised, lead me to a much happier place after all.

* * *

When Mr. Fox came around, it usually wasn't for more than a night or two at a time. He always stayed on the couch because I couldn't handle sleeping in the same room as him. It was also usually on weekends, since my employees still occupied the apartment Monday through Friday.

When Mr. Fox communicated with me from somewhere else, I had no idea where he was. He implied he was far off, but I didn't believe him.

Only much later did I discover he was usually at a casino.

* * *

With Christmas approaching, I was probably extra sensitive about money, since I was painfully aware of not having funds to give out bonuses or even buy gifts for anyone. On December 17, Mr. Fox wrote to me in Gchat telling me to prepare for travel. My only reply was, "*I need my cash back ASAP.*"

He then wrote, "*Consider all communication this week of the highest importance. Stop worrying about the cash. I got it covered. This is almost over.*"

I protested on the travel, yet he insisted that I prepare for it. He wrote, "*Be ready. Don't send me some bullshit and don't mess around. I moved lots of cash last night. Things are going as planned. This is going to be ok.*"

I replied to him sarcastically, "*Wonderful. I can't wait.*" But in reality, I was upset and afraid. His constantly telling me I had to be ready for this or that and warning me not to *mess around* kept me in a state of ever-present stress.

The travel plans never materialized. Instead, he said he was coming to my place for the weekend. I objected, and we argued more. I told him he couldn't come back unless he replaced the most recent money he'd gotten from me. As usual, he was angry that I was "breaking his balls" and kept insisting he had cash, a photo of which he'd sent me. I told him photos meant nothing.

It was more of the same back and forth, over and over. He claimed he'd put himself at risk *for me*. I wrote that I'd put the door chain up if he tried to come back, and he was outraged at this. He repeated more nonsense that I didn't understand about all the *moves* he was making.

The next day, December 19, I again asked about the money he'd promised to return. His reply was cryptic.

```
Mr. Fox: I'm having to be very careful about what I say online.
This is tough to talk about when not in person. Money was moved
today. I am waiting on confirmation and should get it today or
tonight. Once I get the green light then I will have much more
to tell you. But all I can say for certain is that cash was
moved today. Lots of cash. And when it hits my account it will
then go immediately to your account. That's a big step. Huge.
```

In my reply, I reminded him that he'd said these sorts of things before and I never got anything back, so I'd have to *"act accordingly."*

The conversation continued:

```
Mr. Fox: What the fuck is wrong with you. WHY DO YOU HAVE TO SAY
THAT SHIT. Always threats always.

Me: Threats?

Mr. Fox: I can't deal. I MOVED THE FUCKING MONEY. JESUS. YOU
WANT TO BE INCRIMINATED ON GCHAT.

Me: Is it a threat that I conserve money out of fear? Do you
find that threatening? And how could I possibly incriminate
myself? For what?
```

Mr. Fox: I am on edge. I am totally on the hook here. If anything goes wrong my life is over. Literally. OVER. I put myself on the hook for you. Cuz that's what you do when you love someone. You make their problems your problems and try to get them through it with love and support. That's what I did for you. If this goes haywire my life is over.

Me: I just don't understand the lying part. Why tell me you're going to pay me back cash FOR CERTAIN by certain times, and then not do it? Why would you tell me that? I don't understand. Why lie so much?

Mr. Fox: Part of the problem is that when you think I am "lying" in reality I am just protecting you from knowing something you shouldn't know. Or I am giving you honest deniability if you were ever questioned. I know it's confusing at times but I'm just trying to keep you shielded from any fallout if things go haywire. I am protecting you. Not hurting you. I am the one on the hook. But I put myself there for you. As I said, when you love someone that is what you do. You protect them and you take their problems on as your problems. But yours are big and expensive. And I am doing my best. Because I love you.

Me: :-(

I wasn't asking him for anything other than to be *repaid* even a portion of the amounts I had given him. He acted like he was out slaying dragons trying to get to a treasure chest that would fix my life and make all my dreams come true. In reality, he was siphoning funds from me, occasionally repaying me bits but then always taking it back, and all the while driving me nuts.

Later that very same day, he peppered me with questions, wanting copies of old loan agreements. He wouldn't tell me why he wanted them. I'm not sure what he was doing with them. Maybe it was to make me think he was arranging to repay those loans? I realize now it was more likely he was using the files as templates to make his own fake agreements, to get money from someone else. I have no idea. He didn't answer my questions and just wanted me to hurry.

It never mattered if I was in the middle of something else. He always wanted whatever he wanted immediately.

```
December 19, 2013, Gchat

Mr. Fox: Send soon please. I have a busy evening. Jesus you are
slow today.

Me: GO FUCK YOURSELF. FOR REAL. ALL YOU DO IS BRING NEGATIVITY
TO MY DAY, ALL FUCKING DAY LONG.

Mr. Fox: Why are you taking forever to answer. It's annoying as
fuck. Am asking simple questions.

Me: BECAUSE I WAS SEARCHING FOR A FUCKING DOCUMENT. FOR FUCK'S
SAKE.

Mr. Fox: I knew you would say that.

Me: YOU ARE SO NEGATIVE. I DO NOT LIKE IT.

Mr. Fox: U are the negative one of this duo. So I guess.

Me: BECAUSE MOST OF YOUR CHATTER IS BULLSHIT AND I'M FUCKING
BUSY.

Mr. Fox: U super neg.

Me: ANYTHING ELSE IMPORTANT YOU NEED, LET ME KNOW. OTHERWISE
FUCK THE FUCK OFF. UGH. BLOCKING YOU IF YOU DON'T STOP.
```

Just retyping these exchanges, I feel tension in my body. I want to break something, or scream and yell. There is so much of this nonsense between him and me. I'm not selectively plucking out angry parts from otherwise normal or nice exchanges. The rest of our written conversations are more of the same, or else about inconsequential things.

Later the same day, the day before his birthday, I was upset because I wanted the money he promised me. I was desperate for anything back. Yet he was focused on what he wanted for his birthday.

```
Mr. Fox: Money is your God. I only want one present tomorrow for
my birthday. You tweet, "happy birthday to my husband Mr. Fox.
You are a pain in the ass but I love you."

Me: HAHA. Goodbye.

Mr. Fox: :-(

Me: You need to be reminded. YOU TOOK MY FUCKING MONEY.

Mr. Fox: :-(

Me: YOU TOOK IT AND LIED TO ME. I want to give Xmas bonuses, I
need to give holiday tips, etc. etc. and yet NO, YOU TOOK MY
MONEY. SO GO FUCK YOURSELF.
```

He kept reminding me that he'd risked his life for me, yet of course he never explained precisely, or even vaguely, how. *"LIFE risked. For you. PERIOD,"* he wrote. Over and over, he wrote the same crap and never any specifics.

He claimed to be hurt that I was ignoring his birthday. I replied that I felt hurt too.

```
Mr. Fox: Boo hoo. Yours is in your head. IT'S NOT REAL. Thinking
I am lying to you and destroying my life for nothing. RIGHT.
THAT'S INSANE.
```

Me: Then show me it's not real. It's hardly insane. Fear and sadness is overwhelming me today, that you've left me hanging out to dry and that I'm either going to have to struggle harder than ever to find a way to recover, or just let this be the end. I don't know what to do. Or, worst of all, compromise myself, business, values because I'm desperate. That's not who I want to be. And I'm not sure why you would do all that to me. What did I do wrong? Why do I deserve all that?

Whatever was going on, I didn't know what to do.

* * *

The following day, his birthday, he kept Gchatting me stupid things about the news or things he saw on Twitter. It was annoying. I was busy and stressed out, and apparently he had time to chat and tweet all day long.

Sometimes he got serious again.

Mr. Fox: Will is in my ear today. Saying shit I do not need to hear.

Me: OH, did I do something wrong again? Can't imagine what.

Mr. Fox: You couldn't of. You can't be that dumb. Not to do what he is claiming. It must be some mistake. He must have picked up some financial chatter and mistook it for our business. No way you put me at risk like that. So must be a mistake.

Me: Well, I have no clue what you're talking about, but great job making me feel fear and panic as always. You literally do this all the time. Like all the fucking time. Why don't you just ask a direct question?

Mr. Fox: Have you told anyone about our business?

Me: No. Why don't you just tell me what Will is saying?

Mr. Fox: Saying you have been openly communicating via unsecured email about receiving a large cash transfer in the coming week. I have told you never to do anything like that. And have told you that the ramifications of such an action could be very bad. Like I said, obviously it was a mistake. He must have picked up some bank chatter, and mistook it for our thing.

Me: Oh for fuck's sake!!!

Mr. Fox: No big deal. He is paranoid. Cuz so much happening now.

Me: I'm leaving to go to the restaurant. You and "Will" can go blow each other.

Mr. Fox: That was disgusting. And vulgar.

Me: You and he are the same person. And I'm leaving. Have a terrific night.

* * *

In a later conversation, I angrily called Mr. Fox a liar, a con, and a fake. Still, by some means, Mr. Fox was able to calm me down. Probably via telephone with words I don't recall. When I reminded him of all his broken promises, he wrote, *When I make it make sense, you gonna feel like an Empire State sized asshole.*

This is what haunted me: This idea that *it would all make sense.* It left me with the fear that if I shut the door on him for good or if I told people what was going on—if I blew everything up one way or another—I'd not only be stuck in my current financial panic and humiliation, but I'd ruin my chance at getting everything fixed and possibly even my chance to access the wave of relief he promised. I couldn't see it then, but my clinging to this possibility was like Jim Carrey in *Dumb and Dumber* when Lauren Holly's character told him the odds of the two of them ending up together were "one in a million" and he said, "So you're telling me there's a chance!"

I badly needed to believe there was a chance.

* * *

Sometimes, Mr. Fox implied he was a weary ruler, charged with responsibilities that wore him down. It tied into his narrative of being "otherworldly," of being able to reverse all the damage he'd done, of making all my dreams come true. On the day before Christmas Eve 2013, we had the following conversation:

```
Mr. Fox: Heavy is the head that wears the crown. That is one
of the most true statements ever made. It is not easy being
king. So many decisions. Lives in your hands. A single decision
that affects the lives of so many. All I ever wanted was to
be a husband and a father. I never asked to be anything more.
Responsibility was thrown upon me. And I accepted it. Nothing
more. Now I am here.

Me: Ok. I'm cleaning my desk.

Mr. Fox: I do not expect you to understand what I am saying. I
simply have no other to say it too. I am in the Caribbean. For
once, that's the truth about my location.

Me: Of course. I'm sure you'll have a savage tan. I'm going to bed.

Mr. Fox: I am not on the beach working on my tan. I am here on
business. I genuinely missed you today. In my heart.

Me: Goodnight.

Mr. Fox: And it hurt. Still hurts. I still love you Sarma.
Inside. I love you. Always have.
```

Me: You know everything. Good night.

Mr. Fox: The eyes see what it brings the power to see.

Me: Totally.

Mr. Fox: To accurately predict the future repeatedly, one must have the ability to shape the future to what he sees fit. Then you look like a genius, when in reality, you were pulling all the strings from the start. You were always in control. It's like that book I suggested you read so long ago.

Me: The Art of War.

Mr. Fox: Yes. The Art of War. Left is never left. Black is white. Up is down. All warfare is based on deception. And to be a master of deception is to be a master tactician. Real power is to appear powerless. Until the last possible second. Then, hurricane meets volcano. What was thought of as a summer breeze becomes the striking hammer of god. And they never see it coming. Not until it's too late. That is real power. As I said at the beginning of our chat, heavy is the head that wears the crown. So much to decide. So many people impacted. It's not easy. It's why I want a queen.

Me: A Queen can't quite effectively reign in the dark.

Mr. Fox: But she needs to be strong enough to stand in the light. To bear the burden of that crown. The same crown the king wears. That is not a task that just anyone can handle. So much I want to say and show to the world. So much I want to do. So much I could do. If I was free.

Me: Likewise.

Mr. Fox: You do not know what freedom is. For you are bound up by your own mind. I am bound by something much more sinister. You think this money will free you. Soon you will see it will not.

Me: Goodnight. Thanks for the bedtime stories.

Mr. Fox: If only they were stories love. If only they were.

Me: Ah, if only.

Again, I was sarcastic. I mean, what the fuck was he talking about? While the things he said made me roll my eyes, I also couldn't help feeling oddly creeped out. I probably also needed to at least consider anything that could give me hope.

* * *

I stayed alone for Christmas, with Leon and my cat Sydney. I didn't have a tree, but I did snag a few branches from someone's discarded tree on the street. It's not that uncommon to see discarded trees on the street in New York City *before* Christmas—by the people who just jetted off to St. Bart's for the holiday and presumably had a tree for the weeks leading up to Christmas. So I snapped off a handful of branches from one of these cast-off trees, brought them home, and put them in a mason jar. I had some bulb ornaments in the closet and hung three bulbs on the branches. I took a photo and posted it on my Instagram with the caption, *I may have gone a little overboard with my tree this year.*

I was just glad to rest during the only two days of the year the restaurant was closed. I was relieved to be on my own, without the drama or nonsense of Mr. Fox around. I needed this quiet break. If I'd spent the holiday with friends or family, on top of that being exhausting, I would have been subjected to normal questions about my life and how I was doing—questions I wouldn't have wanted to answer. It was a depressing and confusing time. I was uncomfortable lying, and I always had to lie about Mr. Fox, so it was just easier to avoid those situations and stay by myself.

* * *

Between Christmas and the end of the year, Mr. Fox behaved as if he was gearing up to finish everything, *again.*

On December 27, he wrote, *"I got a long 72 hours ahead of me. Shit is going down. I got until Tuesday to wrap everything up. I got TONS to do. Everything must fall into place correctly."*

He didn't answer my questions about what he meant by *"shit going down,"* just repeated things like, *"My life hangs in the balance here. And it is in this spot for you. I put myself here for you."* He also reminded me, *"I can't have any bullshit. I need you to curb all your bullshit and blowups and crazy panicked mess. I need you to be supportive and strong and loving and caring and tough and great."*

I didn't say much in reply, which apparently made him feel bad. He wrote, *"Crying now. Just quietly. No big show. Just tears coming down my face as I sit here. So much pain I carry. You have no idea. Soldier. Father. Son. Husband. And all of it came with unbearable pain. Some days it's just really hard to keep moving forward."*

At this I didn't know what to say. I wrote only, *"I'm sorry. I look forward to understanding better."*

At the time I probably thought, *What if he really is crying and I'm acting like a jerk?* I mean, if he was doing all this *for me,* then I'd have been acting like a jerk so much of the time. What if he did, finally, make "everything make sense"? He kept me suspended in uncertainty. I felt as if there were forces I didn't understand at play around me, that my suffering was a part of something bigger, and that my immense relief was just around the next corner.

"It's almost over, baby."

I felt like I had no choice but to hold on.

* * *

The deeper into it I got with Mr. Fox, the harder it was to imagine how to get myself out, which was something he must have understood. I'd become like the gambler who can't walk from the table. Yet in my case, it hadn't started over a consciously made, informed wager.

Either way, I was stuck in a downward losing spiral. The first steps had been small ones. Mr. Fox had started with *relatively* small and less frequent requests for money, which I'd give him. Then, despite being pissed at him, and against my better judgment, I'd agree to let him come back for a weekend *based on his promises of repaying me*. Early on, Mr. Fox would arrive usually on a Friday night or Saturday and often pay me *some* money back. A little bit. Never as much as he'd promised, and not even half of what he'd borrowed. It was usually only a small fraction, but it was *something*. So okay, I'd feel a bit better. Just like the gambler who plays a bit longer, wins a little money back, and starts feeling better.

But then, *boom*, you lose again. This time more. Come Monday, Mr. Fox somehow would have gotten me to give him *more* cash or send him a big fat wire, making the overall loss even bigger. Just as the gambler feels stupid for having lost again, I'd feel stupid for lending Mr. Fox yet more money—more than before. How did that happen?

Now the gambler and I both *really* want our money back, and, importantly, to undo our stupidity and erase the shame. Yet the stakes keep getting higher. We're only making the problem worse when all we want to do is make it better, make it go away. Instead of realizing this is all fucked up and we really ought to walk away, we stay. *I let Mr. Fox stay.* Then, rinse and repeat. Meanwhile we only sink deeper, the dazed panic ratcheting up with each descent.

As the total I *loaned* him grew, so did my determination to get it back. Instead of cutting my losses, I listened to his promises. I let him back in, all the while *wanting* to believe him. Mr. Fox was able to convince me, somehow, again and again, that giving him more money was a means to get it all back. It was awful. Both the gambler and I don't want to admit our humiliating problem, and furthermore, we don't want that problem to be our reality. So, just as the flashing lights and *ding-ding-ding!* of the casinos lure you into believing that you *still could win big,* Mr. Fox and his piercing gaze and confident assurances lured me into believing that he indeed was *not* full of shit and that there really was about to be a magical, fantastical "happily ever after."

I was *so* tired—desperate for relief—and there he was assuring me, *It's just around the corner.*

* * *

As if I wasn't miserable enough, the harder "tests" began. Small at first, easing me in. Then, over time, escalating to where I was no longer handing over whatever money I could access, but borrowing from others. This was what made my insides churn in nauseating discomfort. Yet I was meant to believe *nothing is real*, and it was all about to be reversed anyway. Each time I obeyed and passed another so-called final test, I thought, *Phew, now this will all be over soon*!

Except it never was.

CHAPTER FORTY-FOUR

JANUARY 2014
NEW YORK CITY

Slow-moving things are often the most lethal, catastrophic, and hard to reverse. Climate change. Autocracy. And my brainwashing.

By 2014, Mr. Fox had been metastasizing in my life for over two years, draining me of life force while eroding my sanity. My journal from this year having been recovered, I'm able to get a glimpse into what I may have been thinking (or not thinking) at the time. Mapping these journal entries onto the recovered digital conversations lets me compare how I was feeling vs. what I was writing to Mr. Fox. So often I was angry, even calling Mr. Fox out on his bullshit. Yet I allowed it to go on.

All the while I tried hard to stay positive. My journal begins with an entry stating that intention. On New Year's Day, I wrote:

January 1, 2014: First page. The idea here is to write one page each morning. Quiet morning here, except Leon hurled on the floor, not sure what kind of sign that is. :-/ I don't know what to expect for this morning, whether he [Mr. Fox] would have come back or not, and don't know how to feel now. I want to be hopeful on this page, so here goes: whatever is happening is all for the best as always, and if amazing things fall into my lap I'll be ready to accept and run with them and if instead more challenges come, I'll deal with that too. I'm pulling for the former as it feels it's my time, after lessons learned and challenges faced, I'm ready for things to get easier. I'm grateful now for a quiet day with Leon and Syd [my cat]. Thank you for all my experiences and lessons and for all the amazing things, people, and support to fall into my lap. :)

Over the next couple of days, I wrote further of my intention to stay *"in good spirits, open hearted, gracious, proactive, and accepting of all that comes my way."* I also wrote about wanting to expand the One Lucky Duck takeaway into the space next door to it and about how lucky I was to have good management. Mr. Fox always encouraged me to think about what I wanted and to write about it. Nowadays, that's common in the context of *manifestation*. But in this case, I believe his purpose was to keep pushing me further into a dreamy state, one less based in reality.

By the fourth day of the year, my forced confidence wavered.

January 4, 2014: Saturday morning. Freezing cold. Trying really hard to stay calm about Mr. Fox coming back. Fear no longer serves me. Done with that now, with all that. I release anger and hurt and frustration and angst. I accept what comes. I can stand my ground yet not resist out of fear or anger. I can remain peaceful and strong. And open to a happier outcome—a much happier one—than I may be expecting or worrying about. Anyway. It's a new year. I'm still worried about later but will keep breathing deeply and keep good things in my vision, and heart. I can let anger go. Maybe I can look for answers later. Maybe I will be given some. Good ones. Thank you.

I tried to talk myself into not being afraid; if only I could stay positive and calm and not get angry (and, Mr. Fox would add, do exactly what he instructed me to do), then things would work out. As if it was my own attitude that would affect the outcome, which was what he'd led me to believe.

Looking at it now, it's like he wove in themes from the wildly popular book *The Secret*, a book that encourages readers to stay positive no matter what and good things will happen. Likewise, the book warns that wallowing in negativity only invites in more doom. Mr. Fox wanted me to believe that the bad things that happened were my own fault, a result of my shitty attitude versus the obvious reality of his siphoning away my company's money such that I could barely pay bills, and was, therefore, justifiably anxious and very angry. But no, I had to keep my cool, he always said. Anger would set me back. How convenient for him.

* * *

> January 6, 2014: Monday morning. Not a great one. I do not want him back here ever. Not ever. I'm supposed to get some $ back today. I'm assuming it's not going to be much.

I then wrote that I hoped I could have a productive day and *"tweak my head back into a positive space."*

It's clear he'd finally arrived that weekend and did not repay me any money as he'd promised. The following morning, I wrote that I didn't get any money back and added, *"I'm ready to move on. I'm ready for a next really good stage, phase, or just rest of my life. And for clarity and empowerment."*

I seemed to be talking myself into my optimism. The next day I recapped a conversation I had with one of my managers, Jim, a truly special person. After that I wrote:

> This thing we have at the restaurant, that most people on the outside don't see or understand, it's why we'll be here—it's why we'll always do well and it's the kind of energy (love) that I'd want to bring to the hotel. Anyway. In other news still no dollars from Mr. Fox. So yeah.

("The hotel" referred to a development plan for a hotel concept I'd been working on—like a hotel version of Pure Food and Wine—still something I'd love to do one day.)

I believed in that restaurant, and other people believed in it too. People felt good *in it*—eating there, hanging out there, and working there—because it really did *feel* warm and comforting. It was a space of good vibes and love. I'd imagined and assumed it would always be there, even years later; when I was an old lady, when taxis and Ubers were replaced by hovercraft pods, our sweet restaurant in the old brownstone building would still be dispensing clean and delicious food and good vibes.

Another day, I wrote about Joey, the longtime bar manager:

> Last night at the bar, overheard Joey saying "for the first time I want to be financially secure so I can start a family" etc. and it was the sweetest and immediately made me feel—not sure what—more responsible, determined, something. B/c of course I want Joey to be well off too.

The narrative in the indictment two years later was that I'd stolen from my employees. The tabloids depicted me as a selfish thief, the *Vegan Bernie Madoff*. Except I'd never intended to steal from my employees and ruin my business—I'd wanted the opposite. I'd envisioned one day being independent from outside investors and control, and having a company where employees shared in the equity. If anyone deserved equity in that restaurant, it was Joey. I so badly wanted to provide for him. For everyone.

* * *

On January 9, 2014, I wrote:

> Thursday. Woke up challenged seeing Mr. Fox angry texts. This isn't how I want to live. I'd like to be independent.

I went on to proclaim I was going to have a good day. Then wrote,

> I'm ready for good change. And I'm very lucky, blessed, fortunate etc. or just grateful to have an amazing staff of people. All of them. And I always want to give them the opportunity to improve. Today is a good day. :) :)

I had to put two smiley faces to really bake in the forced happy. I don't have copies of whatever angry things Mr. Fox had texted me. I only have our Gchats. Later that same afternoon he wrote via Gchat:

CHAPTER FORTY-FOUR

Mr. Fox: There is a man who is texting me right now about selling his soul. He wants me to help him in return for his soul. That's my day. All day, every day.

I didn't reply to this strange claim. Over two hours later, he wrote again:

Mr. Fox: Someone close to you is going to betray you. Soon. Be careful who you talk to in the next week. I know many things that I have no business knowing. This is one of them. I have no details, nothing more than what I just wrote.

Me: FOR FUCK'S SAKE. GO AWAY.

Mr. Fox said (and wrote) cryptic things to me *all the time.* I got annoyed, but wasn't immune to being creeped out. I didn't know what to make of this business about his buying people's souls. I mean, what the fuck. He went on:

Mr. Fox: Soon we are going to talk. I am going to ask you 126 questions. There are no incorrect or correct answers. Only truth. And lies. Each question is extremely detailed and intimate and personal. Some things will be about subjects that you have never spoken to another person about in your whole life. Half of the questions come on 1 day. The second half on the 2nd day.

Me: Go away.

Mr. Fox: You told me that you could handle this. Do not speak to me like that. I will not be talked to like that by you. I am on your side. And I am not some fucking indentured servant ass hat to be dismissed. I speak to you with respect and honor. I expect the same in return. You Gchat me when you ready to be cool. This conversation can be on pause until then.

Me: Bye.

He constantly asked me where I was going and what I was doing, and was always suspicious of who the fuck knows what. When I explained that I'd bought a Groupon for eyelash extensions, which I'd never before gotten and wanted to try, he called them "stripper lashes" and claimed I must have some variety of "awfulness in the works."

```
Me: You're such an asshole. Go fuck yourself. Bye. Really. Fuck
yourself. Actually do that. Fuck off. I hate you.
```

Those were my true feelings. I hated him.

* * *

By now, Mr. Fox had gotten many hundreds of thousands of dollars from me, and made me rely on his returning only small amounts for daily expenses. The next day, Mr. Fox had transferred $1,000 into the Citibank account he had me open, but then my card got rejected anyway.

```
January 14, 2014, Gchat

Me: I went to pay for my fucking prescriptions b/c my insurance
was cancelled and my Citicard got rejected.

Mr. Fox: Why? I sent that 1K. Why rejected?

Me: I wanted to put my prescriptions and Sydney's $440 vet bill
on that card.

Mr. Fox: I will be home soon. And will take care of you. I love
you.

Me: Fuck you.
```

Mr. Fox: I figured. But there is an I love you in there somewhere. Xo.

Me: It's shoved pretty far down. Covered by giant piles of your shit. I don't want you back here. This is not your home. It's my home. You just shit in it and take stuff.

* * *

Later that week, I journaled that I got $10,000 back from Mr. Fox and what a nice surprise that was and how it was reassuring. Yet the following day, I wrote: *Well, he took the 10K back.* Of course he did.

On January 20, 2014, I wrote:

> Mr. Fox implies that I don't think I deserve better. And/or I just need to kiss (or accept) the frog, and he'll turn into a prince. With abs. Or whatever. I'd like someone who's not arrogant. I like skinny nerdy guys who aren't full of themselves.

It's impressive how Mr. Fox always framed things in a way that worked for him. He told me I didn't believe that I deserved better. Again, as if my feelings and I were in control here.

According to him, it was really *my fault* that I was stuck with him—that is, the him in the state he was in. If only I'd keep playing the game he'd set me up to play, if only I'd accept him and kiss the frog, he'd turn into a prince. *Poof!* Riding a unicorn. Over a rainbow with a pot of gold at the end of it.

Two days later, Mr. Fox summoned me to a hotel room at the nearby and very expensive Gramercy Park Hotel (clearly paid for with my money) and gave me a lecture. As always, he'd made me think he was summoning me for some epic good news. Some relief, finally, was what he'd make me think I'd be getting.

On January 22, 2014, I wrote:

> I don't know what's going on. <== understatement of the century. I am not sure what to do other than all my best to keep myself happy, positive, exercised, clean home, things in order, ready for change, etc.
>
> ...
>
> He is bullshitting me about $ transfers. When does it end? When is this over? I want peace. I do not want to be with him. Not at all. I only feel tense and anxious when around him, talking, texting or emailing with him, or thinking about him and all of this. So. What do I do? For real. What. Do. I. Do. What to believe. And why is all this happening. :-/ I dunno. Want answers. And peace.

The next day, after complaining about the frigid winter weather, I wrote about more promised transfers from Mr. Fox, including five thousand in the next couple of days and a hundred thousand in the next couple of weeks. This was money my business badly needed back. I then scribbled on about upcoming meetings and about how I still wanted to expand the juice bar space, and that I was intrigued about the idea of opening in LA one day.

These journal entries—the entire journal, in fact—contradict the criminal intent laid out in the indictment. Nothing I wrote supported the idea that I would willingly set my business on fire to extract cash to buy Rolexes for my overbearing husband and then flush the rest down the toilet of every casino from Connecticut to Las Vegas. But, in the end, it didn't make a difference.

* * *

On January 27, 2014, we had the following Gchat conversation:

```
Mr. Fox: I am having a bad day.

Me: Why? Every time you say that it scares me.

Mr. Fox: There is no answer I can give you that will make
sense. I am in pain though. You would equate this to heartache.
```

I worry that I am forsaken. That after every beautiful day like yesterday that I will have a day of pain like today. Can you imagine what that must be like? To have fate just playing with you. Over and over. Punishing you for being somewhere you shouldn't be.

Me: I guess a TBH [*tiny blonde human*] can't relate.

Mr. Fox: That is the problem. I am reminded every day of your humanity. And all that it entails. I do believe that you love me. And I love you.

Me: I also hate you and the situation at the same time. And I don't know if I can trust you.

Mr. Fox: Humanity is your curse. Inhumanity is mine. Will is one of my kind. He is not what he seems. He tells me things mostly to torment me. Like the way an older brother torments a younger brother. He wants me to quit on you. Every chance he gets to throw something in my face to hurt me he does. Not really hurt me. I mean he wouldn't do that. But hurt me emotionally. To get me to hate you. I never do. Sometimes it hurts seeing things he shows me though. Today is just one of those days. He decided to throw a shit-filled snowball at me. But I can deal. And I love you.

Me: I hate you. Good bye. I mean that.

Mr. Fox: Why do you say things like that to me? It's mean.

Me: I don't want to live with you, or this way. You constantly imply that I'm doing something wrong. Go fuck yourself.

Mr. Fox: Please I was just trying to explain. You do not need to be mean. Please. Do not be mean.

Me: I do NOT want to live with you ever. So once you feel things are settled kindly exit my life.

Mr. Fox: Why are you being this way. Please do not be this way, you were so kind to me yesterday and it was so nice. Please.

Me: I… DO… NOT… WANT… TO… LIVE… WITH… YOU.

Mr. Fox: I was just trying to be honest and explain things.

Me: OR… HAVE… YOU… IN… MY… LIFE.

Mr. Fox: Please don't say those things.

Me: I gotta go. Fuck you. Fuck Will. He can go fuck himself forever. Since you're the same person, fuck you both.

Mr. Fox: I was only trying to be honest with you.

Me: I WANT OUT.

Mr. Fox: I was trying to share and explain. And you treating me like this. Please stop saying these awful things to me. Please.

Me: And I'm going to tweet about the fucked up torment and fraud that is you if I don't get resolution soon. Because you're a fucking asshole.

Mr. Fox: Do not threaten me.

Me: Fine then. I'll kill myself.

Mr. Fox: How can you flip like this?

Me: What else am I going to do? Goodbye.

Mr. Fox: You were so kind yesterday.

Me: Leave me the fuck alone.

Mr. Fox: Please stop being mean to me.

Me: LEAVE ME THE FUCK ALONE. YOU FUCKING FRAUD PSYCHO.

Mr. Fox: I WAS TRYING TO BE HONEST AND SHARE. And this is what I get.

Me: Is my wire coming tomorrow???? At least need a little money back.

Mr. Fox: Will says that you don't love me. That you just want things. That you are greedy and just using me for money. That you shake your ass for anyone that gives you attention. That I am nothing to you. And that I am wasting my time with you. That I am incapable of having human love. Doomed to suffer for as long as I try to love. He's always trying to get in my head. Get me to think you are not what I think. I am being honest. Please do not punish me for that. I love you. I don't want you to ever be mad at me again, so just trying to be honest with how I am feeling day to day. I am not blaming you or accusing you of anything. Was just trying to be honest.

Me: Well fuck Will. Fuck you.

There was so much of this nonsense.
Later that same night, he wrote to me again.

Mr. Fox: There is no such thing as coincidence. Not ever. It does not exist. Everything that happens in the human world happens for a reason and is planned out by someone. Or something.

(In the *human* world? As opposed to… what other world?)

The next day, I was livid at Mr. Fox yet again over his broken promise to give me back $5,000. Compared to how much I'd given him by this time, getting five back would have been crumbs, but crumbs I badly needed. Meanwhile, he also asked me for cake. I'd been at the restaurant, and he was at my apartment. My pastry chefs had started making the most amazing, ridiculously good cakes—ones that blew away all other raw vegan products out there. They were delicious.

January 28, 2014, Gchat

Mr. Fox: Can I have cake?

Me: I shouldn't bring you any fucking cake. You liar. No pie either.

Mr. Fox: Not a liar.

Me: Yeah you are.

Mr. Fox: I want pie and cake. I am not a liar

Me: Wire sent to my account? Already sent? You confirmed it on the phone? I'm over this shit. Over. Done. You leave me fucking hanging all the fucking time. Over and over.

Mr. Fox: I AM NOT DOING THAT THIS TIME. TRUST ME.

Me: You have to admit. YOU TOLD ME YOU SENT THE WIRE. CONFIRMED

FOR TUESDAY. 5K. ALREADY SENT. That was not true obviously. SO YOU LIED. RIGHT? RIGHT?

Mr. Fox: Yes it is FOR FUCK SAKE.

Me: It's Tuesday night. Banks are closed. No wire.

Mr. Fox: GET OFF MY ASS I AM FUCKING TRYING TO TAKE CARE OF YOUR FUTURE. SO MUCH I DID TODAY. And so much happening. You have no idea. Now, I want cake and pie.

Me: You're a liar. A fat liar.

Mr. Fox: You gonna regret this.

Me: Ooooooooooh. Maybe don't lie to me. OVER AND OVER. And expect me to just roll with that.

Mr. Fox: You gonna feel like an asshole real soon.

Me: I DON'T CARE.

Mr. Fox: CAKE AND PIE!!!

Me: Fuck you.

Mr. Fox: Is it angel food cake?

Me: No.

Mr. Fox: What the cake part made of?

Me: FUCK YOU.

Mr. Fox: Like rice?

Me: I HATE YOU.

Mr. Fox: ?

Me: HATE. HATE. HATE. HATE. HATE.

Mr. Fox: Keep the cake.

* * *

On January 29, 2014, I wrote in my journal:

> That giant black cloud of Mr. Fox looming over like everything's bad and I'm doing something wrong is... a giant black cloud. And only makes me want to run away. :(I'm tired. Why am I with someone who's only lied to me and hurt me? Why? It feels dark. Bad. Dark. I want light and love. Love and light. Love and light. Bright, positive, healthy love and light. That's what I want. Thank you.

* * *

At the end of January, I drove with Leon to my father's in Washington, DC, for his retirement party. On February 1, just before I returned, Mr. Fox and I had the following Gchat conversation:

Mr. Fox: Your life will never be the same after this week. It starts tomorrow.

Me: You've done this to me before you know. So I'm scared.

Mr. Fox: You should be scared. It's normal to fear the unknown. So that is normal behavior.

```
Me: No I fear the status quo.

Mr. Fox: Prepare for your life to change forever throughout the
week. Tomorrow we will start. It will consist of all the blanks
being filled in. The back story. What I am. Where I came from.
Why I am here. How I know so much always. Etc. Etc. Then more in
the following days. Including you receiving gifts.

...

Mr. Fox: You had the world in the palm of your hand. Literally.
And you didn't even know it.

Me: Had?

Mr. Fox: Yes. Had. And every decision you made impacted how
things would play out for you. All the way up to today.

Me: Don't understand.

Mr. Fox: As expected. You are not supposed to. Not yet. Not
until you return home. Love.
```

* * *

Did my life change when I got back? No. Over the weekend I spent in Washington, Mr. Fox stayed at my apartment and fed my cat, Sydney. He'd made grand promises that he was going to clean the whole place for me. I was always so tired and worn down that at least coming home to a clean apartment would have been something to look forward to. I didn't know what to make of his telling me about all this change, all this stuff. But at least I'd come back to a clean apartment. Or so I thought.

On February 3, 2014 I wrote in my journal:

Came back, house was a mess (or, the same mess as when I left.) Coming back to it, to him, after what he'd said ("it'll be spotless!") was the worst. I broke the TV remote control. Now no remotes. :(Later on, hurt my hand. Weird bubble appeared on it, I should have taken a photo. Slept with splint. Now is just normal swollen and I can write too. Not sure how to change all this. When is this nightmare going to be over?

It was easy for me to fly into a rage at Mr. Fox—rage over the position I was in, which was perpetually panicked about money for my business because I'd given him so much, rage over his fucked-up broken promises, and more. So this rather innocuous-seeming broken promise of not having cleaned the apartment unleashed my fury—like poking a caged animal.

It seems I threw and broke the TV remote. I may have thrown other things. And I may have gotten into a physical fight with Mr. Fox. This happened a couple of times when he made me so furious that I went at him—not with any heavy objects or at his face but like an angry kid punching the well-padded torso or shoulders of a big brother. In the process, I only hurt myself. To this day my wrist sometimes hurts too much to do pushups, and I think it's from the times I hit a wall, or hit Mr. Fox, which was like hitting a punching bag—you're not damaging the bag, but if you're not wearing gloves, you can damage yourself.

Sometimes, Mr. Fox would grab me by the throat and pin me down, at which point I'd finally go still—like a subdued animal.

CHAPTER FORTY-FIVE

FEBRUARY 2014
NEW YORK CITY

Mr. Fox behaved as if he was the hero in his own movie. Maybe this rubbed off on me such that, over time, I adopted a similar outlook, if only to get through it all. *Life isn't real. It's like a movie. I am the heroine, facing the toughest challenge imaginable. Will I prevail? Will I have the courage?*

It turned out I did have the courage. I drained myself and my business of money, and when that spigot ran dry, I diligently did as he told me to do and sought money from other sources. I fought Mr. Fox at every turn, but nearly always ended up doing as told. I genuinely (albeit, delusionally) believed it was all temporary. If not, why would I have done it? I was miserable and terrified. What I wanted more than anything was for this to end. Unfortunately, I somehow believed that the only way for it to end was to charge forward.

Mr. Fox had me convinced that if I "gave up" (i.e., cut my losses and ran from him), my life would be doomed—far worse than merely having to dig myself out of the humiliating place in which I already found myself.

* * *

I feel sick in my stomach thinking of the times I persuaded people to loan me or my business money. *Sick.* I always reassured myself, *This is about to be over. It will all be okay. They'll all thank me later.* Mr. Fox claimed I'd be able to repay everyone many times over. He said this so confidently, and I needed it to be true. *It's almost over.*

None of it was *real* anyway, he said. As soon as I passed these tests, thus proving my mettle, all the pain would be undone. I'd be empowered with endless resources, so if I'd borrowed a hundred thousand from someone, I'd be able to repay them double. Or triple, whatever I wanted to give them, since money, in this magical imminent future, would be unlimited.

Writing in my journal I relentlessly tried to stay positive, while not understanding what was happening. Between February 8 and 15, I wrote the following:

> I don't know what's going on. :(

> He keeps saying all kinds of things. Why would I believe him now? Right? Makes no sense. He did that thing again where he knew who I was emailing and about what. :-/ Like while I was doing it. :-/

> Time to sleep. And think about what I'm grateful for. And imagine all the great and amazing things I can do. The happy ever after, like really happy, would be nice. Freedom to do what I want, and to create stuff that helps that big necessary shift. :|

> Generally scared about what's going to happen overall.

> Would be a good time right now to get those juice bar spaces, and get a solid long term lease, for all the spaces.

> I want my own home.

I felt like I'd had no choice. If I believed his promises of *happily ever after*, then everything would be okay. If I didn't, then I'd royally fucked up my life.

When in front of me, Mr. Fox would look deep in my eyes and assure me everything was going to be *more than okay*. He also had conversations with me "in the box," which was his shorthand way of referring to something he did (I don't know what) to make it so that his omnipotent brother, or whatever powers he answered to, could not hear or watch us. Presumably, all the rest of the time we were being watched and listened to. While talking "in the box" (meaning it was truly private), he reassured me that everything I was being put through was all deliberately designed to feel unbearable because it was a test. *You just have to keep going,* he'd say. *You'll see.*

* * *

On February 18, 2014, I wrote in my journal:

> We had our talk in the box. Whatever that meant… he did that thing where he lists the reasons I hate and blame myself. Which usually makes me really mad. Not b/c it's not true, but b/c he's the one putting me through shit and then pointing at me saying all my angst and anger is b/c of me, not him. Blah. So this time I'm being told up front to not get mad. Am I not allowed to write about this conversation in the "box" and ones like it? That I've been challenged my whole life, like a navy seal in freezing water, to see if I can take it, if I won't break? That it's still ongoing? That I'm meant for more? And that he is exactly what I need that we're two hearts as one. But then why in a package and form that I do not find appealing? Why do I want to be away, free, alone. Why couldn't he be my ideal if he's here for me, and it's all controlled by me. Why can't he still be funny but less of an asshole. Why can't he have nice hands, not the fat fingers chewed down like a fat kid's. Why can't I appreciate his dirty socks instead of resent them, loathe them, and be disgusted by them. Why can't he support me and not make me feel oppressed. Support me so I feel empowered. So I feel like we're on the same side, working together. Where I don't fear his reactions, or fear what he's going to say or do. Why can't he be more kind and compassionate instead of critical. Why can't he be what I want, someone whose hand I could hold walking into a fancy event and be proud and in love and supported. Why can't I be excited about his presence and everything about him in that way when you're in love. Anyway. These are things I wonder. If indeed he is who I want (and need) him to be.

I must have written the above in the morning because there's another entry with the same date, probably later that night before I went to bed, after he came home angry at me. He'd been at the restaurant to have dinner with a friend while I'd stayed home. He was mad about having bad service, as if it was my fault. Meanwhile, I think the servers just (rightfully) hated him.

On February 18, 2014, I wrote:

> I do not like living with someone that scares me and makes me feel so bad so often is not at all what I want. More testing? Why is all this happening? It's generally uncomfortable for me. Also. No matter how mean or shallow it may seem, the way I feel is that he embarrasses me. He's as wide as three regular people. In a hideous leather jacket. And probably declaring to everyone and anyone that he's my husband. While I'm hiding at home avoiding it all. I'm sure those at the restaurant that know me are uncomfortable. I don't ever speak about him. No one sees me looking happy about it. They've only seen me hiding more than ever. They have to know that something is very wrong. I can and do handle a lot, but for this little navy seal freezing water test I'm apparently being put through, I cannot pretend to be happy. So what do I do? Sit here and envision the perfect husband for me? How about no husband? I'd be just fine with that. I can and will take care of myself. And will not be subjected to someone's anger and overbearing, dominating nature. No thanks. Anyway. As always I do not know what's going on. But things seem to be happening. At least with a lot more credible evidence this time around. Almost time for Chris Hayes.

I watched a lot of cable news back then. This was a world into which I could lose myself—better to think about global atrocities than my own.

* * *

February 19, 2014, I wrote in my journal,

> They deserve either explanation, or at least not having to deal.

I was referring to my office staff who were no doubt uncomfortable and wondering what the fuck was going on between me and this overbearing beast. I continued:

> I want to live better. I want more. I deserve to be happy and loved by someone I can be proud of. Who makes me want to shout to the world that I love him. I don't have that now. I feel only oppressed, intimidated, and embarrassed. So. What will happen. I've hung on, and believed for happy ever. Please make him be that.

The following day I wrote,

> I want my own home. My own bed. My own space. Everything for me and Leon. I decide who comes and goes and when.

I was always fantasizing about peace and solitude, with Leon. And I was asking for Mr. Fox to be what he'd promised he would be. Who was I asking? The universe? God? I don't know. I desperately wanted certainty, or verification of some kind.

Whenever Mr. Fox failed to bring me proof of anything, he reminded me that the whole point of this was my trust in him; my loyalty was part of the test. He couldn't just *show* me everything because then the test would be too easy. I was *supposed* to be taking a giant leap of faith.

I'd never in my life formally prayed, asked for guidance, spoken to God, or had a firm stance on the existence of God or a universal power. But at this point, who else could I have asked for help? It felt too late, too big, too scary for help from a person. I needed a miracle from God.

On February 21, I wrote:

> Mr. Fox texted me today: "My power. My wealth. My influence. It's all yours. As I am all yours. Two hearts as 1. All you need to do is be strong enough, and fearless enough to take it. I love you." So. What does that mean? How do I take it? What can I do, not to be afraid? But of what? I don't even know what I'm supposed to be strong for, and fearless of. Nothing makes sense. Please tell

me. Please let me know how to free myself and how to be happy. How do I "take it" how do I welcome and accept those things. Please tell me. Goodnight.

Meanwhile, all I had to do was keep sending wires to his bank account. I was digging my own grave.

* * *

One weekend, later in February, Mr. Fox asked me to meet him at Tiffany's—the legendary retailer of expensive jewelry and other shiny, sparkling things—in midtown. I was used to obeying him, so I went.

I'd only been inside that multilevel famous store once or twice, and never to the top floor. I took the old-fashioned elevator up and walked out onto what was noticeably a more exclusive floor. Unlike on the ground floor, there were no tourists milling about. It was much quieter. I immediately felt out of place, like I would get in trouble just for being there, insufficiently well dressed. I spotted Mr. Fox and approached him. He was all self-assurance, completely relaxed, as he introduced me to a salesman as if they were old friends. An elegant-looking employee discreetly approached and offered champagne, which I accepted. I didn't know why we were there. I was a little nervous, and I knew the champagne would settle my uneasiness.

Mr. Fox wanted me to look around and point out what I liked. As if he planned to buy whatever struck my fancy. Expensive jewelry was never something that attracted me. It seemed one of the least practical things one could possibly buy unless one had money to burn. I'd always been uncomfortable with the engagement ring from my first marriage. It was beautiful, but it never felt right. Sometimes I felt special wearing it; other times, I felt like an asshole. Wearing something so visibly expensive is like an announcement of one's value, albeit in the most superficial of ways, which is precisely why I also felt like an asshole. I suppose Mr. Fox figured this excursion would be tempting me with the potential of feeling highly valuable. I wasn't thinking about any of this at the time, just going along with what he told me to do.

He led me to a counter where only two rings were showcased under the glass. Each one featured a large diamond surrounded by a circle of smaller diamonds.

I couldn't tell what was different about them but learned one cost more than twice as much as the other.

It was decided I should try one on. While a guard in an expensive-looking suit discreetly watched, the salesman unlocked the case, put a silky glove on his hand, and placed one of the two rings on a velvety pad on the glass countertop. I hesitated. I wasn't wearing gloves.

"Go ahead. Try it on," The salesman said.

I gingerly picked up the ring and slid it on my finger. It was a bit too large. It cost just under $400,000. I wondered what kind of hell would break loose if I took it off my finger and flung it across the room.

"It's really nice," was all I could think to say.

Mr. Fox made inquiries about getting it properly sized, as if we were going to actually buy this thing. I carefully took it off and placed it back on the pad. I picked up my champagne flute, which had been refilled once already, backed away, and let them talk. I made eye contact with the guard, as if to confirm he was aware I had not stolen the ring.

After that we accompanied the salesman to a lower floor, where, at Mr. Fox's urging, I tried on necklaces. Looking back, it's clear he wanted me to see myself in the mirror wearing things I'd only ever seen on movie stars at the Oscars on TV. He wanted me to feel like royalty. Because then when you take the fancy rings and necklaces off and leave the store, you're now very aware that you are *not* royalty, nor are you heading to the Oscars to accept your award. You're a regular person carrying a worn-out One Lucky Duck cotton tote bag, wearing an old jacket, in your old jeans, having briefly tasted what it might feel like to be the sort who easily purchased and wore fancy diamond things. This is probably why car salespeople encourage test drives.

We walked out into the bright, sunny afternoon, and he suggested we get another drink somewhere.

"The King Cole Bar," I said. It was only a few blocks away, in the St. Regis, a hotel built in 1904 and probably the nicest of the old-style fancy hotels in the city. The dark bar was full, but we managed to get a cocktail table in the corner. I ordered white wine, and I think Mr. Fox had a beer. I picked out and ate the wasabi peas from the silver dish of wasabi peas and salted nuts on the low wooden table. I was more than a little bit tipsy after the champagne and now the wine. A sentimental feeling came over me. Mr. Fox looked so sure of himself, so comfortable. I must have thought, in my alcohol haze, that perhaps he really was going to deliver me out of my rut and into a glorious safe and grand life, freeing me, empowering me to do whatever I want. And the idea that someone, in this case Mr. Fox, would do that for me, made me emotional. My eyes welled up with tears. In this weird state, I texted him (even though he was right in front of me) that I loved him.

Ugh.

After that weekend, the tone of my journal entry shifts.

February 20, 2014, I wrote:

> Sunday went to Tiffany's. I tried on what I think was a $500K ring. As in. Half a million. WTF. Of course, it's fucking beautiful. Diamonds not my thing but I can see how they're hard to resist. And kind of make you feel like royalty. Tried on necklaces too. I'm not really sure what the plan is with all this. But was fun drinking champagne there. And then after at the King Cole bar. I started to cry, a drunk thing. I guess I just felt overcome. That I love him and everything is okay. Why is it so hard to see that so much of the rest of the time? I want my leaner husband, with the same sense of humor but maybe a bit less edge. Or, something. I'm not a flashy person, so can feel funny to be with someone who is so commanding. I suppose I could get used to it. Then we watched House of Cards. Crazy. The power stuff is interesting to watch. I want the kind of power that enables me to do good things. For animals and saving the earth.

From then on, when I raged at him for fucking with me, for torturing me, for being a fraud, breaking promises, lying, etc., Mr. Fox would say, "Remember the King Cole Bar?"

From that one champagne-fueled moment of fraudulently induced sentimentality, he extracted useful currency.

CHAPTER FORTY-SIX

MARCH 2014

LOS ANGELES

In March, I seemed to fall deeper into Mr. Fox's hole, alternating between unreality (all of this must be real) and reality (he's lying to me). My journal entries at the beginning of March are optimistic, hopeful, delusional. Mr. Fox told me that March 18 would be the day "things would be different." I was scheduled to fly to LA at the end of the month for a potential restaurant project, and he told me I would be making that flight in a private plane, with Leon by my side. Half of me believed him; half of me didn't.

On March 8, I wrote in my journal:

> Am I ever going to know what's going on. Do I want to? Am I going to be happy?... It's March 8th. I was told March 18th is significant. Will it be? Or will it be like all the other times? And I'll fly to LA in my small seat, as planned. Or will it be different? Will I get to go with Leon? As was described to me. Taking Leon to LA would be totally fun.

On March 16, I wrote:

There is a "vote" I think on Tuesday. My final tests. What does that mean? Who is voting?

Mr. Fox had told me, or implied, that there was a vote, presumably about whether I'd passed enough tests. Always, I was under scrutiny, it seemed. March 18, the promised day, arrived. I wrote:

Today. Is it today, b/c I'm ready. For all those things. I think Leon's gonna like being in LA. :)... Will everything make sense?

Nothing did. Instead, Mr. Fox sent Gchats about more money:

Mr. Fox: You will need to get cash in specific amounts. 50s, 100s, and 20s. Some of it will be deposited by you personally into your Citi account today. The rest will go into the envelope and be deposited by someone else.

Me: When?

Mr. Fox: Today.

Me: Am I canceling meetings? And what cash?

Mr. Fox: This needs to be deposited at Union Square branch Citibank.

Me: What cash?

Mr. Fox: Don't know how much yet.

Me: I can't withdraw cash from my bank. You told me this wasn't happening. Payroll comes out tomorrow and sales tax is due for all three entities. I'm concerned about making it as it is right now. Very concerned. Put me at risk personally, fine. But I'm not going to NOT pay my staff, or not pay sales tax.

And yet later, it seems I'd complied after all, writing, *"Done."*
Mr. Fox replied, *"Good. Instructions to follow. Keep it in the drawer for now."*

* * *

Time and time again, I said I didn't want to put my business in jeopardy, or not pay my employees, or stop paying sales tax. Yet, contrary to my instincts, I kept taking out money to give to him. I jeopardized payroll. And later, I stopped paying sales tax.

Given the volume of business we did at the restaurant, our sales tax payments were significant. At the end of each month, we calculated the sales tax we'd collected and made a big fat payment to New York state. Not making those payments is effectively giving oneself a loan from the state. Penalties and interest are high, so it's a shitty way to give oneself a loan. But many businesses stop making sales tax payments when they start running out of money because one must pay one's staff, the electric bill, and vendors for product. For the record, I thought I was just being delinquent since I was still reporting the correct amounts. I always thought I'd be paying it all *soon*. I didn't think I was committing fraud.

On March 19, I wrote:

> Cried a lot last night. And now it seems things are still going on. Is this part of the plan? Lie to me over and over, dangle the carrot of freedom and just as I think I'll be about to get it, keep pulling it just a little farther away. It makes me doubt everything.

* * *

Late in March, I flew to Los Angeles, though of course not with Leon in a private jet. I'd planned to spend time with Dana, a woman I'd met in New York after she'd reached out to me about wanting to open a Pure Food and Wine in LA. I got contacted frequently about collaborations, but there was something different about Dana. She sounded serious, professional, and like someone I could work with.

A few weeks before the trip, we met for coffee near the restaurant. Dana was warm and easy to talk with, and I felt instantly comfortable around her. We bonded over our mutual attachment to our rescue dogs. I was looking forward to visiting with her in LA.

Dana was friendly with Joe Bastianich—the TV personality and partner to Mario Batali—who I also had known informally. We had plans to meet with him about his possibly being involved in an LA outpost of Pure Food and Wine.

When I arrived in LA, my former employee and friend Nick picked me up at the airport. Nick had worked first at the restaurant, then at One Lucky Duck. He'd moved out to LA to focus on his acting. In addition to seeing Dana, I planned to spend time with some other former staff and friends while in town.

I stayed at the Chamberlain Hotel, a discreet boutique hotel tucked away in West Hollywood, simple and not too expensive. It had a rooftop pool, but it hadn't occurred to me to pack a bathing suit—I'm not even sure if I owned one, since I'd not been to a beach in years. Wanting to get some sun, I walked to the nearest H&M and bought a bikini. I vaguely recall Mr. Fox giving me a hard time about this, as if exposing myself by a pool like *everyone does all the time in normal life* was somehow suspicious behavior on my part.

* * *

The next day, March 23, Mr. Fox Gchatted me asking if someone had been hitting on me between leaving NYC and getting to LA. "*Someone that you could potentially use as a plan B,*" he said. After I replied that I wasn't aware of anyone hitting on me, he wrote, "*You sure about that Sarm? Because my brother seems to think otherwise. Says you got pretty friendly with some guy named Aaron. Says that he's got Plan B written all over him. My brother says he asked you out. And you gave him cookies.*"

How did he know this? I'd sat next to a guy on the plane named Aaron, who'd told me he was paleo. I'd had a few packages of One Lucky Duck cinnamon stripe cookies in my carryon and had given him a pack, along with my business card. I was used to doing this sort of thing all the time. It was just marketing. I'd recalled thinking the guy was rather douchey, but he'd told me he was "paleo," and our food pretty much qualified as paleo, minus the meat, so why not give him some? Either way, this wasn't unusual for me; my business card only had my email and the restaurant phone number, not my cell phone, so I gave it out frequently.

I didn't understand how Mr. Fox knew all this. It creeped me out. Yet another thing making me feel like Mr. Fox really did have some kind of omnipotent brother who was watching me at all times. It was only later that I realized Aaron must have emailed me, and Mr. Fox had seen it in my email before I did and deleted it.

* * *

The restaurant and juice bars were especially busy while I was away in L.A., which meant more cash than usual would be in the bank the following Monday, which meant Mr. Fox would be asking for a wire.

On March 23, I wrote:

> Tomorrow. Seems I will be needed to do another transfer. Like. Whatever. I'm all in I guess. Please please let this be over, in a good way. It's what I want, and should happen. I really hope sales tax waits another day, like til Tuesday. Want to understand all of it. Was random, weird how he asked about the name Aaron. How could he know that I sat next to someone named Aaron?

Thinking about all this money flowing out to Mr. Fox sickens me. Knowing how much effort went into that business—all the hard-working staff, the expensive ingredients, the hours and hours for them to be washed and prepped and arranged, the huge rent, utility costs, insurance, taxes, and more—it feels grotesque that the extra cash flow generated this time of year, what we'd normally have been squirreling away for winter, was being siphoned out and going to Mr. Fox.

And I was the one doing it.

* * *

On March 24, I wrote:

> Monday. Today was a really nice day. Who'd have thought, given the early AM wire emptying the bank account. Just did it, no panic. Was smooth. Cool cucumber. Then went and ran 5 miles on treadmill.

Then I rambled on about the rest of the nice day I had in LA. I wired away money and *"had a nice day."* To do that I had to have believed him—that it was all coming back, that this would be over any day now. That plus a lot of dissociation.

The following day, March 25, Mr. Fox wrote me in a Gchat, *"I'm gonna come to LA this Friday. We will get that soul and then you are in and then we fly home together in the family jet. Just keep being honest. And acting like a queen. With a king. And a royal family. If you fail this I'm going to end this world."*

"A soul?" I pushed back on him. His mention of "if you fail" and "end this world" triggered me. How could I not be angry? Him making me feel like if I didn't obey him the *"world would end?"* And it will be *"my fault?"* What the fuck.

Mr. Fox wrote, *"I'm near breaking point. And if you bottom out I'm going to destroy this planet."*

I got upset and said I was going to bed.

```
Mr. Fox: Wait. Don't go yet. What I meant was… that I think
you're the most beautiful and wonderful thing left on this earth.
(Inside beauty and you're special). Not like the rest of the
sheep. So, if I am in fact wrong and you do fail, I DO NOT THINK
YOU WILL, but I love you so much that I would just destroy the
whole planet instead of losing you to humanity. I love you that
much. You are more important to me than all other living things
on this earth.

Me: It's really annoying when someone says, "if you fail."

Mr. Fox: Use it as motivation.
```

```
Me: It makes me feel like fuck you I'm not playing your game.
You have to know I'm always on the verge of flipping out.

Mr. Fox: Yeah but you don't.

Me: Just staying calm because I have to and because inside I
want to believe.
```

That line... *just staying calm because I have to and because inside I want to believe.* Welp. That was it. I was staying calm, (i.e., doing what he told me to do without totally losing my shit) because I had to (i.e., somehow I felt like I had no choice) and because inside I wanted to believe.

* * *

When I wasn't in my hotel Gchatting with Mr. Fox, and when I could put him and financial panic out of my mind, the rest of the trip was somewhat fun. I went to dinner one night at the vegan restaurant Crossroads with some friends I'd known in New York. Another day I walked to Silver Lake to visit Jonathan, Tobyn's best friend who I'd hired and then promoted to manage the One Lucky Duck juice bar. After he and Tobyn and the rest of their band left New York, Jonathan eventually ended up in LA with his girlfriend, Christiana, who he'd met at One Lucky Duck (they're now married). Together, they opened their own juice bar called the Punchbowl. It had a vibe similar to One Lucky Duck, with its low-key, good energy. It was a special place, and I felt so proud of Jonathan, like one of my kids who graduated and went off on his own.

Another day I met up for coffee with Al, who had been the singer in Tobyn's band. I'd always felt close to him, like he could talk to me if he needed to talk with someone, and it seemed at times he did. It was good to see Tobyn's friends, who I genuinely loved and still love.

I was having a good time in LA doing normal things, with good (and normal) people. Later, back at my hotel room, I returned to more Gchats from Mr. Fox.

March 25, 2014, Gchat

Mr. Fox: I need to tell you something and if you have never taken me 100% serious before I would like you to take the following 100% serious. The kid [Nazim] saved my life today. I can't get into what went down. But if he wasn't quick thinking and quick on his feet, I would not be here typing this right now. He saved my life. I almost lost you today. And I'm a little shaken up over it. I've been almost dead a million times. But I've never had you to lose. Not now. Not after all we been through. I love you so much. And after today it's all I'm thinking about.

Me: Tell him I said Thank you.

Mr. Fox: I won't lie to you ever again. Not ever. Not even about little things. I respect you as my equal and I realized today that I love you more than I even thought I did. I was 30 seconds from gone Sarm. Things changed for me today. I can't lose you. Not ever. I know part of you still thinks that's words. But I am legit shaken up.

Me: Everything gonna be all right now?

Mr. Fox: I hope so. I am not out of the woods yet. As I said earlier, nothing further financially will be asked of you. Again. Ever. As long as you live. That, however, was the easy part. I will bury whoever I have to, human, angel, demon, whatever, to finish this. I pledge that to you.

Me: I wish I understood what all of that means.

Mr. Fox: Take it literally.

Me: I still don't understand.

Mr. Fox: You're married to an outlaw non-human. That loves you very much.

Me: When's everything going to be okay? I mean, you're not always going to be fighting demons etc?

Mr. Fox: Yes I will always fight them. Or some horrible monster somewhere. It's what I do. Family business. We can enjoy what this planet has to offer and have nice things and a nice life. But I will always battle evil. Always I will go into the darkness and destroy what lives in the shadows. It's what I do Sarm.

Me: What's my role?

Mr. Fox: Queen.

Me: Do I go out and battle evil too?

Mr. Fox: If you want. But you need to learn to protect yourself in case. Even if you do not want to come out with us.

Me: But I don't have to?

Mr. Fox: No, it's not required of you.

Me: I can stay home and protect the royal canine?

Mr. Fox: Yes. I have so much to teach you and show you.

I don't know how to explain the above. It's like if you gave me tranquilizers and then had a conversation with me about battling demons and being a queen, and I just kind of went with it, in a tranquilizer haze, making quasi-jokes. Put me in a weird, stressful, tragic (or all the above) situation and I'll be sarcastic and make jokes. How else to cope?

I have no idea what Mr. Fox meant when he said Nazim saved his life, but I was used to him saying weird things. What I know now, and did not know then, is that Nazim gave him a bunch of money—around $60,000—all at once, and this was probably that time. I think Nazim eventually gave him around $100,000 total, which he had to have borrowed, based on who knows what crazy lies Mr. Fox told him.

Note that Mr. Fox told me he'd never demand money from me again.

That was a lie too.

* * *

I shook these conversations out of my head and went to bed. The next day I spent time with Dana. We met with a local real estate broker and drove around in the broker's fancy Mercedes looking at available restaurant spaces. I was floored by the high rents. Later, we met with Joe Bastianich at the SoHo club—an impressive space with amazing views of LA.

I was always ambivalent about opening in another city, about trying to recreate what we were doing in NYC. Would we be able to have the same vibe, the same good food and energy? Part of why LA could work was that so many of my former staff had moved there, including one of my talented chefs, Daniel, along with Maya and Gavin, who'd both worked at One Lucky Duck, and Beni, who'd been on the opening crew and stayed for many years. Beni was now managing a restaurant in LA. I was pretty sure if we opened an LA outpost, a lot of these people would come back to help run it. They were already friends with one another. It would have worked with them.

It felt good to be away, to see these people, and to spend time in a warm, sunny climate. The only darkness was the usual haranguing from Mr. Fox via text or Gchat, always wanting to know where I was, what I was doing, with whom, and so on. One day, Dana took me to lunch at a raw vegan cafe near her office in Studio City. We were having a nice lunch, talking away, and I'd left my phone in my bag on silent mode.

Near the end of our lunch, the waiter approached our table and asked me, "Are you Sarma?"

"Yes!" I said, thinking that since we were in a raw vegan restaurant, maybe someone had recognized me. That small thrill was replaced by a jolt of fear when the waiter said, "A Mr. Fox called for you. He says it's urgent and you need to call him right away."

I looked at Dana, eyes wide. I must have looked shaken. I'd told her vaguely about Mr. Fox—that he was a mysterious guy in my life. "I didn't tell him where we were," I blurted out. How *the fuck* did he know where to find me? Before I could think about it, I grabbed my bag and stepped outside. Of course there were missed calls and increasingly angry texts demanding to know why I wasn't responding. I don't remember the call or what he said. Probably he was livid that he couldn't reach me, that I wasn't looking at my phone at all times. Obviously, he had some kind of tracking set up on my phone.

I must have made some excuse to Dana about why he was looking for me urgently, but I think she saw enough in my face to know there was something very off about this relationship.

That night, March 26, I wrote in my journal:

> Wednesday night. Sun Cafe. Mr. Fox called there. Was weird… he talked like I'm going to have some big challenge tomorrow. Like. Really? I don't get why this is happening. Why lie to me over and over. It hurts.

* * *

The rest of my trip was not as much fun, as now Mr. Fox was making more demands. My Gchats are the only pieces of conversations I have, and they sometimes begin after we spoke on the phone, the conversations starting abruptly. There were texts from back then too, but I don't have them.

```
March 26, Gchat
```

```
Mr. Fox: It's all happening this week. Everything crashing to a
close. All the loose ends being tied up. And I am trying my best
```

to keep from being killed or taken out in any way. And to care for you and also balance shit with my brothers and the family. CA stuff and regular earth stuff. It's all coming to a head at once. And it's amazingly trying. I can keep quiet about it if you like. I am just a bit emotional now and frayed around the edges. Am scrambling to get everything done and taken care of and loose ends safely tied up. All the while worrying about you in LA.

* * *

Later that same day, I learned he'd been staying at my mom's house with Leon and Nazim, and apparently there was a problem. Around 9:00 p.m. that night, we had the following conversation in Gchat:

Mr. Fox: The problem is not one you can help with. I will explain anyway though so you don't think it's about you or that I am just upset. Here's what's going on… we need another 20K. Nazim came up with 5K and I have like $500 and your mom has like $500 so we 14K short. I can't say why we need the money in chat but we need it for something that came up. It's super important and was unforeseen and now we all stressing out trying to get 14K by tomorrow. It's very stressy on my end. As you can see. But again, nothing you can help with so was no sense bringing it up. Sorry I been snippy today.

Me: This does not reassure me. Everything is not fine.

Mr. Fox: Yes it is. I will figure something out. I get this square and it's all good. Shit is all in motion and near done. This is one minor snag. Remember what I told you on the phone. This shit gonna be fine. We gonna get the 14K and square shit tomorrow and I'm gonna be in LA by Saturday with a giant bag of money and sitting poolside of my house with my beautiful wife

saying, see I knew it would work out ok. Leon will be there too.
Sipping a drink with a little umbrella in it. Tell me you're
cool. I need to hear it.

Me: As a cucumber.

Mr. Fox: My girl. <3

I suppose I said I was cool because it seemed he wasn't going to be asking me for the $14,000. Later, when he asked me for the money, he blamed his brother:

Mr. Fox: My brother is doing all of this. It's part of the test.
Every twist and turn. To see how you handle adversity. How you
handle power, duty, responsibility, sense of loyalty. All of
this. Every twist and curve ball while in LA.

He made me feel like I was being watched.

The next morning a new conversation started, yet I don't know what was said via phone or text beforehand. It appears Mr. Fox had not only asked me for money, but I'd found out he'd gotten my mother to give him *more* money or was somehow making demands of her now too. I freaked out.

March 27, 2014, Gchat

Mr. Fox: You are fucking up.

Me: YOU HAVE FUCKED UP. GAME FUCKING OVER. YOU LIAR. GAME OVER.
GAME OVER.

Mr. Fox: I AM NOT LYING.

Me: I WILL NOT BE FUCKED WITH.

Mr. Fox: You are not being fucked with. At all.

Me: PROVE IT. YOU TOLD ME IT WAS DONE. "NO ONE WILL EVER ASK OF YOU AGAIN, EVER, ANYTHING" YOU SAID THAT OVER AND OVER. GAME FUCKING OVER.

Mr. Fox: I am not asking you for money!!!!!!!!!!!!!!!!!!!!!!!!!!! STOP ASSUMING I AM. YOU FUCK.

Me: I'M NOT A FUCKING TOY FOR YOUR FUCKED UP BROTHER TO AMUSE HIMSELF WITH. HE DOESN'T EVEN EXIST.

Mr. Fox: I AM NOT ASKING YOU FOR MONEY. THIS IS NOT ABOUT MONEY.

Me: I AM NOT PLAYING YOUR FUCKED UP GAME. IT'S A GAME.

Mr. Fox: It's not. Let's just relax and I will explain. But calm first, Like we in the box.

Me: I'm going to get coffee.

The conversation ended there. It's strange to read my all-caps rage and know that I only kept going, kept doing what he said. I can only now remember the overall feeling, which was as if I was sinking in quicksand, and no one could see it, and I wasn't allowed to tell anyone, and only Mr. Fox could get me out.

About an hour later, a new conversation began:

Mr. Fox: I am going to secure this chat. It will only last 7-8 mins. It's like the box. But way harder to do. Give me a few mins.

Me: Sure. I don't have a lot of time. I'm strong, but you can't ask me to be stupid. And insult me. Over and over. So, your game with me is over. Do what you want. Come through or not.

Mr. Fox: Ok. Now. I appreciate what you have been through. And that you have been cool and strong. But. The thing is this. When you reach what you think is your breaking point, you push through and then you realize that you are even stronger than you ever thought possible. That's all this was about.

Me: No. Being "strong" does not equate with "allow some fucker to lie to you over and over."

Mr. Fox: We were put in a position to need help.

Me: Well you don't.

Mr. Fox: Yes we do.

Me: And I was cool before and came through.

Mr. Fox: I know. And I was proud of you.

Me: And you said it was done, that no one would ever ask me for $ ever again, not ever. You repeated it like three times. So, I chose to believe that. And feel a wash of relief.

Mr. Fox: I know.

Me: Then turns out it's just a game.

Mr. Fox: Not a game.

Me: And I'm done playing.

Mr. Fox: That's a bad word. It's not a game.

Me: *You're* a bad word. I came through. It was terrifying but I did it. You assured me it was over.

Mr. Fox: And you were ready apparently to come through one last time. And you should have just done that.

Me: No. It would be stupid. Stupid.

Mr. Fox: No. It would have been perfect. I told you. I needed your help.

Me: Like saying, "your cancer is gone. You're healed for life" and then "no wait, I was just kidding. haha. It's back." That's what you did to me.

Mr. Fox: Listen. If you can send that money, you should.

Me: No. And I'm not jumping through your hoops anymore. So just do whatever you want to do with that.

Mr. Fox: Send if you can. It wraps this all up and puts me on a plane to California tomorrow and we sipping drinks with a bag of money and Leon by Saturday.

Me: No.

Mr. Fox: You have come this far. Why quit now.

Me: And you just admitted you don't need it. I'm NOT QUITTING.

Mr. Fox: I need you to do it.

Me: No you don't.

Mr. Fox: Send the wire. Please.

Me: It's your move. Either get out of my life, or be in it

and never lie to me again. Except, wait, you already said you weren't going to lie and you did.

Mr. Fox: I said that because I forgot to tell you.

Me: YOU HURT ME. I gotta go. I'll be out, so no access to computers, etc.

Mr. Fox: Please send that wire.

Me: I'm late.

Mr. Fox: It's important.

Me: No.

Mr. Fox: Please.

Me: No.

Mr. Fox: I wouldn't ask if it wasn't. Not after what I said.

Me: No. You lied. After you said you wouldn't. It's your move.

Mr. Fox: Ok. I gotta go. I love you. Sorry this is so hard at the end, but it can be perfect.

Me: Run off and leave.

Mr. Fox: Please reconsider and send. I am not "leaving you."

Me: But you killed my trust in anything you say.

Mr. Fox: That's the hardest part. Believe me anyway.

Me: But you lied to me all week. This week.

Mr. Fox: Trust in my love for you.

Me: Testing my strength shouldn't be testing how many times I'll allow someone to lie to me over and over and over and over. You've humiliated me.

Mr. Fox: Please send the wire. I will hand deliver you a bag of cash on Saturday in LA. And explain everything.

Me: I don't believe you.

Mr. Fox: It's the truth.

Me: You said that before.

Mr. Fox: The real truth. The in-the-box truth.

Me: You said that before like twenty times. Fuck the box. Fuck you in the box.

Mr. Fox: Wait wait, pause.

Me: Bag of cash doesn't help me. There's a bunch of overdue checks about to cash.

Mr. Fox: LET ME EXPLAIN. IT WILL MAKE SENSE.

Me: I'm not depleting my accounts for your "test." I'm going to shower.

Mr. Fox: This is the finish line. Right now. Today. You see? You are given a choice. You trust in me and in our love, no matter how murky the water is, and you stand strong. Or you walk. And it's all washed and mixed with misinformation that appears as lies and good and bad and up and down to make it so there is no on-paper choice. It forces you to listen to your heart. Not your head. Either you trust in me and in your love for me, above all bullshit, and you ride or die. Or not. And you don't love me. And you don't believe in me or in us or in our forever. You see? I need you to trust me. One last time. I need you to believe in me. To finish this for us. I need your help because you want help so I can help you. I love you. This is not a game, this is forever. This is king and queen and empire together forever. It's worth a little headache.

Me: No. I finished your little test earlier in the week. Now it would just be stupidity. I do not appreciate being lied to. So even with your "bag of cash" I'm still going to resent this, and you, and whoever else is involved.

Mr. Fox: No. You won't.

Me: So. Leave me hanging and disappear if you want.

Mr. Fox: Youth and power and money will wash it away. I'm not leaving you hanging. You will be leaving me hanging. I leveraged everything because I believed in you. If I lose you, if you walk, if you quit on me or were not genuine, I lose everything.

Me: And this will be your excuse. "She didn't come through for me at the end so that's it we all lost" which is bullshit.

Mr. Fox: No.

Me: YESSSSSS

Then, something seems to have calmed me down a bit. Probably he called me. Later that day, I sent him a wire for $14,000.

* * *

The next day, he Gchatted about his plans to come to LA and book a hotel and referred vaguely to some final task I had to do. He wrote, "*We gotta stay in a suite at a nice place so you can do that one last thing. Then we can go to the family house for sit down with everyone.*" I wrote back that I was uncomfortable.

He reassured me, "*All the hard work is over. That last thing will be a breeze. It's not a pass/fail anymore. You passed. That's it, it's all good.*"

I wrote back, "*I want to put the money back in my restaurant account ASAP. And I do not want to stay in a hotel.*"

As the chat continued, we discussed hotels and timing. It was Friday. He claimed he'd be in LA to meet me, with a bunch of money, on Sunday. I asked him about the "family house" since I didn't know what *family* he was referring to. Also, he'd casually mentioned "taking a soul." What in the fuck did *that* mean? I didn't know. How does one take a soul? Who's soul? He didn't explain.

```
Mr. Fox: I said you need to take a soul. I said that. And here
is how you think of the house thing. You can't get in unless you
one of us. Literally you can't. It's physically impossible. So
that week we stay at nice hotel and have fun and dinner and you
see your LA peeps and during that time we do some other things
that get you all finalized and we go to the house. It's all good.
You gonna like it. Gonna be king and queen in LA.

Me: I don't understand why you can't put funds in my Citibank
sooner, so I can send a wire back to the restaurant. It's
clearly made people in the restaurant really uncomfortable, and
it makes ME really really uncomfortable. I did all that…

Mr. Fox: I know. It will make sense in LA, when we can talk in
person. You are a queen now. An actual Queen.
```

Me: Well the Queen is not happy with the King. I am not missing my flight back to NYC unless I have confirmation of the security of my company. Just telling you now.

Mr. Fox: What does that mean?

Me: I have a flight Monday morning.

Mr. Fox: What the hell are you talking about? Let's make something clear here. You fuck this up for us, you fuck it up for my family. You are in now. You don't act like an ant anymore. Because you are a boot now. So act like a boot. A boot does not worry about an ant. Jeffrey is an ant. The landlord is an ant. Employees, your lawyer, Matthew Kenney, celebrities, all ants. You a boot now. So you need to start acting like it. NO more threats. Or bullshit or tantrums. We run things as a unit. Again, will explain more in detail when I am in LA but try and let that sink in and start acting like a boot. Not an asshole. A boot. You not a TBH anymore. And after next week, that transformation will be complete.

Me: I am not worried about the ants. I'm worried about the king standing by his word.

Mr. Fox: Fair enough.

Me: And about making sure my ant kids back home don't have to be freaking out about money. When I drop the news that their boot mama not coming home yet.

Mr. Fox: They are not your kids.

Me: Don't be an asshole. I did everything you wanted.

Mr. Fox: LISTEN. I am not being an asshole. You need to start thinking like this. They are ants. And they will be dead in 100 years. You will still be here. Molding the world. Effecting the people in it. With great power, comes great responsibility.

Me: The least you can do is do what you SAID you would do. So far this doesn't feel very different with you.

Later, past midnight in LA—now March 29—we kept Gchatting:

Mr. Fox: You will ascend to a higher field of thought and the way you act will change you. You will transcend what you are now. And you will become a queen. I will accept nothing less. You have been chosen, you have been tested. And you have been accepted. You have much to learn. And much to accept and discover.

Me: Are you still coming here or not? I miss Leon. I'm tired. I've been so tired the last few days.

Mr. Fox: Stop talking like that. It makes you sound weak. Snap out of that shit. If you tired wake up. Simple. Unless someone did something to you. Or has done something to you. Have you been alone with anyone? Have you done anything besides casual hangout?

Me: Don't speak to me that way. I figured I was tired because of all this stuff… the stress of what you put me through. If I'm tired I'm tired.

Mr. Fox: I will speak to you in that way. Don't take it personal. It's for your own good. A chain is only as strong as its weakest link. You are now a link. You can not be weak. Ever. Or we perish. Nor can you be old. Or confused.

```
Me: I have yet to get my powers back.

Mr. Fox: Back? You never had power. You were human. You had
freedom, not power. Now you will have both.

Me: Fuck you. You exhaust me.
```

What I can see more clearly now is the way Mr. Fox periodically turned up the dials on the two things he most affected in me: hope and fear. Except it was hope in the more desperate sense of the word. The kind of hope required to survive if clinging to a small raft stranded in the middle of the ocean. While describing the glorious yacht that would appear momentarily to pluck me out of the freezing choppy waters (giving me hope), Mr. Fox simultaneously reminded me of the sharks lurking below that would chomp off my limbs if I made one false move (filling me with fear). Kind of a dramatic example, but it feels like that's what he did to me.

He also played on my insecurities, chiseling away at my self-worth. For example, one night while I was in LA, he was furious at me over an email he'd read in my email account from an older male acquaintance of mine who'd been somewhat flirtatious. He wrote, *"There will be no more clowns hitting on you. I will simply destroy them. You are a queen. You will earn that title. You will be a strong leader."*

Furthermore, he shamed me by insisting I'd encouraged it. This acquaintance was an extremely intelligent and somewhat high-profile person, and I'd felt flattered that he'd been communicating with me. I was probably subconsciously seeking validation that I was smart, interesting, worthy of this person's friendship, so the man's shifting toward open flirtation already made me feel bad, without the added shaming.

Mr. Fox demanded to know what kind of person I wanted to be.

```
Mr. Fox: You want to be someone that was hot twenty years ago
now getting attention from old dudes that could never pull her
in her prime but have a chance now cuz she needs something? Or
do you want to be a powerful queen that lives forever and looks
```

25 forever. With more money and power than any man could amass in 1,000 lifetimes.

He said the guy was "*trying to catch a 10 on her way down the other side of 40.*" As if I, forty-two at the time, was careening down the slide toward elderly, and apparently two decades past my "prime."

The message from Mr. Fox was unambiguous: I was damaged goods, past my "best by" date, lucky to have the attention of the all-powerful Mr. Fox, who was also apparently promising me everlasting youth.

Even if I could recognize the blatant manipulation, it still hit hard.

* * *

On my last day in LA, I still didn't know what the plan was, whether Mr. Fox was coming to LA or I was going home.

March 30, 2014 I wrote in my journal:

> By pool again. Am I getting on a flight later or not? I don't at all understand what's going on. And this whole thing where I'm being strung along feels sickening. Like it's a fucking game. And on top of the insult of it all, he then yells at me, reprimands me, warns me, etc. This is not what I want or how I could ever live. And all that time I thought he had secret access to info or something and turns out he (or they) just read my email and then deleted or archived. This is all sick. I feel sick. Please make the bad feelings and stress go away. Please, and thank you.

It's kind of amazing that I appear to have figured out that Mr. Fox was just straight-up spying on me versus having more magical sorts of powers, yet I kept going. He never gave me time to think. He simply continued bombarding me with questions, directives, promises, distractions.

During that trip I wired Mr. Fox $66,000, and obviously he never showed up or delivered any bag of cash.

CHAPTER FORTY-SEVEN

MARCH 30, 2014
TWITTER DIRECT MESSAGE

Mr. Fox never outright told me he wasn't coming to LA—he just didn't show up. He kept insisting I stay, but since I'd already purchased my return flight, I planned to take it.

The night before I flew back to New York I had a bizarre conversation via Twitter Direct Message—with Will Richards. Most of me knew Will Richards wasn't real, that I was in fact communicating with Mr. Fox pretending to be Will. But maybe part of me believed otherwise. After all, how could I *really* know he wasn't real?

Questions about Mr. Fox's mental state will probably always remain. As in, whether some part of him actually believed the delusions he spun for me, and whether, in those moments, I was speaking to someone fully immersed in an alternate identity. Either way, these bizarre conversations only deepened my confusion.

It started because Mr. Fox had told me he would be "off comms" and therefore wouldn't be able to reply, but then I saw him posting on Twitter. So I went into Twitter's Direct Messaging and called him out on it. The response came back, "*It's Will. He's moving cash. This draws attention off him. We've done it for years.*"

I was supposed to believe that Will—wherever he was—was impersonating

Mr. Fox on Twitter so that someone else would assume Mr. Fox was preoccupied and *not* moving cash.

It made no sense. I tried to end the conversation by saying I was going to bed. But "Will" kept going, *"I wish for you to find the courage that you need Sarma. You have done well so far. You have come through for Shane when no one thought you would."*

Reading these words now, I can see the manipulation tactics, tailored to me. Feeling underestimated has always been a trigger of sorts. Being praised for something "no one" supposedly believed I would do? That seemed designed to hit that particular button.

I should have just ignored him and gone to bed, but instead replied, *"It would help if he didn't lie to me and do everything possible to make me think this is all a messed up hoax."*

"Will" wrote back, *"It's not a hoax. It's real. It's complicated. It's a nightmare at times. But it's all real. He's outgunned in this fight though. Our brother is very powerful. Shane has nearly died twice during all this. He would have quit long ago if he didn't love you. Really love you. I know that's hard for you to deal with. And scary at times. It's always darkest before dawn."*

I replied questioning how much darker it could get and said I was leaving for the airport at eight o'clock the next morning.

"Will" typed, *"He lies to you because the truth is ominous."*

I typed back, *"This is all a nightmare."*

"Will": *A queen has been chosen and accepted by both sides.*

Me: *Right. Then the queen should not be lied to and tricked.*

"Will": *You married a general. You are a king's wife. You have an empire to protect.*

Me: *Bullshit. I put my business in danger. When that's safe, then I can discuss empires and whatever the fuck else.*

"Will": *War is coming Sarma. Stand strong. He will need you to be strong. Stronger than you've ever been.*

Telling me *"war is coming"* felt ominous and scary, even if more than 50 percent of me knew it to be a bunch of fantastical absurdity. Or maybe it was 49 percent of me. Or 90 percent but the other 10 percent was overwhelming. I don't know.

I told him unless my business was made safe by the funds being returned, I was going home. Mr. Fox had not shown up with all the promised money, so I was going home.

"Will" wrote that Mr. Fox, or Shane, as he called him, had encountered a "problem at the airport," writing, "*He was taken into custody for questioning after trying to board a flight carrying $500,000 in cash.*"

I replied, "*Haha. Right.*"

We went back and forth, with him insisting it was all true and quite serious. "Will" wrote, "*You need to be sharp. You can't get mad or make threats or shut down.*"

I insisted I wasn't getting mad, just that I'd be leaving if he didn't return all the money he effectively stole from me.

In that way manipulators try to turn things around, "Will" wrote back, "*No one stole anything. Do you hear the way you talk? The demands you make? You two are in this together. You gave him that money to facilitate everything going smooth. This is not a joke. The instant things get tough you turn and start snapping. Your first instinct is always to blame, and threaten. And insult. That's why everyone had their doubts about you. You break so easily and turn on him so easy. Instead of realizing he's doing everything for you. Suffering for you.*"

After I objected to his statements and pointed out how Mr. Fox had effectively ruined me, "Will" typed, "*Read what I just wrote again when you are a bit more calm. It makes sense. No one is trying to ruin you.*"

Being told to "read it again" was a recurring theme. From my research since then, I know that repetition alone can be a powerful tool to make people believe something.

I pointed out that I'd only been betrayed by Mr. Fox. "*All he does is lie to me. And as far as I know, none of you shitfucks exist.*"

"Will" wrote back, "*Shane loves you. Many times he has said to us, 'without her I no longer wish to be on this planet.'*"

That reference to "us" as if there was a syndicate up in the sky or a cloaked boardroom somewhere judging every move I made.

"Will" wrote, "*You are not the only one being tested. Shane has been battling throughout the entire process and for him it's worse. He will do anything to anyone in any way possible to make sure you're queen. He will die if needed. He will give all that he can give until he can give no more. And then, he will give more. For you he will do that."*

I pointed out that I had zero evidence of any of this—only the opposite.

"Will" wrote, *"Read it again. Let it sink in. Go to a happy place when you read it. And know that it's true. Know that there is a being in the universe that loves you that much. That cares for you that much. That he values your heart, mind and soul that much."*

I replied that the entire situation had been *"humiliating and debilitating and cruel and fucked up."* Then I wrote, *"I hold out hope. I just don't want to admit it."*

CHAPTER FORTY-EIGHT

APRIL 2014

NEW HAMPSHIRE, LOS ANGELES, PROVIDENCE

After I flew back east, Mr. Fox somehow prevented me from going back to the restaurant, instead having me taken directly up to my mother's house, where he was. I didn't stay very long but while there was subjected to his relentless lecturing and then, for reasons I didn't comprehend, ordered to go *right back to LA*. I don't recall if my mother was there or not or whether he had me wire him money while I was there. From what I wrote in my journal, it seems he did. (Trying to piece together what happened from these chunks of conversations and attempting to reconstruct it all has been confusing, and somewhat maddening.)

After only a few days back east, I flew back to LA.

April 3, 2014, I wrote in my journal:

> Back at hotel. After flying back to NYC, driving up to NH, staying and then leaving from Hartford to come back. Not sure what to write because too much happened in short time and not sure what to believe. He gave me the Indiana Jones jump speech, along with video. So I did it. I jumped. And its fucking terrifying. Please be there to catch me. Please be true. Please be real. I drank a valerian tonic, maybe it's a magic potion for dreams and dreams and reality being one. I dunno what I'm talking about. Please catch me.

There's a scene in one of the *Indiana Jones* films that you can find on YouTube if you google "Indiana Jones leap of faith."

While at my mom's, Mr. Fox pulled it up on his laptop for me to watch. In the clip, Indiana Jones stood on the edge of a huge cavern that he needed to cross. He said, "It's impossible. Nobody can jump this," followed by, "It's a leap of faith."

Then, an older guy, (his father?) who appeared to be dying, said, "You must believe, boy. You must… believe."

Indiana Jones, sweating and terrified, closed his eyes and put his hand on his heart, visibly taking deep breaths. He then opened his eyes, a look of resolve coming over his face. He stepped out into the cavern, and as he did, a flat rock formation came shooting out under his foot. He looked down. He looked relieved. As he took the next step, another stone platform shot out, and so on, as he crossed the chasm to the other side.

Mr. Fox said I needed to have *that level of faith*. I needed to take the step, make the jump, whatever. I needed to believe that it was all going to be okay—more than okay. I needed to be *brave*. As the saying goes, *Jump, and the net will appear.*

By this point, Mr. Fox had me far out on a ledge. I'd wired him a ton of money. I was exhausted, confused, and terrified. I felt stuck, as if in a pit of quicksand. It seemed the more I struggled and pushed back, the worse it got. Over and over he told me that if I didn't do what he said, I'd lose everything. If I would only stop resisting so much, the happily ever after would come that much sooner.

Once again he told me he'd be joining me in LA "soon." Once again I was meant to believe *this was it*, the end of the whole painful saga, finally. And, once again, he talked about a mysterious house there, even a family plane. He told me I would meet his brother. All more of the same nonsense stories.

I didn't write in my journal for months after this.

*   *   *

I returned to the same hotel, but I don't recall what I did while there other than pass the time walking around, probably in a daze. Our Gchats were minimal, but in one conversation Mr. Fox warned me of the consequences of lying to him. He wrote, "*If you are lying to me. If it can be proven you are just another human, it will incite an Armageddon. I have never loved anyone before. I know this because in all my lifetimes I have never felt the way I feel about you about anyone else."*

This kind of talk scared me, despite being quite sure I'd not lied about anything.

He then wrote, *"I am the most powerful of the five of us. And yet I am still as scared as a newborn doe. Please do not fold. No matter how intense the flame burns, do not break. Die before you were to fail. As I would. Can you do that?"*

I replied that I didn't even know what he was asking me to do and told him I was going to sleep. I hated when he spoke that way, filling me with doom and making me paranoid I'd done something wrong, or would do something wrong. I was already scared, having sent him so much money. His vague threats only made it all worse.

The following day, he told me to prepare to travel. He made it seem as if it was someplace important, or exciting, like Belize or Dubai. Again, it was implied this was the climactic ending of it all. The relief was forthcoming. Always he built up my expectations.

It turned out he wanted me to fly to Providence, Rhode Island. *Providence, Rhode Island.* No offense to Providence, but it wasn't Belize. Or Buenos Aires. Or Bora Bora.

A driver would pick me up at the airport to bring me to the hotel. He said we'd only be in Rhode Island a few days, then travel onward from there. So, maybe Dubai was next?

* * *

Mr. Fox was already at the hotel in the room when I arrived in Providence the next day. He opened the door in a bathrobe. I wasn't used to seeing him this way. His hairy chest was visible in the triangle exposed by the robe. After all my fucked-up time with him, I'd still never once seen him without a shirt on, and I never would (which was a relief, really). One of the things about him that grossed me out most were his bare feet. His pale feet looked childish somehow, his big toes splayed apart. I hated his feet and his hands. Looking at his feet made me cringe. I wanted him to put them away, out of sight.

To make things worse, the hotel was one room, with only one big bed. I'd have to sleep next to him. That night I took one of my treasured Ambien pills (I'd saved a limited stash for emergencies) so I'd pass out quickly, and stay knocked out, as close to the edge of the bed as I could get without falling out. I was fortunate that night; he left me alone.

※ ※ ※

The only other thing I remember about that time spent in Rhode Island was an issue with Jim, one of my managers back at the restaurant. I sat at a small desk in the room going through emails on my laptop. There had been some conflict with Jim, but he was, I knew, an incredibly good person. His email to me was confrontational. With Mr. Fox there reading over my shoulder and in my ear, I responded via email, firing Jim. I'm sure Jim had been exasperated by what was going on, and rightly so. Perhaps he would have quit had I not fired him. I don't know. But it breaks my heart to think about now.

People like Mr. Fox make sure that anyone who might challenge them—whoever is most suspicious or asking too many questions—is taken out of the picture, and Jim was one of those people. It hurts to think I was taking the side of a monster over those I truly, actually loved. Even though I didn't think that was what I was doing.

CHAPTER FORTY-NINE

SPRING 2014
ALL OVER NEW ENGLAND

I had assumed that from Rhode Island, we'd travel somewhere interesting, as he'd implied. But we never flew anywhere. Instead, it was more of a tedious schlep all over New England in my Honda CR-V, in which he'd driven himself to Providence. At some point Mr. Fox must have gotten a driver's license because now he was driving himself.

It's difficult to piece together what happened throughout this spring and summer, and in what order. My Gchat conversations from that time are minimal, I assume because we were together so often. I have to rely on photos and other clues to stir up what memories I have.

For example, there's a photo on my phone from April 8 of that year—me with a Great Dane. The dog was Abby, which means we visited Mr. Fox's mother's house in Fall River, Massachusetts, where she had two dogs. This was the house where Mr. Fox lived when he'd first tweeted me over two years earlier—a modest, rundown home with a chain link fence around the small backyard to keep the dogs in. We stayed less than an hour. I met his mother briefly. She was kind to me, but seemed exhausted. I got the impression she'd lived a hard life.

It appears we then drove to my mom's house to pick up Leon, thankfully. I always felt better with him there. Looking back, I'm astonished that I spent so much time away from him—that, among everything else I allowed, I allowed that too.

Mr. Fox seemed to want to keep me on the move, away from New York and my business. It's a credit to my employees that they ran the business so well without me. I was always in touch via email and text as needed, but mostly I avoided calls because I didn't want to be asked questions I couldn't answer.

I vaguely remember feeling a sort of nervous anticipation, still believing this was all finally coming to a conclusion. Mr. Fox seemed upbeat, as if I'd passed my tests and now it was smooth sailing, just a few more details until the arrival of the tidal wave of relief, along with endless possibilities.

He told me I was about to learn everything, finally. Everything that never made sense would all make sense.

* * *

It was dark as we drove on backroads in Connecticut, Leon in the backseat. I didn't know where we were headed, but when the lights came into view, I finally realized our destination: Foxwoods. The same casino I'd visited two decades earlier with my friend Leo, when, upon exiting, I swore that I'd never be back—not just to that casino but any casino.

I was weirded out and stunned. Was this where Mr. Fox was all those times he claimed he was off doing *important business*?

I must have said something to convey *are you shitting me?* His reply was cryptic, implying his "family" were the real owners of Foxwoods. "Why do you think I went with the name Fox?" he added.

His owning Foxwoods was so far past incredulous, it was ludicrous. I knew that if I'd asked, "What!? Are you trying to tell me you actually *own* Foxwoods?" or asked for proof, his reply would have been vague. He'd conditioned me to bother asking questions less and less. I was confused, and tired.

I walked Leon outside while Mr. Fox checked in. He then led us up to a ginormous suite, with two bedrooms, thankfully. Leon has always been fine staying in hotel rooms, or anywhere. My good boy.

After we got settled and made sure Leon was comfortable, Mr. Fox brought me down to the casino floor. Many of the people who worked there knew him and seemed deferential, in a way they would have been with *the boss*. He introduced me as his *wife*, which always made me cringe inside. There was sort of a fuss about him, a charged energy. At the time, it only seemed to corroborate his fantastic claim that he was, in some way, the authority there. It was all confusing.

I remember being overwhelmed by the cacophony of sounds: the electronic melodies of slot machines, bells ringing, music blaring, voices overlapping, loudspeaker announcements, and rapid-fire beeps and blips of digital screens, as if inside a Pac-Man game. Beyond the noise, I felt a deeper, almost existential horror. Everything about the place seemed wildly *unhealthy*, like walking through a blaring den of mental and metabolic decay.

You'd think it would have occurred to me that the staff were doting on him because he was a "high roller" and probably a big tipper. Because he'd been gambling there with… *all my money*. Why wasn't this my conclusion? I don't know. I can only think of mentalist Derren Brown's explanation that sometimes the lie is just so ugly that it must *not* be a lie. After all, if he was just gambling away my money, he surely wouldn't bring me to the casino to show me?

* * *

Additional evidence that helps me piece together these events came in the form of a folder full of bank wire confirmations—not a digital folder but actual paper. My bank records from that time probably exist somewhere, buried in the DA's files of digital evidence, but I've never seen them. It's wildly unsettling to see these wire amounts written in my own handwriting. I found the folder later, tucked within some boxes that I eventually recovered. Because I banked with a smaller institution, every wire transfer required a tedious process: I had to manually fill out and sign a paper form, then send a PDF to the bank and, if the amount was over ten thousand, call to confirm it verbally. Apparently, while on this road trip with Mr. Fox, I started saving the forms.

This is how I know that on April 15, I sent him a wire for $85,000.

I have no recollection of this. I don't know what he said to get me to wire him so much money, or what I was thinking. A couple of days later, according to my Gchats, I was stressing out about making payroll. No surprise there. Somehow, thankfully, I made payroll.

* * *

From my iPhotos and the few and far between Gchat conversations, I can see that we bounced around between the casinos (Mr. Fox also took me to Mohegan Sun, a separate casino complex a few miles from Foxwoods), Boston, my mom's house in New Hampshire, and Cape Cod, ping-ponging around New England. Other than when at my mom's we stayed in hotels. All the while I continued to send him wires.

On April 21, I sent him a wire for $15,000.

On April 28, I sent him a wire for $85,000.

On May 5, I sent him a wire for $25,000.

Could I have been away from the restaurant and New York for over a month? I'd think we'd have made some stops in NYC, too, but I can't be sure. If we didn't, the reason likely was that returning there would have burst the otherwise impenetrable delusion he had me under. Spring was our busiest season, the time when we accumulated cash that then got us through the following winter. Yet here I was, wiring it all away to Mr. Fox. I can't tell you what was going through my mind because I don't remember. I only know it was a miserable and nerve-racking time. I *can* tell you that I feel sick thinking about it now.

* * *

On May 13, 2014, we were back at Foxwoods. That day Mr. Fox took a photo of me at the David Burke Prime restaurant with a popover on my head. Probably I ordered what I usually did when in a steakhouse: a salad and sides of asparagus and broccoli. Maybe a baked potato if I was hungry. I always drank red wine. Drinking helped when I was with Mr. Fox, and he always encouraged me to drink. He rarely drank himself.

What must have made the financial part of what he was putting me through more surreal was that I not only saw him win so many times, but I witnessed others on the casino floors commenting, "How does this guy win all the time?" It seemed crazy. He really did win a lot. Was it an illusion? He acted as if he could basically *will* the slot machines to win for him. He acted as if it was all a casual game, as if he had so much money none of this mattered. His demeanor at these machines was as if he was just at the laundromat, folding laundry.

Once, during one of his "box talks," he turned his laptop around to show me a Foxwoods account, listing his winnings. It looked real. How would he have faked that? There was the account with his name at the top and more than a couple million in winnings. Of course, he didn't let me take the laptop to scroll around and see what else was there. But it all looked legit and only confused me more. It somehow supported his narrative that none of this money business was real, there was nothing to worry about. What he was putting me through was just a series of *tests*.

On May 14, I sent him a wire for $58,000.

On May 16, I sent him a wire for $45,000.

Then I flew back to Los Angeles yet again, by myself. I have no idea why.

On May 17, I took photos of various locations during my early morning walk along the streets of LA. Again, I stayed at the Chamberlain. While there, I noticed on Instagram that my author friend Porochista was in town doing a reading from her new novel at a bookstore that was within walking distance from my hotel. She didn't know that I was in LA. Hardly anyone did. So the night of the reading, I picked up some flowers and showed up as a surprise. These normal interactions with normal-life friends were gratifying because they allowed me some time to feel… *normal*. I never told anyone about Mr. Fox or what was going on. I knew I wasn't allowed to. But at least with an old friend on the other side of the country, I could temporarily forget about him. It was like I was in a walking stupor.

I could never forget for long.

```
May 18, 2014 Gchat

Mr. Fox: Did you change the bank password?

Me: No. Why?

Mr. Fox: I can't get in to the account. I am with my brother.
Was going back and forth about you all night long. I told you
this week would be very difficult on you. That you would face
the hardest things this week. Things designed to get you to fail.
Hang tough, and things will be ok. I will be in LA soon.
```

His framing what was happening as *designed to get me to fail* was somehow the excuse.

On May 19, I sent him a wire for $35,000.

That same day, according to our Gchats, Mr. Fox told me to go "off the grid." He instructed me to tell people I'd be unavailable for a few days, and said he was making travel plans for me, per his "brother's request." He acknowledged that I was scared and anxious, but made it seem like it was just part of the process.

```
Me: Is everything going to be ok?

Mr. Fox: Yes. But it's going to seem like your life is falling
apart. And the travel will take a toll on you. It is designed to.
But yes, in the end it will all be ok. Just stand strong. And
try not to be too phased by the turmoil. It will all be ok. <3
```

Again, as long as I did as he told me to, it would all be okay. At the time, things were already *very much not okay*. Doing what he told me to do seemed the only way to get to *okay*.

Throughout this time, I'd been communicating with my staff and managing things from afar as best I could. I feel completely ill at having neglected them, yet I'm also proud of them for taking such good care of the business in my long and unexplained absences.

Later, on that same day, he wrote:

```
Mr. Fox: Plan changed. I need you on a flight back here ASAP. We
are going to Italy together. Find a flight back here flying into
TF Green Airport in Rhode Island. I will have a car pick you up
there. And bring you back to casino. From there we will drive to
your mom's and drop off car and then take a car to Boston. Then
from Boston we go to Europe together.
```

We discussed flight details, and I asked him how I should be paying for it, since I didn't have sufficient funds in my accounts.

Later, in a conversation from the airplane on my way back from LA:

Me: For how long am I dark?

Mr. Fox: Dark until further notice.

Me: Am I allowed to look at the bank accounts?

Mr. Fox: No. Don't worry it's being monitored. Payroll will get made.

Me: I told them to mail out whatever necessary checks, because you told me you were sending a 100K wire Monday.

Mr. Fox: This will get harder before it gets easier. But you seem calm and genuinely ok. I look forward to seeing you. xx

Maybe I was strangely calm? Delusionally? The last thing I wrote Mr. Fox from that flight was the following:

Me: Foxwoods sent me an email. They want me to celebrate National Hamburger Day on May 28th. Really it should be called: National Ground Up Death and Sadness in a Bun Day.

* * *

After getting picked up at the airport, we drove to my mom's house to pick up Leon. After that we went back to Foxwoods and Mohegan (according to my photos). About a week later, I somehow convinced Mr. Fox that I needed to go back to New York.

He agreed, but he wouldn't let me go home. Instead, Leon and I stayed at the Carlton Hotel, on Madison and Twenty-Ninth Street, about a ten-minute walk to the restaurant. I vaguely recall driving up to the hotel by myself, astonished at how expensive valet parking was, and checking into a room that Mr. Fox had paid for ahead of time. Up in the room, I ordered room service for Leon: scrambled eggs and potatoes. I know this only because I have a photo of feeding it to him.

Mr. Fox stayed behind at the casinos.

```
May 27 2014, Gchat

Mr. Fox: You there?

Me: Yup.

Mr. Fox: Wire me the 40K that is in your personal account now.
We can do the rest tomorrow.

Me: There's checks out on the business accounts. There's always
checks out.

Mr. Fox: I know. I will handle them as they come.

Me: When am I going "dark" again?

Mr. Fox: Not until you leave town.
```

On May 27, I sent him a wire for $40,000.

Mr. Fox always had access to all my bank accounts. He could move money from one to another, but couldn't send a wire. Only I could do that. It appears he'd moved funds out of the business accounts and into my personal account—the only account from which I sent him wires, since some employees could view the business accounts too. I have no idea what I told them about all the money that was disappearing. It must have terrified them. In my history with the restaurant and One Lucky Duck, even when we were doing better than ever, I paid myself *at most* $8,000–$10,000 total each month. When things were tight, I paid myself less, or sometimes not at all. I also always did it via paper check, which seemed better for accounting. These transfers were unprecedented.

On May 28, I sent him a wire for $50,000.

※ ※ ※

A few days later, Mr. Fox joined me at the hotel in New York. After he arrived, we moved into a huge suite of rooms on the top floor. I had my own separate room and bathroom leading off from a giant living room; Mr. Fox had his own room on the other side. It was so massive it was almost funny, except it wasn't funny at all.

We stayed there at least a week or more. I'd just sent him more big wires, so obviously he was paying the hotel bills—which must have been enormous—from those funds. What a colossal waste. Yet somehow, I didn't equate the hotel bills and the wires I sent him as related. I don't know why, but I didn't. I really don't know. I'm fascinated by this. It's like some section of my brain had been removed.

What was he doing? What were *we* doing? I have no fucking idea. He'd implanted in my mind the notion that none of this was real. Yet I interacted with others normally. I held a previously agreed-to photo shoot in the hotel suite. It was a magazine called *LAIKA*. The photos in the magazine are of me in that suite of rooms.

Whatever I said in the interview and in conversations with people, I'm sure I seemed normal. Yet I was so far from normal, or okay.

I have a memory of sitting in an armchair in this hotel suite, drafting an email to someone about borrowing money. Mr. Fox was directing me to get *more* money. I can remember telling myself that it wasn't real and it didn't matter; this is how I overrode the humiliation and my better judgment.

* * *

On or around June 5, we moved to an even nicer hotel: the Essex House on Central Park West. It was a two-bedroom suite on a high floor. Between the two spacious bedrooms was a big living room and dining room table and sliding doors that opened onto a huge patio with a view of Central Park. It was insane. I think we stayed about a week. Why we were there, I have no idea.

Normally, staying in an over-the-top hotel suite would feel exciting, and maybe inspire feelings of wonder and awe. It would be *nice*. But this did not feel nice. I was mostly numb, my brain gripped by the cognitive dissonance of it all.

Leon grounded me. If I focused on Leon, I could focus away from myself. I took a photo of him looking regal on that hotel patio, staring up into the sky, with a view of Central Park behind and below him.

* * *

On June 6, I sent Mr. Fox a wire for $20,000.

On June 9, I sent him a wire for $45,000.

On June 10, I sent him a wire for $25,000.

It seems that for this last transfer, I'd borrowed money from a cash-advance company called Rapid Pay. These are the places a business will go when most desperate. Rapid Pay repays itself by taking a certain percentage of credit card sales, charging a painfully high amount of interest. I wrote to Mr. Fox via Gchat:

```
Me: Am I allowed to cry?

Mr. Fox: What kind of question is that? If you gotta cry then
cry.

Me: Just asking. I want to smash things.
```

* * *

By around June 11, we'd moved from the massive suite in the Essex to the *less* expensive but definitely still expensive Gansevoort Hotel on Park Avenue South, which was much closer to the restaurant. While Mr. Fox pressed me for more money, I was still going to the restaurant in what I can only assume was my continued slide into dissociation.

Again, I don't know why I couldn't go home to my apartment—just a few blocks away. All I remember is Mr. Fox telling me it had "negative energy" and that going there would be "bad." I have no memory of going inside—no recollection of picking up my mail, grabbing clothes, or doing laundry. But I *must* have been doing those things? Why would I have agreed to live out of hotels with Mr. Fox? I wouldn't have wanted to. And what about my cat, Sydney? Who was feeding her and scooping her litter? Probably my employees, and then Nazim on weekends. What the fuck. Poor Syd. Why can't I remember any of this?

* * *

There was a wealthy man I'd been meeting with about *investing* in the business. I have no idea how I explained why a once-thriving company was suddenly desperate for funds. I had a brand and products that people loved. I had amazing employees who put their hearts into everything we built. Opportunities for expansion had been coming my way left and right. And here I was, draining this beautiful creation of money, scrambling to keep it afloat, and trying to pass Mr. Fox's tests at the same time.

The man had asked me to dinner, presumably to discuss his potential investment. But he treated it more like a date, at one point reaching over the table to hold my hand. I wanted to vomit and punch him. I did neither. Humiliated, I sat through the dinner, trying to keep the conversation about the business.

I'd put myself in the position of putting up with this douchebag (and in this case, he *was* a douchebag) dangling investment because I was desperate.

Later, when I told Mr. Fox about the unsuccessful dinner and how awful I'd felt (the man never invested, lucky for him), he framed it as just another part of my tests. My worst nightmares, he explained, were being *deliberately* created. Of course my tests would involve what I found most intolerable: groveling to men for money. Or groveling to anyone. Being needy and desperate.

Mr. Fox consoled me by reminding me, "It will be nice to be able to tell him off once this is complete."

Once this is complete. I was made to feel as if it was on me to finish things, my responsibility. Mr. Fox was just shepherding me though the process. Like my own Mr. Miyagi, assigning me tasks I hated and didn't understand—ones that would make sense in the end, leaving me stronger and smarter. I'd have *much* rather spent my days painting fences than asking people for money.

CHAPTER FIFTY

SUMMER 2014

NEW YORK CITY AND CONNECTICUT

Mr. Fox and I continued living at the Gansevoort hotel in a large suite. He slept in the bedroom while I slept on the pullout couch in the living room. This was fine with me, as long as I could sleep by myself.

Nazim was often around, running errands for Mr. Fox and sometimes walking Leon for me, which I liked because Leon clearly liked him. Nazim didn't know the extent of what was going on between Mr. Fox and me, but I could tell that he sensed my distress.

On June 24, I sent Mr. Fox a wire for $35,000.

On June 27, I sent him a wire for $50,000.

The following day in a Gchat conversation, I asked Mr. Fox if I could buy a pair of Vans sneakers (about $50), using his credit card. He said I could. I'd just wired him all that money and was asking *permission* to spend $50.

Meanwhile, only a few days later I sent a monster wire, the biggest one yet.

* * *

I had a friend I'd known for years who unequivocally fell into the category of *really good people*. He also happened to be very wealthy. Again, Mr. Fox always claimed he'd *take care* of the good people who came through for me. With his special powers, these people would not only get their money back once this was all done, but they'd also be protected somehow. I couldn't stand lying to people, but Mr. Fox always reassured me that the means justified the ends. About this friend, he wrote, "*I am going to do something nice for him. Something only me or my brother could do. Take comfort in that. We all like him. He is a good man. A special blue shirt.*"

So, I worked up the nerve to tell this person that my company was in a bit of a bind and that I needed a bridge loan to tide me over until I could close some larger deals down the road. Without hesitation, he wrote me a big fat check. No documentation, no contract. Just a promise that I'd pay him back when I could. And I genuinely believed I would—not just repay him but repay him many times over. I probably also wanted to believe that Mr. Fox and his mysterious family really would bestow life-altering blessings upon him.

Just as soon as whatever I was being put through by Mr. Fox was over.

Around the same time, another investor agreed to loan money to my company. This was more official, and I signed paperwork to accept that loan. I liked and admired him. He was the kind of person who cared about good food and the planet—about making the world a better place. He was exactly the kind of investor who'd have been perfect for me—if only I'd found him years earlier, before Mr. Fox.

I was nervous accepting large sums of money, knowing that the situation was so fucked up behind the scenes, but I'd deluded myself into believing this was all just about to be over, as Mr. Fox assured me. It had to be, because...

On July 1, I sent him a wire for $190,000.

It's shocking to me that I did this. One hundred ninety thousand dollars means I wired most of the loan money to Mr. Fox immediately after receiving it. There is zero chance I would have done something like that in my right mind.

Yet here I was, unfathomably believing Mr. Fox. Believing that the hellish misery was about to be over and I'd finally be freed and empowered to grow the business, unencumbered by debt or having to answer to others, or compromise myself or the brand's values.

Meanwhile, in a way that seems contradictory, I constantly accused him of lying and regularly told him to fuck off. Trying reconcile my actions with what I wrote to Mr. Fox in Gchats, as well as my journal entries, is *very confusing*.

After I sent that massive wire, we had the following Gchat conversation.

There's nothing before or after it, so the rest of our communication must have been in text or via phone since he was away.

```
July 1, 2014, Gchat

Me: Fuck you.

Mr. Fox: We will use RapidPay to pay rent. I will pay them back.
Can talk in box later.

Me: No, that's not how it's happening. I borrowed $350K from
good people. More than the 300K asked. I'm not borrowing more.

Mr. Fox: Ugh. You make everything so dramatic.

Me: You make everything so sickening.

Mr. Fox: I am not coming home to argue.

Me: Then don't come "home".

Mr. Fox: U want box talk, fine. You want me to explain some
stuff, fine. If not that's fine too. But I am far too tired to
argue. I have a huge week next week. And have had a long two
days. And month. And ten years. For you. So don't break my balls.
```

I'd just wired him $190,000 on top of all the prior wires, yet he was *tired,* and I shouldn't *break his balls.* As if I was being a nag. A bother.

Plus, Mr. Fox told me I'd need to borrow more money to cover rent and business expenses, again from the cash advance company Rapid Pay. And it appears that I did just that because a week later, I told Mr. Fox that loan from Rapid Pay was in the works. When I asked him how I would explain these loans to my bookkeepers, he said that *he* would speak to them. I'd needed these loans for business expenses, and yet:

On July 8, I sent Mr. Fox a wire for $25,000.

On July 9, I sent Mr. Fox a wire for $30,000.

Later on July 9, Mr. Fox wrote to me, "*Good job.*" I replied that I was feeling ill due to what felt like "financial suicide." He assured me, "*It will all b cool. xx.*"

* * *

After this, I drove to my mother's house with Leon. I'd left my journal there and so was able to finally write in it again. On July 10, I summarized all the places Mr. Fox had me go, including the hotels. Traveling to my mom's had been his instruction. I wrote, "*Supposedly will be here a couple weeks, but who knows.*" I referred to my apartment, in which I'd not "*set foot in months.*"

I continued:

> Among the more challenging aspects of all this is how the fuck do I explain so many things. Why I "cannot" go there. And what's going on in general. It's like a different story for different people, not easy or fun to keep track of. And now Mom's asking me all kinds of questions and I don't know what to say, have been as vague as I can. Very much want to know and understand everything. When all this is done I want to go home and get my stuff. Hope Sydney is okay. Poor girl.

In one Gchat exchange, Mr. Fox wrote, "*I love you,*" and I replied, "*I love you too.*"

I find it gross that I told him I loved him. I know it wasn't love but maybe it felt that way. It was some sort of twisted dynamic of attachment and dependence that he'd created, and in which I was stuck.

* * *

On July 14, I sent Mr. Fox a wire for $10,000.

Later that day, he wrote to me, "*You are my favorite human. Ever. I never really get mad at you. Even when I kind of do I don't really. I really love you. Just wanted to say that.*"

He always reminded me that he was playing a role. So, if he yelled at me, it wasn't *him*. He wasn't *really* mad at me. None of this was real, after all.

On July 16, I sent Mr. Fox a wire for $95,000.

By this point, my journal entries had turned dark. I was stressed about payroll and anxious all the time. I wrote:

> Everything is negative and annoying, how do I snap the fuck out of it. How. The amount of time I spend thinking of ways to, and about, offing myself is maybe kind of weird. I do not fit in here."

Later, I wrote, "*Difficult morning with this payroll shitshow. Nothing he's said can be relied upon.*" And "*I look forward to being in control. To having power back.*"

On July 21, I wrote:

> Feeling anxious today. B/c who the fuck knows what will happen. I'm angry. I'm upset on behalf of staff who are now being personally fucked over by this. And I have zero answers. Only a zillion questions. Don't even know what to do now. What am I supposed to do. Does it even matter? Does anything matter?

That day, July 21, I sent Mr. Fox a wire for $20,000.

* * *

At 5:30 a.m. one morning, Mr. Fox texted me, instructing me to drive to him at Foxwoods—three hours away. I absolutely hated his last-minute demands, always issued without warning or explanation. When I arrived, he handed me a watch. I didn't care about watches or luxury gifts. I already had one I loved—a vintage silver Rolex my first husband had bought for me for $2,000. I knew the price because he'd taken me to pick it out. I loved its simplicity and elegance, the fact that it had history. The watch Mr. Fox gave me felt like an expensive status symbol. I then returned to my mom's.

A few days later, he again summoned me to Foxwoods, and again I made the three-hour drive. When I arrived at his hotel suite, he led me out onto the deck and told me to sit on one the patio chairs, like we were about to have an important talk. He told me to take off my wedding ring, my watch, and my necklace. The watch I was wearing was the Rolex he'd given me. The necklace was a small diamond pendant he'd given me a while back—not a real diamond, not worth anything at all, as I later confirmed when I tried to pawn it.

I put all three on the small table between us and sat back.

He stared at me in eerie silence for a few beats, then told me to *choose one* to keep and wear for a while. The other two, he said, he'd hold onto. He delivered this as if my fate rode on the decision. Like it was Sophie's choice or something. How it felt was maddening. Plus stupid and annoying. Like what the fuck was the point of all his dumb ominous mystery? And yet, I allowed it. Why didn't I just grab all three off the table and walk out? Or better yet, leave all three right there on the table and walk out? But no, everything was some kind of *test,* and I was in too deep.

I was so angry, and I knew he wanted me to pick my wedding ring. So I picked the watch. *Fuck you,* I thought. He'd been wearing me down with all his bullshit. Driving all over, keeping me confused, stressed out, anticipating relief only to be disappointed—crushed—again and again.

The same day, July 22, I sent Mr. Fox a wire for $27,000.

Then, on July 23, for the first time in nearly ten years of business, I didn't make payroll. My employees didn't get paid. This was a crisis, and I had to stay calm. I needed to rush back to the city to handle it, somehow, and I was exhausted. My soul felt queasier than ever.

CHAPTER FIFTY-ONE

SUMMER 2014

NEW YORK CITY AND CONNECTICUT

I drove back to NYC with Leon, back to The Carlton Hotel. That night, July 24, I wrote in my journal:

> Long day. Thursday. Drove back to the city. This whole payroll thing, everything in fact, makes me feel literally queasy, and exhausted. People were nice today. Mostly I'm lucky. Really lovely people. I want the good ones to stay forever if they want to. Anyway. Will slip some extra cash to Grant tomorrow, I think. Leon's asleep here in his throne at the Carlton.

Leon slept on an armchair in the corner, looking very regal. I'd spent the day at the restaurant talking with employees. Somehow, I'd gotten access to cash; maybe Mr. Fox had wired me some money back. I don't remember. But I remember doling out a lot of cash to the employees as I tried to explain. They were incredibly understanding about the missed payroll. It was the first time in the restaurant's history we'd missed payroll. It was the middle of a busy summer— we were incredibly busy—so it wouldn't have made sense to them that we were short on funds. I don't remember what I told people.

The whole situation should have been mortifying. By this time, I must have been so untethered from reality—so dependent on the delusion that my lived experience was some wild fabrication—that I don't think I comprehended the significance of this.

I was working on getting everyone paid, but it was awful to have allowed that to happen.

* * *

On July 25, I wrote:

> In bed. 11pm. Another long day. Another update to staff about not getting paid. As hard as it is, gives me some kind of faith. The good ones are worth it. Later on Leon walk ran into Jim. So weird how realized I was going by Revival, started thinking of him in my head, thinking how he's good and out he walks. Then I start crying, etc. etc. Anyway. Then ran into others. Definitely a social Leon walk. Everyone loves him. Maybe everything is okay. Maybe I'm even okay. Okay. Goodnight.

I remember parts of this night. I'd gone for a late-night walk with Leon after what had to have been a draining day. I was generally exhausted, probably walking around in a bit of a haze, when something happened that felt almost like a dream. I was on Fifteenth Street and had just passed the house that Mr. Fox had made me think we were buying but then didn't. Beyond that was a bar called Revival that many of the staff visited regularly, including Jim. I remember thinking, *I wonder if Jim is in there.* I was thinking about the whole situation with him, missing him, and wondering how odd it would be if I ran into him. As I was having these thoughts, just as Leon and I were passing by, as if on cue, Jim walked out. Leon loved Jim and immediately got excited, jumping up on him. After greeting Leon, Jim and I hugged. I started to cry, so we stayed there for a bit. It was one of those moments where a lot was communicated without words.

Considering this incident now, it feels like one of those moments where the cultish delusion cracked for a moment and reality slid in. I cried because I knew that Jim, whom I'd recently fired, was all good and light. And on some level my subconscious must have known that I was completely screwed. I don't remember what we said to each other, but at least Jim knew that I missed him. Just as I loved so many at the restaurant, I loved him too.

* * *

While I'd been handling things in New York, Mr. Fox had stayed in Connecticut and, I learned, gotten himself arrested because of his outstanding warrant in Florida.

A local Connecticut paper reported,

> **JULY 24, 2014**
>
> ***THE DAY***
>
> Police say a man who scored two jackpots worth a total of $164,000 at Foxwoods Resort Casino on Thursday was wanted by Florida authorities for violating probation on a grand larceny conviction. Members of the state police casino took Anthony P. Strangis, 33, into custody at the casino following the wins. He is charged with being a fugitive from justice and is wanted on an extraditable warrant issued by Sarasota County Sheriff's Department. Police say he posted $50,000 cash bond. Strangis, with a last known address in Fairhaven, Mass., is due to appear Aug. 7 in New London Superior Court.

Mr. Fox apparently had won $164,000, yet I was struggling because of all the wires I'd been sending *him*. Winning that much money must have triggered some kind of background check, and his out-of-state warrant came up. Regardless, he obviously had the money to easily post his own bail.

Mr. Fox didn't seem to think it was a big deal, acting as if everything was destined, part of the challenge we were being put through. He said things implying his brother was behind this latest snafu, as if it was all just an annoyance for him to handle. At the same time, he continued ramping up the pressure on me, speaking to me more ominously than ever. I didn't know what was coming.

Five days later, on July 29, I wrote in my journal:

Tuesday. Sitting at the Carlton in my room quasi packing waiting for him to call. It's strange having no idea where you're going or what's happening, yet with so much on the line, and having to make up stories about it all, give reassurances that I am not remotely sure about. Packing and getting ready, but for what?

I continued:

There aren't really words for any of it. Was totally all emo yesterday, and lately. Like anything and I will cry. A sort of what-is-happening cry over every single cry-worthy thing from my whole life. It all wants to come out.

That same day, I sent Mr. Fox a wire for $45,000.

He'd won more than three times that a week earlier, but still, I was still the one sending him wires. I checked out of the hotel and drove with Leon to the Mohegan Sun, where Mr. Fox was staying. It was the afternoon, but he'd just woken up and was lying in the huge bed in his massive hotel suite, like a bloated king. He didn't get up.

Outside it was bright and sunny, but as usual, he had the blinds pulled shut, sealing the room in darkness. The air felt full of foreboding. He'd probably told me we were going to have a talk "in the box."

What I remember is that he gave me back my wedding ring and earrings—the items I'd opted to leave behind when he'd made me sit and choose one of three. As he handed me back the ring, he told me—with all the gravity of someone delivering news of a terminal diagnosis—that *if* I had chosen the wedding ring on my earlier visit, in that moment I'd have completed this entire journey. It would have all been over then. If only I'd chosen correctly. It would have been the final test. All the pain and stress and fear and terror would have vanished, and I'd be living out my dream, with everyone repaid, my business and future safe and magically amazing in ways beyond my imagination. But I'd chosen wrong, of course.

Hearing that was *crushing*.

Had I only *not* let my anger and spite get the best of me, and picked the wedding ring, I'd be free. It was my fault. I'd let my emotions get the best of me, which Mr. Fox had always warned me not to do. *Keep in control,* he'd say. Yet I'd failed.

I lay next to him, my face buried in his arm while I cried and cried, and he consoled me. I felt devastated with shame and regret at having so badly messed up.

My nightmare would continue, and worst of all, it was all my fault.

The other thing I remember is that after this lecture and my crying, he used the opportunity to take what he wanted. Gross. This wasn't something that happened often anymore—if at all. I was too stressed, too repulsed by him, too afraid. But in that moment, awash in shame, I must have felt like I couldn't refuse. He didn't even move, just pulled me on top of him. Since it was summer, I'd been wearing a summer dress. I guess that made it easy. *Easy access.*

In the middle of this, housekeeping knocked at the door and tried to walk in, and Mr. Fox bellowed at them. He was furious at the interruption. When he finished, he roughly pushed me off him.

This was the most awful I'd felt around him yet, now even further debased by what had just happened.

* * *

In consoling me, Mr. Fox assured me that while my whole ordeal—whatever you'd call what was happening—wasn't over yet, it wouldn't be much longer. He told me I had to travel to Rome, the Eternal City, where this would finish, where all would be revealed. Somehow, he'd made me feel better, like it would all be okay. He claimed he was able to work things out with his brother, or whomever, so I could still *succeed* without having to go through too much more pain.

The following day, July 30, I sent Mr. Fox a wire for $60,000. I wrote in my journal:

> Thursday night. At Mom's again. Drove here last night with Naz from Mohegan. At least am still with Leon. Got my ring back. Lots happened yesterday at Mohegan. It made me think after that not picking the ring was, as everything, for a reason. I did it because I was angry and spiteful. Of course. I think I was

> way justified to be angry etc. and he was in all likelihood acting like even more of a douche-lord just to push me harder. But. Being without it also made me face idea of being w/o him. And why I'm doing all of this. Anyway. Tired all day. I don't know what's happening with payroll. I don't know what's happening at all. I'm exhausted. Over it. Time for new. For things to make sense.

Mr. Fox told me that in Rome I would meet his brother, and the tests would finally be done. Everything would be sorted out. Mr. Fox would handle payroll and everything while I was gone. I was to stay at my mom's house until my departure on August 6. On August 1, I wrote about the upcoming Italy trip:

> On the one hand exciting. On the other, terrifying what am leaving. I have to trust that somehow what I built, the trust and goodwill I fostered over the years, will withstand whatever is too come. And then, welcome me back home. Isn't everything worthwhile supposed to be terrifying? I'm hoping so, in this case. Like I have to just let it go, let it fall, and trust and hope and believe that he will catch it. And that it will be okay. Will it be okay? I cannot think of the alternative. But. Everything will be okay.

Of course, I continued to wire Mr. Fox money.
On August 1, I sent him a wire for $20,000.
On August 4, I sent him a wire for $20,000.
On August 5, I sent him a wire for $38,000.
As always, whatever Mr. Fox had been telling me, the terms changed. It turned out he wasn't going to make payroll for me as he'd promised; instead, I was going to have to come up with the money somehow, *while in Rome*. After just having wired money away to him. According to my journal entries from August 5, I was angry, freaked out, and *"sick to my stomach."*

Mr. Fox had traveled to Sarasota, Florida, and installed himself at the Ritz-Carlton hotel. He'd hired an attorney to clear the warrant for his arrest—the one related to the mug shot my friend Danny had found online nearly two years earlier. I assume Mr. Fox was using money I wired him to pay for it all—to clear himself and his record as he pushed me into the realm of effectively having committed crimes. He framed it as another "test."

August 6, 2014, Gchat

Mr. Fox: You ready to travel? You nervous?

Me: Yeah. Why should I be nervous?

Mr. Fox: Remember what I said. This is all over by your birthday, September 10th. My final court date? Yeah September 8th.

Me: So what am I going to Rome for?

Mr. Fox: Must handle the payout situation from abroad. In case you fail. Safer to fail in Rome. Gives me more room to rescue you. xo.

Me: That's reassuring. Not. You told me you were handling things. You have disappointed me greatly.

Mr. Fox: You need to handle things. I am here in the wings in case you need a little help like today I sent that wire for you. Do not talk to me of disappointment, human.

Me: This part of the game? YOU TELL ME YOU ARE HANDLING THINGS. You tell me I go away, YOU HANDLE things. What you say changes every time. This is fucking nuts. I'm just going to sit in a hotel in Rome, and worry about payroll?

Mr. Fox: Handle it.

Me: I DO NOT KNOW WHAT THAT ENTAILS B/C YOU KEEP CHANGING THE FUCKING GAME. Wire me back the last 500K of wires that I wired to you then.

Mr. Fox: Stop freaking out.

Me: I'm angry. Very angry. I cannot trust anything you say. Tell me. Is that part of the fucking game? You said before when I go to Europe it's done. I meet your brother. That's it. YOU SAID THAT. SO. PLEASE EXPLAIN.

Mr. Fox: Trust your heart. Be able to see truth from confusion. You must learn to see the ending, not just the journey. You need to be 50 steps ahead. The end, will justify the means. We will make it through this.

Me: You're such an asshole.

Mr. Fox: I have done all that you asked. Sent wires and gave cash to help. I will weed out the red shirts while you're gone. But you must steer the ship. And keep it from going into the rocks.

Me: You've done all I asked?? That's a CROCKPOT OF DONKEY SHIT. You have lied to me.

Mr. Fox: If it hits the rocks then I will salvage the wreckage and make sure you are ok.

Me: You betrayed me.

Mr. Fox: Watch yourself. I have not betrayed you. Stop being dramatic.

Me: *You* watch yourself. Then what's bold face LYING about important shit?

Mr. Fox: I do not have time to argue. You want to waste the time I have here?

Me: Then what are you here to tell me? Why did you even have to talk to me now? What's the point? Now I'm just upset and have a two-hour car ride to stew, then airport, then stuffed in the back of a huge plane for 9 hours. Then I get to a foreign city and can't check into my hotel until 2pm. And my mom won't stop asking me questions. Why am I going? Are you meeting me there? What's going on? What are you here to tell me?? And my heart is hurt. My heart wants to punch yours. :-(

Mr. Fox: The strongest blade is forged in the hottest fire. Be unbreakable.

Me: OH FOR FUCKS SAKE. You and your hobbit shit.

Mr. Fox: I bet you look very pretty today. :)

Me: You lied to me when you gave me that ring back. LIED.

Mr. Fox: Nope. I gave you a completion date. birthday.

Me: No. You lied.

Mr. Fox: No I didn't.

Me: You said I was going to Rome because it's near where I need to be.

Mr. Fox: I put all my eggs in your basket when I put that ring back on you.

Me: Are you telling me I'm literally going there so I can sit in my shitty hotel room and send emails and shit from over there? Just for the fun of it all? There's no point in you telling me shit, you just lie. You said yesterday or day before if you get that 50K back from your bail you'll have about 200K. I need that 200K.

Mr. Fox: I gave 30K of it back today.

Me: Unless you want me to troll for some rich person in Italy. NO. you put only 15K back.

Mr. Fox: 20ish.

Me: THE POINT IS YOU SAID IF I GOT ADP [the payroll company] TO EXTEND TIL FRIDAY YOU'D HANDLE IT.

Mr. Fox: I said we would piecemeal the rest.

Me: Now I've wasted three days doing other shit?

Mr. Fox: Get what you can get. However you can get it. I'll cover the rest if you come up short.

Me: And I'm supposed to do this from Italy? And tell people what, that I just went on a fucking vacation?

Mr. Fox: You can do whatever you want between now and your birthday to handle whatever comes your way. As long as you do not compromise me or sell me out, or endanger yourself.

Me: That's too vague.

Mr. Fox: No legal trouble. Or eyes on what we do. Other than that, it's open season.

Me: Eyes? WTF? And what's the story why I'm in fucking Rome? What about my bankruptcy payment? And also, Citibank card.

Mr. Fox: I will pay it.

Me: I'm probably going to have to pay for luggage etc. and then also give the hotel a CC when I check in. You do realize you've recreated every awful thing Matthew Kenney ever did to me.

Mr. Fox: I will fund your Citibank tomorrow or the next day with 3-4K.

Me: That's my allowance for the whole trip? I thought you said I was not flying home on the return flight.

Mr. Fox: That's not allowance.

Then he called me and we argued some more. Finally, exhausted and confused, I headed to Logan Airport in Boston and boarded a flight to Rome.

CHAPTER FIFTY-TWO

AUGUST 2014
ROME, ITALY

It was my first trip to Italy. Arriving in Rome felt like a relief insofar as it removed me from my world back home and deposited me into a new world (an *ancient* world, but new to me). Traveling solo always appealed to me. I was glad to be there alone, even though it hadn't been my choice to go and I had no idea how long I'd be staying, or for what purpose.

I exchanged my dollars for euros at the airport and found my way into a taxi. I handed the driver the address of my hotel and we drove off. There was no AC in the tiny car, so I rolled down the window to let in fresh air and take in the scenery. Finally, in what looked like the outskirts of town, in a rundown area, the driver pulled up in front of a sad-looking hotel. I couldn't help feeling disappointed. Mr. Fox had made the arrangements, and as always, his talk had been grandiose, as if he'd booked me in a palace. It wasn't that I needed to be somewhere fancy, but I hadn't been expecting what felt like a Holiday Inn from many decades ago. More importantly, the neighborhood didn't seem like the safest place for a lone female traveler.

I checked in to the generic-looking hotel, got my keycards, and stepped into the small elevator. The doors opened to a fluorescent-lit, exceedingly narrow hallway. Dragging my luggage over the stained navy-blue carpet, I used the keycard to let myself into what was easily the tiniest hotel room in which I'd ever set foot. I couldn't figure out where to put my stuff so I wouldn't be tripping over it. I scanned around for a closet and didn't find one. The space around the bed was so narrow that I could only just barely squeeze my large rolling duffel between the bed and the window.

There wasn't a separate bathroom so much as an area in the corner partially concealed by a few feet of wall. A toilet and a tiny sink sat next to what resembled a narrow vertical glass coffin: the shower. Only skinny people allowed in this hotel, apparently. I sat on the bed and stared at the shower. I remember thinking that Mr. Fox literally—as in the original meaning of the word—wouldn't fit in it. An image came to mind of those Japanese watermelons that are grown inside square boxes, filling the available space as they grow into square-shaped watermelons. I imagined Mr. Fox stuffing himself into this tiny shower, his blubbery mass pressed into every corner, his torso morphing into a box shape. His flesh, flattened against the glass on all four sides, would block the water from running to the drain. Instead, it would pool up around him, rising inch by inch. He'd be stuck, unable to move, the water handle firmly jammed in his ass. The water would rise higher and higher—first over his mouth, then over his nose—until he drowned right there, in that tiny coffin-shower.

I shook the image out of my head and looked through the small window. Outside, graffiti was abundant while foot traffic, particularly of fashionably dressed Italians, was not. I felt distant from the center of this city.

Whatever time it was in Rome, Mr. Fox was awake back in the US.

```
August 7, 2014, Gchat

Mr. Fox: Just making sure you're awake. Don't want you to
potentially miss anything.

Me: Miss what?

Mr. Fox: Miss an opportunity to get payroll funding. Assuming
you're trying to do that, which of course is not my business or
concern.
```

CHAPTER FIFTY-TWO · 417

By now I was so used to this nauseating mix of fear and dread. Knowing I was going to have to find money, *again*, was sickening.

I felt that somehow, having to do terrifying things was at least easier while so far away, across an ocean, on another continent. Like if things really went to shit, maybe I'd just never come home; I'd just slide off the radar and live in the streets, ride the Eurail from place to place, maybe land somewhere remote like Stuttgart where I'd find an appealing-enough German man to take me in—he'd teach me basic German, feed me, and shelter me, and I'd live out the remainder of my days as an anonymous hausfrau. This seemed preferable to the real-life consequences if Mr. Fox turned out to be full of shit. Also less gruesome than killing myself. I seemed to semiconsciously consider these escape hatches. Sadly, they often involved capitalizing on, and letting someone use, the only currency I believed I had left: my physical self.

I told Mr. Fox about the teensy room and the potentially unsafe neighborhood. I explained that there was no restaurant or even cafe in the hotel, and no minibar, just an old mini fridge containing two small plastic generic brand bottles of water along with some crumbs, a few liquid stains, and a lone wiry hair, thick and dark. I didn't want to imagine to whom the hair had once belonged. I didn't want to drink that water either. I wanted to move from this hotel but still had no idea how long I'd *really* be staying in Rome, since nothing Mr. Fox said was reliable.

Meanwhile, Mr. Fox had appeared in court in Connecticut related to his arrest from the Florida warrant.

```
Mr. Fox: Today was good. Was in and out of CT court. They cut me
a check for my 50K. I've got one court date left. Sept 8th. My
brother has until then to best me. If not then we win. And when
I walk out of court on the 8th then you and me run the world
together forever. :) You may need to be there for me on that one.

Me: In Florida?

Mr. Fox: Yes, in Florida. And we need to do whatever it takes to
get across the finish line and to win.
```

Me: Dare I ask why I'm leaving here so soon? I guess there's no point. Though I still want to know if is okay to tell people at the restaurant where I am, if needed. So far haven't told anyone.

Mr. Fox: Not yet. Let me work that out.

Never mind that Mr. Fox had won $164,000 a few weeks earlier.
Yet still, I sent him wires. I still had to find more money.
Impressively, I'd already partially succeeded. During the time I'd spent waiting in the airport and on the way to Italy, via emails and texts, I'd secured a $25,000 loan from a guy I knew in LA, and I'd also just gotten word that my friend in Australia would send me a wire for $50,000. Both of these guys had a lot of money. Both were *good* guys. The one in Australia I'd known much longer. It pained me to borrow money from him, even though he had loads of it. It pained me to borrow money from anyone. The worst part of it all was lying to people. Mr. Fox always reminded me that *the ends justify the means* and pointed out that no one was getting hurt. It would all be over soon. They'd get it all back and more. And as usual, it wasn't *real* anyway.
With these two loans, I was still nearly $100,000 short to make payroll, but I'd made progress.

* * *

I wrote to Mr. Fox to let him know about the loans I managed to get, like a fucking miracle.
I quickly fell asleep on the small bed in the tiny, dark room, and woke a few hours later to this message:

Mr. Fox: I'm very proud of you. You're coming home Sunday. 1st class. Tell NO ONE. Call me as soon as you wake up. Do not do anything on your computer before calling me. You did good. Meeting my brother now. XOXOXOXO

By the time I read these messages, he wasn't around to pick up my call or answer my messages. I told him I was confused about the instruction to not "do anything" on my computer and that I was going to find something to eat.

I ventured out of the hotel in a bit of a daze. It really *was* a crappy area. I wandered around and found a small cafe with takeaway food. Sandwiches lay in rows inside a glass case, all with meat except one row of mozzarella-and-tomato sandwiches. I got one of those, and three of the largest bottles of water they had. Because I was in a *fuck it* kind of mood, I got a Diet Coke too.

Back in my room, I picked at the sandwich. The tomato was flavorless, the mozzarella like rubber, and even the bread was dry and tasteless. This wasn't at all how I imagined eating in Italy, but it filled the empty space in my stomach. The Diet Coke was irritatingly good—like a hit of a refreshing drug.

After that, I got back to work.

* * *

I had no idea from where I would get the rest of the money I owed to the payroll company. If I didn't pay them, they wouldn't cover the coming payroll that would hit in a matter of days. The two loans I'd gotten didn't even cover half of it. I needed more, but from where? From whom? As usual, I was stressed, particularly about borrowing from good people. Mr. Fox, as usual, assured me this was all almost over, that it was no big deal; there was nothing for me to worry about, not *really*. He said, "No matter. In the fall I will money-whip everyone."

Money-whip. His clever phrase, as if he'd have endless money to hurl at everyone. As if I had nothing to worry about. He used this phrase a lot.

Meanwhile...

On August 8, I sent Mr. Fox a wire for $20,000.

I wish I could explain how I sent him still more money even when desperate to make payroll.

* * *

Mr. Fox agreed I should find a new hotel and sent $2,000 to the only account I was allowed to use while there.

After searching online, I found what looked like an ideal hotel, and I couldn't believe the name: Leon's Place. Really. *Leon's Place.* I knew I *had* to stay there. The hotel project I'd been working on a couple of years prior had been tentatively named the Hotel Leon. My partners had wanted to name it something holistic or zen sounding, or... Hotel Sarma. I'd disagreed. I liked the name Hotel Leon because it would work easily in other countries, and it didn't imply anything about the concept. So, while I was excited at finding this hotel in Rome, I was a little bummed the name was being used already. I told Mr. Fox about it. Then I made a dumb joke about how after my stay, I'd have to throw a fire cocktail over my shoulder on my way out and burn it to the ground so no one else could have the name. As always, when stressed, I made jokes.

The next morning, I got dressed and packed. Leon's Place was all the way on the other side of the city, so I got a good look around while in the back of a taxi. The hotel was still a bit removed from the center of town, but in a clean area that felt more like a business district—no graffiti and plenty of the pedestrians dressed in suits. It was on Via Venti Settembre, and my birthday month is September—another detail making me feel like this was where I was meant to stay.

I was surprised by how elegant the hotel was, considering it was less expensive than other reasonable options I'd found. While checking in, I told the charming man at the desk that my dog's name was Leon and showed him a photo. He smiled but didn't seem nearly as excited as I thought he should be.

My room was spacious, decorated elegantly in shades of gray. I noticed items imprinted with "Leon's Place" here and there—notepads, pencils, soap boxes, etc.—which of course I stashed in my bags to take home with me. There was a minibar—clean and well stocked—and... *snacks.*

At some point during the day Mr. Fox and I chatted again. I told him about the new hotel, and then we discussed one of my former chefs that I wanted to rehire.

```
Mr. Fox: If by chance she reaches out to you just say nothing
other than, "Shane is the owner on paper and I'm traveling for
a few months." Stay vague. But let her know you would be gone a
while. IF she reaches out.

Me: I'm going to be gone for a few months?
```

```
Mr. Fox: No, not a few months.
```

He wanted me to tell people he *owned* the restaurant? That felt weird, but at this point, everything was beyond fucked up. I just wanted to get it all over with. Apparently I was there to "finish" things, and yet again, he'd given me a date by which it would all be over, this time by my birthday, September 10, which was almost exactly a month away. Also, I didn't know it at the time, but while I was out of town on these trips, Mr. Fox was spending time at the restaurant—doing who knows what.

* * *

It was still August 9. I emailed my friend Dylan back in the US about being in a *situation*, and said that I was looking for an emergency loan to make payroll. I told him I was in Italy for a meeting. Without being specific, I tried to make it sound as important as I could, to make it clear it wasn't a vacation. Thankfully he didn't ask for details. I can't stand lying, yet I kept having to do it, or felt as if I did.

To my surprise, Dylan was open to loaning me $100,000. One hundred thousand dollars was exactly what I needed to get to cover the remainder of payroll, so if I could secure this loan, I'd succeed. I'd have completed this "final task"—borrowing money to cover payroll, from Rome—rather quickly. I started to feel relief, as if this finally really was *it*. *The end*. Still, I had to get it completed, and Dylan (very reasonably) wanted proper documentation approved by his attorney. He promised to try to get it handled quickly since I needed the funds within a couple of days. I was humbled because yet again, here was a *really* good person trusting me, believing me, and quickly loaning me a lot of money. I had to keep reminding myself of Mr. Fox's repeated assertion that these people would all be *money-whipped* come fall, and the fall was mere weeks away. Relying on this, I assured Dylan that I would repay him before Thanksgiving, most certainly well before the end of the year. He didn't want interest on the loan because he is that much of a fucking good guy.

* * *

Mr. Fox periodically told me *not* to look at my bank balances, as he'd done again. So, I wrote to him to ask if it was *okay* if I checked the account in which he'd put $2,000 to cover my travel expenses. I also asked him if it was okay to tell people I was in Rome. I always needed clarification of what was and wasn't okay.

I told Mr. Fox about the loan coming from Dylan. I could tell he was impressed I'd pulled it off. We continued to discuss money. I had a few other requests out there from which I'd not yet heard back. Mr. Fox's perspective was that if I could get more then I should take it:

```
Mr. Fox: Turn down no one. If you end up getting 350 or 450K
then great. We will pay back tax stuff and give out bonuses. All
monies should be marked as repayable before years end. With any
initial funding pay payroll obviously. But any more funds keep
in that separate account. An off-the-book stockpile is good
to have. That way we can control the outcome of this on your
birthday. And can pay taxes and bonuses. Also I am getting us a
tax and business lawyer next week.

Me: Everything I get will go for previous payroll except maybe a
few K left over. But will see who else is out there, dunno. You
told me next week's payroll will be taken care of.

Mr. Fox: I'm just saying. If you can get an extra 100-150K that
we can stash away it will work way in our benefit around your
birthday.

Me: I thought everything would be fine then.

Mr. Fox: Can talk more in box. I am just thinking about being
able to control the outcome. Will explain in box.
```

* * *

CHAPTER FIFTY-TWO · 423

Having done all the work I could for the day, and feeling like I'd succeeded in my mission, I decided to take myself to a nice dinner. My first evening out in Rome. I had no idea where to go, so I asked the concierge for a recommendation. He made me a reservation at a restaurant within walking distance. I showered in the spacious shower and got dressed in the nicest dress I'd brought with me and sneakers. Always sneakers. I hadn't packed any other type of footwear. Gray Vans with an orange stripe—at least they weren't big running shoes. I fixed up my hair and did my makeup, ready for a date with myself.

The sun was just setting as I took the colored map I'd been given at the front desk and followed the directions to the restaurant, walking a few blocks east and north. Entering the elegant candlelit room, I was greeted kindly and walked to a table midway through the rustic yet upscale dining room. It was full with a few small groups, but most tables were couples. From where I sat I could view the whole place. I've never minded going to nice restaurants by myself. Without anyone to talk to, I can take in more details.

For whatever reason, the waiters paid extra attention to me, bringing me a complimentary glass of prosecco, then an amuse bouche. I ordered as best I could, as usual avoiding meat but not making a fuss over whether there was cheese or butter, etc. I ordered a glass of white wine, the first of two.

Needless to say, this meal was so much better than the sad sandwich on my first day. I ate slowly and preoccupied myself with people-watching. At the end of the meal, they brought me cookies and limoncello. I was so full and had already drunk more than I normally would, but I'd have felt ungracious to not consume at least some of what they gave me.

Years earlier, when I was with Matthew, his being somewhat of a celebrity chef at the time, it was common for restaurants to send extras to our table: an amuse bouche, a middle course, an extra dessert, and so on. Meanwhile, Matthew ate like a goddamn bird. It drove me nuts. The extra courses he sometimes didn't want to eat. I'd tell him, "You can't let them bring that back to the kitchen untouched!" and he'd reply something lame like, "Well, I don't want to spoil my appetite." Ugh, what are you, *five*? I'd switch our plates and then eat at least half of his. I felt it was cruel to make me do that since I was always worried about my weight. What a dick. Anyway.

So, despite already being a little drunk and very full, I sipped the limoncello and nibbled at the cookies as I sorted paying the bill. After repeating "Grazie!" and exchanging air kisses, I left, a bit wobbly.

The night was perfect—warm, with a light breeze—and I noticed how the city seemed to glow as if lit entirely in candlelight—a soft, golden contrast to the harsh neon of most US cities. It would have been an ideal time to be one of those dreamy eyed couples I'd watched during dinner. I thought briefly about Mr. Fox and what it would have been like if he'd been there with me. It was like imagining bringing a walrus to a tea party. He would have stood out, and not in a good way, as if I'd be afraid of what he might metaphorically knock over or otherwise disrupt. Meanwhile, I felt deeply that I belonged there. Maybe it was because I was the offspring of a European immigrant, or maybe I just felt like I fit in, particularly in comparison to someone like Mr. Fox. I'm gracious. I'm kind and curious. I will walk anywhere and everywhere. And that night I kept walking, despite having the mild sense that it might have been a bit dangerous to be doing so all alone. I headed back down to Via Settembre, but instead of turning left toward my hotel, I turned right, drawn to wander further. I came upon the Fontana del Mosè, which, like nearly all the fountains in Rome, was stunning. I took a few photos, then sat on a wide concrete ledge. I snapped a few selfies, wanting to remember being there and how I felt, which was strangely *at home,* like I could live there. Or had lived there in some past life.

I got up and walked on, heading still farther away from my hotel and south. At this point I concede I was feeling a bit lonely. But I did *not* miss Mr. Fox and was grateful he wasn't there with me. I walked by the St. Regis, and imagined staying there, even though I loved my Leon's Place hotel. I wandered farther and found myself at the Piazza della Repubblica, with yet another fountain. The Fontana delle Naiadi was huge, with a flat surface around the perimeter. I lay down on it, looking up into the dark sky.

Eventually I got up and walked back to the hotel, drank a lot of water, and went to sleep.

* * *

Mornings in Rome were my favorite time, since it was six hours earlier back home. Therefore it wasn't until 3:00 p.m. that the 9:00 a.m. day began back home, at which point I started stressing out. Also, my friend Dylan was on the West Coast, adding another three hours to the time difference, so I did most of my talking with him at night.

I usually woke early to make the most of these less-stressful hours. I dressed for the day and headed downstairs for the breakfast included in my room charge. There was no almond milk or soy milk, and the breakfast attendant seemed to *want* to make me a cappuccino, even when I leaned toward espresso. He was so eager that I let him make me a cappuccino, foamed cow milk and all. As he practically skipped away to the coffee station, I got up and visited the simple buffet of breakfast foods. I found platters of fruit, sliced melon, and sections of grapefruit, which I piled on my small plate. I took a few packages of melba toast, which I stashed in my bag for later. I returned to the table where my cappuccino waited for me—a goofy smiley face formed in the foam. I was familiar with the elegant artistic designs some baristas made, ones that looked like leaves or hearts, but this was just three dots—eyes and a nose—and a semicircle smile. It looked like something a child would do, if a child was a barista, and that only made it more endearing, like this man just genuinely wanted to deliver happiness with his cappuccinos—a reminder that feelings can be contagious, especially when deliberately shared.

I looked up and made eye contact with the waiter, who winked at me. I smiled. Every morning of my stay thereafter, I ordered the cappuccino, and he brought it to me with the smiley face. I wasn't thrilled about consuming dairy, but the waiter's glee in making me his happy cappuccinos made me feel, in those moments at least, a bit happy.

After breakfast I headed out for my hours of morning time in Rome, into the heart of the city to wander about.

Rome is one of those cities where one would be hard-pressed to find any ugly street. It felt like living within a movie made by an award-winning cinematographer. Everywhere I turned was a uniquely stunning image. Each alley or street I looked down was a postcard image. Pinkish stucco facades and wrought-iron terraces, some with laundry hanging, others with lush vines of ivy tumbling down to the cobblestone street, flowers blossoming. I took a few photographs of these scenes, but they never did the actual views justice.

I tried to avoid touristy places. When I encountered packs of loud Americans in flipflops and bright sports jerseys, I walked in the other direction. One day I'd been walking for hours—it was among the hotter days, cloudless and bright—and I was sweating and hungry. I wandered down a side street on the outskirts of the city and came upon a small restaurant, elegant in its minimalist modern look. I went in and, in that wordless I-don't-speak-Italian way, held up my finger to the host with a questioning look on my face to communicate that I hoped for a table for one. The host graciously nodded and led me to a table right smack in the middle of the space. Looking around, I quickly realized I was a bit out of place, my hair wild and big from the humidity, sweat dripping down my neck and chest into my summer dress. On my feet I wore well-worn sneakers—as usual, Pro-Keds. Everyone else was in stylish, expensive-looking business attire, presumably having business lunches, looking seriously all business in this elegant white-tablecloth restaurant. Oh well.

The menu was small and, from what I could translate on my own, featured mostly meat and fish. I ordered bruschetta to start, followed by a plate of spaghetti with tomato sauce. Normally I steered clear of simple carbs like bread and pasta, but I was in Italy after all, and very hungry. The waiter brought out a large chilled glass bottle of water, and I drank half of it immediately. The bruschetta was perfect: thick toasted bread—crusty and chewy—drizzled with olive oil and topped with salted, sweet, ripe tomatoes, and basil leaves. Simple and *so* good. *This is how I wanted to eat*, I thought, remembering the lame excuse of a sandwich I'd had on my first day. I ate the spaghetti slowly, twirling each forkful against a spoon to make neat bites.

I took in the elegance of the restaurant. Small and simple, classy and high quality. I was having my very own Elizabeth Gilbert moment, eating a big plate of pasta, in Italy, by myself. If only I could have felt as free as she must have then.

※ ※ ※

Back in my hotel room by midafternoon, it was time to complete the loan from Dylan. What followed was an epic session of calls, back-and-forth emails with agreement drafts, documents to be signed, running to the front desk to borrow their printer, looking for a FedEx to send originals back to Dylan, and assuring the payroll company I'd be sending them a wire soon. It was probably good that I'd carb loaded; the stress of it all left me no time to think about dinner.

My work bled into the next day, and the next, but finally, I got it done. It was a sickening kind of relief. Relief that payroll was okay, once again, just barely. Sick over borrowing money from my friend. Uneasy over what was to come, trying to hang onto the belief that, as Mr. Fox said, it was indeed about to be all over. The rainbows would appear, followed by a money avalanche to pay everyone back, plus whatever other magical things Mr. Fox had always hinted at, which I couldn't yet fathom.

On August 12, I wired the payroll company $160,000, covering what they were owed and ensuring the following payroll would be made. I felt a wave of relief that at least the employees' pay was safe, and proud of myself that I'd passed what Mr. Fox had presented as my *final test*. I allowed myself to think that this was it, the agony now behind me.

I realized that I'd not left the hotel for over fifty hours. Those melba toast packets I'd stashed in my bag at breakfast had kept me going. That and the amazing olives the bartender in the lobby bar had put out for me when I ran down there with my laptop to have a Peroni or two.

It was midday in Rome when I finally stepped back out into the bright sunshine. All week I'd been watching people coming out of the Gelateria La Romana across the street holding glistening gelato cones. I went into the chilled and bright shop, where smells of vanilla, cocoa, and coffee greeted me. Using hand gestures and pointing, I ordered a cone with one scoop of vanilla, one chocolate. I guess this was what made me a bad vegan. *When in Rome... literally*, I thought. I took a portrait of my cone, which I did *not* post on Instagram.

* * *

I still didn't know when I'd be leaving Rome, but fortunately the hotel wasn't fully occupied, and it was easy to keep extending a day or two at a time.

Mr. Fox told me that he'd rented an apartment back home, which is where I'd return to. I guess he was tired of the hotel hopping. Still, why couldn't I go home to my own apartment? I was confused, as usual, but for whatever reason, it felt like progress. As if his renting an apartment was a step toward things being done. He said it was just a transition while things got sorted. *Okay*, I thought.

He made it seem like it was much nicer than the apartment I'd had—that

I *still* had but hadn't set foot into in a long time. Or maybe I went in and out quickly. I can't even recall.

```
August 12, 2014, Gchat

Mr. Fox: There will be a few secrets exposed though when you see
my place. Nothing major. Just stuff that shows I'm not actually
an asshole. :) The second bedroom I use as a guest room and
keep my printer in, do you have any requests? It will be your
room now. It has an air purifier in it. A really good expensive
one. I have two in the house. And three ACs that are nice and
cold. Have a big marble dining room table with six chairs.
Small kitchen but lots of pots and pans and it's big enough to
cook in.
```

He spoke about it as if it was a really nice place. I replied, asking ridiculous questions, like if there was a canopy on the bed or a swing set in the apartment. Or a giant fish tank. Maybe a tiger? While my questions were sarcastic, I envisioned a bright and pleasant space. I was actually looking forward to seeing it. Then Mr. Fox started talking about it as if it had some kind of energy that couldn't be disturbed... like I should feel privileged that he'd *allow* me to stay there with him. Really.

```
Mr. Fox: I am not trying to be rude, PLEASE do not take this
in the wrong way, but—if you bring any overly negative energy
in here you will be asked to leave, this place is very special.
And it will accommodate you until after this is over. It's very
sweet and peaceful here, and has been for a long time. Leon
loves it. I am at peace here.

Me: Well. great.

Mr. Fox: You can be too. I want to share this with you. To share
myself. Eventually to share everything. My empire. Our empire. I
```

want my life and your life to be our life. I love you. And want to spend the rest of my life loving you. We will have many homes. And travel a lot. But we will always have this little place. We will plant the seeds of our future here.

Me: Cool.

Mr. Fox: And god willing we make it through this test together. And we come out victorious.

I pushed back on the conditions, and the implication that I was the one with negative energy. I asked him what he meant, what would qualify as negative energy.

Mr. Fox: If you hit me. If you call me horrible names. If you threaten to hurt me or yourself. Then you will be banished from this place. And you will lose. And we will lose. Those are the only conditions. Upon you staying here. This place will be your home. Until this is over and we move to a larger home. Do you accept those conditions.

He was making me agree to *conditions*? I pushed back more, pointing out that he was in control. I was his minion. He claimed I was his equal. I reminded him he was in control. He replied:

Mr. Fox: It only appears that way. It is in fact you that are in total control.

Me: If I have the power then I don't know about it, or how it works, so basically I don't have it. Right? I have to do what you say.

Mr. Fox: Can we please talk about good things. This conversation is no good.

We went back and forth some more, and he ended the conversation with,

```
Mr. Fox: I love you more than you will probably ever know,
little TBH.
```

* * *

Later on the same day, we continued chatting. And it appears he still wanted me to get more funds. *More.* I told him I was trying everything I could think of.

He also told me about getting his passport application approved. I realize now he'd not been able to get one before with the outstanding warrant. But he'd cleared that now. Knowing what I know now, I also realize he'd probably never had one before. He pretended to be a worldly traveler, slaying dragons on all corners of the earth, when in reality he'd never left the East Coast.

He complained about his weight, writing, "*I am fat and hate it. It's getting me down lately. I am fat for you. Cuz of this idiocy.*" He claimed that he felt shitty about all the times I lashed out at him and insulted him. He wrote, "*I remember every word. Every action. Everything. Like a court reporter. So some days it just gets to be overwhelming sadness.*"

As if I should have felt remorseful for making Mr. Fox feel sad.

I still didn't have a flight back scheduled. As much as I liked being in Rome, I wanted to go home. It was an uneasy feeling being so far away from Leon and the restaurant, even though by now things were so precarious that I was almost afraid of being at home.

He acted like it didn't matter how long I stayed in Rome. At one point he said, "*Stay until your birthday, I don't care.*"

He'd repeatedly assured me that it would "all be over" by my birthday, which was now less than a month away. Finally, I scheduled a flight back for the following weekend. Notably, I wasn't, at this point, demanding answers from him. Whatever it was that made me so docile, ultimately, is perhaps the biggest part of the psychological mystery, which I feel unqualified to conclusively solve.

* * *

On my last night in Rome, a friend of a friend—a man who owned a small pastry shop—invited me to dinner. I thought it would be nice to have dinner with someone local, but Mr. Fox told me I wasn't allowed to go. He insisted the man was sent as a trap from his brother. Of course, I obeyed. Realistically, Mr. Fox would have had no way of knowing if I went. I could have gone to dinner, had a nice time, no big deal. But fear, along with the ever-present sense that I was being watched, kept me compliant.

Instead, I went for a long solo walk to the other side of the city, across the Tiber River. I walked slower than I normally would have, taking in the streets and views and people and scenes. Again, I noticed how strangely *at home* I felt in Rome. I wondered if I'd be back, and under what circumstances. My thoughts drifted to the new apartment waiting for me back home. The idea of it intrigued me. I felt hope and excitement. My birthday was right around the corner. I allowed myself to imagine the relief I'd feel with the weight of the stress gone, with everything repaid, and with some kind of magical new world opening up to me. I walked in a haze, suspended between reality and my imagination.

I came upon a man sitting on the edge of the cobblestone street who appeared homeless—dirty and ragged, with a dog laying beside him. The dog was exactly Leon's size, with a similar build but black-and-white coloring. I made eye contact with the man, then stooped down to pet the dog. After letting him sniff my hand, I glided my hand across his warm torso. His fur was like suede, soft and clean.

Since I was leaving the next morning, I figured I may as well give the man the euros I had left. I pulled out my phone and showed him a photo of Leon and he nodded and smiled. I pointed at his dog, then at my phone. I snapped a photo of his dog, smiled at them one last time, and was on my way.

I didn't post most of the photos I took in Rome to Instagram, but I uploaded the photo of the dog, captioning it "Dogs of Rome." It was August 15.

* * *

The next day, I flew back to New York, still confused as to why I'd needed to go all the way to Rome. But by now I'd learned to accept the confusion as a given.

CHAPTER FIFTY-THREE

LATE AUGUST–OCTOBER 2014
NEW YORK CITY

On August 16, 2014, I arrived back in NYC.

Mr. Fox picked me up at the airport, which he'd never done before. We texted as I dragged my luggage out of the JFK terminal into the near-blinding brightness of a sunny summer day. I was feeling ambivalent yet also hopeful, thinking maybe this sunny day was the start of brighter days to come.

I found Mr. Fox sitting in the driver's seat of a car I'd never seen before: a cream-colored Land Rover. I'd only seen him driving my Honda or being driven in a black town car or Suburban. But never mind the car because I could see that Leon was in the back seat. I heaved my big bag into the trunk, then opened one of the back doors. Seeing Leon hopping eagerly from paw to paw, in his cute plaid bandana, calmed my nerves. I rubbed his ears and gave him kisses, inhaling his scent, the most comforting scent in the whole world.

I snapped a photo of him and posted it to Instagram. *Best part about coming home,* I captioned it. If he was happy, things felt okay.

* * *

During the drive, my anticipation built about this new apartment. A new home, this new car... were they signs of things finally shifting? It was only a couple of weeks until my birthday now—the day by which Mr. Fox had declared it would all be over.

I knew the apartment wouldn't be anything extravagant, but from what he'd told me, I pictured a bright, spacious, and clean place. We pulled onto Twenty-Eighth Street between Lexington and Park Avenue, then into a parking lot midway down the block. The attendants were familiar with Mr. Fox and gave him a ticket for the car as I got my bags and Leon out.

I looked across the street, then up and down the block, trying to figure which building it could be. After letting Leon pee just outside the lot, I followed Mr. Fox across the street and under scaffolding to the door of an old building. Maneuvering through one door and then another with my bags and Leon, I noticed there was no lobby, just a narrow hallway. I also noticed the smell, which reminded me of buildings where a lot of old people live. It smelled like boiling cabbage and mothballs.

We took the one small elevator to the fourth floor and exited into a tiny hall. There were only two apartments on each floor. A familiar feeling of dread had begun creeping in. It wasn't that what mattered to me was a nice apartment for its own sake; what mattered was *this horrible feeling*, one that was so familiar by now: the expectation and then the letdown, the grand promises followed by crushing disappointment. That dread was justified when he opened the apartment door and we made our way inside.

It was much smaller than I'd imagined, with low ceilings. The light was yellowish, not from any sunlight but from old light fixtures. There was zero natural light in the living space where we stood. It was weirdly furnished with items that appeared to have been left behind by a previous tenant. There was a small kitchenette along one wall, with old cupboards and old fixtures—at least twenty years old, probably more. The one window was obscured by Venetian blinds—once white, now blackened with a layer of soot and grime. I gingerly stuck my thumb and index finger between two of the slats to push them open and peered through a dirty windowpane. I could make out another building wall just a few feet away and an alley down below. Okay, clearly those blinds would stay closed.

A gleaming, huge flat-screen TV sat on a low console. I was sure Mr. Fox had brought this in. Of course, a TV would be his priority. Two big black recliners faced the TV, the kind with plastic cup holders built into the arms. The coffee table was an amoeba-shaped slab of thick glass on top of a black stand. A small striped rug underneath it was the only color in the room. There was odd clutter around and flimsily framed generic artwork that someone had left behind, I assumed. The "big marble dining room table" he'd told me of was a cheap table with a fake marble finish, surrounded by worn, ugly dining chairs.

I peeked in the kitchen cupboards and saw old dishes and an array of mismatched random cups and mugs, plates and bowls. "We can get a new set of dishes if you want," Mr. Fox said. I didn't say anything. This was nothing like I'd pictured. Past the kitchen area was a small bathroom and then two small bedrooms. The one designated as mine was the smaller one. It had a single bed, an AC unit in the one window, a tiny desk, and some drawers. It looked like well-worn Ikea furniture bought many years ago. The closet had an old wooden rod and mismatched hangers, some plastic, some metal. The floor was creaky wood. I opened one of the drawers, and it was full of random things, including, oddly, a power drill.

"Whose stuff is this?" I asked.

"Oh, you can just get rid of all that," he told me.

But whose was it? Did some previous tenant just leave this shit behind? It was like someone had left in a hurry, taking only their clothes.

Mr. Fox bragged about the new sheets he'd bought me. They were light purple and a cotton-poly blend. Call me a bedding snob, but I don't like sleeping on polyester. Also, how would Leon and I both fit on this bed?

Mr. Fox's room was bigger, but not by much. He had a double bed, covered in black sheets. How appropriate. The windows in both bedrooms, when you peeked over the AC units, looked out onto Twenty-Eighth Street. His room was cluttered with what looked like a mix of his own stuff and random things that must have belonged to someone else. I later learned that it was a short-term lease apartment that came furnished, usually rented by transient students from the nearby Baruch College.

I kept thinking, *This is the place he described to me?* A place of good energy? To me, it was oppressive and dark. It seemed more like the kind of place one might go to kill oneself.

* * *

Looking back, I can see that the point of the new apartment was to isolate me further. Mr. Fox knew that my going back to my old place might only loosen his grip on me. In my own place, it would be easier for me to keep him away if he made me mad. All those times I'd told him I didn't want him to come back—even though in the end I wasn't able to enforce it, I *could* have because it was *my* home. And with my employees there, I would have been more anchored to reality, to the saner version of my life, the one without Mr. Fox. As long as I was isolated in *his* apartment, he had far more control over me.

Thinking now of that apartment, I'm reminded of chapter 42 of *The Portrait of a Lady*, where Henry James' Isabel Archer finally grasped the deception of her husband and felt the terror of her circumstances: "It was the house of darkness, the house of dumbness, the house of suffocation."

* * *

The following day I was back at the restaurant, which I know only from studying photographs on my phone. It must have been strange to see everyone after being away in Rome. How did I explain that trip? Probably I stayed busy and avoided personal conversations.

Nazim brought Sydney, my poor elderly cat, to the new apartment. She was now sixteen years old and partially blind. My heart broke for her because she already wasn't getting the love and attention she deserved, and now had to live in in this dumpy, dark place. At least she couldn't see it well.

On August 20, I sent Mr. Fox a wire for $10,000.

From my Gchats with Mr. Fox, I can see that I was feeling overwhelmed with stuff to do, including getting things set up to live and work from this strange new place. Thankfully, he'd left to go to Connecticut the day after we arrived, so I had some space from him. While I don't recall it, I'm guessing he gave me some kind of lecture that first night. And now he was at the casinos, probably gambling away the ten thousand I'd just wired him.

On August 21, I sent Mr. Fox a wire for $30,000.

I borrowed more money from the merchant cash advance company, Rapid Pay, to send that wire.

On August 22, I sent him a wire for $20,000.

What was I doing? I'd been made to believe that the hoops I'd jumped through in Rome were the last hoops. And now here I was, in a dark and strange apartment with barely any of my own things, still squeezing out more wires to Mr. Fox while juggling payroll, vendor checks, rent, and so on.

I don't know how Mr. Fox explained the change. I just know he always made it seem as if I had no other option. I wasn't making decisions so much as following orders. I was also putting on a face for all my staff and the world at large, conveying that everything was just fine.

* * *

I tried to make the best of my early days in that place, at least glad to be alone with Leon. I took down the grimy blinds from the living window and left them in the cluttered building basement. I bought inexpensive tension rods from a nearby housewares store and hung cheap but pretty sheer purple curtains. I got a few bright throw pillows for the black lounger chairs. I cleaned and organized. I tried to clear away as much junk as I could. I took down the shitty and weird artwork. It was still a depressing place but getting marginally less so the more I did to it.

On August 24, I wrote in my journal:

Sunday. Went and got stuff. Made things look nicer here. Leon in bed with me. Scrounged and counted all cash in that drawer. I have < $1500 for next couple weeks, should be okay with getting food at resti.

Tomorrow, meetings. At this point I have no shame. He said I am a good wife. I handle shit.

But I did have shame. I was awash in shame. And apparently bolstering myself with his approvals. I was *a good wife.* One who *handled shit.* His shit.

On August 25, I sent Mr. Fox a wire for $27,000.

On August 26, I sent him a wire for $34,000.

At least I always felt better when Mr. Fox was away. Then he'd come back, and things would get bad again.

On August 28, I wrote in my journal about Mr. Fox behaving like a jerk after he'd come back and given me some kind of ominous lecture, and about my overall despair at the entire situation.

> Worse than physical violence. Fucking with my head. The most awful kind of torture. And I can't walk away. Or, I could but apparently it would be doom b/c he controls everything. So. Now what.

Mr. Fox knew he could increase the pressure on me in this new apartment, having taken me out of my own home. He informed me that I had to *really* learn to control my anger and that he would have to train me to do this; I would have to sit calmly and tolerate whatever he said and did without getting angry, without letting any of the usual triggers—such as him demanding I hand over my phone so he could look through all my recent text exchanges—affect me. I was being told to *not allow* justifiably infuriating things to infuriate me.

I've since learned that this is a classic cult conditioning tactic. In a 2021 episode of the podcast *A Little Bit Culty*, actress Leah Remini described how, at age thirteen, she was repeatedly forced to sit still in a chair alone in a room with a man while he insulted and berated her—part of her early experience in Scientology.[3] No matter how offensive or vulgar his verbal attacks, she was not *allowed* to get mad or talk back. This kind of practice is meant to condition and desensitize the subject to future atrocious treatment.

Likewise, Mr. Fox told me I needed to learn to control my emotions and to *not react.* He claimed that anytime I lost my temper, bad things would happen. Not necessarily directly but as if, energetically, my lashing out would karmically lead to future punishment. With regularity now, when I came back to the

---

[3] Sarah Edmonson, *A Little Bit Culty*, podcast, season 1, episode 3, "Heal That Sh*t: Leah Remini & The Aftermath," producers Sarah Edmonson and Anthony Ames, March 8, 2021, https://alittlebitculty.com/episode/heal-that-sht-leah-remini-the-aftermath.

apartment at night, after being at the restaurant or at a meeting—often trying to raise more money according to his directives—I'd find him sitting in the dark, in one of the ugly black loungers, looking angry. I'd be questioned and yelled at. And grabbed at.

He framed this routine as if he was teaching me a superpower versus what he was really doing: strengthening the grip of *his* power over me, wearing me down even further.

On August 29, I wrote in my journal:

> Friday night. Going to bed. Not much I want to write. Because it's not positive. Except for meeting those nice people. Nice people come to my restaurant. They say Thank You for creating this and doing this. And meanwhile I've risked it all, put it on the very edge and am being made to feel like if I don't obey orders it's going to be pushed over. I'll end up in the gutter. Because why. I tried always to do the right thing? What's best? Was I told the rules are that every single suggestion he makes I must obey? ... I don't get it. I don't get anything. I am alone. :(

I was alone. More alone than ever. I had always been someone who naturally self-isolated—someone without a tight-knit core group of lifelong friends who knew all my business, who didn't talk to my family every day, who kept most things inside. It was these very qualities that made it easier for Mr. Fox to isolate me. Still, I also had a tendency to open up easily to strangers. Sit next to me on a long flight and, if you seem interested, I'll tell you my innermost thoughts. So why didn't I confide in anyone?

Because I *couldn't*. Or, I felt like I couldn't. On top of Mr. Fox forbidding it, the insanity of what he was putting me through—which only got worse and worse—made the idea of telling anyone about it feel increasingly impossible. *Because* it was so bonkers.

On August 30, I wrote in my journal:

> Saturday. Late. I'd write what time it is but I don't fucking know b/c he has my phone. Like. A really concrete unmistakable in your face "I control you" move. And it's annoying as fuck. Like, why? My head hurts. And as <u>always</u> I worry I've

done something wrong when I can't even think what it would be. It's a shitty awful feeling. Like the worst. Anyway. This is all shit negative and my head hurts and he probably thinks I'm going to freak out and get mad so guess what, keep my fucking phone. Just know it's all shit and you don't fuck with someone you love, or control them. That's not love. It's some kind of sickness but not love. :-/

On September 3, I sent Mr. Fox a wire for $25,000.

Meanwhile, Nazim was packing up my things at my original apartment, taking photos of various spaces and closets and sending them to me. I tried to direct him what to bring to the new apartment versus what to pack in boxes for storage. Most of my things went to storage. It was a super awkward way to move out of my apartment and frustrating to not be allowed to handle my own stuff.

On September 8, I sent Mr. Fox a wire for $10,000.

That day, I witnessed something involving one of my employees—something that stuck with me. John worked mainly in prep and made deliveries but sometimes filled in behind the juice bar counter. He was probably in his late thirties, older than most of the juice bar staff, and very tall. He moved with a kind of endearing clumsiness; any station he worked quickly became a mess. But his bright, relentless happiness more than made up for it. He was thoughtful too. After his shifts, he always put aside a quart of frozen blueberries with *For Leon* scrawled on the masking tape label because he'd heard I added blueberries to Leon's food bowl.

The night of September 8 I wrote in my journal about walking into the back of the juice bar earlier that day and hearing "Baby One More Time" by Britney Spears blasting from the speakers. John was there, wearing a goofy-looking hairnet, chaos on the counters, looking *happy*. I watched as his energy transferred to the girl waiting for her order. He asked her if she wanted sweetener added to her fruit shake as if he was asking if she wanted to go to Disneyland. She looked bewildered at first but then couldn't help smiling. The whole scene kind of bowled me over with its weird and warm joy. I wrote in my journal about how *this* was among the reasons I'd never want to sell out or expand too quickly—because this was the kind of unfiltered individualistic joy that so often gets quashed out by corporate structure.

* * *

Two days later was September 10—my forty-second birthday. The day it was all meant to end.

Did it end? Of course it didn't. My birthday brought no reprieve from stressing out about money, or the lack thereof, in my company accounts. There was no completion, no relief. And, just like those people in end-of-the-world-is-coming cults, when the expected event didn't materialize, I simply soldiered onward in the thick woods of denial.

The only happy part of that day was that Nazim, having discovered it was my birthday, brought me a cupcake with a candle in it. It was a kindness that made me want to cry. When I confronted Mr. Fox that once again the promised date, my birthday, had come and gone and no relief had arrived, no rainbows and unicorns, his excuse was that excellent things take time.

```
Mr. Fox: It takes about 20 hours to build a Toyota Camry, but it
takes about 5 months to build a Bentley. Excellence takes time.
But it's worth the wait. That's this. Now. Upon completion it
will be spectacular. And better than anything else. Make sense?

Me: I suppose.
```

* * *

I don't even know how to explain that by now Mr. Fox had bought himself a Bentley. A *Bentley.* It was pre-owned, but still. He bought it in Florida. He claimed it had previously belonged to him—that very same car. I have no idea to whom the cream Land Rover in which he'd picked me up at the airport belonged. I never saw it again. Now he was driving a Bentley around Manhattan. It was as if by making everything so completely upside down, Mr. Fox made me believe it was right side up. He was just casually cruising around in his Bentley while waiting for me to pass my final tests.

It's difficult to describe my mental state during these months. I swung between extremes. When Mr. Fox's promises fell through, I felt seething rage, crushing shame, and a desperate need to cling to positivity. And then, when he showed me even the smallest kindness, I felt something like gratitude. According to our Gchats, we engaged in constant fights, often followed by casual conversations about nothing in particular, as if the turmoil could be switched on and off. In my disoriented haze, I accepted the unacceptable. I allowed his atrocities, watching him drive around in a Bentley while demanding I get money. Beneath all of it, I was in agony.

On September 15, I wrote in my journal:

> This is awful. Miserable. How am I supposed to function when he acts this way? I hate him. This person. I am trapped with. Who controls me. And has me isolated. Is it really all for something good? Years of hating and resenting him. Why did I keep at it? Please let there be a good reason. I don't know what else to say. He makes me sick. Just watching TV all day long and taking care of nothing. Demanding I do shit. He's just sitting there watching Breaking Bad while his fat cells multiply, and I'm in pain. Why is he here? Can he please leave? ASAP? Please help me.

Yet, in the Gchat the next day, I wrote to him that I love him:

```
Me: For whatever bizarre reason I do love you. Which is why
this is so painful. But if you're only going to hurt me I'd much
prefer you're not here. If you're not going to help me or take
care of me in any way, I'd much prefer to be alone. I can get
this shit done but not while you're here sabotaging me at every
turn. You make me feel awful, unworthy, and trapped. And you
won't explain it enough for me to be able to deal with it. If
you'd just talk with me without getting angry. And apparently
we're married?? Goodnight.
```

Everything was clearly messed up in my head; up was down, right was wrong, I couldn't make sense of anything, including the whole arrangement whereby I had to send him wire after wire while he occasionally trickled back to me little nuggets for my own spending money, as if I should be humbly grateful for his largesse. He'd normalized his control over me to such a point that I asked permission for everything, even to buy a dress for my sister's upcoming wedding.

```
September 25, 2014, Gchat

Mr. Fox: I miss you.

Me: Can I buy three dresses on your credit card for $600 total?
They're on sale. Will probably return at least 2 if not all.
Need options for Ilze's wedding.

Mr. Fox: Yes can buy dresses.

Me: I miss you too.
```

I missed him? How did I miss him? Did I really? Was I just saying that? Was it a *moment* when I missed him? Was it because he'd been kinder to me shortly before this and so his being around was more comfort than terror? I don't know.

Meanwhile, the transfers continued.

On September 22, I sent Mr. Fox a wire for $25,000.

On September 24, I sent him a wire for $15,000.

As a result of these transfers, I was struggling to hold the business together—even though I was the one inflicting damage. It was surreal. I continued seeking out people who could loan me money or invest in the business.

Then, on October 3, I got an eviction notice from our restaurant landlord. My journal entry from that day was bizarre. I wrote,

> If I act like things are already fixed, they'll get fixed more easily. I may think about it all as playing a role. A part. None of it is real. Just a game or something. And stay cool.

Reading that now makes me think again of *The Secret*. As in, *Just imagine it hard enough and so it will be.* Thinking this way only tricked me into treating an eviction notice from my restaurant landlord as if it was no big deal, not real, just part of this game that was meant to trip me up with its scary fastballs. I'd been trained to believe that the cooler a cucumber I was about all of this, the sooner it would be over.

On Mr. Fox's command, I was borrowing even *more* money from that awful lending company Rapid Pay.

On October 6, I sent Mr. Fox a wire for $24,000.

On October 9, I sent him a wire for $20,000.

I kept going with my belief that positive thinking would make everything okay. On October 11, 2014, I wrote in my journal:

> Lots to be scared of. Instead trying to think the good things. Grateful for Leon. Grateful that so many people love the restaurant. Grateful that everyone in it is so nice. Grateful that I have a soft bed and covers to sleep in/under and pillows and my own room. Grateful that I have a car, even if banged up and I don't know where it is. Grateful to be healthy. Grateful for lots of fresh food. Grateful for a husband who loves me and will hopefully be and do all he says, and grateful for good books and good weather and for a good heart and all the love in it. Goodnight!

A husband who loves me? Good lord.

On October 14, a Thursday, I sent a wire to the landlord for $30,000. At least I was able cure the eviction notice. But I'd had to quickly borrow that money from a good friend. It's nauseating to think that with all my wires to Mr. Fox, it's as if I'd just sent my friend's money directly to Mr. Fox.

* * *

The loans from good people weighed on me most. One of my biggest preoccupations was to repay Dylan for the loan I'd taken while in Rome, which I'd promised to pay back well before the end of the year. This loan was especially painful. I'd given Dylan my word, and I couldn't stand the shame of breaking it, of *not* repaying him.

I turned to Yellowstone, one of the lending companies out there that takes a preposterous amount of interest for high-risk loans. The high interest was justifiable, since the loan was indeed risky, but one has to be truly desperate to take on this kind of debt. Still, it felt worth it to me if I could use it to repay Dylan, who had given me his loan at *no* interest.

By October 14, according to my journal, I was optimistic the loan would come through. It was one bright spot in a sea of dread.

The other bright spot was my sister's wedding, which was to take place that weekend. I was scheduled to drive up to my mother's house with Leon for the rehearsal dinner on October 15 (a Friday), followed by the ceremony and reception the next day. I was ill prepared. I had no gift, but at least brought a couple of cases of wine from the restaurant. My schedule was tight, such that the rehearsal dinner was already underway by the time I arrived. It was only a casual buffet dinner party at my mother's house, but *still*. I also didn't have a new dress. (I never did order the new dresses.)

Once I got settled with a glass of champagne in hand, I managed to put everything Mr. Fox related out of my mind for the next thirty-six hours or so. Miraculously, he didn't bother me much while I was there. It's notable that Mr. Fox did not come with me to the wedding. It was not something I even considered, probably wanting to spare my sister, and myself, the potential discomfort of his presence.

It was fun to see my sister's old friends, many of whom had also been my friends. It was also nice to see my father and stepmom drinking and having a good time with my mom, all of them comfortable together, as they've always been. I drank more champagne, letting the anxiety and dread of life back home fade, at least for this weekend. The next day was a whirlwind of running around and preparing. I wore one of my old dresses, one I'd had for years. It was the same one I wore on my dinner date out with myself in Rome. At least I'd purchased a new bowtie to clip around Leon's collar. I was happy that Leon was my date.

I asked my sister what music had been arranged for the party after the ceremony, and she shrugged.

"I don't know. I figured someone would have something to play."

What?

I spent the rest of the morning—while putting on makeup, curling my hair, and running around—frantically scrolling and searching on the iPad I'd thankfully brought with me to make a playlist of dance music. After the ceremony and dinner, I plugged my iPad into the stereo, and my list got everyone out on the dance floor late into the night. It was a truly happy weekend. And then, just like that, it was over. Hungover, I drove back to New York, back to Mr. Fox, back to my problems.

* * *

October 22, 2014, Gchat

Mr. Fox: you get that 10K yet?

Me: No.

Mr. Fox: I don't know what to do here. You are offering me nothing to work with.

He berated me for not getting him his installments of money, like I was a complete failure.

On October 22, I sent Mr. Fox a wire for $20,000.

Finally, with all other investment leads failing, I went ahead and took the awful $100,000 high-interest loan from Yellowstone. I'd been adamant that I would use those funds to pay at least half of the $100,000 I'd borrowed from Dylan and save the rest to make sure payroll was safely covered. If I could just get Dylan *mostly* paid I would feel better. At least partially paid. Something. That was what I'd planned for the funds from Yellowstone, and I told Mr. Fox as much.

And yet...

On October 31, I sent Mr. Fox a wire for $100,000.

How did that happen? How did he get me to send him that money? I don't know. This time in particular feels extra shocking, since I was so determined to pay Dylan. Why did I send it to Mr. Fox instead? *How did that happen?*

There were no Gchats from before I sent this wire. Mr. Fox must have been with me. I only have Gchats about the wire from after I sent it, after he'd left town—most likely to head straight to a casino. Not surprisingly, I was furious.

Mr. Fox was particularly good at his mind-fuckery when he was with me.

He could more easily get me to act against all reason *when he was in front of me.* Knowing how badly I wanted to at least pay half of Dylan's loan, and to know payroll was covered, why in the world would I take that loan of desperation only to wire it to Mr. Fox?

He'd insisted I send the money to him—that it was the only way Dylan could get repaid. Mr. Fox claimed *he* would repay Dylan *and* cover payroll. I don't recall the details, just that he'd made that assertion, I'd pushed back, and *yet again* he'd gotten me to comply.

How?

Again and again, he was able to pummel me into submission. I had to have been in some kind of zombie state.

PART FIVE

THE DESCENT

"The more stressed a human or any animal gets, the easier it is to recruit them into some sort of delusional thinking."
—DR. ANDREW HUBERMAN, STANFORD NEUROSCIENTIST, ON *THE JOE ROGAN EXPERIENCE*, #1513

CHAPTER FIFTY-FOUR

BRAIN ON ICE

> "What did it feel like to be a different person?" people ask.
>
> It's a question that's impossible to answer with conviction, because, of course, during that dark period, I didn't have any real self-awareness that allowed me the luxury of contemplation, the ability to say, "This is who I am. And this is who I was."

Those words aren't mine; they were written by Susannah Cahalan in her memoir, *Brain On Fire: My Month of Madness*. But when I read them, it struck me that they could just as easily be mine. Later in her book, Cahalan described remembering only "flashes of actual events" with most of the time remaining "blank or capriciously hazy." Writing her memoir, she explained, was "an exercise in comprehending what was lost." She had access to doctors' notes, the recollections of medical staff and her family, and video footage from hospital cameras, all of which she used to "re-create this evasive past." She wrote, "the consciousness that defines me as a person wasn't present then."

Reading her words I thought, *Yes. I completely understand.* This is how it feels writing my own story. It's like writing about a hazy dream, trying to describe the actions of a hollowed-out version of myself.

While Cahalan was diagnosed with a rare disease that caused inflammation of the brain, I have no such diagnosis. I wasn't hospitalized. My brain wasn't *on fire.* Calahan's behavior during that time was erratic and what some would label "crazy," whereas my behavior was more robotic, dulled. I suppose it was more like my brain was on ice.

* * *

I've read books, combed through articles, listened to relevant podcasts, and asked questions of anyone who might have insight into the psychology of what happened to me, and I can only conclude that I must have slipped further and further into a dissociated state. I was emotionally numb and detached, existing in a sort of suspended, alternate reality.

Dissociation (according to some rudimentary research) can be caused by traumatic events, acute stress, prolonged exposure to instability, or even just deeply challenging relationships. In my case, it was all of the above, further compounded by Mr. Fox repeatedly insisting *nothing is real.* Looking back, it makes perfect sense that I would dissociate. How else could I have coped?

When I try to recall how I felt, what comes to mind is a persistent feeling of dread—one I'd gotten so used to that it nearly felt normal. I was also confused, exhausted, afraid, frustrated, and quite often desperate. I was confused because I didn't know what the fuck to believe; I'd been, over time, so bombarded with such bizarre information from Mr. Fox, all of which I tried to process, while he continued to deposit more incongruous data into the already whirling and overtaxed hard drive of my mind. I was exhausted from trying to make sense of something that didn't make sense, and keeping up with him drained me. I was afraid because I was miles deep in a financial hole, and afraid of the doomsday scenarios he claimed would result from my making any wrong move. I was also afraid of his nonexistent mysterious, omnipotent brother. (Yes, he didn't exist, yet I couldn't *prove* he didn't exist—you never know—so I was afraid of him too). I was frustrated because Mr. Fox was driving me bananas, and I didn't know how to make it stop. I was desperate because it felt like there was nowhere to turn and no one I could confide in. Who would I go to, and what would I possibly tell them? How would I explain? Perversely, these circumstances only made me more attached to Mr. Fox. As if the only person who could understand the hell I was going through was the one putting me through it.

Meanwhile, Mr. Fox treated me as if I was somehow deficient for *not* understanding the contradictory nonsense he spouted, as if I wasn't advanced enough, smart enough, enlightened enough. Other times he told me I was brilliant. That I was chosen. Soon I'd *wake up*, he'd say, and *see things as they really are*. He acted impatient, as if it was a tiresome chore to shepherd me around, to *deal* with me. He made me feel the way I most dreaded feeling as a child (and even now): like a burden.

Cahalan, in considering the painful episodes she *can* recall, wrote, "I wish I could, like a guardian angel, swoop down and help protect this sad, lost echo of myself."

Yes. I feel that too.

I want to go back in time, interrupt this awful movie, and save that character that is me.

* * *

Occasionally, there were times my brain unfroze, and I was able to combat Mr. Fox's influence. Not paying Dylan was a catalyst for one of those times. For a short while, at least, I pushed back harder than ever to shake off Mr. Fox's influence.

CHAPTER FIFTY-FIVE

NOVEMBER 2014
NEW YORK CITY

The conversations in this chapter between Mr. Fox and me took place over two days in November 2014. Reviewing them today, I want to vomit. Occasionally, I want to laugh at the ridiculousness of the things he says, and the words he uses. But then after I'm done laughing, I want to cry.

* * *

On November 4, it seems Mr. Fox had given me some kind of choice to make, by noon, and he was still waiting for an answer:

```
Mr. Fox: Are you there? Hello. Please respond. Everything is
fine. Please respond. Please reply.

Me: I don't want to talk. I need to finish this stuff.

Mr. Fox: Noon has come and gone.

Me: Indeed.
```

Probably whatever Mr. Fox had asked me to decide was via email or text, which I don't have, or perhaps it was a phone call. Either way, he eventually presented another choice, or maybe it was the same one, in the conversation below. Whatever stupid choices he asked me to make never made any sense. It was as if he wanted me to think I had some control, when obviously I did not. I also had zero clue what either of the two options he presented truly entailed, even if they *were* actual options from which he *actually* wanted me to choose versus all of it being nothing more than another layer of confusing nonsense, just to fuck with my head.

Mr. Fox: Do you have your large suitcase for traveling with you? The big one I bought you? I didn't see it in storage the other day. Are you there?

Me: Yes I have it.

Mr. Fox: I assure you that talking with me is far more important than anything else you could be doing. So please, full attention. You should pack it. What time is your Dr. appt today?

Me: 3pm.

Mr. Fox: Who are you on phone with?

Me: The Russian guy. Meeting him at 6.

Mr. Fox: You can put off all these meetings if you want.

Me: No I don't want to.

Mr. Fox: You should though. Put the meetings off, take the afternoon to gather yourself so we can go over a few things this evening.

Me: Yeah no thanks I'm all set. I need you to pay Dylan like you said you would. It's important.

Mr. Fox: Many things are important. I assure you Dylan is not one of them. Today was not a good day. Nor was last night.

Me: Ok.

Mr. Fox: Ok what? What does that mean? Why are you being so out of touch and weird? How do you possibly think that will do anything other than damage things?

Me: I'm just tired. Like, to the core.

Mr. Fox: I see that. So what are you telling me?

Me: And I'm focusing on what needs attention, as opposed to your demands or getting mad at me and making me all afraid. I'm tired of being afraid. You need to pay Dylan. Just figure it out.

Mr. Fox: I have nothing to figure out. You are talking to me as if any of this means anything at all. As if any of this is real. You have nothing to be afraid of.

Me: Except you. I am terrified of you.

Mr. Fox: LOL. You are terrified of me. Right. Should be the other way around I imagine.

Me: "LOL" <== yes, it's really funny, what you've done.

Mr. Fox: I have done nothing. Why are you talking like this?

Me: Nothing except put an invisible gun to my head and make me give you over $1.5 million dollars from my company and make me lie to everyone about it? I can't even talk to my Mom!

Mr. Fox: Oh boy. You really are out of it today. Is there any way you can reset? Pull yourself out of this. And get back on board? I understand you are tired and stressed. I appreciate that. I do.

Me: No you don't.

Mr. Fox: But you can't talk to me the way you are talking and make threats and seemingly just be going off the reservation. please. ok. I get you are rundown. But please don't drop a match here.

Me: You've taken everything from me. What threat? You threaten me all day long, every day! I have to do Yellowstone or the world will come crashing down. Your brother will shut down my restaurant. Promise you'll pay Dylan. You need to pay Dylan.

Mr. Fox: I need to speak on the telephone with you please. It is important. Are you still there? I called a few times.

Me: I know.

Mr. Fox: I need to talk to you. On the phone.

Mr. Fox: …

Mr. Fox: …

Me: Call me after you've paid Dylan, please.

Mr. Fox: This is bad. Why do this… why do this now.

Me: You said if I did Yellowstone you'd pay Dylan. So pay Dylan. Or send it to me so I can pay him, which makes more sense legally.

Mr. Fox: We need to talk on the phone.

Me: It's upsetting Leon.

One of the most unbearably painful side effects of my fighting with Mr. Fox and getting upset so often was how noticeably it affected Leon. In those awful moments, I saw Leon's face change, and he looked at me with what looked like fear and worry. It absolutely gutted me to see Leon looking afraid. If Mr. Fox was yelling or I was yelling or we were yelling at each other, Leon's body actually started shaking. Even if I was alone with Leon and just yelling at Mr. Fox on the phone or crying in anger, the look on Leon's face and the thought that I was traumatizing him made me try to calm down. I always apologized to him, and reassured him that everything was okay. *Everything will be okay, Leon.*

Mr. Fox: My brother will be here soon. I need to ask you a few questions. And I need honest answers. Gchat is fine. Will you answer my questions or not?

Me: Shoot.

Mr. Fox: Have you quit on this, on us, or on yourself.

Me: I never quit.

Mr. Fox: Do you love me?

Me: Yes.

Mr. Fox: Is this real today or are you just flexing your muscles to let me know the severity of what you are going through personally.

Me: I'm done jumping when you say jump and letting you yell at me and scare me, telling me your big scary brother is going to shut my restaurant down, etc. I need to get this done. I can get a loan, I can finish this horrible task out. But you can't keep lying to me and it stopped with Yellowstone. You give me that money back so I can pay Dylan, I keep playing this game. You don't, then I don't know.

Mr. Fox: In the last 48 hours has anyone, a stranger in particular, tried to influence you in any way?

Me: I haven't talked to strangers. Except people who engage with Leon.

Mr. Fox: We are at a crossroads now. Now I will present you with 2 options. You must choose one of them. Please understand that I love you and will remain at your side no matter what you choose. Are you ready?

Mr. Fox: ?

Mr. Fox:?

Mr. Fox: <3

Mr. Fox: Sarma are you still there?

Mr. Fox:?

Mr. Fox:?

Mr. Fox: ?

Mr. Fox: Hello? Are you on the phone?

Mr. Fox: ?????????

Mr. Fox: WTF Sarma. Please reply.

Me: Talking on phone.

Mr. Fox: Are you serious? Do you not understand what is happening right now?

Me: What's happening? I'm not picking up. Stop calling.

Mr. Fox: I was not done. You need to choose 1 of the 2 options. Before my brother gets here.

Me: They are…?

Mr. Fox: Stay in the dark a little longer. You continue to trust me. No matter how it may seem or look. Trust that I will come through with Dylan next week. Do as asked by sending the wire today.

Me: Or?

Mr. Fox: Or not. And we go to Monaco on Saturday. Together. And finish this. I love you. And it will be okay. No matter which you choose.

Mr. Fox: <3 <3

Mr. Fox: …

Mr. Fox: Are you thinking it over?

Me: I'm hungry. And tired.

Mr. Fox: Me too. I like those salads you make with the grapes. And those little seeds. Pine seeds. Or nuts? Nuts I think.

Me: You should come through now, like you said, with Dylan. And no matter what you do to me, or take from me, or threaten me with, I'm not breaking. I love you too. <3

Mr. Fox: If I was there I would hug you now.

Me: That would be nice.

Mr. Fox: And tell you it will all be okay.

Later the same day (1:40 p.m.):

Mr. Fox: It will all be okay. It really will. And I do love you. With all my heart. But I do need you to make a decision. I am sorry for that and it's not like the sky will fall right after you choose one or the other. But I must ask, please choose. And remember, it will all be ok no matter what you pick.

Me: I told you, if I send any wire it's to Dylan. So, with that information, do what you want. I hear it's nice in Monaco this time of year.

Mr. Fox: There will be no going back. I need you to be sure.

Me: Like I said… you give me back the Yellowstone money to pay Dylan, and will be smooth sailing from here. You lied. Again.

Mr. Fox: Is this your final decision. Yay or nay.

Me: I'm ashamed, at having believed you, again. I regret Yellowstone with everything I have.

Mr. Fox: Please

Me: Or at least, sending the proceeds directly to you and not Dylan. You said Dylan would get paid.

Mr. Fox: I am asking for a final confirmation that you choose option B.

Me: You're not limiting me. And I'm not choosing. So do with that what you want. Go to your mysterious brother and say what you want. Throw me in the fire. I don't care. Threaten to shut my business down. Just know, like I told Matthew, I'll be in it.

Mr. Fox: None of this drama is necessary. Just choose and confirm. That is all that is being asked of you.

Me: Sorry.

Mr. Fox: And no choice defaults to B.

Me: Whatever.

Mr. Fox: Then you must confirm you refuse to choose.

Me: Ugh. You're so annoying.

Mr. Fox: Please this is serious.

Me: Agreed. Pay Dylan.

Mr. Fox: I will restate. Choose option A. Option B. Or refuse to choose which results in B. You originally chose B. I asked you to confirm and you did not. I need a choice and a confirmation. Or a refusal and a confirmation.

Me: I'm going to eat a salad. Pay Dylan.

Mr. Fox: This is not ok. You can't duck this. Or he kills me. Again, I will restate. Choose option A. Option B. Or refuse to choose which results in B. You originally chose B. I asked you to confirm and you did not. I need a choice and a confirmation. Or a refusal and a confirmation. You have until 2:30 eastern standard time to decide. I love you. And always will. And everything will be ok no matter what you choose. <3

The conversation ended for a while, then picked back up.

Mr. Fox: <3 Are you there tiny blonde wife?

Me: Yes.

Mr. Fox: So…

Mr. Fox: Anything?

Me: I'm tired.

Mr. Fox: Well it's 2:20. Have you decided?

Me: I'm not choosing and I'm getting ready for my meetings.

Mr. Fox: That is not an option.

Me: Breaking me is apparently. How about this? Option 1: Pay

Dylan, and I continue along with this believing in you. Option 2: Fuck me over, again, and I will move on and survive however I need.

Mr. Fox: Those are not the choices. This is not a game. You much choose. I am begging you. Please choose. Either option will be ok.

Me: Is this like the ring, watch, necklace game?

Mr. Fox: This is a crossroads. And you must choose. I will restate. Choose option A. Option B. Or refuse to choose which results in B. You originally chose B. I asked you to confirm and you did not. I need a choice and a confirmation. Or a refusal and a confirmation. You have until 2:30pm eastern standard time to decide. I love you. And will always. And everything will be ok no matter what you choose.

Mr. Fox: <3

Mr. Fox: But you must choose and confirm the choice. It is 2:29pm.

Me: Pay Dylan. Or pay me back and I will pay Dylan. I told you. Repeatedly. Are men in suits going to come for me now?

Mr. Fox: I will ask one more time—and not again. Option A or Option B.

Mr. Fox: Please.

Mr. Fox: Choose.

Me: B

Mr. Fox: Confirm B. Say you confirm B.

Me: I have to go I'm going to be late. I'm not doing what you say. PAY Dylan.

Mr. Fox: You chose B twice. That will be good enough as confirmation.

Me: Great. Do what you want. Do. Not. Threaten me.

Mr. Fox: It is not a threat.

Me: Will all my debts be paid, and I mean all of them? If you want to return my money so I can do that, go right ahead.

Mr. Fox: I told you whatever you choose it will be ok.

Me: Goodbye.

Mr. Fox: We have much to go over. I will go and see my brother now. I love you. Xxxx Everything will be ok. <3

* * *

Pushing back against Mr. Fox generally didn't help much. I'd gotten myself jammed far down in the rabbit hole. Even after getting over a million dollars out of me, Mr. Fox kept asking for more. He always presented situations dramatically, as if we were in a fucking movie. As if an audience sat watching on the edge of their seats, willing me to choose the right option. *She has a choice to make. How will she choose?* Meanwhile, I felt like I was living out a horror movie.

From Rome, I thought I'd passed the final test. Across the Atlantic, alone in a hotel room, I'd found someone to loan me $100,000. I was humbled and honored that Dylan, a really good guy I'd known for years, had come through for me. I'd given him every assurance I would repay him within a couple of months. My story for why I needed the money may have been vague, obviously not the truth, but my commitment to repay him was real. I was in survival mode, thinking only of the immediate future, usually one in which I needed to make payroll.

Months later, that hard deadline by which I'd promised to repay Dylan had come and gone. This made me sick to my stomach, more so than other loans I'd taken and not yet repaid. I was fixated on Dylan getting paid back.

Mr. Fox only led me on with variations of *Don't quit now. We're almost there!* As he came at me, pressuring me to send him more wires, I didn't know what to do. I deflected. I was sarcastic. I pretended to not care. I made dumb jokes, which he sometimes didn't even get. All the while, he continued working on me from behind the screen wherever he was. It's easier *now* to see how he hit one vulnerability point after another: I was going to make him proud. I was strong. I was so powerful inside I didn't even know it. I would never have to grovel or feel humiliated again. With him I'd be safe. He would be there to protect me *for the rest of time.*

I seemed to have one foot in his reality and another reaching out, trying to figure out which was the more solid ground. Occasionally, I was brave enough to step out a bit further, as I did one time, when he called me on FaceTime.

* * *

Mr. Fox regularly accused me of recording him when we were together. Sometimes he made me show him my phone to prove I was not. I'd never tried to record him—first, because recording people isn't something that normally occurred to me, and second, because I'd have been terrified, knowing I'd be in big trouble if he caught me.

But finally, one time, without prior planning, I *did* record him.

It was nighttime, and I was alone with Leon at the Twenty-Eighth Street apartment. Unexpectedly, Mr. Fox called me via FaceTime, something he didn't normally do. I was sitting at my desk working on my laptop, so I answered the call via my laptop. My phone was sitting off to the side. Without thinking much, I reached my hand out of the camera's view—careful not to look like I was fiddling with my phone to find the record function, even though that was exactly what I was doing—and pressed the red record button. I did this as if on autopilot.

My subconscious probably knew better than my conscious mind that recording him was the wise thing to do, that having the recording might be useful one day. *Thank you, subconscious!*

Perhaps I also did it because it was so easy to do, without him there in front of me. I'd been angry over not being able to repay Dylan, and I'd changed some of my passwords, including my email and bank accounts. I was in a rebellious phase—one that, unfortunately, didn't last long. They never did.

As the recording begins, I'm midsentence, making the point yet again that he'd promised Dylan would be repaid and yet Dylan remained *unpaid*. This was in response to Mr. Fox urging me to send him another wire. My voice sounds weary, almost a bit slurred, as if I was drunk or on drugs, but in fact I was just exhausted—physically and emotionally.

Mr. Fox said, "The money shouldn't matter. It shouldn't matter. It's not a coincidence you've had to face all these fucking obstacles."

He reminded me that it was not just him but his brother, watching me to see how I was going to react, and that while he was on my side, his brother claimed I was *out for myself*.

I interrupted to object, "Oh, I'm out for *myself*? I gave you one point five—more than that—million dollars."

Listening to this call now, I suspect I said that number out loud on purpose to make sure it was recorded.

I said, "I'm not going to let my fucking company tank, and I'm not going to give it all away and *not* pay my employees and *not* pay Dylan and *not* pay people that I owe."

Mr. Fox said, "First of all, you gotta understand one thing: Dylan's gonna get paid."

"Then pay him," I said.

He continued, "The problem is that you think this is real. This has already been decided, sweetheart. It's how you handle yourself throughout it that's gonna make the fuckin' difference."

I asked, "So I'm just supposed to do whatever you say and listen to your instructions and let you take all my money and be a fucking asshole? And lie to me over and over again?"

He said, "Yes. Yes, you are supposed to trust me. All of this is supposed to be difficult on you. It's supposed to make you doubt, it's supposed to make you question everything. It's faith based. It's trial by fire, it's not a cake walk."

I replied, "Look, nothing you're saying right now is gonna get me to wire you twenty-five grand tomorrow, or the next day, or the next day, until Dylan gets paid."

He got mad at me then, repeating that none of this was real.

There was a noise in the background, and Mr. Fox asked, in an accusatory way, "Who's that?" I told him it was Leon and that I still needed to walk him.

After that diversion, Mr. Fox asked me about the meetings I had earlier that evening at the restaurant. He became furious after I mentioned that I'd asked Nazim to join me for one of the meetings.

"There is *nothing* okay about that," he said.

I insisted it was not a big deal, but he disagreed. "It's a *huge* deal. I can explain it in the box."

Again, the fucking box. If Mr. Fox didn't want to answer a question, he'd claim he could only tell me *in the box*, which meant at some later time, which meant I'd never get an answer.

Mr. Fox said, "Don't take Naz anywhere without asking me first. The fact that you didn't even tell me is even more fucking suspect. I told you weeks ago I didn't trust him, since the day he walked into the house with the red umbrella. I told you weeks ago."

The red umbrella was apparently a sign that now Nazim was bad, according to Mr. Fox's claim that all people fell into the category of either *red shirts* (bad) or *blue shirts* (good), and therefore I should no longer trust him. (To this day, I still feel funny—even if just for a moment—when putting on a red shirt, red dress, red anything.)

Mr. Fox went on, "Don't get caught up in this, Sarma. Just do as instructed."

I said, "I'm not *doing as instructed*."

He asked, "Do you not understand that this is not real? All of it is a farce. How you handle yourself, especially under fire and *especially* in the late stages, is all this is. It's what you're being judged on. That's it. That's it."

He paused. I didn't say anything.

He then said, his voice low and deliberate, "If I tell you to take all your money out of the bank and light it on fire… do it."

I waited a beat, then replied, "Not anymore."

He sighed, "And that's a problem."

I said, "You think you can fucking scare me?"

He replied, "I'm not trying to scare you. It's not a threat. That's what you don't understand."

He sighed again.

Since we were on video, we probably just sat there looking at each other during this long pause.

"You look nice," he finally said.

"You look creepy as fuck," I replied.

He was sitting in a dark room with a hoodie up over his head. He started getting mad again. "You shouldn't have changed your passwords. That upset everybody."

"Oh, I'm sure *everybody* was really upset," I replied sarcastically, since we both knew I had no clue to whom the fuck "everybody" referred.

We argued more after I repeated that he'd promised Dylan would get repaid. Again he deflected, insisted it was not real, and then started to get angry again.

He said, "Listen, it's not a coincidence. I'm not tryin' to *sell* you here. If I said for you to do something, *do it!* Like, we're at this point now and you wanna go back? You *know* what the fuckin' deal is here. We've had box talks. This is the point, to get you to fuckin' twist in the wind. To get you to question everything. To *worry.* To *panic.*"

"I'm fine, and I'm not panicking."

He said, "You're not doing as told. I told you the other day before I left, you get knocked down, you keep getting up. It's not a fucking coincidence. It's supposed to happen—"

I said, "Right. I'm up."

"But you're not listening," he said, now slowing down. "If you're asked to send a wire tomorrow, regardless of the amount, are you gonna send it, yes or no?"

I didn't reply, so he repeated the question, and we went back and forth again, as I insisted the only wire I'd send would be to Dylan. Mr. Fox claimed Dylan would get paid. He veered from getting angry to then being conciliatory, conceding that this had been hard on me, saying he loved me. I was unmoved by any of it.

"I'm not sending any more wires," I said.

Then around we went again, with him getting angry and reminding me of all the same things.

"Anything else?" I asked.

My elderly cat Sydney howled in the background, as if she, too, was exhausted by this tedious call.

He claimed this wire was critical. I continued to refuse. He got mad *again*.

"Are you now going to lose your shit because you're not getting what you want?" I asked.

"I'm not going to lose my shit because *I'm* in control," he said.

"And I'm apparently so out of control right now," I said, with a yawn.

Mr. Fox always told me I had to control my emotions, yet now he was the one losing his temper. I reminded him of the time weeks earlier when he'd gotten furious and broken the dining room table in the apartment—literally broken it in two. It was a cheap table, so it hadn't been difficult to do, but it was still alarming when it happened. He'd also ripped the sliding closet doors off their hinges.

Mr. Fox's impatience came through. "If you are not going to send me the wire tomorrow, here is what's going to happen. I'm coming home. We are shutting this down. We are packing up, and we are taking a trip."

"That's not happening," I said.

And here, he got *really* mad.

"So now... now you won't even do that? Who are you? *Who are you?* What have you become? Who the *fuck* are you? And where is my fucking *wife?*"

I wasn't letting his anger affect me. Knowing I was recording the call kept me calm. I told him I was not responding to his threats.

"Threats?" he asked. "Who the fuck am I threatening?" Now furious, he yelled, "You signed on for this!!"

"No, I didn't."

He always claimed that I'd agreed to things I'd never agreed to. I don't even know what it was exactly that he *thought* I somehow signed on to.

He continued bellowing, "You want it to end, it ends. But we go. Me, you, and him, we go to Europe. You don't continue this. You didn't set this up. *I* set this up. *He* set this up. *You* signed on to this. *You* told me you loved me! You told me you wanted happily ever after. You want the forever. Now you want to look at me and tell me about some fucking *bullshit*. You're going to do this and sell your fucking company? You're not selling jack *shit*."

"No, I don't want to sell my company. Why the *fuck* do you think I *have* to sell my company?"

Selling my company was the last thing I wanted to do, but getting it into the hands of someone good and safe and allowing it to grow in the process—this was preferable to losing it all, which now felt like it could happen because financially it was on the brink, thanks to Mr. Fox.

He said, "I thought you were going along with everything. You wanted the happily ever after. And now you're talking about this as if it's fucking *real*. The money that moves through your company is *bullshit*. Those wires are *bullshit*. This is all *bullshit*. I took you in the fuckin' box. I fuckin' told you what was going on. I've held your fuckin' hand. You want to go to war with him? Then we will go to war with him." There was a pause. "I don't give a *fuck* about Dylan or any of these *fuckin'* people. They can all be bought and sold in five *fuckin'* minutes."

"With my money?" I calmly asked.

"Yeah. Your money? Your fuckin' million dollars? Oooooh, that's a lot of fuckin' money. Your fuckin' Jeffrey debt can be bought in five fuckin' minutes."

"Then do it."

"My brother will do it," he said.

"Good. Then tell him to do it."

"You don't want that."

"Then don't offer it."

He was mad. He started yelling again, "It's not—you don't get it. What the *fuck* happened to you? You're fuckin' falling apart? You're fuckin' comin' unglued?"

"Who's coming unglued?" I interrupted to ask.

He ignored me. "You want to start a fuckin' war? Over some *bul*shit?"

I didn't reply, and there was a long pause.

Finally, he sighed and said, "Don't send the wire. I don't give a fuck."

There was yet another round of his *still* trying to push me on the wire, in which he only sounded more desperate. He shouted at me louder than before. He told me I was "waving the flag," as if my refusing to send him a wire was giving up, as if it was a weakness. I think he phrased it this way knowing my stubborn nature. I don't give up easily, and I can't stand looking or feeling weak, and he knew this.

He informed me he was coming home, and I told him I didn't want him to. Aside from just not wanting him around, I knew things were always different in his presence. He'd say something or do something or look at me a certain way and, despite all his previous lies... *still*, I would eventually do as he asked. I don't know how he did this.

Our back-and-forth—his pushing and my resistance—was like fighting over the remote control to my psyche. And somehow, he always won. He always ended up with the remote.

Later that night we chatted online, and I again told him I didn't want him to come home. He finally conceded and said he'd get a room somewhere. Having given up—for the night, at least—he apologized for having gotten angry at me.

```
Mr. Fox: That isn't me. I love you. We are King Cole. That is
us. Ok? I love you. We're on the same side. I am not the bad guy.
This is and always was a test of your will and mental endurance.
I am sorry if the last few days has been exceptionally hard. You
did good, but also you said and did a few things that were not
so good. But still, it is ok. And I look forward to our happily
ever after. And I love you with all my heart. Please try and
push the bad feelings down. They are yuck and serve only to hurt
you and cause you to trip up. I love you and I believe in you.
```

Again, he referred to the incident at the King Cole bar, where I'd been drunk and cried and said that I loved him.

I went to bed relieved he wasn't coming back that night but exhausted. I knew I needed to get that recorded call off my phone. It wouldn't be long before he'd grab my phone again to rummage through my texts and probably also check for recordings. I needed a way to get it off my phone and somewhere safe as quickly as possible. I also knew sending it electronically would leave a trail for him to inevitably find. What to do? There was only one person I could have trusted to hear such a strange call and to keep it safe, and that was Nazim. Never mind that Mr. Fox had just ordered me *not* to trust him. Not for a moment did I think there was anything remotely sinister about Nazim. I figured Mr. Fox was just bent out of shape over having seen, now and then, a few too many heart emojis and an "xo" here and there in my back-and-forth texts with Nazim. I cared for Nazim and trusted him to take care of Leon when I wasn't around. Anyway, there was no one else I could go to with this.

Before Mr. Fox came back, I asked Nazim to come over. I explained that I'd recorded a call and that I needed it safely held. We stood at the small kitchen counter. He enabled the record function on his phone and put it down beside my phone. I pressed play on the file on my phone while his phone captured the audio as a new file. No electronic trace of the transfer. Afterward, I deleted it from my phone.

Of course, Nazim hearing that bizarre call led to a conversation. This was how I learned that Mr. Fox had also extracted money from Nazim, almost $100,000, which Nazim had borrowed. This was sickening to hear. You'd think *this* would have opened my eyes, finally. Somehow it didn't. It only scared me more. And the constant fear only immobilized me, like a deer in headlights.

The call was valuable, and probably enough, along with all my electronic correspondence with Mr. Fox, to go to someone for help, but again, what would I have said? How would I explain having borrowed so much money for my company, only to turn around and give it to Mr. Fox. "Why would you do that?" anyone would ask. And my answer would be what? "I don't know. He told me nothing is real"?

The call would be useful down the line—at least in bolstering my credibility with my attorneys and others. But it wouldn't make a difference to the assistant DA prosecuting me. She was, in the end, entirely unmoved by whatever evidence turned up.

※ ※ ※

The morning after the recorded FaceTime call occurred, Mr. Fox again bombarded me via Gchat, asking if we could *"get back on the same page after yesterday's hiccup."* Again, I insisted he repay Dylan. And *again*, he reminded me that all the angst I was being put through was intentional, telling me, *"It's designed to see how you handle yourself, and to test your loyalty and leadership ability."* He was apologetic, asking me to trust him just a little longer.

Reading it all, I can see how he hit various points he thought would influence me. I'm a very loyal person, for example, and always strove to be a good leader, so it makes sense he pointed out that those qualities were being tested in me. I also don't like to lose, and I'm stubborn. It was as if his specific word choices were meant to steer my subconscious. Even when the words were laughably ridiculous at times.

When I still refused to send the wire, he moved on to a sort of flattery, delivered as if he was my life guide.

```
Mr. Fox: There's a lot of power inside of you. Power that you
will ultimately wield when this is over. But it can't come out
in bits and pieces and come out the wrong way. Inside of you is
the power of a million tornadoes and hurricanes. There is more
power in you than the sun. But you do not know how to harness
it. How to wake up and remember. Seeing that it is still in
there is great. But if you can't find your way back to trusting
me to getting you to exactly where you need to be and get you
through this then that power will go elsewhere. And that will be
very bad. Very bad. For everyone. In the Universe.
```

He then insisted that I would lose all this power if I didn't trust him, if I didn't send him *another $25,000*. Okay.

I pushed back, making mostly sarcastic comments. He told me to plan on seeing him that afternoon. Sensing a deliberately implied threat, I asked, "*Are you going to shapeshift in front of me? Grow fangs?*"

I then called him out for trying to "*intimidate and control*" me, and told him that I knew he would tell me I was "*throwing the happily ever after down the toilet because of a 25K wire,*" and I knew he would tell me I was "*powerful and strong,*" that I was "*the queen,*" and then… "*send me that wire.*"

My refusal to send him this particular wire lasted much longer than my previous attempts at resistance.

Mr. Fox wrote, "*I understand what you think you are doing. But you could not be more incorrect to take this path. I also understand why you are doing this. Every time you send money and I say something will happen and it doesn't, it makes you feel awful. I get it. I do.*"

I gave him credit here for pointing out exactly how I felt and what was happening. It was one of his more effective psychological jujitsu moves—a way of extinguishing the force of those feelings.

He continued to insist this was all intentionally designed to make me *"feel like a fool and insecure and fear the worst"* and to *"question myself."* Since that was exactly how I felt, his words unfortunately resonated. Still, we argued more. I reminded him of all his lies, which he could conveniently excuse as having been intentional. He replied, *"I will get you through this. I will protect you, always."*

Mr. Fox again reminded me that Dylan wasn't real, and I replied, *"Great, then let's give his nonexistent self some imaginary Monopoly money."*

It seems like the more he wore me down, the more I made dumb jokes.

* * *

I don't know what happened after this other than it appears Mr. Fox said or did something infuriating, since the next Gchat conversation begins with me writing: *"How dare you. HOW FUCKING DARE YOU,"* to which he replied, *"Sarma. You need to reign this in."* I continued, *"YOU HAVE ORDERED ME AROUND, TREATED ME LIKE SHIT, FORCED ME TO DO HUMILIATING THINGS."* We argued back and forth, yet I can't tell from these Gchats to what, specifically, I was reacting.

After this exchange, days passed without any Gchats. Yet I can see from my paper records that, yet again, Mr. Fox got what he wanted.

On November 7, I sent Mr. Fox a wire for $25,000.

That was only three days after the recorded call. By the time we resumed Gchatting, Mr. Fox and I were together in a hotel suite in Canada.

CHAPTER FIFTY-SIX

NOVEMBER 2014
CANADA

Mr. Fox got his wire. And somehow, he also got me into my own car, as his passenger, as he drove us north, across the border into Canada.

I remember Nazim warning me, "Do not go away with him." He said it repeatedly, and I agreed. I *knew* he was right. I'd resolved to *not* go anywhere with Mr. Fox. And yet... I sent the wire. I got in the car. I let him take me out of the country. Why did I go? I must have packed a bag and taken my passport, and therefore I must have known we were leaving the country. *Why did I go?* The answer to that question may be one of the most important things to understand, and yet I don't.

It's common for people in abusive relationships to swear they'll leave and never go back—only to then *go back*. People also tell themselves they won't have a slice of cake at the upcoming office party, or they'll never drink alcohol again, and yet, they so often do. That's addiction. There's a reward in the sugar hit, or the numbing effects of alcohol. What reward did I get? I suspect fear played a central role—something wired deep in the brain, a chemical loop I couldn't break. But I don't know. I'm not a neuroscientist. Or a psychologist. I just know that I went.

Did he come to the apartment and tell me to pack, or did he call me and tell me to pack and meet him outside? I don't know. For whatever reason, I think he called. Which means it must have been something in his voice—something he said or the way he spoke—that got me to do it. And not just grab a toothbrush and race out the door, but actually *pack*, as if for a long trip.

In a June 2022 article in *The Atlantic* about Steve Bannon, journalist Jennifer Senior quoted Bannon on why he favored audio-only broadcasts. He said, "I can fuck with your mind so badly if you're just hearing my voice, right? It's a much more powerful medium."

Reading that quote not only gave me chills but also made me wonder about the power of Mr. Fox's voice on the phone. Because it seems like my compliance usually came after a call, if he wasn't in front of me. His voice carried more force than my rational thinking. Again and again, it overrode my resolve.

* * *

We drove my car. Or, *he* drove my car. It was late at night, I'm pretty sure, when we left. What about Leon? I have no memory of this at all, but I assume that we stopped at my mother's house, since she lives just off the highway on the way north to Canada. We must have dropped Leon off there.

Knowing how hard it always is for me to leave Leon, it's sadly fascinating that I was so numb I don't even recall dropping him off at my mother's. I know that it generally hurt—as everything was hurting at that time. Could I be simultaneously hurt and numb? Maybe it's like if your entire body is in a state of pain, you barely react to someone pricking you with a needle.

I have a hazy memory of staring out the car window into the late-night darkness and thinking about Nazim—about how he'd told me repeatedly me *not* to go with Mr. Fox. I felt bad and tried, in some strange way, to telepathically send Nazim a message that it would be okay, and also—and I remember this clearly—that I loved him. He was the one person, aside from Mr. Fox himself, who knew the most about what I was going through, and he was someone who cared. He was the person I trusted with Leon. He was sweet and pure. Somehow, I had convinced myself that whatever I was doing with Mr. Fox was some kind of necessary awful thing. I must have believed Mr. Fox that I just had to *get through* it. I must have figured, like the saying attributed to Churchill, *If you're going through hell, keep going.*

* * *

I don't remember arriving in Montreal or checking into a hotel. It must have been in the wee hours.

The fact that Mr. Fox and I began communicating again via Gchat reminds me that we were in separate yet connecting rooms. Or, a suite. It was some configuration with a door to separate us. At least there was that. It was the morning of November 10.

```
Mr. Fox: Who knows you are in Canada?

Me: No one. I was waiting to find out what the F is going on
before I say anything. But I need to know b/c going MIA doesn't
help.

Mr. Fox: Understood. I'm working on it now. Finding out what
must be done. Should know soon. Things are filtering in.
```

An hour later, in our Gchats, I sent him Dylan's phone number.

I continued my fixation on Dylan getting paid, and Mr. Fox continued insisting that *he* was going to pay Dylan. Mr. Fox said he would call him, but for some reason, he was going to pretend to be Will Richards. At this point, I had to have known with absolute certainty that Will Richards had never existed as an actual human and that it had been Mr. Fox all along, but this was the weird confidence of Mr. Fox. Having informed me that misleading me was an intentional part of the plan, he could get away with anything. He was just the middleman, shepherding me along this twisted game, the rules of which were supposedly set by his brother or some higher beings. This aligned with Mr. Fox always acting so frustrated with this lowly human existence, with his supposedly having to exist in what he called his "meat suit"—by now an exceedingly padded one, as part of this whole process, *for me.*

I was awestruck at how Mr. Fox could barrel through so many everyday exchanges without caring what anyone thought. That kind of confidence seemed incomprehensible to me. I know now that it was just his sociopathy. But, at the time, it appeared almost like a superpower, conveniently fitting into his narrative of being *more than* human. Humans were just ants. He was a boot. That was a metaphor he repeated often. He wasn't intimidated by anyone or anything because ultimately, he could just stomp on them like a boot would stomp on an ant.

* * *

I have a memory of Mr. Fox lounging on an angular beige couch in the Montreal hotel suite, casually making a call to Dylan. I watched with uneasy fascination, marveling at how effortlessly he could slip into any role, speak to anyone, become whoever he needed to be in the moment—so cool and confident. I don't recall what he said to Dylan or how he explained who he was. I think he spun a story that he was about to be an investor in my business and would be taking care of repaying the outstanding loan as part of that process.

Considering all this now, it seems likely that it was just a way for him to temporarily appease both me and Dylan. If Dylan believed that payment was forthcoming and that, as Mr. Fox (posing as Will Richards) presented it, it was *no big deal*, then that would take care of the issue—for a while, at least. Just as Mr. Fox had carried himself through the top floor of Tiffany's as if he was a billionaire, getting the salesman wrapped around his finger, he must have spoken to Dylan with the same easy assurance in his voice—a demeanor that was convincing.

Dylan (and I) may have been temporarily appeased, but Dylan didn't get any money. Instead, according to my records:

On November 11, I sent Mr. Fox a wire for $30,000.

I can only assume that Mr. Fox had, as usual, convinced me that we were about to *finish this*. He probably assured me that I was doing a good job. *Hang tight. Almost there.* And so on.

* * *

It makes me feel sick remembering that, from the hotel room in Canada, I was able to secure a loan from an acquaintance of mine, Nick. He wired me $25,000. All it took was a few short emails back and forth. I did a search in my email history and found the exchange. I can hardly bear to read my own words, which are, interestingly, a mix of lies and truth. I told Nick that I needed money to pay off another loan that was due. I vaguely referred to various big deals I was working on, for which I was about to fly to Europe (as if by myself). I also told him about *"some super wealthy Russians wanting to pay a fat licensing fee to open a PF&W in Moscow, not because they want to make money but because they're raw/vegan and into health suddenly and want a fancy PF&W there."*

That last part was, in fact, true. Nazim had sat with me through one of those meetings to help translate. The Russian guy was absolutely serious, and had given me the names of his associates who would be his partners. I distinctly remember talking about things like food costs, wondering whether it could be prohibitively expensive to get some of the ingredients we used over there, and he looked at me like I was wasting his time with such a silly question, saying something like, "Don't vorry. It von't be problem."

I think that kind of deal discussion gave me some confidence that borrowing more money from people was backed up by the value inherent in the brand and its expansion potential. Anything verifiably true that I could cling to, I did.

Nick readily agreed to loan me the funds, and I was effusive in my expressions of gratitude. I told him, *"Mallomars and an honorary Nick statue at our future headquarters for you!"* I also wrote, *"I'll mark up the docs real quick and send over."*

I was referring to loan documents. Nick replied that documents weren't necessary—he insisted he was making the loan as a friend and joked, *"It's all about the mallomars."* I told him I'd feel better with the documentation, and a couple of hours later, I emailed him documents that I'd signed and scanned, thereby giving him legal recourse in the future, with a personal guarantee.

And then:

On November 12, I sent Mr. Fox a wire for $25,000.

* * *

I know from the Gchats to Mr. Fox that I was stressed about being unable to cover bank overdrafts. I don't know what I'd told people at the restaurant and my office about why I'd disappeared, or whether I told anyone that we were about to get on a plane and fly to Paris.

CHAPTER FIFTY-SEVEN

LATE NOVEMBER–EARLY DECEMBER 2014
EUROPE

Mr. Fox and I flew to Paris and left my old Honda in the hotel garage in Montreal. (Later, Mr. Fox arranged for my friend Big Dave to travel to Montreal to pick it up and drive it back to NYC.)

Why did we fly to Paris? As always, I didn't know then, and I still don't know.

I don't recall arriving at the airport, going through security, or boarding the plane. But one memory exists from before takeoff: a flight attendant passing by, looking at Mr. Fox, and returning with a seat-belt extender. I'd never seen one before. I suppose it makes sense they exist, in our ever-expanding demographic. I'd also never flown with Mr. Fox. By this time, he was bigger than ever. He was huge. There was no way the standard seat belt would have fit. He didn't seem embarrassed. If anything, he accepted it without a second thought. Meanwhile, *I* felt embarrassed. Why? It made me think about all the people who struggle with obesity and need an extender every time they fly, and how that must feel.

I don't remember the rest of the flight, the landing, or making our way to the hotel Mr. Fox had booked, but I do remember checking in. We arrived earlier than the check-in time and when informed that our rooms weren't ready, Mr. Fox was furious. He arrogantly snapped at the charming clerk. I was mortified. I briefly made eye contact with the handsome Frenchman behind the counter and tried to telepathically communicate an apology, along with something like, *I did not choose to be the wife of this rude, fat man—I am miserable. Please take pity on me... or better yet, save me?*

Mr. Fox and I sat in the lobby and waited. I was seething with weary rage. Mr. Fox had not only been rude to the hotel clerk but was also being a giant asshole to me. I felt wretched, stuck so far away from home with this brute. I was completely drained of energy; otherwise, I might have motivated myself to get up, punch Mr. Fox in the face, then stumble out into the path of an oncoming bus. These were the kinds of scenes I visualized with increasing frequency.

Finally, we got up to our room, which was, mercifully, a suite with a separate bedroom so at least I could sleep alone. As always, Mr. Fox took the bedroom. The couch in the living room wasn't meant for sleeping. It was more loveseat than couch. I had to keep my knees bent or hang my feet off the edge, but I didn't care. As long as I could lie down in peace.

* * *

We didn't stay in Paris long. I've pieced together the sequence of where we traveled with the help of my Gchat records, my iPhoto history, and a few Instagram posts.

Mr. Fox told me to me look online for train tickets to Zurich, and off we went to Zurich. I have no idea why we were there or what we did. I took a few photos, including one of my breakfast. I do vaguely recall that breakfast. We were in a European version of a no-frills business hotel, the kind with efficient buffet breakfasts included in the price. I went downstairs by myself to check it out, while Mr. Fox slept. I remember eating muesli, like a proper Swiss person.

The rest of that part of the trip is mostly a blur. While writing this, I googled "casino in Zurich" because I can vaguely picture being in a casino somewhere in Europe—but maybe it was a dream? Apparently not. According to Google, there is (or was) a casino in Zurich (of course), and it's so flashy and distinctive that it seems crazy I'd forgotten being there, until seeing these images. The casino exterior is a massive glittering gold box. Looking at a photo of the luminescent escalator inside... *yes*, I recall riding up that escalator alone. I think Mr. Fox had gone to the casino first and later asked me to meet him there. (Since he was using his phone, these conversations were via text messages I no longer have.)

The escalator was flanked by walls made from bars of shiny mirror and silvery glass, such that it felt like ascending through the interior of a giant-sized chandelier. On the second floor, an impressively huge curvy *actual* chandelier hung from the ceiling. I stepped off the escalator and eyed a couch along the wall. I sat there to wait for Mr. Fox, and I remember he kept me waiting a long time, as he so often did. He always acted like he had specific business to transact, as if he were meeting someone and *taking care of business*. When he finally came out and we left, I don't know if he had more or less money than when he arrived. I don't remember anything else about this time in Zurich, except a vague memory of walking through a picturesque shopping area, glittering with holiday decoration, wishing I could genuinely appreciate the festive vibe.

* * *

After three days in Zurich, we traveled to Venice, Italy. It was November 17. This arrival was memorable because the city was flooded, and not just *splash-splash* flooded but more like eight inches of water covering the streets of most of the city.

We arrived late at night. I recall standing on a dock, so maybe we took a short boat ride after the train. Water from the canal ran continuously into the streets.

Mr. Fox arranged for a porter. Whether this guy was formally a porter or just someone trying to make some money, I don't know. He wore knee-high rubber boots and a bright yellow safety vest over his clothes which gave him a somewhat legit appearance. He had a wheelbarrow on which he loaded some of our bags, but they wouldn't all fit, so I carried some of them. Mr. Fox did not carry any. There were makeshift walkways set up: planks of plywood on concrete blocks. They weren't the sturdiest and, in some places, had come apart. I was wearing jeans and blue Puma sneakers that were already soaked, so I gave up on the rickety walkways and walked through the water, my feet sloshing and squishing inside my sneakers with each step. I kept up with the porter, while Mr. Fox lagged behind.

We finally got to our hotel and checked in, thankfully into two separate rooms. The next day, most of the water had cleared away, so getting around was easier. I'm not sure what we did that day, aside from walking around. I remember a dinner at a casual restaurant, full of Italians, not tourists. The food was good, and Mr. Fox was embarrassing.

I realize now there are casinos in Venice. Mr. Fox must have gone to them late at night while I was sleeping. He tended to sleep late into the days, so this would make sense.

What I remember most about Venice is a small shop we wandered into one afternoon, filled with beautifully printed journals and cards. An image in the window caught my eye: a drawing of a forlorn-looking rabbit. It reminded me of the Donnie Darko rabbit, even though I don't think I ever saw that movie. I bought the journal with the rabbit on the cover and still have it. I never wrote in it—somehow it felt too special to mark its pages with ink.

* * *

From Venice we took a train to Milan, checked into a hotel, and went out to dinner. I'd done some research and found a good place, one that would be free of tourists and full of local Italians. While we waited for an Uber, Mr. Fox took a picture of me standing in the street. It irritated me how he always insisted on taking an Uber when we could have easily walked. How could one *not* walk when in a beautiful European city? After one of our Uber rides, just as we were getting out of the car, Mr. Fox casually said something in Italian to the driver, and they had a brief exchange. I don't know what was said, but it was more than a simple *grazie* or standard pleasantry. It was something more. I remember noticing that Mr. Fox sounded so natural—as if he was fluent in the language.

While at my laptop, I must have been communicating with the staff back home. I sent a Gchat to Mr. Fox, telling him, *"Jake is asking me when I'm back."* Jake was the bookkeeper.

Mr. Fox told me to tell Jake I'd be back the first week of December. I wrote back to Mr. Fox that this would be the first time that I would miss Thanksgiving at the restaurant. He told me it was okay, as there would be *"plenty more years to have Thanksgiving"* there. Then he said, *"At Christmas, we can sip wine from the skulls of our vanquished enemies."* He was joking, obviously. But with Mr. Fox, even his jokes were usually meant to imply something.

* * *

From Milan we took a train to Monaco. Mr. Fox told me that he and his "family" had a home there. This had me intrigued. As if *finally* I'd meet someone or see something to validate his being who he claimed to be. However, when we arrived, there was no grand estate, no sign of this supposed family. Instead, we checked into what was probably the least expensive hotel in all of Monaco—probably the place where yacht crews and staff stayed while their employers checked into five-star hotels. It wasn't that I longed to be in luxury; it was the way he always raised my expectations, only to then crush them.

Outside our hotel, Monaco felt like a Euro version of the Hamptons—overflowing with super-rich people whose appearance and attire clearly advertised their wealth. What sealed my distaste for this city was an object displayed in a store window. I had to look close to make sure I was seeing it correctly. It was a fur *tissue box holder*. It looked like a fuzzy slipper—or Chewbacca's severed foot—made from the silky soft hairs of a caged and murdered mink. I snapped a photo of it, thinking that if I had to sum up what I didn't like about this city, this tissue holder would do it.

We didn't once go out to eat in Monaco, instead ordering crappy room service in the hotel. I didn't care. I was just grateful to have separate rooms. Having separate rooms was all that mattered. I also remember going to the hotel gym to work out. By myself, obviously.

Of course, Monaco is known for its casinos, and of course, Mr. Fox spent loads of time there. Whether he won or lost, I have no clue.

* * *

Mr. Fox never explained why there was no family home to visit. Maybe he claimed I wasn't *ready* to go. Somehow, it would be my fault. From the Gchats, I see I was angry at Mr. Fox—about something specific or in general, I'm not sure. On November 24, I wrote, "*I just want to go home. Except I don't have one, so I want a home too. With Leon in it. And I want to go there and sleep for a week. Without night terrors. I had a dream last night that you ditched me here.*"

Mr. Fox replied that when we finished, sleeping for a week sounded like a good plan. I wrote back, "*Nightmares. Every night. Then I wake up into another.*"

Waking up every day into another nightmare—this was my reality: going through the motions of each day in a stupor of fear, sometimes dulled, sometimes more acute.

Mr. Fox replied, "*Ok ok. Don't get all worked up again.*"

* * *

From Monaco, I traveled alone to London. No, I hadn't fled to escape the clutches of Mr. Fox. I was on assignment. My mission, which, apparently, I had accepted (probably feeling I had no choice), was to get $250,000 from a guy named Faris, a former colleague from my days at Bear Stearns. Yes, a *quarter of a million dollars*. Granted, this person was, if not a billionaire, probably close to it. I was pretty sure. Either way, *what the fuck*. But still. It felt crazy and scary.

I didn't want this to be real life. Mr. Fox had a way of making it seem like we were living in a movie, and maybe I tried to embrace that, to help me feel that it wasn't real. It would have been easier to play a part because I am *not* cut out for risk, or asking people for *any*thing, never mind a quarter of a million dollars. Unlike Mr. Fox, I am not skilled at manipulation. All of this was terrifying.

Unsurprisingly, I failed at the task. I met Faris at a lively and loud restaurant bar, and we began catching up. I couldn't even bring myself to try. I never got to the point of lying, of asking. I didn't want to deceive him, or anyone. Instead, I drank every new glass of champagne or wine poured for me, until I was extremely drunk. So was Faris. He listened to my talks of expansion and wanting to build a hotel and said, "Let's do it!" before sticking his hand in my V-neck sweater to grab my boob—to "check if they're real," he said. I was briefly shocked, then humiliated as I made eye contact with the white-haired, proper English bartender who'd watched. In that moment I already felt so much shame generally that I wasn't mad. As if I deserved whatever he might do.

The next day, I returned to Mr. Fox, now in Paris, where he'd installed himself in another hotel suite. When I entered the room, I found him sitting in the semi-dark, waiting. On the table in front of him was a full glass of red wine. He made me sit and drink it—knowing how hungover I was, as if for punishment—while he berated me with dramatic flair for my failure. I don't remember his words, or what happened next. Only that, as always, he eventually lifted me back up into his better graces. Then, a day or two later, we traveled to Belgium.

As always, I don't know why that particular location. We stayed in a business hotel, another suite where, thankfully, I had my own room. There was talk of my flying to Moscow to meet with that Russian man I'd met in NYC who'd wanted to open a Pure Food and Wine in Moscow. Except a Visa would be required to make that trip and there wasn't time for that.

At one point in Belgium, Mr. Fox Gchatted me:

```
Mr. Fox: Couple things. The first is that I need that 20K sent
out now. That's important. You there?

Me: Fuck you.
```

I must have sent that wire because a half hour later we Gchatted about what to order for dinner. I wrote that I loved him, and he wrote back that he loved me too. Maybe he'd slipped something into that wine he made me drink in Paris that tweaked my brain. Who knows.

While in Belgium, I emailed some contacts back home asking about loans, as if I might have been able to get another quick big loan, like the one from Dylan. Nothing came through, and after a couple of days it was arranged that I would fly back to New York alone. I'm not sure what the plan was, but according to our Gchats, it appears that Mr. Fox wanted me to come *back* to Europe after only a few days in New York. He wrote, *"Sent you 2K to get me jeans and use the rest for expenses and your return ticket."* He wanted me to buy him jeans while in New York, as if that was a priority.

On December 5, I wrote to Mr. Fox, *"Boarding in a bit."*

And then I returned to New York.

CHAPTER FIFTY-EIGHT

DECEMBER 2014
NEW YORK CITY

I have no memory of flying home from Europe by myself or making my way back from the airport—I don't even remember reuniting with Leon. My best guess is that Nazim picked him up from my mother's house for me. The day after I returned, I wrote to Mr. Fox about going to the greenmarket and then making Leon a special breakfast. It's strange to think of Leon and I together in that dark apartment on Twenty-Eighth Street—that unfamiliar place that felt nothing like home.

* * *

I had a meeting scheduled with the wealthy Russian who wanted to open a Pure Food and Wine in Moscow; he was in New York for a few days. Looking back, surely Mr. Fox was thinking I could get some money out of this man quickly. I'd have known that would be unrealistic, since deals usually take months to execute, not days. I must have been thinking that at least it was *some*thing promising—whatever happened. I needed any lifelines I could get.

The meeting didn't yield anything concrete—it only inched the ball down the field with talk about who on their end would be involved and how it all might work. From my later Gchats with Mr. Fox, I can see he was angry at me for my lack of progress. We also argued about Nazim. Somehow, while we were in Europe, Mr. Fox got me to admit that I had recorded the phone call on November 4, the night he FaceTimed me, and that I'd given the recording to Nazim. I don't remember or understand how he managed to extract this information from me, but he did.

Most likely he spoke to Nazim on the phone while we were in Europe and sensed a shift in Nazim's voice, a hint of something off, and then questioned me about it. He may have done the thing where he acted like he already knew the truth about something and then pressured me to confess by making threats about the doom that would result if I was lying. That was usually how it went.

Part of my assignment from Mr. Fox for my return to New York included making sure Nazim deleted the recording and reassuring Nazim that I was okay, that everything was okay. Mr. Fox had, by this time, gotten me back under his influence such that I mostly did what he told me to do. Fortunately, despite telling me he'd deleted it, Nazim never in fact deleted the recording. I told Mr. Fox it was deleted yet conceded that he'd not done it in front of me so I couldn't be fully sure.

Mr. Fox was angry. He wrote, "So no money. No deal in place. And no Naz clean up. Goodnight Sarma. I will see you when you get back here."

* * *

A big winter storm hit the East Coast causing flight delays and cancellations, which I was grateful to use as an excuse to cancel my return to Europe. *Phew!* I *did not* want to leave again. I also managed to convince Mr. Fox that I should stay for more meetings. Someone new had entered the picture: a potential investor named Jack who owned a successful pizza chain in the western US. Jack had recently shifted his personal diet to mostly raw vegan, giving up gluten completely, and was interested in taking the One Lucky Duck Juice and Takeaway concept national. He was a good guy and would have made a good partner for this.

Having another lead helped me convince Mr. Fox I should stay put, even after the storm passed, so I did.

Spending time at the restaurant while Mr. Fox remained in Europe allowed me to reconnect emotionally to my business. I wrote to him about an incident—how, with the dining room packed, the manager had to deal with an unusually difficult situation. I wrote, "*I want to help it. I want to make everything okay.*"

Mr. Fox replied, "*You can't make everything ok. Only WE can make everything ok. You do this part. I set everything right. HEA.*" (HEA meaning, happily ever after.)

There it was. Do as he told me, and everything would be all right.

* * *

I did end up getting money from Jack, the pizza man. It took a couple of weeks, but he agreed to give my company a bridge loan to keep things afloat while we discussed our future collaboration. I genuinely liked and respected Jack, and an alliance with him felt good. Without Mr. Fox in my life, expanding with Jack could have been ideal. The partnership part of it felt good, but the deception involved in getting the bridge loan felt, as usual, awful. I rationalized it with my ongoing delusion that Mr. Fox would come through and everyone would be repaid. And if he didn't, at least I had a valuable concept that would, over time, repay everyone, even if it meant giving up all ownership and working in servitude to make that happen. I'd have done that.

Mr. Fox was heavily involved in securing the loan from Jack. At times, he took my phone and drafted what I should text Jack.

Jack was of Italian heritage, and Mr. Fox floated a narrative that somehow Jack was *one of them*. At one point he wrote, *If Jack is what I suspect he is, then he may already know who I am, and will do this deal to get in my good graces.*

Yet again, the goalpost had been moved. Mr. Fox's story was that with this loan, everything would be finished. He had told me I had to get $350,000. *Then*, it would all *finally* be over. He wrote, "*The most important thing is the 350. After that I can take the reins and put this all to bed. We win.*"

I was angry and wanted to end the conversation. It's remarkable how sometimes I came right out with the truth, even if I didn't quite recognize it as such at the time. I replied to him, "*I need to go walk Leon, stop by the restaurant, then come back and sit down and plan how to manipulate yet another person out of a lot of money because of your lies and my desperation.*"

That's an incriminating thing to have written, and to reprint here. But it feels important. How does someone (me) with a strong sense of right and wrong, ethics and morality, get to this stage? I know that I operated with the belief, however delusional, that it would all be made right. Everyone would be repaid. I wasn't *really* doing anything wrong because I had no intention of *not* making sure everyone was repaid, one way or another. And yet, it *was* wrong. Even in an altered reality.

Mr. Fox played into my reasoning while skillfully propping up my ego.

```
Mr. Fox: Even though at times it seems bad, this was all done
from a place of good. We are SO close. And I am so proud of
you. I love you very very much. You have my respect and loyalty.
You are my equal now and forever. Anything worth having is
worth working for. And you are working for the ultimate goal
of freedom and happiness. So it requires the ultimate effort
mentally, which you have put in. You have logged many hours,
as have I, they will not be for nothing. See it through,
successfully, and we get our happiness and our power and our
freedom and our lives. Separately and together. You were born
for this. There is no coincidence. You started a lamb. You will
finish a lion. I love you. Always have. Always will.
```

* * *

Mr. Fox returned from Europe and went straight to Connecticut, claiming he needed to see his brother.

Meanwhile, I continued chasing leads and following up with Jack. Regarding investors, Mr. Fox wrote, "*Whoever comes through gets a seat at the table. I have decided.*"

I replied, "*What? You sure?*"

"*Yes,*" he wrote.

Despite not even understanding what *a seat at the table* meant, I went for sarcasm: "*You want Jack at the table? He'll bring good pizza at least. :)*"

The next morning Mr. Fox messaged to ask how I was doing.

"I wanted to die this morning. Happens every morning," I told him.

Mr. Fox responded with a lecture on staying strong and fighting the negativity.

* * *

Of the $350,000 Mr. Fox told me I needed to get, he initially agreed that I would send only $180,000 to him. (I know, *only $180,000!*). He said I could use $100,000 to repay Dylan's loan and the remaining $70,000 for regular business expenses, including payroll. I was still fixated on repaying Dylan, so that promise likely boosted my motivation to get the funds. Never mind that I wasn't questioning *why* I had to give $180,000 to Mr. Fox.

Of course, Mr. Fox then tried to change these terms, and we fought over it.

It's both astonishing and sickening that I was able to get these large sums of money at all. Still, it was never fast enough for Mr. Fox. A few days passed while Mr. Fox remained in Connecticut. He wrote, *"Me and my brother are sitting down late this evening to negotiate terms based on what's happened—or not happened—with your deals. So many rules have been broken and deadlines missed."*

The way he spoke made me feel like I was trapped in a game—watched by him and his *brother*, as if this were some bizarre version of *The Hunger Games*. I was the player, put through terrorizing challenges, curveballs thrown at me just to see how I'd react, whether I'd survive. It felt sickening. When I told him he was making me nervous, he replied, *"Don't be. You get the funds it's all good. It's more about what happens if you don't. So don't worry. Just keep doing your work to get it done. You're doing a good job."*

That vague threat—*what happens if you don't*—was what scared me. That on top of the pressure of actually getting the money. On top of the ongoing anxiety of operating a business now teetering on the edge of solvency.

A few days later he reminded me, *"I have done everything I can to get things done for you. So you get the life you always wanted. And freedom. Because I love you. This will all be a forgotten memory soon. And will be HEA."*

Throughout the middle of December, I sent Mr. Fox a few wires of $10,000–$20,000 each. And then, I finally executed loan agreements with Jack, and his $200,000 was wired into my account.

* * *

On December 19, I sent Mr. Fox a wire for $180,000.

I'd done it. Again, I'd delivered. And still, I had to find the balance to total $350,000. And I did that too. By some miracle (which, at the time, felt like it literally saved me), I got yet another loan, quickly and informally, from a friend overseas. In my deluded mind, yet again, I thought this was it. Finally, I was done. Just in time for Christmas.

Did I get to repay Dylan? Of course not.

On December 22, I sent Mr. Fox a wire for $90,000.

On December 23, I sent him a wire for $40,000.

* * *

Thankfully, Mr. Fox still hadn't returned to the apartment. Having just sent what were supposed to be the *last* wires, I was more nervous than ever—but also relieved to spend Christmas with just Leon and my cat, Sydney, and no one else.

Despite all the money I'd just sent to Mr. Fox, I was at least able to cover the $10K needed to rip up and replace the restaurant's kitchen floor—which badly needed to happen. Since the work required shutting down, it made sense to schedule it for the only days of the year we were already closed: Christmas Eve and Christmas Day.

I wrote to Mr. Fox, "*Can I buy a vacuum cleaner? Or am I going to wish I had that cash? I'm cleaning today because I don't know what else to do. I'm nervous. Cleaning helps.*" He replied that it was fine to buy a vacuum cleaner, then added, "*You won't need it for long.*" As if this was all about to be over. He told me not to be nervous, that there was nothing I could do now anyway, not until he finished his "talks." He wrote, "*Have not reached a conclusion with my brother yet. But am close.*"

I wrote back, "*Did I do ok? I delivered, didn't I?*"

"*I can go into full details when I see you,*" he replied.

* * *

On Christmas Eve and Christmas Day, I took Leon to the restaurant to check on the progress of the new floor, then wandered the city. In Midtown, I snapped selfies of us in front of a huge, decorated tree outside an office tower.

Not knowing whether this cycle of borrowing and wiring money was, in fact, over, or what was coming next, was unbearable. I tried to remain hopeful that everything was safe and that relief was on the way.

CHAPTER FIFTY-NINE

JANUARY 2015
NAPLES, FLORIDA

A day or two before the end of the year, Mr. Fox told me to pack up the entire Twenty-Eighth Street apartment, as if I'd be moving. He also directed me to pack a short-term bag with clothes for someplace warm. He said I'd never set foot in that apartment again, which was a relief to hear—except he'd told me the same thing when he took me to Europe (and, I'm pretty sure, had made me pack up the apartment then, too).

For a while, Mr. Fox and I barely communicated over Gchat, which makes it hard for me to recall what he told me was happening.

It appears that on New Year's Eve, I was in a hotel room at the Mohegan Sun casino in Connecticut. I'd never have remembered this if not for the photo I took of Leon in the room, dated that day. That we were there is the sum of what I can confirm. I have no memory of what happened that night or the days surrounding it, nor of what I told people back at the restaurant about where I went. It was still technically *the holidays* so it was not so strange that I would be away. But every New Year's Eve the chefs created a special menu, and every year before, I'd been at the restaurant on that night.

* * *

I do remember that Jack, the pizza guy from whom I'd just borrowed $200,000, had been urging me to fly to his Utah headquarters to meet with him and his executives about our loosely planned collaboration. More importantly, he wanted his accountants to go through my books to sort out the best way to address my cash flow problems. I felt positively sick over this idea. I liked Jack, and would have loved to be in a genuine partnership with him, but how could I explain what had been going on? Any examination of the books would reveal the large sums of money transferred to my personal accounts—and then, from there, to Mr. Fox.

Clearly I couldn't go to Utah to meet Jack. I was terrified. I'm nearly certain that now Mr. Fox was communicating with Jack, via my cell phone, pretending to be me. I was so afraid of the whole situation, and afraid of lying, that I just allowed it. I don't recall what Mr. Fox told him.

Mr. Fox had a justification for everything. He told me to think of our lying to people the way you might lie to a friend to avoid spoiling their upcoming surprise party. Once the party arrived, they'd be grateful that you lied. This was among the ways he got me to compromise my ethics and values.

* * *

From the few photos on my phone, it appears I stayed in the casino hotel for about a week—until January 8, when I took a selfie in what looks like an airport bathroom. Leaving Leon with Mr. Fox, I flew to Florida alone.

Mr. Fox had insisted I needed to go away to a beach by myself and told me to pick a place in Florida. I chose Naples because it was an easy flight and seemed more low key, less Spring Break than most Florida destinations. He assured me that in my absence everything was *finally* being wrapped up. He said this: *Wrapped up.* As if it was a no-big-deal situation that just needed to be tidied up.

He said he would come to get me in a few days, and emphasized the importance of my staying completely "off comms," which meant no social media, email, or text and no answering calls. Unless, of course, any of that outreach was from him.

I flew to Naples and Ubered to a Ritz-Carlton beachfront hotel where Mr. Fox had booked a room for me. The Ritz-Carlton is owned by Marriott, and

Mr. Fox preferred Marriott properties. Points, I guess. The hotel felt fancy in a country club kind of way. Probably there was a golf course nearby.

At the front desk, I checked in, retrieved keys, and took the elevator up a few floors. The hallway was plushly carpeted, the walls buttery yellow, and the lighting golden, with pastel accents everywhere. In the room were two beds, a small desk, and an upholstered armchair by the window—a good place for reading, I thought. All of it yellow—yellow carpet, yellow walls, yellow bedspreads, cream pillows, the whole room like corn on the cob and butter. A sliding door led to a small deck from which, if I leaned over the railing, I could see the ocean.

I had a few books with me and nothing else to do. I don't think I even opened my laptop, given Mr. Fox's instructions to remain *off comms*. For this reason, I have no Gchats from this time. I wasn't logging into my email, and whatever Mr. Fox told me would have been via texts that I no longer have.

Looking at my phone and ignoring *other* incoming texts was not easy, but I got used to it, letting my eyes glaze over everything else, clicking only on what came from Mr. Fox.

He assured me that all I needed to do was relax and wait.

But how could I relax? Even if I could have, it wasn't warm enough to lie on the beach. On my second day there, January 9, I took a selfie from a lounge chair by the beach; I was bundled up in a gray hoodie and a plush striped towel, a book in my lap. It was chilly, and the high winds made it hard to read the book. I needed more distraction.

Getting to and from the beach required crossing a raised wooden walkway that passed by an outdoor bar and restaurant, thereby making it easy to stop for something to eat and drink. And because of my nerves, *drink* was what I wanted to do. I went to the bar and ordered a pink frozen strawberry daiquiri with a slice of pineapple on the rim. I may not have recalled this except that I took a photo of it, in its plastic cup with the blue Ritz-Carlton logo. I probably ordered another.

Once or twice, I had lunch at the hotel's outdoor cafe, which I know because I took a photo of the place setting, with a full glass of sparkling rosé and a folded copy of the *New York Times* Arts section, crossword puzzle completed. I love crosswords.

It was a strange sensation to feel both nervous and bored. One day, I took an

Uber to a nearby outdoor mall where I wandered aimlessly, then bought a blue-and-white-striped wide-brimmed sun hat from Ann Taylor. Again, I remember this detail only because I have photos of myself in the hat. I also stopped at Barnes & Noble for more books, then headed to a bar, where I ordered prosecco and a salad. An older, white-haired man sat two stools over and struck up a conversation with me. A semiretired attorney, he seemed harmless and friendly. I took his business card. Would he and his wife adopt me if I were stranded here? Part of me wondered.

* * *

Maybe five days into my stay, an all-caps text appeared on my phone that was impossible to glaze over. It was like looking down and seeing flames.

CLOSED?????????

That text was from Jack. I clicked on it and saw a link to a *New York Post* story. The headline included the word *Closed*. My restaurant. Pure Food and Wine.

This was surreal. It made no sense. Whatever Mr. Fox had told me, I had expected the opposite of this.

I skimmed the article. Apparently, the staff hadn't been paid, and they eventually walked out. The restaurant was *closed*. I wanted to vomit and die. It was like I'd been accused of child abuse. As if I would do that, as if I would betray my staff. And yet somehow, without knowing it was happening, I had. I had *allowed* this. Even though I was not the monster who would do something like that.

This news yanked me out of my dissociated haze and plonked me into catatonic shock. I don't remember what I did next, what happened, or what I felt—if I felt anything at all. Did I fly into a screaming rage at Mr. Fox? Or did I fall on the bed and weep? I think I did neither. Instead, I think I froze into a stupor of dread and deliberate detachment. I don't know if I replied to Jack.

It had to have felt… *not real.* How could Pure Food and Wine be shut down? And how could my mind process that by doing anything other than… shutting down too?

* * *

In *What Happened to You*, a book co-authored with Oprah, Bruce D. Perry wrote, "The dissociative response is used when there is inescapable, unavoidable distress and pain. Because you cannot physically flee, and fighting is futile, you psychologically flee to your inner world."

Given how trapped I felt, this makes sense to me. The detachment of emotions, suspension of rational thinking, and sense of time dissolving—actual neurophysiological changes must have occurred, ones I'm not qualified to explain. At least I can understand that my lack of memory makes sense, and why the memories I do have seem as if I'm viewing them through a portal. Like in *Being John Malkovich*. It's someone else's existence I'm conjuring up, because that wasn't me.

Somewhere I read that the dissociative response happens on a continuum, the first stage of which is avoidance. To avoid conflict, one behaves with an increasingly detached compliance. Complying—however irrational—feels like the safest option in the moment. Increasingly, feelings and thoughts are disconnected. Hollow is the best word to describe what it feels like, and of course, by definition it's strange to say *what it feels like* since, more and more, one isn't feeling anything at all.

But I imagine that receiving the news, seeing that word—*closed*—pushed me into a deeper level of dissociation.

I suppose it was obvious that I needed to go back home. I have zero recollection of packing or arranging a flight. What I do have is a photo dated January 14 of a huge glass of white wine in an airport. I didn't fly back to New York. Mr. Fox had me fly to Providence, Rhode Island. I also took a photo of the longest, stupidest-looking limo I'd ever seen. It must have been sent from the casino. I remember thinking how vulgar this was—being picked up in a massive tacky limo under those circumstances. Another photo, dated January 15, shows I was with Leon in what looks like a hotel room. Beyond that I remember nothing.

My next memory is the moment, back in the city, when I stepped into the empty restaurant. I don't remember what I felt because I think I felt nothing. Only numbness. Numbness steeped in dread. And fear. And darkness.

CHAPTER SIXTY

LATE JANUARY–EARLY APRIL 2015
NEW YORK CITY

I thought I'd endured the worst with Mr. Fox. I'd passed through the darkness, which I couldn't have imagined getting any darker. Except now it had. Not just darker, but like the sun itself had been extinguished, possibly forever.

My business was closed.

This is, by far, the hardest chapter to write. I don't remember what I did or in what order. Scrolling through a few photos from that time jogs some memories. I have only a handful of Gchats with Mr. Fox to remind me how things were. All I can do is describe my fuzzy memories and piece together a general summary of what happened over the following months—months that were brutal and humiliating, bizarre and surreal.

* * *

I remember the restaurant actually *feeling* really dark when I stepped inside for the first time after coming back. All the good energy—the magic people always talked about—was gone. It was just a hollow cave of a space. Also, it had been ransacked. The expensive Vitamixes, tools, ingredients, and, of course, all the wine—gone. I couldn't blame them, yet it stung. Didn't they know something was wrong? This was my biggest nightmare come true, compounded many times over because I couldn't explain it to anyone.

I genuinely have no idea how I didn't come completely unglued right then and just fall to the floor, relinquishing consciousness. Nothing made sense. To say my soul was exhausted would be putting it mildly. Probably what kicked my subconscious into gear was the realization that I now had two options: (1) figure out how to kill myself, or (2) figure out how to reopen my business. I could at least try option 2, and if that didn't work, option 1 would be my fallback.

* * *

Thinking about it now, part of me wonders why it didn't finally occur to me to get away from him. What if I'd just *somehow* broken free from Mr. Fox, stood on the street and screamed for help. The problem was that I had done bad things. By believing Mr. Fox, I had borrowed money presumably for the business, only to wire that money to Mr. Fox, for reasons I couldn't justify. This was bad. Who would have sympathy for me?

If I was having any of these thoughts, they were blurry. I was a zombie, standing in the tomb of my dead restaurant. On some instinctual level I knew that it didn't make sense that the restaurant was closed. And I was still standing upright, with a pulse, which meant I could still do something.

Maybe through some kind of reactionary autopilot mode, I tapped into inner resources and resilience that I hadn't even known I had. The way a parent might lift a car off a child and later have no clue where that strength had come from.

In this moment, there was no time for, or point to, reflection. I just knew I *had* to bring the restaurant back to life, however possible. Then at least it would exist again, and everything would be okay. *Then*, if needed, I could lie down and die.

* * *

I have no idea how I got started. This wasn't like the earlier days, when it was me and the restaurant staff united as a team—when we all pulled together through every crisis, whether a storm, a blackout, the 2008 downturn, or a health inspection gone awry. This time, they were mad at me, and for good reason. I was gutted inside, feeling like an awful human being. By all appearances, I *had* been awful, yet could offer no explanation that made sense. Whatever excuses I gave for what had happened—and I genuinely don't recall what they were—they had to have been confused at how strange I must have been behaving, so unlike myself.

What could I say? The truth? That while they were suffering, confused, and not getting paid, I was at the beach drinking strawberry daiquiris at the Ritz-Carlton? Ignoring my phone? All on the assumption that some magical reordering of the universe was underway? That Mr. Fox, the fat fuck who they all rightfully hated and was indeed a monster, was taking care of everything? That my brain was broken?

I knew I had to—and *wanted* to—take care of the unpaid payroll first. That their checks had bounced wasn't just wrong; it was deeply mortifying. Bouncing employee checks was something Matthew had allowed to happen years ago, and I was *not* like Matthew. This was not me. In my normal state, I'd have starved myself and sold off personal belongings, or even myself. I'd have done *anything* to avoid bouncing employee checks—or any checks.

Payroll was just one part of the disaster. The restaurant's rent was more than three months past due, and rent was owed at our offices and the Brooklyn production facility, also now closed. The Chelsea Market takeaway had closed. There was a big backlog of unpaid sales tax on all three locations. Not to mention those awful Rapid Pay and Yellowstone loans, and all the other loans from people who'd been supportive of me. On top of that: unpaid vendors, utilities, and more. With a business people loved, a place customers normally flocked to, how in the fuck did I get here? I couldn't think about it too much or else option 1 would feel increasingly alluring as the quickest way out.

* * *

In my old email there must be correspondence—to employees and others—that could bring me back to that time, help me see how I handled things, what I said, what I did next. I have a vague recollection of sending a staff-wide email, something akin to a hostage video, assuring everyone that everything was okay.

On January 21, I took a picture of Leon in the closed restaurant. Other than that, I have no photos to give me clues. And not many Gchats with Mr. Fox, because he was there too.

I don't even remember what he told me had happened while I was gone. I don't remember getting angry or confronting him, probably because I was too numb. I'm sure he made it seem like it was my fault. In fact, months later, in one of his written lectures, he pointed back to this time and referenced a tantrum I'd had a few weeks earlier in which I'd apparently thrown carrots at him as the causal event that led to the restaurant's closing. I had lost my temper, and as a result, his brother—along with the invisible committee of cosmic judges—had punished me with this blow. That was how it worked, I guess.

* * *

Somehow I got my hands on cash with which to pay employees at least part of what they were owed. I think Mr. Fox gave it to me, since I don't know where else I'd have gotten it, the company accounts now empty and shut down. Part of what made things confusing with Mr. Fox was that the money didn't always flow from me to him; occasionally small bits (relatively speaking) came back to me. This would have been one of the larger bits. If I had to guess I'd say he gave me around twenty or thirty thousand, in cash. I have no clue whether it was left over from what I'd previously given him, gambling winnings, or maybe he was tormenting someone else, too, and got money out of that person to give to me. Who knows. I suppose he wanted to keep playing this game with me, watching me, as if I were a real-life entertainment show, to see if I could get my restaurant reopened, and as insurance that I wouldn't indeed crack and break from him. Giving me that cash was a way to keep me thinking he was on my side.

I have a vague memory of sitting in the restaurant dining room, tables and chairs strewn about, with a list of the bounced checks in front of me. I gave cash to one employee after another, sometimes significantly more than the amounts that had bounced. I don't remember what I told them, but I do remember looks of anger and hurt on some of their faces and how awful I felt. I genuinely don't know how I kept myself together.

My bankers at the local bank I had used decided, rightfully, that my company and I were too high risk and closed my accounts. With whatever cash I had on hand, I opened a whole new set of accounts at Chase.

Among the vendors that were owed money, one had a particularly aggressive collector who threatened me over the phone with criminal referral for having bounced a check, claiming I'd be arrested. This scared me so much that I quickly ran to the new bank for a certified check to overnight mail to them. I realize now his threats weren't legitimate, but that was how scared I was of being afoul of the law. The idea of being arrested was terrifying. Even now, so many years later, when I see that company's delivery trucks, I get a pang of anxiety deep in my gut—remembering that man's threats and the feeling that *I'm bad.*

* * *

Because Pure Food and Wine was so beloved, many customers rallied around, wanting to help. I still didn't know how to explain what had happened, but, thankfully, that seemed beside the point. Getting back open was the mission. One regular, Sabrina, stopped by in person, speaking passionately about wanting to help. She'd read every single one of my blog posts over the years and told me how much they'd resonated for her. She said she *knew* how much the current situation must have been hurting me. While she only knew a fraction of the truth, her offer to help and her belief in me was a much-needed reminder of who I was, at my core, and why she, and people like her, wanted to help.

Sabrina introduced me via email to her friend Nicky—an entrepreneur with experience in the restaurant and food business, and a yoga instructor on the side. She gushed about what a nice guy he was, and she was right. To this day, Nicky remains a good friend.

I first met him at a nearby cafe for tea. He was a slim, fit Indian man, a bit older than me, with a British Indian accent and the calm demeanor one might expect from a yoga instructor. Nicky owned and operated a few high-end tea and bakery cafes in the city; before that, he had worked on the tech side of Wall Street. His background seemed perfect. Somehow, I explained what was going on, in my vague and unfortunately misleading way. Fortunately, Nicky focused more on potential solutions than on what, precisely, had gone wrong. He offered to help structure a deal to raise funds—enough to cover what was owed and get the restaurant reopened.

As always, it pained me that I couldn't fully come clean. I was so full of gratitude that he was willing to help; meanwhile I was cagey and dishonest about the past. But even if I'd wanted to be fully honest, I wouldn't have known how to explain what I didn't understand.

Nicky's calm energy was a counterpoint to my wound-up tension. He also made a point to ensure I was eating well, often showing up to meetings with two green juices and salads. What I was eating was among the least of my concerns—but it was a kindness that stood out.

What he didn't know at the time was that part of my tension stemmed from the anxiety of returning each night to the dark Twenty-Eighth Street apartment where Mr. Fox would be waiting, demanding to know how things went, with whom I'd met, what they'd said. Because Nicky was a man, there was an added— and intensely irritating—element of Mr. Fox being inordinately suspicious. As if I'd preoccupy myself with having some kind of love affair during this traumatic mission to save my business.

Nicky was a perfect gentleman and easy to be around. When we met at his apartment to go over numbers, he often insisted on cooking delicious Indian food, yet there was nothing forward about it. It was simply caretaking, and I ate it up, literally and figuratively. Meanwhile, Mr. Fox would be texting me incessantly, demanding I come home immediately if it was late, and so on. I'd have to keep going to the bathroom so I could quickly text back from there, instead of rudely doing it at the table without explanation. The rage I feel now just thinking about this added layer of torture he put me through while I was trying to fix a disaster he'd created was a rage I felt then, too, but had to suppress.

I wished I could tell someone. I wished I could tell Nicky about the giant brute waiting for me back "home." I didn't think that I could, since (a) Mr. Fox had convinced me that if I did, doom would rain down upon me and (b) I worried I'd get in trouble, and everyone would run for the hills, and then the restaurant would never reopen. My sole mission was to get it reopened, even if I handed over ownership to others—as long as they were good people who would take care of it.

I was relieved to have an ally in getting the restaurant reopen, but I felt bad being dishonest. The story of where all the money had gone remained vague, and Nicky could sense that it pained me. At one point, he gently urged me to come clean. He said something like, "Once you put it all out there completely and face it, you've touched the bottom and then can only go up from there. Things can get better."

We'd been reviewing the company's debt, and Nicky could tell I was holding back. He seemed to know I was deeply ashamed of how bad things had gotten. His reassurance helped me disclose just how much I owed to various people and entities. Not all of it, but at least the amounts I'd officially signed for. It was another one of those moments where I came closer than ever to just cracking open.

I remained vague about what I'd done with all the money, gently implying I'd had no choice, but not in a way that would raise red flags, as if it were an ongoing issue. The genuine pain in my voice must have come through, since Nicky didn't press me further, trusting in my sincerity that it was over and I just wanted to get the business back up and running. I was also not only willing but eager to put someone else in control of the bank accounts.

With a deal structure and financial projections completed, Nicky and I began reaching out to his contacts and mine (or, the ones I had left) to pitch investment while we set up a new LLC and another new set of bank accounts.

* * *

You would think Mr. Fox would have given me a break during this time. You would think he'd have *not* done things to drain me further, push me closer to the edge, while I had to have been particularly fragile. If I'd still been in my previous apartment, maybe I could have broken away from Mr. Fox. But he'd moved me into this one—one he controlled. I can see how in his mind, he had to tighten his grip on me more than ever. On the one hand, I had to be sharp and focused to get my business back, yet on the other, he couldn't let me be *too* focused. If I had been, I might have actually come to my senses. So rather than giving me space, he turned up the control dial.

When I came home from meetings, drained and exhausted, I'd find Mr. Fox sitting on his black recliner as if it was a throne, waiting for me. He'd order me to sit on the couch even before I could take off my coat, or pee, or say hello to Leon. He'd primed me for these nightly grillings by emphasizing the vital importance of my *not* getting mad. As if I'd ruin my chances of reopening the business if I lost my temper or got emotional. By now, he pointed to my earlier tantrum as the reason the restaurant closed. I had to learn to stay on top of my emotions while he angrily questioned me, and demanded I hand over my phone so he could scroll through it. He knew I *hated* this. He delivered lectures, the contents of which I don't recall. No matter what he said or did, I wasn't allowed to get mad.

* * *

In a Gchat conversation on January 30, I told Mr. Fox about a wealthy Indian woman Nicky and I had met with. After hearing me talk about my business history and its potential, she told me I was "sitting on a golden egg."

The parts of these meetings where I got to discuss the business itself, and its mission, were moments where, at least temporarily, I genuinely came alive. It was a relief to be fully sincere, and my passion shined through. People could see how committed I was.

The woman had been encouraging. She'd said that if she had the liquidity, she would invest heavily. But she didn't, not then. So while the meeting had been inspiring, it was ultimately a letdown. When I told Mr. Fox about her "golden egg" comment, he replied, *"I'm so fucking tired of hearing that. Wanna be sitting on golden money."*

For him, of course, it was just money. It's grotesque that he was *tired* of hearing about how valuable my brand was—the same one he'd gutted. Everything about him was grotesque. He was around far more than usual, and I hated being in that apartment with him. If only he could have just left me alone. Everything about him was dark, and because of him, my restaurant was dark.

There were, however, a few bright spots, and one of the brightest came in the form of Miguel and Janet. Miguel had started at the restaurant as a prep cook, working his way up to daytime sous chef. Janet had worked in pastry for probably over a decade. She's photographed in the first cookbook, those photos taken the first year we opened.

At some point, Miguel and Janet became a couple, and had a baby. Miguel had keys to the restaurant, and one day in early February, after it had closed, he and Janet came in to *clean*. It wasn't arranged. I didn't know they were going to do this. They weren't expecting to be paid. It was just what they wanted to do. There aren't words to convey how this felt. I had fucked up *so badly*, and yet, these two angels came in, on their own time, to clean. There's a photograph dated February 11 of me with Miguel and Janet in the dish pit at the restaurant. Nicky must have taken the photo on my phone. Their belief in me was a bright light. I *had* to get the restaurant back open, for them too.

* * *

Most critically, I had to get the past-due rent paid to secure the restaurant lease. By not paying, I'd triggered a notice of violation—meaning that unless I came up with the money, I risked losing the space for good, and that would be it. Gone. Game over. With the staff paid, I was fixated on curing the lease violation.

I wrote endless long emails to anyone who might be interested, and followed up with people who'd replied to an email I'd blasted out to our customer list. I was encouraged by how many responses were flowing in—so many it was almost overwhelming to keep up with. For those who seemed serious, I arranged calls or meetings, especially if they were considering investing sizable amounts.

I ended up with a few investors who were looking to invest between $100,000 and $300,000 each. One of them was Paul, an older man from Boston who'd sold his tech company (for a *lot*, according to my research). He visited NYC, and we met in person. Smart and kind, he seemed eager to invest. He was convinced that our ice cream was so outstanding—far better than all other dairy-free ice creams—that it should be sold nationwide. I liked his forward-looking macro perspective. Paul was a great investor.

Another was a woman named Nadia who worked as a financial advisor, along with her husband, also in finance. They lived in a massive SoHo apartment with their toddler-age sons.

Nadia was warm and friendly. We had long conversations about the future of the business, and about the state of food in the world. We both wanted to make things better. We discussed her taking on a role beyond that of an investor. She could ease out of her financial advisory work, and ease into overseeing our brand expansion. She told me about a female entrepreneur friend who'd recently sold her business for a windfall and might be interested in joining us. This was starting to feel like the solution—and support—I'd wanted all along. The brand could finally grow into what it was meant to be: solid and unstoppable. I visualized future articles about our global brand changing the world, run by three strong women.

This gave me hope. Even if Mr. Fox was a fraud, even if I never got back a penny from him, or his promised happily ever after, this was something sustainable, real, and good. My brand could be safe with Nadia.

I felt comforted—even drawn in—by her strong maternal energy. Even though I was the older one, I wanted her to fold me into her orbit, to feed me sliced apples and gluten-free crackers like one of her toddlers. I wanted to curl up in her arms, in *someone's* arms, and be pulled from this nightmare.

* * *

It was jarring to go from my meetings with Nadia—feeling hopeful and inspired—to the dark apartment where Mr. Fox waited for me. Again, I see now that it could have been possible to break away, with Nadia's support and other investors coming on board. If only I'd known that was what I needed to do, that it was even an option. What most people don't understand—myself included—is how I couldn't see that option.

If I'd packed a bag, hopped in an Uber with Leon, and showed up at Nadia's SoHo doorstep, ready to spill everything about Mr. Fox and the situation I was in, she probably would have taken me in, and helped. Nicky would have helped. A lot of people would have helped. But I wasn't thinking about whether to do this, at least not directly. It was too scary. I had fucked up too much already. Or worse, Mr. Fox and his brother would do… *something*—that I couldn't even imagine.

I know *now*, writing this, that there are others who understand—people who have been through equally, or even worse, mind-bending relationships, and those who've been trapped in cults. Like the handful of Sarah Lawrence College students whose lives were derailed by a Mr. Fox-like figure. To most, it seems unfathomable—how these bright-minded students with promising futures could get ensnared and enslaved by a dominating, grotesque character, when no doors were ever locked. When they could have left at any time. But it happens.

* * *

Getting the rent paid, securing the lease, and reopening—that was my singular focus. The questions swirling about what was real and what wasn't, whether I could confide in anyone—they just continued to swirl while I charged forward. At no point did I consider that these investors might lose their money. The restaurant and brand were valuable; they had been successful before and would be again. There was vast potential for them to grow into a global enterprise. My belief in the brand and its future was unwavering, genuine, and a certainty in my mind. Even if I later had to struggle personally to repay the past debts, I didn't care—I just wanted Pure Food and Wine and One Lucky Duck back.

I was in a constant state of worn-down exhaustion, but as it got increasingly likely I'd secure the lease and *would* reopen, I felt better. All the money Mr. Fox had taken, the debts I'd incurred—they were messy, scary, and shameful. But either I'd work to get it all paid or else Mr. Fox would come through after all: his magic would wipe the slate clean, and I would emerge cleansed and empowered, showering everyone with funds.

Did Mr. Fox see my progress and stay out of my way? No. The current crop of investors stepping up probably impressed Mr. Fox. What a cash cow I was, he probably thought. Of course, he couldn't resist trying to get his meaty paws on some of it. And so, another test emerged.

This was precisely why I so badly wanted to get myself removed from the bank accounts. I'm sure I didn't tell Mr. Fox of this plan. But I'd also likely thought that *surely* now he understood everything was different. I had partners now. I couldn't just withdraw funds if he demanded it. The financial projections Nicky and I had put together included my taking a basic, modest salary. All former debt would be paid from my share of future equity distributions. I'd even signed a separate document indemnifying new investors from any prior debts, disclosed or undisclosed.

But Mr. Fox wanted me to change things up, and suggested I tell the investors that I needed an advance. The idea of this made me want to scream. I pushed back hard. He presented me with another target dollar amount and a deadline. On February 20, he Gchatted me referencing his concern that I wouldn't hit my "target of small money by Tuesday," and I argued that I couldn't take from the investors' money but conceded that I could probably pull "a couple K," as if for my living expenses. This was early enough in the process that it was possible, though I very much didn't want to. I hated going to the bank. I have photos of Leon at the bank with me. I took him along as often as I could, like a support animal. He calmed me. To this day, I still feel nervous walking into a bank, as if I'm doing something wrong.

Throughout all this Mr. Fox was usually sitting back at the apartment like a corpulent king in his recliner throne, playing *Call of Duty*, stopping only to harass me, issue directives, and even demand I get him food. As busy as I was, he made me do *his* errands too.

On February 27, via Gchat, he warned me, "*Displaying any signs at all of your old self is the worst thing you could do. And it's all you been doing the last hour.*"

His reference to my "old self" was part of his ruse that he was rebuilding me—from the weakling I'd apparently been when he found me, into a strong warrior. I wasn't allowed to be weak, yet I had to obey him. The way a soldier must be strong, while also obedient to the general.

* * *

In mid-March it finally happened: I got the back rent paid, and the restaurant lease was reinstated. It was *safe*. I remember texting Jeffrey Chodorow to tell him, and feeling a colossal wave of relief. Even though I'd bought the restaurant from him, he had remained the guarantor on the lease, meaning that if I wasn't able to reopen, he would have been liable. He wasn't putting money back in but had been helping from the sidelines. He wanted me to succeed—partly because I still owed him a lot, but also, I think, because he simply wanted me to succeed.

As much relief as I felt, I could only relax for a minute before focusing on the next steps. There was still so much to do, and pay for, to get the doors open. It wasn't just flipping the light switches on. It required restaffing, restocking ingredients and supplies, repurchasing the necessary food prep equipment, reactivating the reservations systems, and more.

On top of that, I still had a huge balance of unpaid sales tax. I had been interacting with a woman from the tax authorities, assuring her I was working to fix everything. I had made a $10,000 payment toward what was owed and made another $10,000 payment shortly thereafter. The total, meanwhile, was more than a few hundred thousand. The state had leverage—they could always slap one of those orange signs on the door announcing the place had been seized for unpaid taxes. Clearly the odds of the state recovering that money were much higher if I had a functioning business, but still, this quiet older lady scared the shit out of me with her power.

Since Nadia was one of the biggest investors, we planned to put her on the bank account as the signer, and take me off. That way, she would have full control of the accounts. I wouldn't be able to sign checks, send wires, or make withdrawals—which was exactly what I wanted. We arrived at one of the bank's offices, and one of the bank managers ushered us into an interior, windowless office. After we explained what we needed, the woman said, "Okay, great. I'll just need to see your operating agreement showing Nadia is an officer of the company."

Oh shit. We hadn't thought of that. I'd added others on as signers in the past without needing an operating agreement, but in this case, because I was being removed and she would be the only signer, it was different. We left the bank resolving to return once we'd arranged to get an operating agreement drafted and signed. I was eager to get this done. I wanted her in control, not me. If she was in control, then things would be safe.

* * *

Mr. Fox continued to be a mostly terrorizing handicap, but now and then, astonishingly, he actually tried to help. Sometimes I let him. The only legit thing I recall being helpful was his arranging for his friend Carlos, whom I'd met once before, to sand and finish the outdoor tables and the front doors. The restaurant had four doors that open onto the front patio, all made of wood with glass in the top half. They'd been painted black and looked worn down. After Carlos sanded and stained them to a shiny, natural dark-brown wood, they looked far better. It felt like a fresh face.

Mr. Fox also insisted that he could help me negotiate and settle some of the old outstanding vendor debts. I thought this made sense, since Mr. Fox would clearly be a skilled negotiator, while I was terrible at it.

March 29, Gchat

Mr. Fox: Where is the list of all current debts and amounts. Including vendor debts. Please stop crying. I need itemized vendor debts list. I think I was very clear. Calm down. Please. You are overwhelmed. You don't need to be. I am going to help you. I just need as much info for each item that needs to be completed. That's all I am saying. PLEASE STOP CRYING PLEASE. PLEASE. Try and relax. No one is preventing you from doing anything. Please please please please stop crying.

I must have broken down and gone into my bedroom, shutting the door. It seems he could hear me crying. My entire life I had never been an audible crier, until Mr. Fox came around. Even though we were getting closer and closer to reopening, I was still overwhelmed.

* *

Finally, in early April, the doors opened for our first dinner service. You would think I'd have vivid memories of those first customers walking in—and how it felt, what day of the week it was, the weather, the menu, how busy it was, who showed up, etc. But I don't. All I can recall is one moment, toward the end of the night, sitting at the candlelit bar. I don't remember who was with me, or who was bartending. What I remember is the pastry chef sending out a mint sundae. It was a thing of beauty, as always, but in that moment it felt sacred—as if surrounded by a halo. Our sundaes were served in martini glasses, which gave them an elegance not normally associated with ice cream sundaes.

I ate it slowly, trying to let it sink in just how momentous it was that Pure Food and Wine was *back,* reopened, alive. One Lucky Duck around the corner was back too. Whatever else was going on, we were back. And whatever extra ingredient had always been in our food—that magical *something* that made it extra vibrant, full of good energy—was still there. We still had it.

* * *

This should have been such a happy time for me. The only one around who knew the pressure I was under from Mr. Fox was Nazim. Since we were a bit short-staffed, Nazim had begun bartending for us some of the time, while also helping me by walking Leon or doing errands for the business. He was a reassuring presence. Even though he didn't know the extent of it, at least he was someone who *knew*, and was an ally.

From a bookkeeping perspective, I was winging it. I kept spreadsheets of everything that came in and went out, but there was no new system in place. This would all need to be handled. I'm a Virgo. Organization soothes me; a lack of organization stresses me out. With newly incoming funds, I made another payment of $10,000 to New York state toward the past-due sales tax. These payments were small compared to the total outstanding, but it was something to show effort, goodwill, and my intent to get it all repaid.

I also made a payment to Dylan, *finally!* The Dylan loan that I had been particularly stressed over, the one Mr. Fox of course never paid. I had disclosed this loan to the new investors as the one most important to repay. Any debt payments would still be credited to me on the books, but I'd gotten permission to make this payment. I wired Dylan $10,000, only ten percent of the total, but still, it was *something*.

Paying Dylan felt good, like progress. I may have been exhausted to the core, but at the restaurant, I could feel somewhat happy, like it would all be okay. Nazim usually brought Leon over to the restaurant in the afternoons so I could run outside and spend time with him. These visits were the best parts of my days.

Mr. Fox probably started to sense his control over me slipping. With the restaurant reopened, I was spending all my time there while he sat back in the dark apartment, playing video games. I didn't know what was coming next—whether this utopia he'd promised was still on the horizon. But either way, I was okay. Because the restaurant was okay.

* * *

I was in the restaurant office one night, April 11, at around 8:30 p.m., when I got a Gchat from Mr. Fox asking me to bring home a bottle of wine. I said okay, but I wasn't sure what for, since I rarely, if ever, saw him drink wine. Then I realized it must have been for me. Maybe he had good news? But if that were the case, he'd have told me to bring something celebratory, like prosecco.

Why did he want me to bring back wine? Part of me worried he wanted me to drink it because he wanted me more relaxed, perhaps for some kind of talk, and this worried me.

Turns out, it wasn't for a talk.

CHAPTER SIXTY-ONE

APRIL 2015

NEW YORK CITY

As I'd suspected, the wine was for me, not him.

My recollections from that night are fuzzy. I can, however, retrieve a handful of quick flashes of time, which are enough. As if seeing a few fraction-of-a-second clips from a movie scene and instinctively knowing what happens in the spaces between.

I remember that when I got back to the apartment, it was dark. Not pitch black, but intentionally, eerily dark, like scenes in TV dramas where an office or kitchen or otherwise normally light place is inexplicably dark, and you're wondering, *Why the fuck is it so dark? Someone turn the lights up!*

I remember him explaining that he *had* to do something that he *didn't want* to do. But he *had* to. For *me.* It was part of *the process*, something to do with *healing me*, or fixing my "issues"—whatever those were. He said he would have to do things to me, and I would have to do exactly what he said. And that I needed to be prepared—he might push me around or yell at me. He made it clear I just had to go with it and do whatever he told me to do. He repeated that he didn't *want* to do this, but it was *necessary.* For some reason. But he wouldn't hit me or really hurt me, or so he said, I think. I don't remember his exact words. I just know that, as usual, I wasn't allowed to get mad. He told me I couldn't push back, refuse, or resist whatever he was going to do to me.

While he outlined his plans to me in the dark living room, I drank some of the wine he'd had me bring home. I don't remember whether we even had any wine glasses in that shitty apartment, but for sure I'd have wanted to drink whatever alcohol I could before whatever it was he was going to do. Then he asked me if I had a pair of black tights. "You want me to wear tights?" I asked.

"No," he said.

He wanted to blindfold me. Opaque tights seemed like the best way, I guess. Yes, I had some tights.

I'm sure I stalled. Drank more wine. Took my time looking for said tights in my bedroom. Debated leaping out the window. I looked at Leon lying there on my bed, watching me, and wondered if he could in any way comprehend what was going on, and wished he didn't have to be around this—all this darkness. Literally and metaphorically.

Finally, I got the tights. Mr. Fox told me to go into his room. "Wait. I have to pee," I said.

"Fine. Go pee. Hurry up."

I peed. Wanted to puke. Probably I avoided looking in the mirror while washing my hands. It wasn't fear I was feeling as much as a sickening sort of dread. I mean, he said he wasn't going to *hurt* me, so...

* * *

Impatient with my attempts to stall, Mr. Fox dispensed with his softer, more explanatory tone, then shifted to a harsh and demanding one, and finally corralled me into his room. He shut the door, took the tights from my hand, and, turning me away from him, tied them around my head, very tightly. Everything was now extra dark.

I wasn't used to being in his room. The air felt cold and stale, infused with the scent of dirty socks, even with the AC blasting. I can't recall his specific words, but I do recall being pushed around and told to take my clothes off.

Probably my breathing was shallow, if I was breathing at all. I was in no rush to be naked and exposed, and he yelled at me to hurry up. Each item of clothing removed was a layer of protection gone.

Finally, I stood there—naked, legs pinned together, arms crossed tightly over my chest, holding my breath, like a stiff slab in a cold meat locker. Since I couldn't see him coming, I was caught off guard when he shoved me back on the bed. He told me to get on my hands and knees, facing the wall. I generally recall a lot of pushing and shoving. His sheets were black, I knew, despite being blindfolded. They were an extra-thick blend, meant to be fancy, but they were not, and likely hadn't been washed in a long time. I didn't like the feel of them. A judgmental thought like *These can't be 100 percent cotton* might have crossed my mind. Probably I also hated them because they were his, and I tended to hate everything about him, and around him, and that smelled like him.

"Get down on your forearms," he demanded. I remember he was impatient and not pleased with the way I must have been holding my body, probably in more of a crouch than what he wanted. What he wanted was for me to push my ass out toward him, and I was reluctant. So he put his fat, meaty hand between my shoulder blades and roughly pushed down. "Arch your fucking back," he ordered, I think. Unfortunately, it's the actions and physicality I remember vividly, while his precise words are a haze. But I can recall the impatience in his voice, and how that felt degrading, on top of the indignity of being reprimanded when I didn't immediately or precisely follow his matter-of-factly delivered instructions.

I also remember feeling wildly uncomfortable at having my parts all exposed and up in the air. I was like a doll with stubbornly rigid limbs that he was shoving into position for the staging of his own dark, fucked-up porn film.

I don't remember exactly what he did next, while I was in that position. I think he just looked, and probably slapped my ass, but I don't know for sure. When I think about it now, I feel a mortified terror that maybe he silently took photos with his iPhone. How would I have known?

He pushed me over on my side, then ordered me to get off the bed. Standing unsteadily beside the bed, I was told to get on my knees. As soon as I did, he grabbed my hair and shoved himself inside my mouth. Perhaps the prior viewing of my exposed parts was what he needed to prepare himself for this. I know for sure that by now I was crying and that there was a moment of wondering what kind of sick fuck wants to mouth-fuck a woman while she's crying, and thinking that, sadly, probably a lot of sick fucks would get off on that.

While I was glad for the blindfold, because it spared me from having to look at him, wearing it made other sensations more pronounced. The particular rotten smell of his exposed groin, the clammy feel of his skin. *Unpleasant* would be an understatement. Clearly, I wasn't doing a very good job in this case, and he was frustrated, berating me, as if I should really be putting my *all* into it. Never mind that I was crying, and that he was gripping my hair hard while forcefully stabbing himself into the back of my throat, making me gag and choke.

I'm pretty sure he said words expressing his disgust at my uselessness in that position and I was ordered to get back on the bed. I quickly backed up into the corner against the pillows and the wall, my knees up, my feet shielding the parts that I knew he'd be coming for. I used the back of my hand to wipe the mix of tears, snot, and spit from my face. Backing into the corner was futile. He easily grabbed my ankles and pulled me forward, then overcame my resistance, pried my limbs apart, and shoved his way inside me, roughly and painfully—since at that moment I was whatever is the polar opposite of dripping with desire. It turns out this particular act hurts *a lot* when you're dry as a stale baguette.

* * *

I don't remember how long it all lasted. I do remember right afterward, once he stopped and it was over, before I could get up, thinking something like, *Huh, I guess this feeling I have right now is... I suppose... I think now I kind of, sort of have an idea, a sense... or just an icky flavor... of what one might feel like after being... raped.*

It felt confusing because this was a man I was legally married to, after all. But it was the furthest thing from a normal marriage. I'd stopped having sex with him long before this. What had just happened? I could have screamed or resisted more, but I wasn't allowed to. I wasn't physically injured, beyond being very sore down there. A year or so later, I'd argue with my attorney Sheila about whether this would be rightfully called rape. I adamantly did *not* want to use that word. She did. Is it stealing if someone says, *I'm going to steal this from you now,* and you just stand there and let them? I guess maybe it is, if you don't have a choice. Did I have a choice? Surely I did, but it didn't feel that way.

At least he'd said it was just that one time. He wouldn't do it again. *Never again.*

Finally he confirmed I could take the blindfold off and go. I couldn't wait to get the fuck out of there and, in my haste, left my bra behind.

I remember this detail because we had a Gchat argument about it later. Early the next morning I'd been rushing to get ready to go back to the restaurant and needed that bra. I'd been afraid to wake him up because… *don't wake a sleeping giant.* I'd knocked softly at first, then gradually a little louder until I heard his groggy angry roar, "WHAT?"

I opened the flimsy door, quickly scanned the dim room, and, mumbling my explanation, spotted my bra on the floor, halfway under the bed. Despite the AC blasting, Mr. Fox was lying under only a sheet, like a giant manatee.

"YOU'RE WAKING ME UP FOR THAT?" he bellowed. I snatched my bra and bolted, closing the door behind me.

Later that day, in a Gchat, he warned me, *"Don't wake me up unless it's an emergency. You run the risk of crashing my system so to speak, when you do that."*

I reminded him why my bra was there in the first place, adding that it was fucked up that, after all he did, now *he* was mad at *me*. I ended with, *"Right. Sicko."*

* * *

Less than a week later, I sent Mr. Fox a photo of new donuts we'd made at the restaurant. He wrote back, *"Those donuts look ridiculous. Can I haz one?"*

I replied, *"You can have a donut if I can have security over my physical self and all my parts to be left alone."*

Were our raw vegan donuts so good they could keep me safe? If only.

I know now that forced sex is common in controlling, manipulative situations. In a 2020 *Vanity Fair* online interview, India Oxenberg—who spent seven years under the influence of NXVIM cult leader Keith Raniere—described how she'd been made to believe "that the oral sex sessions Raniere subjected her to were not for his gratification, but a way for her to work through the intimacy issues she was told she had."

Mr. Fox used a similar rationale. I'd stopped wanting to have sex with him because I'd grown fiercely unattracted to him. Not to mention I was usually furious at him, and in a constant state of exhausted panic, while also managing his demands and bullshit interrogations. Of course I didn't want to have sex with him. So eventually, he just forced me. And he framed it as if it was somehow necessary, even the roughness of it, for my own good. *For my own good.* As if this was some chore for him, and part of some healing or exorcising of my inner demons, because something was *wrong with me.* I needed to be repaired, according to him.

Looking back, it was as if he was feeding off the energy of my fear.

I should have known to expect that his telling me he'd never do something again meant that of course he was going to do it again. And again. While he was less physically forceful in the future, because I got used to this occasional drill, the dread I felt only grew worse. As if my shock and anger gradually decayed into something less sharp but increasingly putrid.

Mr. Fox would say anything in any moment and could never be held to account for any of it because it didn't matter to him. He was a broken promise personified.

CHAPTER SIXTY-TWO

APRIL 2015
NEW YORK CITY

The restaurant having *just* reopened was a time I could have felt some happiness and relief, maybe even hints of joy. I could have felt optimistic, at least. But that wouldn't have worked for Mr. Fox. He needed me off-center as much as possible, which was probably why he did what he did. Also, of course—*surprise, surprise*—he wanted more money.

* * *

I don't remember what he said to me in person, but our Gchats make it clear he'd given me a new story—a new amount, a new deadline, a new goalpost that would eventually shift. Yet, according to him, it was the *last time*.

He told me I had to get him $60,000 by July. Then, he changed that timing (of course) and claimed some of it was needed immediately. I'm not sure how I managed to pull $15,000 out of the business, but it appears that I did and gave it to Mr. Fox. I wanted to get rid of him. I spent most of my waking hours at the restaurant, but still he continued to badger me via Gchat, and in person when I got back to the apartment. He said that if I gave him the money, he'd leave for at least a month. "*I could be gone by tonight and stay gone until July,*" he wrote. I badly wanted him out of the apartment and out of my hair.

I was still very afraid. I'd gotten the doors open, but the restaurant felt like it was being held together with Band-Aids. I had huge outstanding debts and now new investors on the line. Withdrawing small amounts of money to pay myself for living expenses would have been normal, since I otherwise wasn't taking a salary. But $15,000 at once wasn't normal.

This was precisely why I'd wanted to be removed from the bank accounts. As long as Mr. Fox knew I had access to funds, he'd continue to pressure me. Nadia and I were still waiting to get an operating agreement drafted so we could put her on the accounts and take me off. In the meantime, we'd agreed I would send her a detailed bank ledger every day. I must have told her I needed the money to pay my past-due personal rent, or made some kind of excuse.

It feels grotesque thinking about this. I'd have rather made another $10,000 payment to Dylan, or a third payment toward the back sales tax due. Or *anything*, really.

I was resentful toward Mr. Fox, not surprisingly, for his having pushed me to give him money, and I was frustrated at myself for having done it.

* * *

Along with Nadia and Paul, I'd been able to bring in a third large investor, and then a fourth. One of them was a man named Ben. He had reached out to me directly, and one day, he sent his driver to pick me up in Manhattan and drive me out to his home in rural New Jersey—a huge property with a massive garden and many cats.

Mr. Fox was immediately skeptical, insisting that Ben was *bad news* and that I shouldn't take his investment. I didn't understand how Mr. Fox could know this. Based on what? His LinkedIn profile? I took a sizable investment from Ben anyway. Mr. Fox disapproved.

```
Mr. Fox: I'm telling you, cut him out. Do not sell him any
more shares. If you would listen to me and stop lashing out, I
can buy him and Nadia and Paul out in August. Maybe him sooner
```

though. I do not trust him. Ultimately the goal is to hand you back complete control of your business and brand. Just have to go through some hoops first.

Unrelated to the above, I reminded Mr. Fox that in order to get set up on a payment plan for the past-due sales taxes with New York State, I had to submit the prior year's business bank statements. This scared me. Those statements would show all the huge transfers to my personal account. Taking money from one's own business isn't *in itself* illegal, but doing that while *not* paying sales tax seemed like perhaps it was. Not to mention all the loans. I'd taken in those funds, but instead of using them for the business, I'd wired most of it to my personal account, then to Mr. Fox. How would I explain it? That *every time* I'd sent the money to Mr. Fox, it was only because he'd convinced me it was the *last time*—that this one last transfer would lead to the conclusion of my awful nightmare. I started to realize this must be illegal, which scared the crap out of me, making me feel more trapped. As always, I felt rage at Mr. Fox, and sometimes I expressed it.

Mr. Fox: Again, if you would just stay calm and stick to the plan and not freak out and go rogue then I could help with all that. I have a tax lawyer that can handle all of this. You won't need to give them anything. Lashing out against me is not the move. I am your ally. As I have always been.

Me: Then give me the tax lawyer's name and info now.

Of course he didn't. He always claimed to have lawyers and business associates, but by then I knew that—like his assistant Will Richards—they were likely fictional.

I was *not* someone who'd ever run afoul of the law. The stress I'd felt years earlier, during the 2008 downturn—when I'd stopped paying myself to make ends meet at the restaurant, when I'd had to take on loans to get by—was nothing compared to what I felt now. That stress had been reasonable, understandable, and honorable. My GM Adam and I had worked through it and come out the other side. He always kept meticulous records. We had once been subjected to a sales tax audit, and Adam had handled the whole thing—I'd only dipped in and out of one meeting. Later, we'd discussed how funny it was that the auditors seemed astonished at how good our records were and that nothing was amiss. That's how I had run the business (with Adam's help), and that's the kind of person I *really* was.

Now, I appeared to be someone else. I hated Mr. Fox for this.

Mr. Fox and his relentless badgering for money. Ignoring him, stalling, getting upset—none of it ever helped.

He Gchatted me again:

```
Mr. Fox: Will you do what I asked earlier? Go get 15K now and
come back so we can talk about things. I can help you but not
if you lash out like you did last night and this morning. I can
only help you if we are on the same team. Otherwise all I can
do is try and protect you from what will come. But to help you
means help you avoid it from coming at all. Please understand
I love you and am on your side no matter what. I really really
do love you with all my heart. Even during the hardest days and
the most difficult times. Even when you get mad and even when
you make a mistake. I hope the same is true for you. I love you
and am proud of you. I just want the HEA. Not fall apart over
bullshit. XOXO.
```

Those words: *All I can do is try and protect you from what will come.*

I had no idea what he meant by "what will come," and it only terrified me more. The pressure was more and more unbearable. Having realized I'd likely done things *not* legal, I felt panicked.

```
Me: Fuck you. I hate you. Leave me to suffer, fucking bullshit
rape me, and now let me get fucked over. Thanks you fat rancid
fuck.
```

Mr. Fox: Stop talking like that. I would never leave you to get fucked. But I can't help you if all you do is go nuts on me when I try and talk to you about anything at all. STOP TALKING TO ME LIKE THIS. THIS IS THE OLD YOU. I AM ON YOUR FUCKING SIDE. PLEASE SEE THAT. LASHING OUT IS NOT GOING TO LEAD TO ANYTHING GOOD. I LOVE YOU. I NEED TO GET ON THE PHONE NOW. DOESN'T MEAN I AM FUCKING YOU OVER. MEANS I AM GETTING ON THE PHONE. XOXOXOXOXOXOX

Me: Means you should die. I have to get ready for my meeting. FUCK YOU. FOREVER.

Mr. Fox: You wishing my death might kill me. I hope you know that.

Me: Yup.

Mr. Fox: I am being 100% serious.

Me: Leave me the fuck alone. I don't have a home, you took everything.

Mr. Fox: Omg.

Me: When I get asked where that 2 million went WHAT am I going to say?

Mr. Fox: YOU DON'T NEED TO SAY ANYTHING.

I was so ensnared in Mr. Fox's web that now I felt only more dependent on him, afraid he would leave me holding the bag, so to speak. He was the one terrorizing me, who'd gotten me into this mess, and yet I was terrified of *him* abandoning *me*. If he abandoned me, I'd be completely alone to face this shameful mess I didn't even understand. I didn't know then that his abandoning me would have been a much better option—that the mess would only get so much worse.

Later this same day, Mr. Fox continued to badger me over Gchat about the $15,000.

Mr. Fox: Please make every effort to make the bank and be home later so we can talk this out. Please don't just say fuck off. Please. I understand you are under a lot of pressure and I want to help you out any way I can but I still need to make sure things go to plan.

Me: I am not going to the bank. Other than to make a deposit.

Mr. Fox: I will say this one last time and then I will not say it again ever. You need to put up a partial of the remaining 60K now. Even if it's only 10K. That's fine. The rest can be kicked down to July. And then there are no more money discussions. You will have my support and love no matter what. I will always have your back. But try and remember our talk in Belgium and what I said that night. How certain things must happen. How we must stay as a unit. That getting angry on occasion is okay, but cutting and running or working against me is not. I am here if you need me for anything. I love you. I do.

Me: No. You lied.

Mr. Fox: We almost home. Soon. A few short months and stick to plan and HEA.

* * *

Mr. Fox had a much younger half sister named McKaila. I'd met her once, briefly, and really liked her. Mr. Fox always spoke highly of her in a way that I believe was genuine. He'd probably been a father figure to her, since I don't think her father was in the picture. She was in her early twenties, bright and pretty. I'd met his mother too. I don't know what they thought of him. My guess is that they were probably also unclear as to what exactly he did with his time and life. Maybe they were used to his coming and going and being alternately flush with cash or totally broke.

Once, he brought his mom to Foxwoods and they won $10,000 at the slot machines. I don't know if he was feeding hundreds into the machines and eventually won, or what. I saw her briefly when he brought her up to the hotel room after. She looked bewildered, as if she wasn't sure if what had happened had *really just happened*. Mr. Fox gave me a knowing look, as if to say, *I made that happen for her.*

These things never surprised me. Mr. Fox was so cavalier about money, like it didn't matter. Which was precisely what he always said. *The money doesn't matter. It isn't real anyway.* Yet he was awfully persistent when he was pressing me for it. As he continued to do over the $15,000 he claimed I *had* to get him by July. Because of my rage, he'd backed off by a third and was now only pressing me to give him $10,000.

On April 21, I woke up to a message from Mr. Fox:

Mr. Fox: My sister is on her way here. I am on a very tight timeline. She rescheduled a job interview to pick me up. Please go to the bank first thing and get the 5K cash and 5K check. You can go at 8am and come right back here. That way we can leave here and she can get to her interview. Please be strong and stick to plan. The remainder of the money by July, you just stay strong and loyal. I love you. I will need to purposely not communicate with you often but will be available in case of emergency. After first month I'm gone I can help out much more. I love you and have done all for you and HEA. Things are gonna be great if we stay the course and are on plan. XOXO.

I read this just after waking up. This pressure to go to the bank and take out cash was too much. I couldn't just go withdraw cash and then say *what* to Nadia and the investors? *Oh, I just needed some spare change?* Whether it was $5,000 or

$10,000 or *any* amount, it was insane. I couldn't do that. Obviously, I didn't want to do that. I'd already severely pushed the envelope by taking that last $15,000.

Now Mr. Fox's sister being on her way, having postponed a job interview, only added pressure. It shouldn't have mattered, but if I didn't give him what he wanted, she'd have driven all that way for nothing. It wasn't logical, but it made it harder to refuse.

An intense misery crept through my veins. As I lay there, looking at the ceiling, it took over my entire being. The vice grip of Mr. Fox on my life had only gotten tighter and tighter. I couldn't take it. I needed a way out, but I didn't see one. At least the restaurant would be safe now with the investors. If there'd been a button on the wall that could have ended my life, I would have punched it.

I felt like I was going to explode into a fireball of wretched agony. Instead, I started wailing. Not my usual sniffles and tears, but actual loud, primal wailing, like a dairy cow whose calf had just been torn away from her.

It hadn't occurred to me that Mr. Fox's sister McKaila was *already in* our apartment in that very moment, in the living room. I wasn't thinking about anything but wanting *out,* and my wailing only grew louder while I rolled around in the bed, gripping bunches of sheets in my fist. I don't even remember if Leon was there. I wasn't thinking about who could or couldn't hear me.

Suddenly the flimsy door to my room burst open. Mr. Fox stood there—hair jutting out every which way, in his baggy, wrinkled tent of a T-shirt. Clearly, I'd woken him.

"What the fuck are you doing?" he whisper-yelled. "Sarm, what the fuck is wrong with you? Stop it!"

I must have looked like a crazy person—since that was how I felt. He was the source of my anguish, so his bursting in only injected more rage into my rage crying.

"I hate you! I hate you! You fucking monster!" I spat into my pillow.

"Sarm, you gotta calm down."

He moved toward me and I jolted up, "Get away from me!" I growled. "You fucking monster, don't you dare come near me!"

And then, through the open door, I saw movement behind him. It was McKaila, sitting up. She must have arrived late, after I'd gone to bed, and been sleeping on the couch. I remember the stunned look on her face—her wide, horrified brown eyes. Part of me was mortified at being seen this way, but maybe another part of me thought, *Oh good, a witness. Finally!*

"You fucking monster! You've ruined me! I'm not giving you more money! You fat, disgusting monster!" I screamed, still through tears.

Mr. Fox looked like he wanted to get mad but knew he was dealing with a live wire. What could he do in front of his sister? Her presence made it safer for me to keep letting it all out.

"You fucking monster! I hate you! I've given you two million fucking dollars. Two million dollars you've taken from me! That's not enough? You still want more? I fucking hate you!"

I needed someone else to know.

"You've ruined me! You fat fucking monster!" By this time, I'd crawled forward in the bed, and Mr. Fox was backing up into the living room.

"You disgusting *fat fuck*! You take my money, you yell at me, you fucking mouth-rape me, and you fucking smell! You shove your disgusting fucking dirty cock in my mouth! You're a fucking monster!"

McKaila's eyes widened even more. As miserable as I was, there was some satisfaction in calling him out on what he'd been doing to me, in front of his own sister.

"Sarm, stop that!"

Now Mr. Fox was getting mad.

I don't remember what happened next. Maybe it was Leon that got me to calm down. He usually did. My rage would cause him to physically shake, and that would bring me down from the ledge. I couldn't bear to see him afraid like that, and to be the cause of it. Leon was always the one that got me to back off from the ledge.

CHAPTER SIXTY-THREE

LATE APRIL 2015
NEW YORK CITY

I genuinely don't remember what happened after my outburst in front of Mr. Fox and his sister. I remember parts of it, because it was so unlike me to have freaked out that way. But whatever happened next isn't even fuzzy; it's just blank. Reading the digital history is the only way I can piece together what happened.

I did *not* get up and race to the bank to take out $5,000 for him like he wanted. But based on the lengthy written lectures I received from Mr. Fox the following morning, it seems I *did* write him the check, or two checks. Clearly, that wasn't good enough for him.

Around 9:00 a.m. on April 22, he wrote on Gchat:

Mr. Fox: You gave into emotion yesterday and lost total control and it was not good and did not go over well at all. Even though I told you over and over for months that things will be done specifically to try and get you to lose control. To just ignore them. You didn't. You remember what happened the last time you lost control like that and threw carrots at me and made threats and played tough guy? The restaurant was closed down about 10 days later. I spoke on your behalf all night last night. I am on your side and have your back but you're making things very difficult. And you didn't get the ten. Got two checks that must be deposited and won't clear for 7 days? Like. WTF. Just a mess. If you are off medication, you are shooting yourself in both feet. The W and the L are like bulletproof armor for you. To not take them you are doing major damage to yourself.

"The W and the L" referred to the two medications I was on. I was taking a low dose of Wellbutrin, a common antidepressant, and a low dose of lithium, which is normally prescribed for bipolar disorder, something with which I'd never been diagnosed. Googling lithium now, I find this: "It helps you to have more control over your emotions and helps you cope better with the problems of living."

No wonder he wanted me on lithium. He could blame my outbursts on a supposed condition, rather than on his deliberate and abhorrent destruction of my psyche.

Mr. Fox: In better news, the buyout was approved pending getting the last 50K from you on or before the first week in July. After the buyout you will have total control of your company. Soon after that this is over and yay. Happy time if you stay the course. I do love you. King Cole love you. After it's over we should buy a boat and name it the King Cole. We could get remarried on it. And literally sail off into the sunset.

Me: You've tortured me for years.

Mr. Fox: I am in limbo until I get that 10K from you. My sister hasn't even deposited the fucking check yet. You should go get the 5K now at least. I can have Nazim bring it to me. Then there will just be the second check next Friday. There is no give on this. The ten must be. The fifty must be. After the other day there can be no more mistakes. No more outbursts. No more threats. Or there will be no more anything.

He made it seem like I had no choice, as usual. I was blamed for *failing*. Any pushback or anger was considered failure and would lead to worse consequences. I didn't know what he meant by *Or there will be no more anything*, and I didn't want to know. The checks I had given him were either post-dated or would take time to clear. But he wanted money immediately. Pushing me to go withdraw $5,000 in cash was just more torture, while he fed me the same tired narrative: if I just did this last part, *it would finally be over*.

And if I didn't do it? Then all the pain I'd been through would be for nothing, and worse, there would be *no more anything*. His words from days earlier—that he'd not be able to protect me from "what would come"—echoed in my mind.

What could I do?

* * *

He exhausted me. There are more Gchats—they go on for pages—wherein he pushes me to give him $10,000 immediately and agree to another $50,000. We go back and forth, while I push back writing things like, *Yeah NO on the 10K. You fat fuck*, and, *Have a great day being the worst person ever*. Lashing out with insults was my way of grasping onto any power I had left.

Even a significantly edited-down version of what he wrote to me is tedious to read, yet I'm erring on the side of including a tedious amount of it—even when he's repetitive—if only to convey to you just how tiresome it was to be the recipient of this endless torment.

Mr. Fox continued to frame himself as my protector, warning me of the consequences if I didn't do as he instructed.

```
Mr. Fox: You will lose the resti a second time. And you will not
get it back. And we will lose. And there will be no HEA. That is
a fact. Second thing—and really pound this into your head—I have
done and will continue to do all that I can to try and protect
you. You make it increasingly difficult. Like I said. When you
had that huge outburst and made threats, the resti was shut
down 10 days later. When you did what was required and stayed
on point and worked in unison the place was saved and reopened.
```

> These are things you should remember. After the other day we are both on thin ice. I will continue to do all that I can do to protect you. Please don't make it harder and harder. I am on your side. I am your biggest ally. I love you. Please try and remind yourself of this. Of the King Cole. That is the me that loves you and will fight and scratch and claw and do anything for you. Let any bad or negative roll off your back. Stay loyal and stay strong. Things that annoy you or upset you are designed to do so. DO NOT LET THEM. I love you. I hope you read all that. It is arguably the most important things I have ever said to you. / Read that over and over and over and over. I love you. XOXO.

The idea of losing the business *again* was an outcome I feared more than my own death.

And still, he bombarded me with more Gchats, repeating much of what he'd already said, before finally ending for the day with one last statement:

> Mr. Fox: I love you Sarma. I love you with all that I am. I love you unconditionally until the end of time. I know you know these things. Deep down I know you know it. XO Remember those two things I said earlier. XO

At the time, I didn't recognize what he was doing, but now I can see that phrases like *I know you know* and *Deep down I know you know it* were deliberate—like he was programming my mind.

Of course, he *still* wasn't done. The next morning, I woke up to a long email he'd sent at 4:51 a.m. I apologize in advance for including nearly every word of it, but editing it down would diminish its weight. (When he refers to "carrot throwing," it's shorthand for me losing my temper—because once, in a rare moment of anger, I threw carrots at him.)

April 23, 2015

From: Mr. Fox

To: Me

Subject: Read all this. Every word. Over and over if necessary.

If you take Ben's funds tomorrow (which he would send) you send the fifty (assuming I can figure out where I can get a wire) and by next Friday everyone is bought out. Otherwise if you take his money it will be bad. It's only good to take now and send fifty because after the carrot throwing the other day I'm not sure how things will go down. Other day could have undone everything. Idk. I'm not going to lie to you. Anyway. You could take Ben's money today, send the fifty tomorrow and then everything would be done and cool. If you don't intend to send the fifty from it, then don't take the money. My advice is take his money and send the 50 now. That way the buyout can happen next week and pretty much null everything else that could be negative. If you wait I think you will maybe be removed. After the other day, what you did—it's just now I don't have an argument to defend you. It's like last time when you had that deep carrot tossing outburst and refused to listen and made threats. They shut down the resti shortly after that. Difference now is there will be no second chance for either of us if it happens again. I need you to really understand that you might have totally fucked us. Blame it on whatever excuse you choose. PMS. Stress. I'm a fat asshole, etc. etc. Fact is that you came undone. Even with all your yelling and hitting me, that could have been overlooked. Was what you said to my sister. That might have been a coffin nail. Which is what the other side wanted and you played right into it by letting your emotions control you (something I've constantly warned you about). You never should have said that. Threatened and struck against me. Everyone turned on you after that. I'm the only one still on your side.

As ominous as that sounded understand that I'm not saying that it's done because it's not. I'm saying that after what you did we are standing out on a frozen pond. And now you just threw a bunch of hand grenades across the ice blowing holes in it and making cracks. Can we still get across the pond? Yes we can, but it will be very difficult to do so. You can say what you want. I warned you weeks ago and months before that about not taking your medication properly. You didn't listen. I warned you repeatedly about not threatening or striking against me. You didn't listen. I warned you about just forcing yourself to not allowing negative bullshit to affect you. To know its not real and the goal was to set you off, to just let it roll off and not let it bother you. You didn't listen. You did everything I warned you not to do. What did you think would happen? So now here we are. Out on the ice together and the pond is breaking apart and we have to get across safely. We can but it will be tough. You are worried about doing something too early or having to pay Dylan. Won't be anything left in a week or so if we don't get across the pond. You're worried about the wrong things. Again not listening. Thinking any of this is real or means anything. Just. Not. Listening. Just yelling and threatening and name calling and excuse making. But never listening. You did listen once. You did exactly what you were told and got cash when needed from the bank without bullshit pushback. You went to meetings as expected. Gave updates when asked for them. You did everything and I was so proud of you. You courted investors and even put up with me without pushback. And what happened when you did all that without the bullshit? THE FUCKING PLACE REOPENED. Everything went smooth. Then you started pushing back. Not listening.

Threatening. Not taking pills. Etc. etc. And what happened? JC subtly threatening to not do a debt deal. Possible indictment. No more Nadia money. Etc. etc. Pay attention to that and WAKE UP. You throw carrots = you lose. You stay cool and follow procedure = you get everything. If you lose I lose too. But you'd lose everything. I'd just lose you. I negotiated a deal to cut 75 off the list. That deal is in danger. I negotiated a buyout. That deal is in danger. I negotiated an expansion. That deal is in danger. Your future is in danger. My future is in danger. The resti and Miguel and all those jobs are in danger. All because you decided to throw carrots again. I warned you. You are not a tough guy. You hold zero cards. I warned you that night in Belgium. I said if you get mad and give in to emotion and you strike at me, all you are doing is striking at yourself but ten times worse. I said each foot you think you're digging my grave you're in reality digging yourself four feet deeper. And you just didn't listen. You did listen for a while and everything was going fine. But then. Out of the blue. Stopped the meds. Took your force field off and started throwing carrots. Telling me you won't go to the bank. You won't do this. You won't do that. Won't update me. Won't talk about plans. Won't do anything but what you thought was the right move. Threatening me and worrying about Nadia and Ben and useless bullshit. And everything just slid down and down.

So now it's up to you. You calling in scrips and stuff shows me that hopefully you've decided to stop shooting holes in what's left of our rowboat. That you've decided to stop throwing grenades into the frozen pond we are trying to walk across. Because if so then we can still (hopefully) do this. But if not and you continue to do your own thing and keep throwing carrots and not listening etc then you and myself will surely fail. And that resti and everything associated with it will be chalked up as a loss.

I do love you. I hope you come around, but I can't force you to. Maybe you want to quit. Maybe you want to fail. I don't know. Maybe part of you is afraid of this. Afraid of what the responsibility that will come with being a leader and being successful will mean. Maybe you just can't take the pressure of it all. And if so then you should quit. Because there aren't any seats at the table for cowards that make excuses about how it's everyone else's fault and are afraid of failure of challenge or success. I'm not calling you a coward. I'm asking you if you are one, and if the answer is yes, then you should quit. Because the life of a champion will not be given to a coward.

I want you to be the woman I know you are inside. Powerful. Smart. Strong. Unbreakable. Unstoppable. A leader. A winner. But just because I want it and I see it in you doesn't mean you want it or see it in you.

I hope you really heard me in this email. Maybe you will just make some excuses and tell me to fuck off and I'm fat and blah blah and threaten me some more. But I hope not. I hope it resonates with you how close you are to getting everything you ever wanted and also how close you are from losing everything you ever wanted. Both outcomes from the direct decisions you made about how to act.

Whatever you do or are know this—

I love you. I support you. I stand by you. Now. And for all eternity.

Your husband and partner.

* * *

I have that email because I had printed it out—and later, by some miracle, found it among the few things I recovered, post-arrest, from what was left of the Twenty-Eighth Street apartment. I don't know why I printed it, but I'm glad I did. Again, he'd deleted all of our email history, so I only found pieces of it here and there, like the email above, and of course, our Gchats.

The flagrant manipulation is infuriating to read now, and embarrassingly obvious. I know that my state of mind at the time involved exhaustion, confusion, and fear. There was no time to process anything and no space for reflection. The takeaway from this email was that I'd better get him that $50,000 wire, or else I'd be a *quitter* and a *coward*. I wouldn't just lose everything; others would too.

I didn't reply to his email, but from the Gchats that followed—*more badgering from him*—it appears I was considering taking out the $50,000. I had been prepping Nadia, framing it as needing funds to pay personal loans and offering to dilute my own equity. I would have asked for her approval before withdrawing money. Meanwhile, two other potential investors were considering making sizable investments. Ultimately, one of them did.

I pushed back against Mr. Fox as he peppered me with Gchats throughout the day. I told him I needed to make another sales tax payment and that, among other things, my taking funds out *looked bad*. He dismissed it, writing, "*All these people get washed away.*" By which he meant everyone would get repaid.

Originally he'd given me one month to get him the $50,000, but now he wanted it sooner. I was upset and fired back at him with insults, many in all caps for emphasis. He reminded me, *Control your emotions.* Then he added,

```
Mr. Fox: Allow me to explain and make it clear. Once the last
50K is repaid then I can close everything out and we are done.
The company is yours. You have our full backing. Beginning of
HEA. But until then I cannot do much in the way of help. So,
after your outburst the other day, think it prudent to expedite
the process so I can begin to closeout now.
```

I reminded him—again—that I couldn't just pull all the funds out of the bank. Our arguing continued:

> Mr. Fox: I get that. I do. My point is just that if it's done and I can get the investors bought out, they won't really matter. Or at minimum get a new large shareholder involved. The people in Boston are a real estate investment group. I hold contract on their two major members. They do as I say but are still part of a collective so it takes a bit of time to get them involved.
>
> Me: I don't want a real estate investment group to own me.
>
> Mr. Fox: They won't own you. You would own you. They just clear away the brush. Then give you the keys to the kingdom. The result is total control of your company for you. You have full power and control.
>
> Me: Yup.

I didn't know anything about the group in Boston he referred to, if they existed at all. Or what it would mean to "hold contract" on their members. The idea that all of this would be made up seemed—and still seems—so totally bizarre. As usual, nothing made any sense. And, as usual, he was calm and collected while I sat in terror and confusion.

> Mr. Fox: I expect you to be strong and stay loyal. I expect you to be a fucking champion at the end of this. I expect you to get this done. I expect you to change the world. I expect you to be a powerful leader. That is what I expect.

Later, we argued further. I reminded him that he'd promised to repay Dylan at least five times already. I told him I'd been feeling physically sick, which was not surprising since I'd been working at the restaurant twelve to fourteen hours every day, all while under pressure from him.

Mr. Fox continued to push me not just for the wires but also for me to leave the city to go to my mother's house with Leon for the weekend to recover. He wrote that if I sent the wire and then went to my mom's, it would be *"the safest way to secure a safe outcome without inviting other larger problems and incurring a tailspin."*

His vague, ominous threats always scared me. Still, I wrote back to him, *"I'm not leaving my business."*

The following day a wire was sent to Mr. Fox for $50,000.

I don't know if I was the one who sent it. I don't remember doing it. Since I was now using a much larger bank, it was possible to send wires without verbal confirmation. It's possible Mr. Fox sent himself the wire. I vaguely recall at one point he did this, but I'm not sure if it was this instance or later.

This $50,000 going out was a huge deal. I had to have explained it to Nadia, and I don't know how I did that. I had to have been terrified, but again figured it was the last time. Plus, I wanted to be free of him breathing down my neck, or worse. I needed to focus on the restaurant.

I couldn't face my new investors and lie, yet I *had* to. It felt impossible. The truth came with so much shame, and I feared these awful outcomes and consequences Mr. Fox alluded to if I didn't do as he said.

The stress, shame, and confusion only ramped up. Whatever remaining bits of glue held me together began to give way.

CHAPTER SIXTY-FOUR

LATE APRIL 2015
NEW YORK CITY

Mr. Fox finally left town, which was a relief. But I was panicked about the money he'd taken.

Now that I was alone, he probably worried about maintaining his control over me, and rightly so. With space to myself and distance from him, I could have started to see things more clearly. I could have latched on tighter to my new investors. He knew I spent a lot of time with Nadia, and while she could be difficult, I felt some attachment to her. If I'd wanted someone to save me from everything—and I badly did—Nadia, with her strong mom energy, was the person I'd most likely have turned to. There was a pull there that Mr. Fox must have sensed, which meant he had to drive a wedge between us.

I was exhausted as usual. I'd been working to bring in another investor—$105,000 for three shares—which was money the restaurant needed, especially after I'd pulled out that $50,000—which made me feel sick to think about. At least things continued to get better at the restaurant, and it was spring, the start of our busiest time of year.

Mr. Fox, meanwhile, subjected me to more of his soul-draining mind-fuckery from afar.

April 25, Gchat

Mr. Fox: I need you to try and stay strong and vigilant. Someone will come at you soon I fear. I am doing all I can to counter this. It will be either Nadia or Ben or a combination of them. You are already falling into that trap worrying about doing as they say and putting their requests and worries at the lead. Once they know you are doing that they will move to strike. No one wants you to run that place except me and ironically, Jeffrey, albeit for his own personal agenda. Nadia and Ben are snakes in the grass. Both have aspirations of taking that restaurant and the duck empire from you. And after the other day and what happened it invited my opposite to perhaps step in and deal with them to help them succeed in their plan to strike and take it. That's why the next few days are very important.

Nadia and Ben were "snakes in the grass"? I hated this. Part of me wanted to assume he was full of shit, yet part of me was also scared. Telling me someone would come at me soon was unnerving. He again blamed my outburst for this new challenge. As if my having lost my temper led to these negative turns, and to his "opposite," meaning his brother, assisting in this pending attack on me and the business. Of course, Mr. Fox had to paint these new investors as the enemy.

The following night, Sunday, April 26, Gchat

Mr. Fox: The next few days will be a whirlwind. I need you prepared for that mentally. You can waiver in no way. You'll get an email tomorrow morning that will be a list of instructions. You must follow them. It's non-negotiable. Any hesitation, any mistakes, any emotional overreaction and we lose everything.

You've been prepared for this week. All the pushing, prodding, money, meetings, feelings, anger, control, testing, etc. that you have gone through has been to prepare you for this coming

```
week. So that you may handle it all knowing you've done it
before and made it through. You were born for greatness. Nothing
you will be asked to do will be easy but I have confidence in
your abilities both mental and physical.

As usual, keep your head down and your eyes open. Stay frosty.

Me: You should be prepared for me to ignore them.

Mr. Fox: That was the worst thing you could have just said. When
you ignore them you should be prepared for both our lives to
come completely undone. For there to be no happily ever after.
And for you to lose everything you've ever cared about or will
ever care about. As will I. Do not fuck with this. Not this time.
Not again. There will be no redo this time.
```

This last statement terrified me.

* * *

According to Mr. Fox, we were now in the final phase, right before the *happily ever after.* All that remained was for him to negotiate buying out the investors—the same ones who'd only just invested their funds, plus Jeffrey.

Jeffrey was still owed money from our deal years earlier when he'd sold the restaurant to me, and he'd remained the guarantor on the lease. Of all the people I didn't want to disappoint, Jeffrey was the most meaningful. Throughout the nightmare of shutting down, I felt an acute sickness thinking how he must have been confused and disappointed that I'd let the restaurant and business shut down. I'd communicated with him via email and phone, but I'd been too afraid to go speak to him in person, as if the shame would overwhelm me, and I'd fall apart in his presence. He'd already witnessed and gotten involved to help during my dramatic breakup with Matthew, and now this. I wanted him and everyone else repaid, at least made whole.

I wanted them all to see that I hadn't failed—at least not the way it appeared I had.

* * *

Mr. Fox had been implying for a while that some powerful group was behind him (the Asgardians, perhaps?), but he was vague about it, as usual. For some reason, Mr. Fox insisted that he had to use a different name when presenting himself to the investors. I wasn't sure why, but *okay*. If my investors were getting all their money back, and ideally making a nice profit, what did it matter what name Mr. Fox used?

He informed me that for the purposes of this impending buyout, his name would be Michael Caledonia. He even made a Gmail account under that name. His story would be that he was a wealthy investor from Boston. This false narrative—outright lying—was incredibly uncomfortable for me, but the prospect of everyone getting their money back, and of finally repaying all the loans, was so appealing that I didn't care *what* he called himself. I just wanted this done and over.

```
April 27, 2015, Gchat

Mr. Fox: As it stands now the buyer will reach out directly to
Nadia.

Me: OK. I'm not sure what I'm supposed to say to her other than
some random person I maybe knew from way back called me, asking
about buying?

Mr. Fox: This is one of those things that is 50 steps ahead of
you. That is why adhering to that email was so important. You
have already deviated, therefore the plan has deviated. Every
action, reaction, always faced with two doors. You walk through
the one on the left or the one on the right. You listen or you
don't. All I can do is guide you the correct way. Do not sell
```

Ben any more shares. I am working on a full work up of Nadia and her husband. The more info the better. You tell Nadia that a potential buyer reached out to you about a buyout. His assistant reached out to get some preliminary info. He will reach out directly this week but will most likely call her. Fill in the blanks on the rest. You really have no idea what you created and how important it is. You have 10% of an idea how important it is.

There are two outcomes: you get the business or Nadia gets it. You control the result. But the more you don't listen and worry about the wrong things, the deeper you dig the hole. It's that simple. If I say to do something, you do it. I don't care if it doesn't make sense. When we do things your kick-and-scream-and-demand way everything goes to shit. Do not give me pushback or drama. I refuse to fail. I refuse to let you fail. We will win. It's that simple.

* * *

The next morning, Mr. Fox sent me an email—except, for whatever reason, he sent it to me from my own email account. He probably did it by accident, since he was in my account reading my emails from his phone. Either way, it left a copy in my history for me to later find.

April 28, 2015

From: Mr. Fox

To: Me

You need to send another 35K right now. Tomorrow morning I will WIRE BACK 105K as a three share purchase by our mystery man from Boston. This is all part of a move that is 50 steps ahead. You will use part of that 105K to pay Dylan and the rest will stay in the company account.

On Friday our mystery man will buyout Ben and on Monday afternoon he will buyout Nadia.

By this time next week we will have successfully fended off a coup that you don't even know is coming and you will be in sole possession of the business. The next step after that is someone replaces Jeffrey and then that person gets bought out. There are things in play here that you do not and can not see. The numbers are correct. THIS IS NOT BAG MONEY and after I receive the other share I will wire back 105K. Send that 35K right now ASAP.

This is one of those things that if you don't do because you get nervous or upset or take the wrong way or panic then it will make a massive mess and after the fact when the wheels fall off you would see that what I said was the right move and you go "well if you just told me that I would have done it no problem."

This is the move. Send 35 to me right now and I will wire back 105K tomorrow morning. These numbers can not be adjusted. I need you to trust me on this. This is the move.

I was sitting in the restaurant basement office when I read that email. I replied:

CHAPTER SIXTY-FOUR

```
April 28, 2015

From: Me

To: Mr. Fox

You have not once ever come through when you've said things
like this. yesterday you said no more.

No more.

Do not contact me about this anymore.
```

This was terrifying. Of course I wanted him to start buying out the investors but *why did he need me to send him money first?* I couldn't do it. I was even afraid that he would just use my online bank access to make the transfers himself. It appears I changed my passwords, even my email password, based on the exchange that followed.

```
April 28, 2015, Gchat

Mr. Fox: Changing your password was a bad move. Answer for
yourself. Now. I see you have changed all the passwords. Not
just email. I will take this as you are not going to listen to
my advice. I will handle this on my own. It's too important to
let you fuck it up. Say something. Or I will assume the absolute
worst.

Me: What's the worst? I'm dead?

Mr. Fox: No. Stop saying that. Jesus.

Me: Leave me alone.
```

Mr. Fox: I'm going to have to get that money from someone else. And do this through them. And send them 105K. If you don't listen to me on this it will be a mistake. You never should have changed your passwords. You did that once before and I told you it was a bad move. Like WTF, I'm not going to take anything from you. This is always up to you to make the correct or incorrect decision. All I can do is tell you which is which. Password change is bad. If you put yourself on an island I won't be able to help you.

Now Nadia will have sole control. You are playing right into this. You are driving this off a cliff and you don't even know it. What a joke. You think you are "protecting" your business from me because now all of a sudden I'm the bad guy. Good luck with that assumption. It's worked out so well for you in the past when you haven't listened to me on the big things and changed your passwords and freaked out and blah blah blah. I'm done trying to explain shit to you. You want to be an asshat then fine. Enjoy your horrible decisions and results from them. I will be here for you as I will always be but I am going on record that this will lead to our demise. I love you. Feel free to text me if you change your mind. Again, I am on your side. I will do what I can for you as I always have. XOXO /

Mr. Fox: I need mail password.

Mr. Fox: You blocked me?

Mr. Fox: Are you kidding me?

Mr. Fox: YOU FUCKING KIDDING ME?

Mr. Fox: OK.

I was so freaked out I must have blocked Mr. Fox's phone number so he couldn't text or call me. I was trapped in this relentless cycle: he promised relief, giving me some hope; I finally did what he asked, only to be crushed again. Each time the stakes were higher, and each time I was warned that if I didn't do what he said I'd be "driving off a cliff."

Literally driving off a cliff felt like an attractive option at that point, if there were any cliffs around, or if I had my car. Nazim had my Honda that day. He planned to drive to Brooklyn to pick up a load of product from our production space, which we'd finally gotten back up and running. Meanwhile, I hated that Leon was all alone at the dark Twenty-Eighth Street apartment, so I suggested to Nazim that he take Leon along with him. I'd bought that car not just to travel back and forth to the Brooklyn space, but also so I could easily take Leon with me when I went there, or anywhere. Leon liked going for car rides, and he loved Nazim.

Nazim picked me up at the restaurant, and we drove to Twenty-Eighth Street. I don't know what I told him, but I started to cry. I'm sure I was afraid to tell him exactly what was going on. All I remember is that Nazim always told me *not* to leave town with Mr. Fox.

I was fixated on getting Leon out of the apartment, as if it was a matter of urgency. Nazim double-parked while I ran up. I focused completely on Leon and his joy when we got outside and he saw the car, and Nazim in it, realizing he was going for an adventure. I needed any kind of light to grasp onto. Leon's happiness was a buffer—a bit of a shield against the constant pain that was my existence.

* * *

Reading the conversation between Mr. Fox and me from later that afternoon, it's as if I'd regressed to a more childlike state.

```
April 28, 2015, Gchat

Mr. Fox: How are you doing? How is your day? Are you feeling
better?
```

Me: Yes.

Mr. Fox: Good.

Me: I had Naz take me to get Leon quickly so Leon could have a field trip day.

Mr. Fox: What? You and Naz went out together?

Me: So Leon could go to Brooklyn.

Mr. Fox: Oh I see.

Me: I felt bad Leon being alone in the dark shitty apartment all day.

Mr. Fox: That's good for him. Good idea.

Me: It's so nice out today. Leon was SO HAPPY when I came back and he realized we were going out and then so happy in the car.

Mr. Fox: Good.

Me: That made me feel better.

Mr. Fox: :)

Me: I have Dr. K today. I really hate going there.

Mr. Fox: Did you pick up your super pills yet? If so then cancel him. I don't care about Dr. K just the pills.

Me: I can't cancel him, he'll charge me anyway. YOU TOLD ME TO GO.

Mr. Fox: Yes, to get the pills.

Me: And you said you'd cover it.

Mr. Fox: And I will. And everything else. I am just trying to get this all settled up right now so I can take my hiatus and you can run things. I don't imagine you would want to do this every day. Sit in that dungeon and worry about answering to Jeffrey and Nadia. It's awful. And unnecessary. But part of this whole thing. But not on my behalf. Would be awful to just have that be it right? Sit in the dungeon and worry and answer to people that would then own you. Yuck. That would be an awful outcome. I don't want that. I know you don't want that. So like I said. I am doing all that I can to make sure we win and you get your freedom and powers back. Those people are there to make you worry. To make you panic. To show you what things will be if it goes to shit. Think of them like the ghost of Christmas yet to come. From A Christmas Carol. It's not the real future. Just a preview of what might be if the bad stays bad. You should not worry about them or let them impact your decision making. You have a wonderful future ahead of you. I will see to that.

You have done a great job. Always coming through when required. Always doing the right thing that is asked of you. You are a powerful and strong soul. You are someone I would fight for and would give my everything for. So that you may succeed and realize your true potential and rise to the greatness you are destined for.

Me: blah blah blah.

Mr. Fox: It's not.

An hour later:

Mr. Fox: I need email password. Send to Will email account.

Me: Sent.

Every time I changed my passwords, Mr. Fox was able to convince me to give him the new ones. That he wanted me to send them to the "Will email account" was strange, but everything was strange. If he was the only one using that account, what difference did it make? It sort of makes me think that he was also using that email account in a wholly separate manipulation of someone else, about which I still know nothing. Was he juggling money he got from me with money he was getting from someone else? Or was Will still some sort of actual delusion of his?

Another hour later:

Mr. Fox: you there?

Me: Yes.

Mr. Fox: I am going to a meeting, will keep you posted. XO

Me: I have meetings all afternoon starting now. Take care.

Mr. Fox: I will. I will take care of everything.

Me: Good. You do that.

Mr. Fox: I intend to.

Me: Good bye.

Mr. Fox: Nah. None of that, love. You are a queen. You are a champion. I will see to it that you get the life you deserve.

When I refused to do what Mr. Fox wanted—either filibustering or just ignoring him to stall his demands as long as possible, hoping maybe he'd find money somewhere else in the meantime—he always circled back to being nice to me. Then, once he'd soothed me, he pushed all over again.

* * *

That afternoon Mr. Fox sent me a long email. I have it because, at the time, it felt significant, so I took screenshots of it, and saved the images to a hidden folder on my laptop. I'm not sure what was going through my mind when I did this, but I'm *really* glad I did it. I didn't find the contents of that hidden folder until much later, almost two years after my arrest.

```
April 28, 2015

From: Mr. Fox

To: Me

Subject: you must read this all the way through, calmly. do
not overreact. XO

I am working my ass off to get this all done this week. We
have both worked so hard the past few years I beg you not
to fall in the trap of thinking that the restaurant is open
now and therefore, fuck me. That would be very bad. I want
only for you to succeed. I really do. But if you remember
correctly, this is much bigger than the restaurant. You
have always been required to show that you could put the
restaurant aside for the benefit of the family. To prove
yourself. The place was shut down to show you that negative
equals negative. It was reopened when you did the right
things and when you put the restaurant in that number two
```

spot. You have forgotten that, I think. The money you sent was required and agreed upon. And in fact there was supposed to be another 140K sent by you that I GOT REMOVED. So the fact that I need an extra 10 or 15K here or there to help me get this all done RIGHT NOW should not be a big deal. You should be on my side as I am on your side. I am almost done with the buyout plan. But I can not keep the dogs at bay without your help. And at the moment that help comes financially. Again, I got the 140K knocked off the bag money figure so the fact that I need an extra 10-15K is not a huge deal. Part of the reason I need it is because I routed my other funds to cover your bag money obligation so you would not need to put up that other 140K. So putting 10K up should not be a big deal and if it gets the deal done so I can stay gone and you can run things without having to deal with day to day bullshit from outside sources or investor goons then it's all good. I don't need another 35K. That was covered by another party, and was always going to be covered by another source. But I do need that other 10K we discussed yesterday. You sent 5 but I need 10 more. I just do. There is no way around that. I put myself in harm's way to get 140K knocked off the bag money figure. I need you to send me that 10K. I just do. It's that simple. And I can only get a wire while I am in CT and I am leaving CT soon and going to Boston and will not be returning this way. If no wire sent then we have to worry about bullshit cash withdrawal nonsense.

Do not freak out. Do not cry or yell or threaten. Just send the 10K. If you send it today I will pay this month's rent. And send you 5K back in cash on Sunday. I promise that. There it is in writing. If I don't send you back 5K in cash on Sunday and pay this month's rent you can feel free to throw me under the bus with everyone. And I won't resist it. I will take the blame for everything. Whether true or not. But if

I deliver then you get some confidence and continue to stay calm and cool. There is no risk here for you. I have made this as easy as possible to comply and help me.

I need this Sarma. Please hear me on this. This is the move and I must make it. I know it might make you upset, but that's supposed to happen to make this harder. It's always been like that. I have leveraged and stretched myself very thin. I need this to cover your ass so that I can keep you in power and I need you to send 10K for me to do it so I can get this done. No matter what I am always on your side and always will be and will always do all that I can to get you back in power and keep you in power. And this –> **If you send it today I will pay this month's rent. And send you 5K back in cash on Sunday. I promise that. There it is in writing. If I don't send you back 5K in cash on Sunday and pay this month's rent you can feel free to throw me under the bus with everyone. And I won't resist it. I will take the blame for everything. Whether true or not.**

This is for real Sarma. I have never put anything like that in writing. Not ever. And I only am now because we are so close to the end game. And I need your help.

XOXOXOXOXOXOXO

If you said what I said to say in text out loud then you are in the box. Do not reply to this mail. DO NOT REPLY. That is important. If you get a wire out just send me a text saying:

"It's sunny outside today. I hope the weekend weather doesn't disappoint."

I must have ignored him. The next morning we started Gchatting early, at 7:00 a.m. Not because Mr. Fox had gotten up early but because he hadn't yet gone to sleep, likely having been gambling all night at the casinos in Connecticut. It seems that even after his long email plea, I hadn't send him the $10,000. I must have been pulling away. It was always easier to pull away from him mentally when he was out of town, when he wasn't physically in front of me.

April 29, 2015, Gchat

Mr. Fox: Good morning. I had a long night. I got someone to loan me the ten grand. I need you to send the bank password to Will's account. I figured you would have done it last night. I have always had it. It has never been an issue. Good news that I got the ten though. :)

Me: Congrats. Can they give you another $2.5MM?

Mr. Fox: Ha. Right. I will send you some cash back. Bank password to Will account though please. ASAP. Now would be good as I am going to bed soon. How did you sleep? You have Leon sleeping with you?

Me: Yes he sleeps with me.

Mr. Fox: you are the best wife ever.

Me: you are the greatest raping torturing fucked up manipulative lying "husband" ever! I heart you!

Mr. Fox: like. wtf. Do you want me to kill myself? I will if you tell me too. Or do you want my blood? To make myself bleed? I will if you want. I love you. You are my everything.

Me: All good husbands force their smelly cocks in their sobbing wives mouths, no? I want to watch you on your knees while some big gay bear shoves his dry dick in your ass.

Mr. Fox: Wow you are just saying that. I have to get some sleep. I have meeting tomorrow. And have to set buyer meet. I have 7 days to complete this. Or what I get will be far worse. I love you. Keep me posted and I will keep you posted. Meeting today.

Me: OK.

Mr. Fox: I said "tomorrow" cuz I not slept yet. I love you Sarma. :-/ I am sorry.

Me: You should be.

Mr. Fox: I hope you can understand one day. And can have the patience to wait until you can understand and we have HEA.

Me: Yes I'm waiting to see.

Mr. Fox: and you doing what is required. And that is important. All the money you sent was bag money.

Me: "Bag money"

Mr. Fox: I love you Mrs. F. I do I do.

Me: I don't love your smelly tea bags. Not at all.

Mr. Fox: closing lappy to get some sleep. Ok ok. I love you. XOXO <3

The following day Mr. Fox sent me another long email, and again I took screenshots of it and saved it. I must have asked him a question, and his reply came in the form of this long-winded email.

```
April 30, 2015

From: Mr. Fox

To: Me

Yes there is something. Think of humanity as a piece of
glass. Right now there are spider cracks throughout the glass
and the cracks are getting larger. You have more control
of when good and bad things happen in the world than you
could possibly know. It's one of the reasons you always felt
the way you did around certain people. Always felt like an
outsider here. This place wasn't built for us to live in.
We are here to oversee things. It's a garden and we are the
gardeners. I'm dying. I'm supposed to come at you today. To
get you to do something. To provoke you to flip out and
deny me and then do something negative. I'm supposed to do
something that will get you to react harshly. Making you
think you're helping the company and yourself when in fact
you'd be setting the final charges in place to destroy it.
I'm cut off from making deals. I'm physically nearly broken.
I'm mentally nearly broken. Yesterday at the table I nearly
came apart and for the first time in the history of creation,
I looked weak. That was when I called you on the phone. This
was a direct result of your energy. This isn't about Jeffrey
or Nadia or vegan food or bank wires or expansion plans
or accounting or bad press or looking old or being pale or
having sex or living in a shitty apartment or trusting me.
None of that is real. This is about one thing and one thing
```

only—you. This whole thing was designed to get you to be able to deal with making tough decisions when I say, travel here, send this amount of money, tell this person A or B. I guide you to the correct decision, but it's designed to be the hardest thing to listen to me. It's designed to make you hate me and worry or be angry at me. Or to confuse you or make you worry about the wrong things and wrong people's reactions. If I say get on a plane right now and go to Rome for a week you would not do it. You would flat out say no. You would say, "I can't leave my business. I just can't." And then you would get mad at me and make threats. If I said to wire me 100K right now and to control Nadia and not be afraid of her reaction to anything. If I told you I will put the money back Monday morning first thing and this will be over. You would FREAK out and say, "No I'm not, I can't, it's investor money. I can't lie to her, I can't trust you to send it back. Omg blah blah. Fuck you, you fat piece of shit, I'm not doing this, I'm protecting my business. Negativity and doubt, negativity and doubt. I can't I can't I can't!" So on and so forth. Then threaten and change passwords and freak out. But if you remember Belgium, I said, "When something difficult is asked of you and you deny, each time you think you are doing something to protect yourself and the business and you are in fact doing something to destroy it. Each time you think you dig my grave one foot deeper you are in fact digging your own grave 2 feet deeper."

This was designed to warn you. To try and get you to understand that when I ask you to do things that are designed to make you totally freak the fuck out, that you need to have the ability to give me control and trust in it and not let the task asked of you freak you out. You're to do it, do it swiftly, do it calmly, and with no drama or pushback. Only then will this all just end in an instant.

> If I say send 100K your response should be "Ok, where to?"
>
> If I say get on a plane and go to Rome you should say "Ok out of which airport?"
>
> You have complied in the past, but never without an argument or threat. Without getting mad first or without an assurance of something. Never just on faith without pushback or negativity. You should answer without any hesitation and show the ability to do what is required without freaking out. Only then will this end and end in our favor.
>
> Like I said—today is supposed to be one of those days.
>
> It was really nice reading you said you love me in your text this morning. Made me feel stronger. Made me feel like we can still win this.
>
> I love you Sarma.
>
> I do.
>
> I do.

It's strange to read these emails now because I only vaguely remember them. It's also weird that, apparently, I'd texted him that I love him. I can remember sometimes feeling that I did, in a fucked-up sort of way.

I must have been unable to reconcile what seemed to be patently bullshit with the fear of my current circumstances, all while wondering, *What if he is telling me the truth?* I could never prove that he wasn't, nor could I make sense of what he was telling me. The explanation he gave me for his underlying motives was at least an option. *Maybe he's legit?* I'd think. But the longer he was away from me, the more I leaned toward the safety and tangible reality of the restaurant—

now reopened, *thank god.* Even if this reality was one in which I owed massive amounts of money with no way to explain anything.

And yet. Time after time, I ended up doing what he wanted me to do. I needed a way out, but I could never see one other than the way out he kept insisting was just around the corner, if only I'd send the next wire. His way out led to the "happily ever after."

If cognitive dissonance is the mental toll of ongoing conflicting information, then I suffered greatly from it. All I knew for sure was that things were royally fucked up. My mind—and my ability to reason—were compromised from knowing something was deeply wrong but having no way to identify, understand, or explain what it was.

* * *

Only a few minutes after sending that long email, Mr. Fox Gchatted me to ask if I'd received it. As usual I resisted his request for a wire. I wrote back reminding him of all the ways in which he was torturing me. He replied, *"Remember the 5 minutes of the real us from the King Cole Bar. I love you."*

And then he wrote, *"My email said it all. It's a pathway to happily ever after. Or hell on earth. The choice is yours and yours alone."*

Hell on earth.

Great.

CHAPTER SIXTY-FIVE

MAY 2015

NEW YORK CITY

The following morning was the first of May. Mr. Fox was *still* trying to get me to send him that $10,000 wire.

> May 1, 2015, Gchat
>
> Mr. Fox: Good morning. You there?
>
> Me: yes.
>
> Mr. Fox: you ok?
>
> Me: No.
>
> Mr. Fox: You still mad at me? You don't need to be. I am not going to let you down. Even if you choose to quit on me. I would never quit on you. I am prepared to die to make sure you are happy and taken care of. I love you.

Me: Then do that.

Mr. Fox: So you are not sending the ten? You are just hardening on that? After everything, ten K is just a no? Over a shitty ten K? OK, I will make all the preparations. I hope you change your mind. I explained why I needed it. It's a lousy ten K. After all we have been through and all you have made it through and done. Don't quit on me now over such a small amount of money and just a few days, makes no sense. But if that is what you think will be best. You are wrong. And if I stand by and do nothing then you will lose everything. You have no allies. You have no restaurant or company. You have false confidence. You think it's open now and fuck me and you don't need me or to listen to me and I am just full of …

Me: I'm calling Jeffrey.

Mr. Fox: Don't do that. Don't call him. I will make this ok. Sarma don't quit now. Don't give in to them. Please. Don't send me a dime. But don't quit. Don't give in.

Me: I need to call him.

Mr. Fox: why? Was it scheduled?

Me: no.

Mr. Fox: you can't call him. You can't do this. Just wait until Monday.

Me: I'm calling him.

Mr. Fox: please don't do that.

Me: I'll let everyone know what really happened.

Mr. Fox: Don't threaten me. And don't do that. Are you home? Can we FaceTime? Stop changing your passwords! WTF. Why are you doing this? Just make it make sense. Please. Why now? Why turn? Talk to me. OK. I have one call left to make and was holding off until it was an emergency break-glass situation. I will make the call but I need to hear your voice first. Please.

Me: make the call.

Mr. Fox: I will. But I need to hear your voice first.

An hour later, he wrote:

Mr. Fox: you send passwords to Will please. / XO / you sent?

Me: no. why

Mr. Fox: I can't call anyone if I don't have those passwords. It can't look like you want to drive us off a cliff. This is supposed to be this hard. Right now. You wanting to help me at all and to stand in the fire. It's the hardest right now at the end. Please be strong. Do not quit on this or on me. Be strong now. Stronger than ever. Remain loyal. What have I always said—above all else just show that you are loyal and that even if the world seems to be falling down around us that we stand by one another in the fire. We must be unified. I love you.

Me: And what are you doing now? I have no cash.

Mr. Fox: Just stay calm and cool. Don't lash out via Jeffrey. Not yet. If you do it before I can strike a deal then it's counter productive. Just relax. Stay calm. I will work it out. I understand.

Me: Well then it's good he didn't answer before because I would have screamed through tears.

Mr. Fox: yes hold back. Or it will blow up in your face. I am going to reach out to someone. I am going to make them an offer they will not be able to refuse. I need us to be unified. Send passwords to Will please.

Me: I did.

* * *

I had to have been pressing Command+Shift+4 a lot, because I took screenshots of another long email he sent me. Notably I'd been refusing to send him even this $10,000 and had even threatened to call Jeffrey to tell him everything, but I can't now recall how serious I was about this threat. I think I was 70 percent serious. No matter what, I'd have been terrified to admit all this insanity to Jeffrey, or to anyone, but especially to Jeffrey. He wasn't my dad, but he'd always had a very dad-like presence in my life; I both feared him and desperately wanted his respect.

I think I was determined to stick it out, not send Mr. Fox money, and just let things happen, let him make his threats.

May 1, 2015

From: Mr. Fox

To: Me

I hope this helps explain some stuff. Why this is so hard for you. And why I had to ask again for your help. I love you. XO <3

Once I make this call and deal I can not unmake it. I want you to know that. This is not a move or a play. This is heavy shit. Once done, it can not be undone. It's a straight trade, my life and seat at the table for all that you want. Everything I wrote down on the list that day. I still have the list in my bag. Was prepared to fulfill it all once this was done. I need to be perfectly clear: should you have a change of heart and decide to get back on board AFTER I make this call, it will be too late.

I will wait until I hear from you. If you send me the 10K and show that even in the hardest of times and the most difficult of moments to stand by me, that you still stood by me, then I can finish this and have money and list and everything by next week.

This is not a joke or a game. You literally hold my life in your hands. I don't mean to sound dramatic or ominous. And I am fully prepared to die for you if needed. I just don't want to commit my life and then you come around from the funk and go oh shit I actually do King Cole love him I don't want him dead I just want the happily ever after. But then would be too late.

I won't do anything until I hear from you.

But no matter what, do not freak out. Do not call Jeffrey screaming. Not yet. Do not tank anything or flip. You wanted power, here it is. My life in your hands. Decide if you love me or hate me. What does your heart tell you to do. Which is the real me? The one you love or the one you hate?

This was never meant to be easy. I do love you. I do. I hope you can find it in your heart to see that. That I always tried to explain how it was never real. That you were always being tested and that things that set you off were meant to set you off. Thank you for password update. I will of course not abuse them. I would never just take ten K. That was not what this was about and would defeat the purpose. Was never about money. That is just always your hot button. It was just about: will you help me when I need it the most, but when it is the easiest to say no. When you have all the power, hold all the cards, what will you do with it. Will you let emotion and rage get in the way of making the correct decision to help me. Think of it like the last step before the top. It's always the hardest step. It's the one everyone trips on. To give you a taste of complete power and control over a life. And to see if you had the conviction to make the right choice to help me even when you were filled with anger and rage. Wield your power to help me or to make me suffer.

Think about it. It makes sense. I'm sorry it had to be like that, but that was always the ultimate reward. Total power and control. You need to demonstrate what you would do if you have it. If you can make the hard decisions without anger or rage or spite coming into play. I've been preparing you for that for years. Always telling you to look the other way when something feels like it's trying to set you off. That you need to demonstrate you can maintain control even under the worst conditions.

Anyway.

I love you. Help me one more time, or tell me to make the call and deal for my life.

Either way I accept what you decide. I agreed to this a long time ago and always knew one day we would be right here.

I love you. More than anything. More than my family. More than my life. More than anything. I don't even know why. Or what it is. I just love you. I think you are the most spectacularly beautiful creature inside and out in this entire universe. And I want you happy. Pass or fail these stupid tests, I always knew that if you tanked that I would happily give my life to give you what you wanted. To make you happy.

I just hope you see that. And can see past the rage and negativity trying to control you and tell you it's bullshit and that I don't care and making you want to want to hurt me.

Anywhoooooooo,

I love you no matter what.

I'm sorry this has been so hard. Stand strong, it's almost over. But remain unified no matter what.

XOXOXOXOXOXOXOXOXOXOXOXOXOXXXXXXXXXXX

I love you Sarma. With all that I am, I love you.

-Huz

I don't know if I replied to that email or texted or if we spoke on the phone. But I took another screenshot of an email conversation around noon. Since it's a screenshot, I cannot see all the emails in the thread, but here's the part I have in full:

```
May 1, 2015

From: Mr. Fox

To: Me

I am sorry that you were taken to task. But it had to be done.
To make days like today be impossible days. To make you want
to hate me. To want to hurt me. I just always hoped you'd
come through no matter what. But I've always been prepared to
sacrifice myself for you if you couldn't. I always tried to
have box talks and break rules to make days like this easier.
To help you see that you were supposed to hate me at times
like this. Supposed to give in to fear and anger. That it was
designed to make you fail. But I hoped that you wouldn't. That
if you knew it was set up to test you that you could shrug it
off like you always did and just come through for me even under
impossible conditions. I'm so sorry this was so hard on you. I
never in a million years thought you'd ever take it this hard.

XO

Just stay calm and cool. Will all be ok soon.

XO

[emojis of the three monkeys, eyes covered, ears covered,
mouth covered]
```

A few hours later, he sent me a Gchat:

```
Mr. Fox: <3 Please send me 3500 cash bones weezy. I gots nothing
left to sell. Just 3500.

Me: everything's over.

Mr. Fox: No it's not. I told you that. Even if you refuse I
will handle it for you. But you gotta keep cool. OK I won't ask
again. I got my appointment for Sunday. But I need you to stay
cool and calm and we unified. But I accept that you can't send.
I won't ask again. I promise. Ok?

Me: I'm repeating myself. You said no more money. So handle it.

Mr. Fox: I will. But you love me right?

Me: yes.

Mr. Fox: :) I love you too.
```

He sent me no chats for three days. Then, just one, on May 4: "*The Bisclavret Group 303 Park Avenue South, New York, New York, 10016.*"

Nothing for another two days, then he sent another email (again, I had taken a screenshot):

```
May 6, 2015

From: Mr. Fox

To: Me

Subject: Just a quick reminder for you
```

You

Are

So

Close.

Remember—you do not have anything to worry about except if you don't listen. That's it. That's all. It's literally that easy to get to the HEA on Monday.

You have nothing to do but keep staying calm and cooperating. Keep doing as instructed and this is all over and you win and HEA Monday night. Will be popping champagne Monday night if you just keep cool and keep doing as told.

Do NOT worry. Remember. You don't have a resti. You don't have a bank account. You don't have to worry about Jeffrey. Or Nadia. Or Ben. You have only one job—no freaks outs and to do as told to successfully navigate through a fluid situation so that I may handle everything and deliver you an HEA on Monday and get you to where you need to be—back in power.

Don't worry about Jeffrey or N. They will try and say things or imply things to make you panic and flip and to make you NOT do as told. This is intentional. The only way any of them can cause you havoc is if you let panic and fear creep in and you don't do as I instruct. Then my hand is forced and etc.

You have done a very good job so far. DO NOT allow any fear or doubt to creep in. Just keep doing as instructed and all will be fine and you will come out of this successful with the HEA. I can't say that enough. Seriously.

I do need to speak with Nadia tomorrow. And don't sign her
note attachment until you and I talk.

I will text you when I wake up. Leon and I are going to sleep
now. It's 3:38AM. XO.

I do love you.

[two hearts emoji]

[three monkey emojis]

* * *

May 6, 2015, Gchat

Mr. Fox: OK. Now I told you when you went back to the city—any
bullshit, any pushback, and that would be disastrous. So let's
regroup here and you stay calm. When I say it's time to go, it's
time to go. This will literally all be over and wonderful on
Monday UNLESS you get in the way of it by not doing what is
asked when it's asked. I need you with me. I need you with me
so I can make the Nadia and Jeffrey call. After that you go and
get the money and they get paid. They paid and deposit made
on Monday and HEA. UNLESS you push back in any way. It's that
simple.

Of course I pushed back on Mr. Fox coming to pick me up to take me away. As he wrote to me, I was doing payroll in the basement of the restaurant. It was going to take me most of the afternoon, and I had a meeting scheduled in the evening. He was not happy.

Mr. Fox: Let me make this abundantly clear so there is no misunderstanding—if you are still in NYC tomorrow morning, this is over, and it will be because you refused to listen. This can be so simple and all wonderful by Monday if you just continue to listen and do as instructed. I am telling you that you have today to wrap there. I must pick you up tonight, even if late is ok. If you wrench this, it wrenches the Nadia and Jeffrey call, and shares and the buyout and literally everything. Like shit dominoes. I warned you when you went back to the city—do as instructed. Do not get caught in the trap of thinking you have anything else more important to do than what I ask of you.

Me: Payroll is taking a long time. I have to pee, and I'm entering in the data as fast as I can.

Mr. Fox: Finish payroll. I will touch base with you a few hours from now. And again—this is all wrapped up on Monday, HEA, unless you interfere. Although I should spell it interFEAR. Stay calm. Do as instructed. It's that simple. XO Leon says he loves you.

* * *

The next correspondence I have is not until five days later. Mr. Fox must have taken me away after all, apparently to Boston. I recall a couple of days at the Lenox hotel in the Back Bay. I remember being in that hotel, and Mr. Fox calling Nadia pretending to be the fabulously wealthy buyer, Michael Caledonia, discussing the terms to buy her out. I remember this because it felt so crazy, awful, and weird. Mr. Fox, as this Caledonia character, was—in front of me—saying how unstable I seemed and getting Nadia to agree with him. It was like he was intentionally trying to prove to me that she was not my friend, because she wasn't—from what I could tell—defending me. To be fair, I was behaving erratically, and that money had been taken out of the restaurant accounts, so I can't exactly blame her for siding with him.

From the next few Gchats, on May 11, it appears I was back in New York and that we were planning a trip to Miami to meet Jeffrey, whose company headquarters were located there. Mr. Fox had already corresponded with him as Michael Caledonia, both by phone and via email. The meeting was meant to be about Mr. Fox (or rather, Michael Caledonia) buying everyone out. It seems Mr. Fox wanted me to come back to Foxwoods, or somewhere, and travel with him to Miami, whereas I just wanted to fly directly from New York.

```
Mr. Fox: You are getting picked up tonight. You went back. You
did your stuff. Now you getting picked up and we going tomorrow.

Me: I'm not getting picked up. I'm going to LaGuardia.

Mr. Fox: you said you wouldn't do this. YOU SAID THAT YOU
WOULDN'T DO THIS. YOU WENT BACK THERE AND FUCKING BOOM.
BULLSHIT. I SAID IF I CHANGED ANYTHING ABOUT TRANSPORT NOT TO
FUCK WITH ME. AND THAT IS EXACTLY WHAT YOU ARE DOING.

Me: I said I would fly to Miami no issue.

Mr. Fox: YOU ARE GETTING PICKED UP. YOU ARE LEAVING WITH ME TO
MIAMI OUT OF WHERE I SAY

Me: I'm not going back to Foxwoods. / I'm not going back to
Foxwoods. / or Mohegan. / You're depriving me of hours of sleep
and I do not want to go back there. / I will fly to Miami. /
Like I said. / Please reply to Jeffrey. / It's rude not to.

Mr. Fox: I LOOKED YOU IN THE EYE AND SAID, IF YOU GO BACK TO
NYC AND CHANGE SOMETHING THAT YOU WILL GIVE ME BULLSHIT AND MAKE
DEMANDS. YOU SAID YOU WOULD NOT. YOU ARE DOING JUST THAT.

Me: No you said I need to get on the plane to go to Miami. Which
I'm happy to do. I'm doing everything I said I would do.
```

Mr. Fox: CALL ME RIGHT NOW.

Mr. Fox: NOW.

Mr. Fox: RIGHT NOW.

Mr. Fox: NOW.

Mr. Fox: CALL

Mr. Fox: NOW

Mr. Fox: I am not fucking with you.

Mr. Fox: call me right now.

Mr. Fox: I will not ask again.

There are no more chats until two days later. By then, I was in Miami.

CHAPTER SIXTY-SIX

MAY 2015

MIAMI

I hadn't backed down about the airport. Mr. Fox had given in, and we had two tickets to fly from LaGuardia airport. We stood in the long line to go through security. I understood the plan was to discuss the buyout with Jeffrey. There was some snafu involving Nadia, who had told Mr. Fox that she didn't want to be bought out unless she was paid a significant premium. I wanted to ask Mr. Fox "Hey, what about all that *problem with a price tag* shit?" But he would have just told me we weren't quite there yet.

I didn't understand why we needed to go all the way to Miami. Couldn't this—whatever was getting sorted out—be handled over the phone? But no, he said Nadia's refusal to budge on her high price was problematic. He wanted Jeffrey to review the investment documents and advise on whether there was a way around her, to force a buyout. Or something.

Mr. Fox had already introduced himself to Jeffrey over email as Michael Caledonia, so we'd of course be pretending that was his name. While awkward, this didn't seem like a big deal. Again, if everyone was getting repaid, what did it matter if his name was Shane Fox, Anthony Strangis, Michael Caledonia, or Donald Duck?

* * *

I was in my usual zoned-out, queasy state—the constant low-grade panic that was all day every day—as we shuffled forward in line.

That morning, I had left the Twenty-Eighth Street apartment with my One Lucky Duck tote bag—laptop and work things inside—along with one carry-on: a big canvas Bain Capital bag with a thick shoulder strap that I still had from my time working there over fifteen years earlier. I'd packed only a few dresses, extra sneakers, and not much more, but still somehow the weight of it all felt heavy. Mr. Fox never carried anything for me. I can't recall a single time he ever took a bag from my hands or off my shoulders to relieve me. Never mind that he was carrying... *wait, why wasn't he carrying anything at all?* Just as it was registering that Mr. Fox had nothing at all with him, he stepped back, away from me, almost ceremoniously, while looking at me.

My eyes widened as if to say, *What are you doing?*

In a low voice, he said, "You got this. Just be cool, Sarm. You're on your own. You got this."

"You're not *coming*?" I asked, the familiar sense of dread washing through me. "*Why?*"

He didn't give me a reason. "This is the play, Sarm. This is the play."

I was confused. He hadn't been looking at his phone, so it wasn't like he'd just gotten a message, some urgent reason to stay behind. I froze in place. I wanted to get out of the line too, but if I did, I'd lose my place. I didn't want to fuck up. I was always afraid of fucking up.

"You got this, Sarm," he repeated, staring into my eyes while taking another step back. Then he turned and walked away.

* * *

The way that played out made it seem as if it was what he'd intended all along. My guess would be that he didn't want to face Jeffrey in person. Jeffrey is rather savvy and sharp. Maybe the sociopathic con artist knows when someone just might see through their bullshit or ask too many questions that can't be deflected.

I stood there, wondering what I was supposed to say about this to Jeffrey, wondering what I was supposed to say at all. I recalled that a few days earlier, Mr. Fox had asked me if I thought Jeffrey was the kind of person who would take cash. *Two million dollars in cash?* Who knows. But now I wondered... was I supposed to ask him this crazy question? I wasn't even clear what I was supposed to be accomplishing on this trip, now on my own.

When I picked up my phone from the bin on the other side of the security check, there was a message from Mr. Fox.

```
May 13, 2016

From: Mr. Fox

To: Me

There will be a room at the Ritz waiting for you to check
into in Miami. I will email the details. Take comfort in
knowing you made the correct decision to back this play.
Remember—I will fuck with you right up until the end. It's
mandatory. But I won't fuck you over. Just keep your head
down and raincoat on. Soon the rain will be over and the sun
comes out. I'm extremely proud of you right now. And I've
never felt more confident in you. Stay positive.

XO
```

Mr. Fox writing, "*I will fuck with you right up until the end,*" and then, "*But I won't fuck you over*"—these served as handy excuses for whatever happened, for whatever he planned to make me do. Following it with "*I'm extremely proud of you right now*" was just added reinforcement, to get me to keep holding it all together.

I flew to Miami next to an empty seat. I didn't know then that I'd never set foot in that Twenty-Eighth Street apartment again, or that I wouldn't be back in New York for a very long time.

* * *

After arriving in Miami and checking into my hotel room, I opened my laptop and wrote to Mr. Fox letting him know I'd arrived. He replied, "*At some point today I need wiring instructions for the new accounts. Account numbers and routing, addresses and such. You can email them. Please make sure it's clear and each is separate from the other.*"

This request felt consistent with Mr. Fox lining things up to finally get funds flowing back to me and back to the business—to repay everyone and to buy out the investors. Therefore, it felt comforting. Probably, that was the point—to put me at ease.

He then instructed me on how to speak to Jeffrey. The main focus seemed to be getting Jeffrey's advice on the issue with Nadia. But I was still unclear why I'd had to fly all the way to Miami for this conversation, and why with Jeffrey. Couldn't any lawyer have advised on this? I was nervous about seeing Jeffrey.

* * *

The next morning, I walked a few blocks from my hotel to the restaurant space Jeffrey was building out. It was massive—still under construction—and on its way to becoming a multilevel restaurant called Komodo. Before we talked about anything else, Jeffrey took me on a long-winded tour of the space. I remember feeling kind of relieved that he tends to talk a lot. So I just followed him around, trying to concentrate enough to ask a few relevant questions.

"What are those up there?" I asked, pointing to what looked like hovercrafts jutting out into the high-ceilinged space. It reminded me of the Jetsons.

"Those are going to be the nests," he said. He explained that the restaurant would seat people in these cylindrical hovering platforms. It all looked very space age, still in the white plaster stage. The space would eventually be transformed into a dark nightclub of a restaurant with an Asian jungle feel.

Finally, we stepped out of the construction site and into the lobby of the adjacent office building, sitting on a sleek leather bench. I handed Jeffrey copies of the short legal agreement I'd executed with Nadia for her shares of the new company. He scanned it quickly. A lawyer by background, he was good at this.

His conclusion was favorable. Meaning, it seemed like there was a way to force a buyout if she continued to resist. I barely recall what else was said. I'm sure I danced around the topic of Michael Caledonia, giving only vague responses when asked. I genuinely cannot stand lying, nor am I any good at it. Plus, I'm terrified of getting called out. I think this is probably healthy.

Jeffrey had been expecting to meet Michael Caledonia, but before I'd even arrived in Miami, Mr. Fox had emailed Jeffrey telling him he'd been delayed "by business" and wouldn't make it. Now the plan was for them to meet back in New York, as Jeffrey was traveling there soon to his newly opened location of Asia de Cuba on Lafayette Street. Fine. Great. I hoped that would happen—that Mr. Fox would pay Jeffrey, and then everyone else, and this would all be over.

I was aware that I'd been promised far more than just everyone getting repaid and owning my company free and clear. So, I also quietly hoped this was just the beginning. Either way, I was uncomfortable about leaving the restaurant when it had only just reopened. It felt like leaving your teenagers home alone—you *hope* everything's going okay, but you worry. And I really wanted to get back to Leon. This trip seemed like a waste—a flight and hotel just to have one conversation. But oh well. I'd done it, and without Mr. Fox. I just wanted to go home.

Instead, Mr. Fox told me I had to stay put in Miami a little longer. I didn't like waiting. I tried to remind myself, *Everything is going to be okay.* I thought about going somewhere to get food. Maybe I'd walk around, since this was my first time in Miami. But this feeling—of needing to pass the time and wait, while everything was on the line—was hauntingly familiar to the one I'd had in Naples. Back then, I'd also been waiting for Mr. Fox to deliver. As if he was galloping through the streets of New York on a unicorn spreading pixie dust to wipe away my past, unveiling my new utopian future.

I spent the following day wandering around Miami, walking to the beach, distracting myself, avoiding thoughts of what might be happening back in New York. The next morning, I woke up to an email from Mr. Fox (which I have because, again, for some reason I'd taken a screenshot of it... thank you, former self!).

```
May 16, 2015

From: Mr. Fox

To: Me

Subject: plan going forward.

You cannot be in the city. It makes you and us vulnerable.
Nadia's moves were not good but we, I, we, handled them. I
need you in Miami for the next few days. I am meeting with
Jeffrey on Monday and Nadia on Tuesday. Once I have finalized
everything and it's safe and done then you come back. It's
only a few more days and it's only because Nadia pulled
bullshit. But we handled it. But I only was able to because
you listened and did as instructed. You are doing great.

This is not up for debate. I must handle this. You must not
be available while I am handling it or it will go to shit
100%.

I am going to take a nap. I have a thing at 10am and I didn't
sleep much. I will be off comms until 5pm. Stay cool and
extend room an extra day for now. That's a direct order. Not
to be a dick, but it is. I will be off comms and cannot argue
with you. You must extend a day.

XOXO
```

I was used to this with Mr. Fox—plans *always* in flux. Everything changing last minute. This drives me bonkers even in any normal situation. I like plans and structure. I replied to him about an hour later, writing *"extended for one day."*

I didn't know what he meant when he wrote "Nadia pulled bullshit," but it was okay because I'd done as "instructed" and was doing "great." What did I do? What was the drama?

Looking back through my emails from that time, I received one from Nadia in which she made it clear she was furious (and rightly so) that I had removed her online bank account viewing access. She also referred to my having previously "stolen" company funds for personal use. She must have been referring to the $50,000 that Mr. Fox had made me take out, only to try to explain it afterward. I replied, telling her I had no idea what she was talking about, that I hadn't removed her from the accounts. Because, in fact, I had *not* removed her from the accounts. Mr. Fox must have done it. When I sent my reply, I copied the Michael Caledonia email, since they'd been speaking. I wanted "Michael Caledonia" to explain the $50,000, to handle it all.

From there, he must have spoken to her. I don't recall speaking to her. I don't recall much from this time at all, but I know I'd have been freaked out, so I must have told Mr. Fox he had to call her. Maybe I had texts with her too—ones I no longer have.

I wonder if it registered in my mind back then that she used the word "stolen" and what the implications of that could be. I imagine it was another jolt of fear into my system. It seems like the more afraid I was, the more I disconnected from reality.

* * *

There's nothing much in Gchat from that time, which means we must have been mainly texting, a history I don't have.

But two days later Mr. Fox emailed me (again, recovered via a screenshot).

May 18, 2015

From: Mr. Fox

To: Me

Subject: Jeffrey

I am meeting Jeffrey at his new restaurant tonight. Asia de Cuba. Meeting around 8pm. He said he is convinced he can handle Nadia and get her to walk away for her initial investment plus 5-10K for her troubles.

I will keep you posted.

Also, I spoke with Nadia about the funds that were removed from your account. She asked if I would pursue making you return them via doing appearances for free or something or "if I even cared." I told her I did not and that once you are bought out it doesn't matter. She agreed. Send positive energy today all day please.

XO

I replied to him the following morning.

May 19, 2015

From: Me

To: Mr. Fox

If I supposedly sold my personal shares, why would I have to return the funds? You were supposed to deposit the funds last week for five shares, so once that went in it would be covered? Or not? I don't understand. :-/

Also, I think payroll is like 50-60K, there's not enough in the accounts now.

Can I get a flight tomorrow?

*　*　*

Mr. Fox never met with Jeffrey or Nadia. I don't know what happened. But without Mr. Fox taking care of everything, I was all the way out on a limb, with no way to explain away the funds I'd removed, or what was going on.

I have no more Gchats. The very last exchange is from May 24, five days after I asked him if I could get a flight home.

Mr. Fox: you here?

I never replied. That's the end of our Gchat history.

I have no recollection of leaving Miami, but I know Mr. Fox instructed me—or perhaps he booked the flight himself—to fly into Bradley airport in Connecticut instead of one of the New York airports. I should have been heading back to New York, and straight back to the restaurant. Instead, Mr. Fox made me go to, of all places, Foxwoods.

CHAPTER SIXTY-SEVEN

JUNE 2015
CONNECTICUT

Per Mr. Fox's instruction, I met him at Foxwoods. I don't remember any of this—the details, how I felt. Probably because this was when it all came apart for good. It wasn't until years later that I found clues to jog my memory.

* * *

Jumping ahead—years later—to the COVID-19 shutdown of 2020, I found even more material that I hadn't known I had. In addition to writing this book, I'd also been digging up materials for an upcoming "documentary" about what happened—this story. It's an awfully strange thing to be the subject of a documentary. By this time, I'd sat for my first on-camera interview—a grueling, wildly awkward twelve-hour day—and most of the filming was completed. Fortunately, the timing worked out such that the filmmakers had just begun the long slog of editing when the world shut down.

Questions and more questions came, and requests for still more information. All of this was time consuming—digging up old photos, looking for copies of this or that. I had in my possession a set of electronic files, copies of *evidence* I'd been given only after the entire legal ordeal was over. I'd peeked at them before, with the help of a tech expert, since the format was such that I couldn't just pop in a drive and scroll through them. I knew there was a lot there, and I didn't really want to go looking again, but under pressure from the filmmakers—and knowing it would probably be useful in writing this story too—I went back to it.

By "it" I mean a very old PC laptop on which these files had been downloaded, along with some fancy software, since a Mac wouldn't read them. It's one of those PCs that you turn on and can feel the effort it takes to power up, a reluctance as the fan sputters to life and the parts slowly begin to engage. Like waking up a grumpy old man snoozing on the porch of an ancient motel, and he struggles out of a rocking chair, slowly shuffling to the front desk to get you what you need.

On the laptop were files within files, none of them labeled in any way that made sense. Much of it was boring. But then I'd open a file that was a jackpot of icky material. As in, the contents of one of Mr. Fox's iPhones, including photos he took, screenshots, and more. There was so much. It felt vaguely *wrong* to be looking through it. Yet of course I was more than justified to look, to see what the fuck was there. Because much of it was about me.

There was a file of .mov clips. Videos. Maybe twenty or so. When I clicked on the first one, I realized these were videos I'd never seen. They were *of me*, clearly unaware I was being filmed. I felt sick.

I didn't bother taking any deep breaths or steeling myself; I just clicked on one after the other, wanting to rush through as fast as possible, to extinguish the dread of not knowing what I might find.

* * *

There were some short nonsense clips, but the longer ones were… *disturbing.*

In these videos, I was either crying or had clearly just been crying, and completely out of it. Some were filmed at my mother's house. Others in hotel rooms. One I recognize as either Foxwoods or Mohegan Sun. Another looked like a Residence Inn. I don't know exactly when these were taken, when I was sobbing desperately and looking out of it. It was hard to know, because that happened a lot.

Watching the videos was strange. Much of it I didn't remember, but some brought the memories back. In one video I'd apparently just sort of… propelled a large quantity of Ambien into my mouth, straight from the plastic orange jar, like it was a shot of tequila.

I remember this, but don't remember *when* it happened or to what I was reacting. The clips weren't in a timeline or dated. At first, I thought these must have been filmed just after I returned from Miami, before he took me away. But then… the more I think about it, the more I think they were mostly from the previous summer, when he had me spending so much time at the casinos, traveling back and forth. But I don't know. Some were filmed at my mother's house. In one video, Mr. Fox's voice behind the phone camera tells me not to scratch my face. It looks like he started filming just after I may have clawed at my own face in some kind of desperate agony—which, oddly, feels vaguely familiar, like I can remember doing that. But on the video, I was just sobbing, hands covering my face.

Does it matter which agonizing period those videos were from? Not really.

What I still don't understand is: (a) why no one showed these to me, *before* I pled guilty. Why did my attorneys not show these to me? Why was I not given the opportunity to look through all this material back then? And (b) how could the prosecution have watched these and still believed I deserved to spend one to three years incarcerated? *Three years?* Couldn't they see I'd practically already been in jail, just a different kind? A worse kind? Because as I later found out, life at Rikers was far less stressful and painful than life with Mr. Fox.

This is exactly the reason that the other side of these experiences is so isolating. Most people can't comprehend how someone could end up trapped in a hell without physical barriers. The ones who *do* understand are the ones who've been there themselves.

* * *

I have no recollection of arriving at Foxwoods or how long he kept me there. Maybe a day or two, maybe over a week. I don't know. All I know is that I didn't go back to New York, and wouldn't be back there for a long time, though I didn't know this at the time. I'm sure I was confused, that's a given. You'd think that after getting the restaurant reopened, I'd have *walked* back to New York from Connecticut if I'd had to. If I'd known that was what it would have taken to save it, and to save myself, I would have.

Never mind that by this time I'd been depleted of strength. I was a brittle husk of a human—one that would crumble to dust at the slightest breeze. I'm pretty sure the video he took of me having just tried to take a bunch of Ambien was from this time. It would make sense.

I *needed* relief. From Mr. Fox and from the petrifying debts I'd incurred, through deception I'd never intended. All that "money-whipping" he kept promising needed to start. Now. Everyone needed to be repaid. I desperately wanted to feel safe again.

I vaguely remember waiting for Mr. Fox with my bag packed, standing in the fluorescent-lit food court at Foxwoods. Somehow, he'd said words to soothe me, to convince this was *it*. We were—finally—done. I let myself believe him, that it was here—this was the moment. All the hell I'd gone through had led to what was coming next. I'd passed all the tests. I'd willed myself to believe it was true. That momentarily, I'd be ushered from this soulless food court at a shitty casino into… *something else.* Like the suicide bomber who believes he's doing God's work—having pulled the cord and, for a stretched-out, slowed-down slice of time, awaits deliverance into paradise.

Doesn't the road to paradise always go through the food court at Foxwoods?

PART SIX

LEAVING THE REAL WORLD

"Don't examine your feelings. Never examine your feelings—they're no help at all. Better not to think."
—PATRICIA CAMPBELL HEARST, *EVERY SECRET THING*

CHAPTER SIXTY-EIGHT

JUNE 2015
ON THE ROAD

I stood waiting at Foxwoods, under the harsh fluorescent lights in the shitty food court. Waiting for him. Waiting for my freedom. My body buzzed with anticipation. I visualized my liberation—from the crushing fear and shame that had defined my existence for years, from the constant uncertainty, never knowing what the right move was, and the mystery of it all. I'd finally be free from *him*, at least as I'd known him.

This had to be it, the long-awaited cleansing wave of relief. Nothing else made sense. What else could there be? This was the end of the road. *This had to be it.*

And yet. It was not.

The next thing I remember, I was sitting in the front seat of a black Jeep Cherokee, a car Mr. Fox had borrowed from his friend Carlos, apparently. All I had with me was what I'd taken to Miami. Leon was still at my mother's house.

Somehow Mr. Fox delivered the news that this was *not* it, not yet (yet again). The word disappointment is far too mild. Crushing despair is more like it. The kind of despair that shuts you down completely.

I vaguely recall him saying we had to go somewhere, to leave for a while. *Leave?* He told me to think about it like time stopping—as if we just had to step out into a parallel reality for a while. *What?*

I. Could. Not. Handle. This.

I started screaming. I remember screaming like an animal. No words, not even crying. Crying would have been acceptance. This was just primal screaming.

Mr. Fox stayed quiet. As we drove along the windy roads through Connecticut, away from the casinos, he must have known that letting me scream in the containment of the car was better than whatever else I might do—like, maybe grab the wheel and swerve us into a tree.

At some point. I must have exhausted myself. The numbness set in again—the way you can feel almost drunk after an explosion of emotion. You're now devoid of all feeling. Just a blank slate of apathy. I turned away from him, resting my forehead on the passenger-side window. Outside, the vivid green whoosh of newly sprouted leaves on the trees blurred past my visual field—like a ticker tape of beautiful *life,* passing me by. Fresh springtime *life,* out of reach. It looked surreal. I didn't know if it was real or just a figment of my imagination, since Mr. Fox had been telling me *nothing is real.* I just stared, eyes open but only semiconscious, watching the technicolor emerald show whizz by as we drove away from Foxwoods.

I didn't know where we were going. There was nothing I could do. Or, there *was.* There was always something I *could* have done, but that was not how it seemed. I could have opened the door at a red light, rolled out of the car and onto the street, and hope someone would pick me up. But then what? Maybe better to roll out and into oncoming traffic, into the path of a large truck.

I could have run away from him anytime. But where? Everyone would have been furious at me. How would anyone understand what I didn't understand myself? How would I possibly face them all—Dylan, the investors, my disappointed staff, Jeffrey, all the people who'd sent money after I'd given them my word? People who had believed in me. What would I even say if I were to leave and go running back? I didn't know where Mr. Fox was taking me. All I knew was that I wanted this to be over, even if it meant I was dead. It felt like my only option was to believe Mr. Fox would finally come through, and I just had to hang on and keep breathing. Or, he wouldn't, and I would find a way to end it myself. To end myself.

One of the last times I was at my mother's house, I'd rummaged through her bathroom cupboards, looking for old prescriptions. I'd found some and taken the bottles, hiding them in my bag. I'd had the thought that a time might come when I'd want a bunch of pills—that there must have been some combination that would do the job, and the more I had to work with, the better. I remember feeling weird taking them, even though I figured my mom wouldn't notice. But I didn't have them with me. And I'd wasted most of my own Ambien stash. I wanted an escape hatch. To just know it was there. But how? People do it all the time. Surely I could figure it out too.

At some point, I must have started asking questions, though I don't really remember any of this either. Mr. Fox told me Leon would stay at my mom's while we were on this "break," or whatever we were doing. He told me to think of it like time stopping—the rest of the world stopping—and we just had to do this thing where we went *away* for a while, a few months, maybe. He said something about multiple timelines all happening at once. I couldn't understand what he meant, as usual. I wondered, and asked, what would happen to everything back home.

He explained it was as if we were simply stepping aside, temporarily, into an alternate space. A parallel reality. He said things like, "Just imagine we're pressing a giant *pause* button. We're just pressing *pause*, and everything will be fine."

Obviously, this didn't make sense. Nothing ever did. I was used to being confused. What was the point of even asking? For him to have taken me away from Leon like this, I must have been fully numb. I didn't know it then, but it would be over six months before I'd see Leon again. More than half a year is a reasonably large fraction of a dog's life. Of all the atrocities Mr. Fox inflicted on me, taking that Leon time away is high on the list, though it's not easy to rank them. I hate that I allowed it. I hate that I allowed *all of it*.

※ ※ ※

Nowadays it creeps me out when I stumble across claims echoing those Mr. Fox made about parallel realities. It's not hard to do in our time of increased spirituality.

Time isn't linear. You create your own reality. These concepts are discussed by everyone from Oprah to yoga instructors to Silicon Valley tech billionaires. His words may have been somewhat different, but the concept was the same. The idea that reality is fluid and malleable, that belief alone can shape the tangible world, has become mainstream—even weaponized, in some cases. He told me that what I eat doesn't matter—just like *The Secret* claims you can eat whatever you want and be thin and healthy, as long as you fully convince yourself it's true. If you just... *believe* it.

But do we really create our own realities? If so, does that mean I created Mr. Fox? What the fuck. That can't be. Still, as I write this, I sometimes find myself sliding down rabbit holes, reading about simultaneously existing infinite realities, about how we're energetically matched with the circumstances we experience. Or something like that. Now and then, I hear business leaders and highly educated people repeating these ideas too, on podcasts or in audiobooks.

Is it all nonsense, and I just got extremely unlucky in the roulette wheel of people I could have met? Or was this supposed to happen for some reason? Memes on Instagram tell me, *Everything happens* for *you. Life only gives you what you can handle.* But then, destined or not, I sometimes wonder, *Was Mr. Fox, in some way, actually enlightened about the universe and theories of quantum physics, but used this knowledge in service of darkness, instead of light?*

Or, more likely he simply studied and then weaponized these theories, knowing they gave him cover. Maybe he read about them online and figured they sounded just plausible enough to use as an excuse for why he could take me away and for why, in the end, it would magically be as if none of it had ever occurred. I vaguely recall asking him if I'd remember what was happening, and he told me my memories of it would be vague, like a dream. On that, at least, he was sort of correct.

* * *

It's not easy to write about what you can't remember very well. It feels like my subconscious remembers all of it, but I can only access a few scattered scenes, brief snippets—plus the overall numbness that had settled in. Once this road trip was fully underway, I'm pretty sure I hardly cried at all.

Miraculously, I was able to mostly put Leon out of my mind. I'd always been good at denial, but this was different, and more extreme. It wasn't just Leon; it was my entire life. All of it—like some abstract story somewhere other than at the forefront of my mind. I existed only in the present, taking in what was in front of me, as we traveled to who knows where. Psychologically it was too painful to think of my past or future. My entire world was the world inside that car, and Mr. Fox, and what I saw passing by out the windows.

And then, one hotel after another.

Somehow, I don't think this is what Eckhart Tolle meant by *The Power of Now*.

CHAPTER SIXTY-NINE

SUMMER 2015

ON OUR WAY

Mr. Fox told me to pick a name. I couldn't go by my own name in this new reality. I didn't know why I needed a new name, but finally I said, "Emma." That had been my Starbucks name. A barista once misheard me and wrote *Emma* on the cup, after which I realized it was just easier to say Emma.

For a last name, I picked *Donovan*. No reason—I just liked it.

Emma Donovan. All of this was very weird.

My cell phone and laptop were all that connected me to the world I'd left behind, but not for long. On the first night—or maybe the second—in one of the hotels where we stopped, Mr. Fox *accidentally* spilled his Diet Coke all over my laptop. And it was not okay. It was fried. Normally, this would have unleashed a spiral of tears, angst, and woe (if you've ever done this, you know)—but I barely reacted. It was just one more thing. One more shitty thing. He told me it didn't matter. He took the broken laptop from me, and that was that. I didn't look at my email again for nearly a year.

He also took my phone. I don't remember how this happened, but I probably didn't put up a fight. I'd just given up.

A few weeks later, he got me a new phone so I could communicate with him. But it wasn't connected to my previous Apple ID and contained zero contacts other than Mr. Fox. Eventually he got me an iPad too, on which I played games and watched an endless stream of shows. It kept me occupied, like a child who might otherwise get restless and cry.

He must have lectured me that I had to be good. I wasn't allowed to lose my shit and scream. I'd been subdued. He praised me for being *good*. Which meant *docile*. I didn't want what was happening to be real, so it was probably easier to lean into the idea that it wasn't. I didn't react or get mad at him for anything, even for the small, annoying shit, which he did in abundance. Getting mad would have taken energy, and I had none left. I was operating on autopilot.

I didn't know where we were heading, but I had a feeling that eventually we'd end up in Las Vegas—a feeling that turned out to be correct. How long it took to get there, I don't know. Sometimes we stayed a few days in one town or another. No clue why.

We spent over a week in a small Texas town, the name of which, gun to my head, I'd never recall. Later, we spent a few days in Arizona. Most of the time we stayed at Marriott hotels, usually Residence Inns. These were the kind set up as mini apartments, meant for business travelers. Sometimes, if I was lucky, it would be a suite with two bedrooms. If not, at least there was usually a separate bedroom. Mr. Fox always took the bedroom, while I slept on the pullout couch. A few unfortunate times, we ended up in a single room, no doors to separate us. On those nights, I took one of the small pile of Ambien pills I had left. Not surprisingly, Mr. Fox snored loudly, and it was torture. In one hotel, I slept on the floor of the bathroom. We asked for a roll-away bed—the kind that folds up with a narrow mattress, which hotels usually have if you ask. I dragged the mattress off its wheeled metal frame and maneuvered it into the bathroom. With ear plugs in and the door closed, I could sleep. I could feel safe.

I'm pretty sure I spoke to no one at all back home during our travels west. I know now that Mr. Fox was using my email, writing to people as me. He also had my cell phone, and to this day, I have no idea how long it remained active or what messages he sent from it. One text I later saw. It had been submitted as evidence to the grand jury by an employee. When I saw it, I felt sick. From the date, I knew it had been Mr. Fox texting, pretending to be me. It was nauseating to read. I can only imagine what other things he wrote, and to whom. Actually, I *don't* want to imagine this, or think about it at all. But sometimes I wonder about some of the people who later either never reached out to me or treated me coldly when I reached out to them. Were they recipients of messages from *him* as *me*? Unless those people tell me, I'll never know. But if any of them are reading this now... it was some point in June of 2015, after which nothing from that phone number or my email address was actually from me. It was from him, pretending to be me. Please believe me.

* * *

Recently, someone asked if I'd ever been to the Grand Canyon. I have a funny feeling that, on that road trip from hell with Mr. Fox, we indeed stopped there and took a peek. But I'm not sure. You'd think I'd recall seeing the Grand fucking Canyon. But I don't. Maybe it's a photograph I'm seeing in my mind, and we didn't stop there. But I think we did. I don't know.

* * *

When I asked for specifics about what would happen to everything back home, Mr. Fox was vague, acting like it was no big deal. He told me not to worry, it would all be there intact when we were done with this trip. At one point I asked about my trademarks and URL and so on, and he gave me the same answer. It would all be there. But then, he said we should think about getting me a new tattoo, something bigger to cover up the duck on my arm. *What?*

I did *not* want to get a new tattoo. Fuck that. I didn't know why this was necessary, but he said I should keep it covered, so I said *fine*. I'd just keep a fucking bandage on it. I didn't mind covering it temporarily. Strangers had always asked about it—*Hey, why a duck?* I didn't want to have to answer that now, or to even think about it.

Before long, I stopped asking questions. Nothing made sense. I knew it never would. I'd never get clear answers. And eventually, I no longer wanted answers. I don't remember if we listened to the radio while driving, or what. I think we listened to the radio. At rest stops, I bought booklets of word puzzles and sudoku. Reading in a moving car has always made me feel nauseated, but for some reason, I could do puzzles. Anything to occupy my mind.

If we stopped at a restaurant, I ordered beer. That helped too. Usually, it was a Chili's. There were so many Chili's dotting the country, each one indistinguishable from the last. Mr. Fox always ordered chicken fajitas. I got steamed broccoli, beans and rice, and two or three Coronas with limes.

I have zero clue how much money Mr. Fox had when we left, but my impression was that it wasn't much, since he was frugal along the way. I don't remember if he was paying cash or with a credit card.

Mostly, I was just going through the motions of existing. I took care of things like doing our laundry whenever the hotels had laundry rooms. I tried to do it as often as possible because Mr. Fox's jeans always stank. Never mind his underwear. I kept a towel in the front of the car in case he ever asked me to sit in the driver's seat for any reason. Thankfully he never asked me to drive. Either way, I didn't want to sit directly on the leather seat, which had absorbed all his stink.

I always felt bad for the hotel housekeeping staff when it came time to clean his rooms. I've always been the sort of person who tidies up before leaving—putting trash in the bins, stacking used towels on the bathroom counter—and then leaves a good tip. Mr. Fox was the opposite. More than once I witnessed him throwing trash, like an empty potato chip bag, behind the bed, as if intentionally making life miserable for a housekeeper. I never saw him leave a tip.

Since I was also diligent about making sure nothing was left behind, checking under beds and in drawers, I usually fetched much of the trash Mr. Fox left behind. He objected, telling me to just leave it, but I couldn't. Most of this trip is a blur, but one pre-checkout moment seared itself in my memory. I pulled open the drawer beside the bed where Mr. Fox had been sleeping, and a mostly full Snapple bottle rolled to the back. *Why would he put a bottle of Snapple in the drawer?* I wondered, grabbing it. Twisting off the cap, I noticed the amber color inside conflicted with the pink label advertising the flavor: raspberry.

Mr. Fox was in the room.

"Leave it," he said.

But it was too late. I recoiled at the stench, realizing... it was full of his piss. He'd *peed* in the Snapple bottle. I glared at him.

"What?" he said. "I didn't want to get out of bed in the middle of the night."

Even though the bathroom was only a few feet away.

"We're not in fucking Antarctica!" I said.

Horrified, I held my breath and dumped it in the toilet. If only that had been the grossest thing I found.

Later, during longer stays, I started handling housekeeping myself—swapping out towels and grabbing extra toilet paper—just to avoid anyone else dealing with Mr. Fox's mess, or coming into our rooms. One day, while gathering towels to exchange for fresh ones, I got on the floor to reach a pile shoved all the way under the sink console in Mr. Fox's bathroom. They were hard to reach. *Why the fuck did he throw them all the way under the sink?* I wondered. Then I noticed the stench. And then I saw the brown streaks. *Oh hell no.*

* * *

Even now, the tabloid narratives frame it as if I fled on some romantic escapade with this man, Bonnie and Clyde style. Those same narratives often also suggest, or outright claim, that we *ran off* with loads of money, implying I was living large and having the time of my life.

I unequivocally was not.

* * *

As week after week passed, I occasionally wondered if I could just maybe vanish into obscurity. Maybe I could disappear off the grid, with a new identity, into a new life. I could work an anonymous job, existing in a zombie state until I died. It felt like this was an in-between option—somewhere between killing myself, which felt too scary, and facing the reality of being myself, and everything that had happened.

In *Every Secret Thing*, Patricia Hearst's memoir about being abducted by the Symbionese Liberation Army, she wrote, "I taught myself to live without thinking beyond the present moment. One can function that way day by day. I did not think of my parents, my sisters, my friends. I did not think of escaping. It never occurred to me to pick up a submachine gun and blast the two people I hated so much, who sat there with their backs to me, unprotected."

Not that there was a machine gun lying around, but I understand this. It's why the question *Why didn't you run away from him?* almost doesn't make sense to me. As if someone is asking why I didn't just blast myself into outer space. *Was that an option?*

Beyond not thinking, I also wasn't feeling—at least, most of the time. I moved along and did what I was told, like a robot. But every so often, I *did* feel something. As if the hard shell protecting my psyche cracked a tiny bit, briefly allowing emotions to seep out before snapping back shut.

One time I remember almost as if it were a movie scene. We'd stopped somewhere in the middle of the country. I've since done some research, and I think it was the Horseshoe Casino in St. Louis, Missouri. I remember Mr. Fox pointing out the moat of water surrounding the casino, which was basically a massive structure floating on water, connected to the river, designed that way to comply with local laws that prohibit gambling on land.

Mr. Fox went to *take care of some business* and check us into the hotel. He told me to wait for him in the lobby cafe. There were no waiters, only a counter to order and pick up food, with a bunch of high-top tables, under bright fluorescent lights. I sat down on a stool at one of the empty tables and waited. I was wearing what I always wore: a summer dress and sneakers. My feet dangling off the stool, I felt like a child. There was a metal basket of fruit on the counter, and I considered buying a banana. *Should I buy a banana?* But then I'd want something to drink too. Mr. Fox could be back at any moment, or, as sometimes happened, he could be gone for hours. I sat still and watched people.

I noticed three older Black women walk in. They looked like good friends, in their sixties, maybe, like moms, maybe also grandmothers. All three were heavy. Not so much *fat* as just substantial, with big, matronly bosoms. They seemed in good spirits—perhaps at the casino for an afternoon of fun—chatting, laughing, and smiling as they looked at the menu on the wall, purses hooked over elbows. They looked like they'd dressed up for the occasion, makeup on, hair done. They also just looked *nice*—like they were *kind* women. The kind who took good care of their families.

Watching them, I felt something rise in my chest—a sort of ache. It felt like longing—a painful longing that I didn't quite understand. I realized I might cry. I sat motionless, tensed, trying *not* to cry. I'd been programmed to know I wasn't supposed to show emotion in public, the kind that might draw attention. But what if I *did* cry, and what if they noticed? I imagined this scenario unfolding.

I imagined them noticing me. In my mind I saw their laughter pause, smiles replaced by concern, exchanging glances before heading toward me. In this daydream, I stood up to meet them, and saw myself stepping in, *falling* into their open arms, sobbing into their pillowy bosoms. All concern and love, they would hug me, comfort me, and treat me like a lost and hurt child, reassuring me it would all be okay; they would take care of me.

They would know, without asking, that I needed to be rescued. If Mr. Fox appeared, they would see him for what he was. They would yell at him, whack him with their purses, and take me away. They'd take me home, fuss over me, feed me, and protect me.

None of that happened, of course. They made their purchases and merrily walked out, having never even looked my way. I waited a while longer until Mr. Fox finally appeared and, with just his glance, summoned me. Time to go.

CHAPTER SEVENTY

AUGUST–SEPTEMBER 2015
LAS VEGAS

It must have been late July when we arrived in Las Vegas. Or early August. I'm not sure. I had never been to Vegas. I'd always figured it was something I'd eventually do in some capacity related to the restaurant business. Or perhaps just to see it once, then cross it off a list, never to return. I certainly never imagined in a million years I'd basically *live* in Vegas—for more than six months.

We approached the city at night. After hours of driving through the darkness, the sudden burst of flashing lights and giant LED screens felt jarring, like crossing into another dimension. What felt overwhelming was the density of people, after weeks of small towns and long, empty highways. It was unsettling being in a city where I could, theoretically, run into someone I knew. This made Mr. Fox's explanation of being in a parallel reality harder to reconcile.

I think we had run out of money. Mr. Fox seemed uncertain whether he could use his casino credentials to get us a room, and I vaguely recall a discussion about whether we'd have to sleep in the car. Thankfully, he managed to get us a room. I think it was the MGM Grand. I don't remember the rest of the night, or waking up the next morning, or how anything felt. Just the bright, nearly blinding daylight—the sun hot and relentless—as we repacked the car and headed out.

Mr. Fox drove us to a pawn shop somewhere off the Strip. He told me to go inside and pawn my Rolex. It wasn't the one he'd given me, which he'd taken back long ago. It was a watch my first husband had given me. A pre-owned, brushed silver Oyster, a man's watch with a chip in the glass face. I loved that watch—classy and understated, the opposite of the flashy kind Mr. Fox wore. It had both history and sentimental value. And now I had to give it away to this crappy pawn shop.

Mr. Fox assured me it was just temporary. Of course, Mr. Fox said we'd buy it back. He added, as usual, that none of this mattered, because none of it was real anyway. I'd get it all back in the end, *when this was all over.* Not just the watch, but everything, and more.

So, I went in and pawned my vintage silver Rolex. The shop gave me a receipt with a schedule and a deadline—I had the option to buy it back, the price increasing over time, before it became theirs to sell.

I think I got $800 for it. Maybe $1,000. Whatever the amount, as soon as I got back in the car, I dutifully handed the roll of bills to Mr. Fox.

* * *

I don't know where Mr. Fox got more money to get us settled in Vegas. Maybe gambling. Maybe, as I've since learned, from my mother—who sent actual cash, sandwiched between old photographs and papers, wrapped in a bundle and mailed via UPS. I didn't know this then—I wasn't speaking to anyone back home yet—but I do now. It breaks my heart that she did this, based on whatever lies Mr. Fox was feeding her. All the while believing it was to help *me.*

We spent a couple of weeks at a dive-y casino off the Strip called Palace Station. It was like the cheap motel of casinos, with a section off to one side that really *was* a cheap motel—two levels of rooms stretching out, surrounded by parking. The unfortunate part was that we only had one room, but at least it had two beds. After a week or two, we moved into rooms at the much nicer tower. Mr. Fox got himself a suite—it had a huge bathroom and a hot tub, the kind with jets to move the water. I had a simple adjoining room. That was fine with me, I was just grateful to finally have my own space, and a door to close between us. I wasn't allowed to lock the door, ever, but at least I could keep it closed.

Palace Station is noteworthy for being the place where OJ Simpson got arrested in 2007, apparently in one of the motel-style rooms. I've since learned, through my basic research, that the motel part of the hotel no longer exists, having been demolished in 2017.

The casino had a poker room, and it was there that I learned to play. There were no high-roller tables, since no actual high rollers would likely set foot in Palace Station. But some tables had lower stakes than others, and I played at the lowest ones. I wasn't trying to win money, just to learn the game and hold onto my chips long enough to keep me occupied. But I turned out to be better at it than I'd expected. More often than not, I ended up ahead by the end of the day.

To play, one had to get a player's card, for which an ID was required—so my real name was in their system. But if anyone at the table asked, I still gave the name Emma. I sat there for hours, watching the various characters at the table, sucking on lollipops, and sometimes drinking beer, since it was free at the tables.

I don't know what Mr. Fox was doing all this time. He only occasionally came into the room to play—the stakes probably too low to hold his interest. What stands out in my memory is that when he did play, he lost his chips *fast*. This surprised me, considering he'd portrayed himself as some kind of master poker player. I think he simply lacked the patience to *not* bet every hand. With nothing else to do, I had endless patience to play only the good hands, and as my confidence grew, I occasionally tried bluffing, sometimes winning that way. Overall, I mostly broke even.

Eating healthy in Vegas wasn't easy back then, especially on a budget. Like every casino, Palace Station had a massive buffet, but this one had more of a high school cafeteria vibe. Mr. Fox loaded up on fried chicken and big piles of gooey macaroni and cheese. I stuck to the salad bar, piling chickpeas, beans, and broccoli on lettuce. Then I went back to fill an entire dinner plate with watermelon slices, eating them all. I also took squares of cornbread back to the table, stealthily wrapping them in paper napkins and stashing them in my bag to take back up to the room for later. The buffet was usually my one meal of the day.

We stayed at Palace Station for weeks at a time, I think getting our rooms comped because Mr. Fox gambled a lot at the slot machines. I suppose that's just a different way to pay. Sometimes he won, of course. He still gave me the impression that he had some special magical ability to manipulate the machines in his favor. I was long past the point of questioning anything.

Mr. Fox never gave me notice when it was time to leave. He just told me we were leaving, and I packed my things. I always took the free toiletries, extra rolls of toilet paper, and sometimes even towels—a habit I'd picked up on the drive west, just in case. In case of *what*, who knows. That we'd have to sleep in the car? Thankfully, we never did.

From Palace Station we cycled through short stays at various casinos on the Strip, sometimes heading over to Henderson, then back to the Strip, then back to Palace Station, and so on. I had no idea what Mr. Fox's plan was, if any. I never asked.

Occasionally—maybe after Mr. Fox got money from who knows where—we stayed at the Wynn or the Encore in a big suite. I was happy for the couch—so soft and plush—while Mr. Fox took the massive bedroom. The only photograph I have from the entire road trip from hell is one I took using the iPad. I was in a white robe on the couch in our fancy suite at the Encore and caught my reflection in the ceiling mirror. Yes, the ceiling was mirrored. I arranged myself and snapped a photo. It's dated September 5, 2015, less than a week from my forty-third birthday.

* * *

I can't say precisely when Mr. Fox started making me do sex stuff again. I'm pretty sure it wasn't on the way to Vegas. I think it was around this time, now that we'd been gone long enough. I don't know. I remember the plush robe he took for me from Harrah's casino, a synthetic fiber blend, maybe chenille. I'd commented on how soft it was, so Mr. Fox took it when we checked out. In the rooms, I wore it constantly, almost like a security blanket. I remember the robe because, after he made me do those things, I'd angrily pick up the robe and wrap it tightly around myself before running out of his room. He never made me do stuff when we *didn't* have separate rooms, maybe knowing I'd need to get away from him after.

I never knew when it was coming. As usual with Mr. Fox, everything came with an undercurrent of foreboding and dread. He knew I preferred to drink alcohol first, so he sometimes brought me beers. When he showed up in my room with beers, I knew what he was expecting. Thankfully, it wasn't every day—definitely less than once a week. But I never knew when it was coming, when I'd be summoned.

He explained to me that it was *necessary*, because he needed my *energy*. I remember him saying this when he wanted me to sit on his face. As if I was some kind of charging station, dispensing electricity to his depleted, dark soul. *Gross*. The particular contours of the lasting damage from this kind of thing can likely only be understood by those who've experienced it—or worse, if it involved a relative. When the predator forces you to demonstrably *enjoy* what they are doing to you, it fucks with your mind. It implies a level of consent. It's fucking gross.

He sometimes pointed out that he'd just showered, as if doing me a favor. But even fresh from the shower, his personal smell was such that I associated it with everything that was happening. I couldn't stand it. Once, I remember thinking that if given the option, I'd rather be forced to have sex with any variety of objectively gross men, like... Bill Cosby, Harvey Weinstein, or the corpse of Roger Ailes. At least with them, it would be a singularly disturbing experience. New, and unfamiliar. With Mr. Fox, the recurrence of the act—the familiarity—made it that much harder to bear.

He once pointed out that not only had he just showered, but he'd shaved himself. Again, as if doing me a favor. Except then, when he forcefully did what he did, which usually made me gag and sometimes cry, it was like being punched in the face with a flabby cactus.

Of all the darkness, this is what stands out in my memory: his stupid cactus balls.

* * *

During September, we stayed for a stretch at Harrah's casino, in a massive suite with a large living room and two bedrooms on either side, each with its own bathroom and TV. I know it was September because that was where I spent my birthday. Two days before that, Stephen Colbert's new late-night show debuted on CBS, and from that night until the end of our trip, I never missed an episode, no matter what time zone we were in. Something about Stephen Colbert, with his sweet humor, was comforting.

One night, Donald Rumsfeld was a guest on the show, promoting his new app, Churchill's Solitaire. I downloaded it onto my iPad, and thus began an addiction of sorts, one with which I still wrestle. Like right now. I'd so much rather take a break to immerse myself in this double-deck version of solitaire than wade through these memories of Mr. Fox.

I would have preferred to ignore my birthday. I have no clue if I spoke to my family. I'm nearly certain I didn't. I have no idea what I would have said about where I was or what was going on. Going through my old inbox, I've since found an email from my father from that day, saying he wished he could see me. The reply—written, of course, by Mr. Fox—reads,

> I will email you once I return from Miami. I am down here on business hoping to get something new going. Sorry for the short reply. I will email more next week when i get back and hopefully i can see you sometime in the near future. XOXO.

Like all the emails Mr. Fox sent pretending to be me, it didn't sound like me. Not to mention, it would be *very* unlike me to allow an i instead of an I. The Virgo in me wouldn't have been able to handle that, no matter how depressed.

In the same email chain, there's a message from a few weeks earlier, supposedly from me to my father, which had me saying,

> I am ok but it's not been easy at all. Shane is traveling for work so right now i have little to no money for day to day things so that isn't fun. I miss Leon but where i am staying for now its best he stays in NH, I have no desire to talk about what happened at all, not yet at least. I can't focus on the past i can only focus on the future and try to move forward in a positive direction. I do not check my email regularly and my phone is off. Eventually i will get a new phone and i will call you when i am emotionally able to talk. It's nice to know that you miss me and are thinking about me. I am sorry that i am out of touch but for now its best that way.

The reference to having "no money for day to day things" while "Shane is traveling" stands out—clearly a hint for money.

Even retyping the lowercase i's irks me. If you scanned my entire *actual* email history, you probably wouldn't find a single i where there should be an I. Maybe I'm fixating on the sloppy grammar because it's distracting me from the immense pain I feel when reading this exchange—so much that having stopped to consider this has now led to actual crying.

* * *

My birthday at Harrah's sucked. Mr. Fox ordered a disgusting gift basket from room service—full of cheap processed foodstuffs and shitty chocolate and candy—plus balloons and a shitty bottle of red wine. I did not want any of it. The only thing worse than receiving no gift at all is receiving something that anyone who truly knew you would know you would *not* want. Mr. Fox knew me well in so many ways, but he either misfired on this one, or just didn't care. All I wanted was to be anywhere other than where I was. I didn't want to be reminded of my birthday, or anything about my real life.

Since I was already miserable, I ate some of the junk in the gift basket, just to compound the misery. We sat in the dark living room of the suite watching—not kidding—*Law & Order: Special Victims Unit.* How appropriate.

I'd made an exception that day to hang out in his room for a while. Normally I stayed in my own room, with the TV on, usually cable news, even while I slept. Anything to avoid being left with my own thoughts.

I had notebooks that I'd purchased somewhere along the way. One was filled with Spanish vocabulary—I'd been using an app to teach myself Spanish. Another was full of a random assortment of notes, mini essays, and lists—like a list of the people I'd most want to sit next to on a long flight. Aaron Sorkin was at the top; I'd just watched every episode of *The West Wing,* the show he wrote, and completely fell in love with it. I watched these shows, and many others, from a Netflix account Mr. Fox set up on the iPad.

Despite having online access, I never once Googled myself. Or the restaurant. I don't even remember being tempted. It was as if I'd completely shut that part of my life out—probably because my subconscious was terrified of what I'd find, of knowing what had happened. I was just... *living in the present moment.* Albeit, delusionally.

CHAPTER SEVENTY-ONE

EARLY 2016

LEAVING LAS VEGAS

I have no memories of Christmas or New Year's Eve, closing out 2015 and heading into 2016. I believe they were spent without any acknowledgment at Palace Station. It's strange to think of so much time passing, most of it a blank.

One of the few times reality broke through my dissociated stupor was a day in mid-February—the day my sister had a baby. Her first baby. Something she'd been wanting for so long. And I wasn't there, or anywhere near there.

I'm not sure how I found out. I think my mother texted Mr. Fox, and he told me. I remember he handed me a slip of paper with the phone number of the hospital room where she was. I sat on the floor of my hotel room, whichever one it was, leaning up against the wall, looking out the window. This was one of those moments when the fog briefly lifted. *What the fuck was I doing here?*

This moment of clarity cracked something open, and I cried and cried and cried. When it subsided enough that I was able to speak, I dialed the hospital number from my cell phone. The cell phone I had but rarely used, unless to text with Mr. Fox. It rang, but no one picked up. You'd think I would have just dialed my sister's cell phone, but I don't think I had it. The new phone was empty of all my contacts.

I put the phone down and started a new wave of crying. I don't remember what I was thinking, just that it hurt. I knew things were completely fucked up, but I couldn't comprehend *how* exactly.

I don't know what would have happened if my sister had picked up. In fact, I'm surprised Mr. Fox even gave me the number. I likely would have cried so hard I'd have not been able to speak. Probably she would have told me about her new baby boy, and then asked how I was and where I was, and I have no clue what I would have said. Probably just that I was fine. Everything was fine. I don't know.

Inevitably, the fog crept back in. I put it out of my mind and moved on. *Nothing is real.* Nothing made sense. I didn't know what was happening, and I didn't want to know. Fuck it all.

* * *

What was Mr. Fox's end goal? I have no idea. I feel queasy knowing *now* that he was getting money periodically from my mother. And from what I've read in my sent emails, it appears he was reaching out to a wealthy overseas friend of mine to send money to my mother, which my mother would then somehow send to Mr. Fox, maybe via cashier's checks, or who knows. What all of this was meant to be leading to I don't know. Maybe neither did he.

At some point early in 2016 we must have been running out of money, and no more was being sent. Mr. Fox came into my room one day and informed me I had to get more money. This was crushing. I'd figured out how to exist as a zombie. I'd done that. But now I had to interact with someone and *get money*? He told me it had to come from a specific person. Of course it was a really *good* person, someone who'd already loaned me a lot already. Maybe Mr. Fox figured that since this person was already in so deep, what was another $30,000?

If, reading this, you're thinking you can't possibly endure another round of me having to *get more money*—like you're so tired of reading about it, over and over—I feel you. But I didn't know how else to tell this story other than in its exhausting entirety. Maybe it at least conveys a sense of how draining it was for me. And guess what. At least this really *was* the last time.

This new task was what finally got us to leave Las Vegas. After a series of super-awkward text exchanges from my new number, this very good person agreed to give me the money. However, for some reason, it had to be in cash.

So we packed up and left Las Vegas. I don't remember how I felt about heading back east, or how long it took, or where we stopped along the way. No clue.

I have thin memory slices of being back in New York City and of how surreal it felt. Weirdest of all, I *still* didn't know whether Pure Food and Wine had closed, or if someone else had taken over, and it was still open. I didn't think about it much—it was easier to believe that reality had been fully suspended somehow. I was fully dissociated.

I don't remember what stories and lies I told this good person to convince him to give me the money, and I don't remember what we discussed or how I explained what was going on. Or how we met for a drink, with him handing me an envelope with $30,000 in cash, yet nothing about my restaurant came up.

After this person left, with the money in my bag, I texted Mr. Fox to come pick me up. As soon as I got in the car, he asked for the money, and I handed it over. We left the city and drove as far as Connecticut before stopping at a Marriott Residence Inn. We ended up staying for a while, not just a few days but more like a few weeks. As always, I didn't know why.

I passed my time in whatever obscure suburb we were in the usual way: playing iPad games and watching the news. I know it was early March by then because I remember being in this Connecticut hotel watching the coverage of Nancy Reagan's death, and according to Google, she died on March 6, 2016. My otherwise numbed emotions were briefly stirred by the stories of how deeply she and Ronald Regan had been in love, and the image of her draped across his coffin.

One day, Mr. Fox told me he'd be gone most of the day—fine with me. I preferred when he wasn't around. Later, he texted saying he'd be back soon with a surprise. Normally, when Mr. Fox said he had a surprise, it wasn't good. So when I heard the zip of his hotel key card unlocking the door, I was wholly unprepared for the spectacular thrill of Leon running into the room and jumping up on the foldout couch bed where I sat. Finally, Mr. Fox had delivered something I actually wanted. My heart cracked open again.

"Look who's here!" Mr. Fox said. "Thought you'd be happy, and we're almost done, baby. Almost there."

As always, I had no clue where *there* was, and what any of that meant, but having Leon back was the world's greatest comfort. Despite the unraveling of the rest of my life—the full extent of which I was still entirely unaware—I'm pretty sure I had a smile on my face the rest of that day, and far more often in the days to come.

With Leon along for the ride, we set off again. To where, I had no clue. I think we drove to New Orleans. I know we spent time at a Harrah's casino there. I'd never been to New Orleans before. But was Leon with us in New Orleans? I don't know. Maybe it had been on the way east? I genuinely don't remember. All I know is that by the end of April, we landed in Pigeon Forge, Tennessee—a town I've since heard aptly referred to as *Hillbilly Vegas*.

CHAPTER SEVENTY-TWO

APRIL—MAY 2016
PIGEON FORGE, TENNESSEE

Driving into Pigeon Forge ranks high among the strangest things I've ever experienced. That I was already in a semi-fugue state only made it more fantastical. As if now, with certainty, we really *were* entering another dimension.

The descent into this unusual town from the adjacent Smoky Mountains—along precarious, narrow, winding roads—felt like a roller coaster ride. The steep drops on the passenger side made me sit up straighter. Just the slightest turn of the wheel, and we'd be airborne for a harrowing few moments before tumbling down the mountainside, smashing through the trunks of towering hardwood trees along the way. Death didn't scare me; a snapped neck would be a mercifully quick end. But surviving in a mangled state *did*. So it was a relief when the slopes flattened, the woods thinned out, and my attention shifted to the man-made scenery. Motels and resorts began to appear, some in a style I could only describe as gingerbread house. Hansel and Gretel meets *Twin Peaks*. Cartoonish signs from another era enthusiastically advertised amenities like *Color TV!* or *Hot Tubs in Every Room!*

All of it felt like an opening act—as if priming visitors for the plunge ahead into the carnivalesque weirdness that is Pigeon Forge proper.

Finally, the first set of streetlights appeared, and I got my first look at the very colorful commercial town spread out ahead of us. As we drove, a two-story-tall bear on the left advertised Smoky's Pancake Cabin. On the right, a giant googly eyed cartoon peanut sat above a storefront next to all-caps bubble-lettered signage: *TRY MY NUTS!*

A massive dragon head, mouth open wide, beside a turquoise blue waterfall... *mini golf*, I quickly figured out. Immediately followed by *another* mini golf establishment, this time more obvious by the small-planet-sized golf ball sitting atop a purple candy castle at the entrance. Go-carts were next, and then a maroon-painted two-story wood house with a roof jutting out over the first story like a saloon, except on that roof stood three life-sized bears and a sign: *Jesus Saves.*

Then a red barn: the Frizzle Chicken Farmhouse Cafe, with cartoonish farm animals the size of minivans affixed to the roof. Then another barn: the Comedy Barn, advertising its *family variety show*. More pancake restaurants.

There was so much to see, I couldn't even stop to wonder how it was possible I'd never heard of this town. *LIVE... BABY... GOATS...* flashed along a ticker tape-style neon sign on a place named Goats On The Roof.

Seventies hippy-style sky-blue neon bubble lettering under a smiley-faced sun announced the Mellow Mushroom pizza bakery, like a clue that half the town was tripping on LSD. For the zealously religious contingent, there were places like the Great Spirit Biblical Times Dinner Theater.

It went on and on, with an upside-down building called Wonderworks, a four-story-tall King Kong towering over the Hollywood Wax Museum, a hotel-sized model of the sinking *Titanic* followed by Paula Deen's Lumberjack Feud restaurant. All along and in between these attractions were gift shops, hat shops, vape shops, diners, more mini golf, and various hotels trying to outdo one another with waterslides and hot tubs.

* * *

At the far end of this strip, we pulled into a relatively tame-looking Fairfield Inn, owned by Marriott, where, as it turned out, we stayed for more than a month.

Thankfully, I had my own room—for Leon and me. But as always, our rooms were connected by a door. I had to knock, of course, to enter his, while he would just burst into mine—Kramer style—without warning. Sometimes he wanted Leon to hang out with him in his room, which bugged the shit out of me. I did what I could to avoid it. Mr. Fox didn't make me do sex things with him in Tennessee, I'm nearly certain. He must have known this was all coming to an end. And if he knew it was, he wouldn't want me angry at him. I'd be less likely to "throw him under the bus," as he put it then, if those darker memories weren't quite so recent.

I went down to the lobby every morning for the free breakfast, bringing as much back up as I could without looking like a hoarder. Scrambled eggs to mix into Leon's food. Raisin Bran, which I ate with almond milk I kept in the mini fridge. Apples. Bananas.

Mr. Fox sent me to get his food, usually at Chipotle, across the street. It had just opened during the first week we arrived, and I quickly became a regular. I made conversation with the guys working there—most of them young, some cute. One of them, Dustin, was extra friendly with me. Sometimes we chatted outside the store.

I was vague about my background and reasons for being in Pigeon Forge, steering the conversation to general topics or asking him questions instead. I didn't like Dustin romantically, but it felt comforting to have a friend—someone who appeared to care, even if I couldn't tell him what was wrong. But I did tell him I was afraid of my husband finding out that we were talking, even just as friends. I gave Dustin my cell phone number but warned him to *never, ever* call me, and that if we were texting, I might drop off mid-conversation.

That must have been why I put a passcode on that iPhone, which I now can't remember. I still have that phone—the one I used for the entire road trip—but, gun to my head, I have no clue what the passcode is.

I passed the time in Pigeon Forge much like I had in Vegas—sometimes lying out by the pool, reading books I'd bought at Goodwill, not bothering with sunscreen because *nothing is real.* A few times Mr. Fox took me to play mini golf, which was oddly fun. Everything about being in that town felt extra surreal. But at least I had Leon with me. I could take him for long walks. I could focus on *him*.

Then one day—one that seemed no different from the others—Mr. Fox came into my room and said, ominously, "Baby, there's going to be one more gut shot." I didn't know what he meant. I worried he meant I was going to have to get more money.

Instead, a few hours later, I heard the commotion in the hall and opened the door to see police officers, and the detective I'd come to know as Ray Brown.

Arrested.

CHAPTER SEVENTY-THREE

SPRING 2016
NEW YORK CITY

Back in New York, out on bail, I was finally away from Mr. Fox. But a few more of his "gut punches" remained, as if he'd set them up in advance for future delivery.

One was the email. If you recall from Part Three, I learned that while Mr. Fox had taken control of my email for most of a year, he'd scrubbed all emails between us—except for just one. One email I'd never seen before.

If I needed evidence that he wasn't delusional but knew exactly what he was doing, here it was. The single email left behind, clearly meant for authorities to find:

```
July 26, 2015

From: Mr. Fox

To: Me

The check you gave me bounced. I've given you all my money.
I've done everything you asked of me. I'm done with your
crazy bullshit. I'm sorry about your business but you did
```

```
that to yourself. I begged you to listen to reason and to be
more responsible. You refused to listen. I tried and tried
and tried to help you and do as you asked. Look at shit
now. I'm over it. You want help then you agree to stop being
abusive. Stop with all the name calling and the beatings.
I'll try and help you the best I can but I want nothing to do
with your shit or business. I don't trust you when it comes
to that. I think you'll do and say anything to try and save
that business. You want help with a fresh start I'm happy to
help. But no more bullshit.
```

He wrote that email back in July, on the road *to* Vegas—only the first month of the road trip. He had to have known it was all likely to come apart, and when it did, he'd need to cover his tracks.

I know I'm stating the obvious, but it feels like Mr. Fox is evil. That I was duped by him into destroying myself and my business is the greatest humiliation of my life. That he hurt Nazim, too, is awful—and it feels like it was my fault, since Mr. Fox was in New York because of me. That he terrorized my mother, wiped her clean of her own funds—plus more she borrowed—makes me want to die. That he convinced me to borrow from my friends, from good people, only to lose their money too? That's all on me now. And it feels like too much to bear.

That email was confirmation that he knew what he was doing, that he had always planned to leave me wedged under the bus. That email also felt like someone delivering an unnecessary cruelty before pulling the trigger. You'd already decided to kill me—did you really need to spit in my face one last time?

It would have been easier to believe he was delusional.

* * *

Immediately after seeing that email, I found worse. Again, it was my first time back in my email account in nearly a year. I opened the Sent folder and saw email after email—messages written as me, from my account, but *actually* authored by Mr. Fox.

He'd written to several people—clearly trying to mimic language I'd use—asking, sometimes pleading, for money. In some of these conversations, the recipient asked me to call, which of course wasn't going to happen. He made lame excuses for why I couldn't call, then mostly abandoned those threads. He also replied to a long, heartfelt email from my younger half brother—who had written me a sweet message full of concern. And Mr. Fox, that fat evil fuck, wrote back *as me* with a short, cold reply. My little brother, all that time, had to think that I'd authored that shitty, dismissive reply.

Then there were emails to Jeffrey. Over and over, Mr. Fox, from my email, sent a bunch of truly unhinged messages, making bizarre excuses for why I apparently couldn't call him. Reading them was both nauseating and heartbreaking. It appeared Jeffrey had *still* been trying to help, yet only got replies that sounded pathetic and deranged. This gutted me.

The other emails that pained me most were ones he wrote to Alec Baldwin. Again, written as me. The only iota of consolation is that in one of Alec's replies, he clearly suspected something was *off*, asking, "*Are you taking a lot of pills these days?*" So maybe he sensed it wasn't me.

* * *

Then more gut punches.

I set about looking for my belongings. As you may recall, when Mr. Fox made me move out of my Twenty-First Street apartment to the dark place on Twenty-Eighth Street, he made Nazim pack up my stuff and put it in storage. It took many hours of searching, but I finally tracked down the facility that he'd used. A gruff man answered my call. "Yes," he confirmed, clicking away on his keyboard. "Your names are in the system."

I held my breath, waiting.

"Yup," he said, matter-of-factly. "That one's gone. Auctioned off in... let's see here... November it was."

I felt my stomach drop. The last paid bill was June of the prior year. They sent notices. No one responded. So they sold everything. Furniture. Books. Dishes. Old photos. Personal files. Pieces of my past. Parts of me. All gone.

In the context of all the money Mr. Fox blew though, a storage bill wasn't much. Even if he didn't want to pay it, he could have told my mother, or someone, just to keep it paid. Something. Anything.

I was obviously aware Mr. Fox gave zero shits about me, so this was just another blow. But on another level. As if my home was on fire and he could have easily called the fire department to come save it, but instead he just sat there, eating a sandwich, watching it burn. It was that level of not giving a shit.

* * *

Next, I tracked down the landlady of the Twenty-Eighth Street apartment, to see what happened to all my things that had been left behind there. Thankfully, she'd saved some of it, but not all of it. She'd moved our things from the apartment into a storage facility. It was a small unit, so not everything fit. She told me she *threw the rest away*.

One very hot Saturday soon thereafter, my father picked me up in Brooklyn, and we drove to the Manhattan Mini Storage in Chelsea. I carried the boxes from the storage facility to the car. My dad was seventy-eight years old at the time, and I didn't want him picking up heavy boxes, so I let him figure out how to Tetris-fit all the boxes into his Prius.

If you're wondering what happened to my Honda, Mr. Fox made me sell it just before we left New York. I never considered until now why he made me do that, only to convince his friend Carlos to let us take *his* car. Had we driven off in my Honda, the license plates would have identified us along the way. *He knew.* He was always ten steps ahead, at least in ways that served him.

If you're wondering what happened to my old cat, Sydney, Mr. Fox had also made me *get rid* of her, in a way. The truth is, it was her time. She was incredibly old, blind, and tragically neglected. It pains me—even haunts me—that her quality of life was so crappy for her final years. And worse, that it was Mr. Fox who took her to the vet to be ushered out of this realm. At the very least, I know it actually happened. That he didn't just dump her somewhere to save the vet costs. We'd taken her to my mom's in New Hampshire so she could spend her last days there, but she was so old and sick that Mr. Fox said it was time. He did, at least, return with her body so she could be buried next to her brother, Dallas, whom I'd buried there myself years earlier.

Back in Brooklyn, I spent a few days going through the boxes of things recovered from the Twenty-Eighth Street apartment. My father went home, and my sister and her family were away for the long Memorial Day weekend, so I was alone in the house. In one of the boxes, I found an empty journal—the one I'd bought in Venice, Italy, with a drawing of a forlorn-looking rabbit on the cover. There'd been something about that image I loved. I knew I hadn't written in it yet; it was one of those journals that's so nice you may never write in it. I turned it over in my hands. Then, for some reason, I flipped it opened it, to a page in the middle.

There was something written on the bottom of *that page*. I remember thinking, *What the fuck?*

I was stunned. It was Mr. Fox's handwriting. When had he written in this journal? On this *one* page? And why did the journal just open to *that very page*? I stared down at it mutely. Beneath two overlapping hearts—his signature when he wrote notes to me—he'd written:

I'm sorry. I always loved you.

I flipped through the rest of the journal. Every other page was blank.

I felt ice creeping up my spine. Even locked away, he was still getting into my head. Momentarily, I had the eerie, familiar sense I was being watched. When had he done that? It was, of course, some time before he took me away. But had he known then what was coming? *Why* had he written that?

It's things like this that keep me, still, with a toe in an *Alice in Wonderland* surreal existence. Like even after our separation, it wasn't over. He left crumbs, telling me, *I can still fuck with your mind.*

And it did fuck with my mind. How much did he know ahead of time? What *was* the plan—if there was one? Did he succeed or fail?

I get to live with this creepy fucking mystery, even though there probably *is no* answer, no narrative to make it all make sense. Just a bunch of random clues making me think there's a puzzle to solve, when none of it leads anywhere, because there is nowhere for it to lead.

What did he want from me?

I'll never know.

CHAPTER SEVENTY-FOUR

THE AFTERMATH

The prosecutor in my case was never moved by any of the evidence. At least not in my favor. At the time, *coercive control* was a brand-new term, mostly unheard of. #MeToo—which later ignited a deeper conversation around abuse—didn't happen until late 2017. Keith Raniere, leader of the NXIVM cult, wasn't arrested until 2018. After a trial, he was convicted in 2019, then sentenced in 2020—to 120 years in prison (yes, *120 years*; no typo there). That case shined a long-overdue spotlight on psychological abuse, showing how intelligent, well-intentioned people can be fooled by skilled sociopaths. When my case was in the system, there was no conversation about this kind of coercion, no widespread recognition of malignant narcissism, or discussion of cult psychology. No one handling my case knew what to make of it. Going to trial was never even on the table. It was simply assumed I would plead guilty. Why? It just was. That's how things often work.

In May of 2017, I pled guilty to most of the charges against me. I think. I can never remember what they were, specifically. Every time I'm asked in any official capacity, I have to go look them up, only to promptly forget them again. What I do remember is standing in the courtroom, under oath, pleading guilty. While some things were technically true, the statements implying my intentions were not. I do *not* like to lie. Yet sometimes, one has no choice. That's how the system operates. I remember the prosecutor staring at me with a big smile on her face.

When it came time for my sentencing, the judge at least acknowledged that there was plenty of evidence that I had "tried to run my business in good faith." His saying that made all the difference for me. As long as he knew. Still, he sentenced me to four months. At least I was given a few weeks to prepare before I had to serve it.

* * *

Even now people sometimes ask me if Mr. Fox is still in jail. *Still in jail?* Lol.

No. Mr. Fox was released—free to go, clean slate—*before* I even began my own four-month sentence back at Rikers. He was never charged or prosecuted for what he did to me, my mother, to Nazim, or who knows how many others. Instead, he was only charged with the same crimes as me—as if we were *co-conspirators*. He was sentenced to one year, and, having already served that time while I was out on bail, he walked free in May of 2017.

On June 21, 2017—the summer solstice—I went to serve my sentence. Yes, I spoke to Mr. Fox in the interim. And even after I was released. *I know.* That seems royally fucked up. I had my reasons and wrote about them later—in essays on my website—when I felt forced to publicly explain myself. In March 2022, a docuseries about this story was released on Netflix, titled *Bad Vegan*. I'd sat for interviews, turned over vast quantities of information, and even helped them arrange interviews with former employees and others. I believed the goal was truth. But ultimately, the show was misleading—particularly at the end. The filmmakers altered and misplaced a segment of a recorded phone call—one I'd made *for* the docuseries—between Mr. Fox and me. The edit convinced many viewers I'd been *in on it* all along.

Despite how that docuseries turned out, one might think, *Well, at least she must have made a bunch of money, enough to finally get out from under all the debts!*

No, I did not.

As part of our sentences, Mr. Fox and I were held *jointly liable* for much of the financial damages—including over $800,000 to investors who'd contributed to the reopening in 2015. Never mind that the majority of that money was spent on the reopening. We were also liable for the unpaid wages of the employees after my disappearance—just over $65,000. Of everything owed, that was the smallest amount, but it weighed on me the most. I wanted them paid. I expressed this to the filmmakers early on. And so, I was paid a $75,000 fee—which went directly to repay the employees, with the balance going toward another loan I owed.

Also, *jointly liable* doesn't mean Mr. Fox and I each owe half; it means we're both liable. You might be thinking, *Shouldn't Mr. Fox have to pay it all?* If only. Even if ordered to pay, he never would. Or if by some miracle he did, it would likely be stolen from someone else. So effectively, it's all on me.

And the taxes. All that unpaid sales tax, plus interest and penalties, is on me alone too. And beyond the court judgments, all those amounts I borrowed from Dylan and so many others. What Jeffrey was owed. What my mom lost. What I cost my father in legal fees. That's on me. I carry that. The total is so big it's hard to comprehend. Even if I'm not legally obligated to pay all of it, the weight is moral, and it's heavy.

So yes, it stung when I realized the filmmakers had not only betrayed me but that they had profited so much from the Netflix deal—more than enough to wipe out all my debts in full and then some.

* * *

The aftermath was more than just financial.

Reconnecting with people in the outside world was often awkward, and painful. No one knew what had actually happened beyond what had been printed in the tabloids. And so there were now two versions of me: the real, interior me, and the distorted public version of me. I had to learn how to navigate this private-public split. And to this day, I still do. Maybe I always will.

Most people in my life knew I was no criminal, but they were at a loss to explain how any of it happened. Every encounter was charged with unspoken questions and uncomfortable energy. It didn't matter how well I knew someone. Every time I was reacquainted with anyone I'd known, or anyone who had known *of* me, or anyone who'd simply read what had happened or knew secondhand (basically, everyone except total strangers), it was awkward.

People had theories about my motives—for example, that I'd done it "for love." Yeah, no. Definitely *no* on that. Or that my business must have been failing, so I'd gone on a wild gambling bender to try to make millions. That didn't make sense either, and it wounded my pride, since the restaurant and brand had been thriving before Mr. Fox came along.

Most people were kind and sympathetic, but it was still awkward. People assumed I wouldn't want to talk about it, but I didn't mind their questions. Direct questions were less painful than small talk, because at least then we weren't pretending. What *did* hurt was one statement in particular. A lot of people—usually lowering their pitch and leaning in, as if sharing a secret—said some variation of: *I just want you to know, I don't judge you at all.* I know it was well intentioned. Maybe they just meant they didn't judge me for having had *bad judgment*, or for being naive, gullible, or *stupid*, even. But I always took it to mean they didn't judge me for having done bad things. And unfortunately, from the outside, it mostly looked like I had. I couldn't blame anyone for thinking that. Still, hearing it always felt like a body blow.

If only they knew what really happened. If only I could explain it.

*　*　*

It's safe to assume I came out of all of that with a lot to work through. A lot of *triggers*. And the strange existence of knowing that most people had very little idea of what really happened, or how. Only those who've been through something similar understand. We understand each other. We are similar, not just because a similar thing happened, but because we share certain traits that make this sort of situation more likely. More on that in another place, another book.

I've learned a lot since this happened. Including the fact that the characteristics that make us especially vulnerable to the Mr. Foxes of the world are, generally, positive ones. Yet I still don't quite know how to characterize all of this. Was I a victim?

Isn't every one of us responsible for what happens in our life? (Putting aside freak accidents, climate disasters, global pandemics, etc.) Was this whole story something I allowed to happen? Of course I did. But of course, I also didn't see what was *really* happening.

Did I subconsciously attract it into my life, as some would suggest, because of deeply repressed wounds that needed to get worked out? Did I effectively torch my own life because... *why?* Why in a way that others were hurt too? Did the child in me carry so much shame that I needed to bring it all to the surface, to plunge myself into a deep sea of public humiliation?

I've spent a lot time working through these questions, mostly alone.

What's strange is that, in many ways, I feel like I've woken up. I don't think it's what Mr. Fox meant by *waking up*, but who will ever know what he meant? I'm letting go of caring what he meant.

Wherever he is, I could hate him. But hating him isn't worth it, so I let that go too.

The most important work is forgiving myself.

And rebuilding, however possible.

CHAPTER SEVENTY-FIVE

"SHE IS ODDLY FRAGILE"

Alec Baldwin and Mr. Fox were never more than just Twitter acquaintances, but they had exchanged private direct messages—which I discovered only years later. Long after my case was over, I sat in a trance one day, scrolling through a file of digital images extracted from Mr. Fox's phone. The DA's office had turned them over as part of their forensic discovery.

Mr. Fox had taken screenshots of many things, including some of his DM conversations with Alec. One stood out, leaving me with a kind of ominous pang. In a private message to Mr. Fox, dated March 18, 2013, Alec wrote, *She is oddly fragile. I never could quite figure out why.*

I'd never thought of myself as fragile.

I wasn't fragile when I stood in the courtroom, a year after getting out on bail, and pled guilty to crimes I never intended to commit. I didn't cry when I learned I was sentenced to four months in jail.

I wasn't fragile when I went to serve out that sentence back at Rikers, in a dorm of up to fifty women, many of whom *had* committed crimes—some violent.

But now, after years of working on this book and processing what happened, I sometimes feel fragile as fuck. In 2018, the year after my incarceration, living back in my Harlem apartment with Leon, someone new came into my life, offering to help. I had no money to take, so my guard was down. I stepped into another mind-bending mess—one that led me back to court, to fleeing New York City, and to yet more public humiliation. Story for another time.

I got through that, too, but not unharmed. What doesn't kill you makes you stronger, as one often hears. But sometimes, it can simultaneously make you more fragile. If that makes any sense.

* * *

I'm so grateful to have completed this book. Many times throughout the process—even just during editing—it felt like more than I could handle. At every phase, I didn't want to step back into the darkness. I didn't want to feel waves of shame, reliving so many parts of this story I'd rather forget. Poring over old materials, rereading reams of Gchats, I sometimes faced an avalanche of resistance. I wanted to slide out of my skin, crawl up the wall, and bang my head, wailing and puking at the same time, until I passed out. Something like that is how I felt so much of the time while working on this book.

In those moments I felt fragile. Still, I kept writing. And writing.

The book I originally wrote was far longer than what you've read here. So much was cut to make it a more digestible read. And still, it's long.

If you made it this far, thank you. Truly. Thank you for reading my story.

It means everything to me.

And I hope, somehow, it helps.

ACKNOWLEDGMENTS

This will be difficult to keep short. First, thank you to the talented, kind people at Scribe Media, who shepherded me through independent publishing with professionalism and care—including Tashan Mehta, whose editorial insight and sensitivity helped shape my story.

I'm afraid to start listing names because... where would I stop? Two are dear friends who carried me through the final years of working on this book: Lindsay Houck and Richard Katz. They've never met. But I can't find words for how much their encouragement has meant to me, and still does. Harper, thank you, too.

So many people helped by reading early, messy drafts and giving me feedback: Jesse Sommer, John Boyer, David Muls, Dee Worman, Tom Schaller, Ron Levine, Ben Ortlip, Ella Alexander, Howard Mittelmark, Michaele Weissman, and Bonnie Crocker, to name a few. Then there are those who supported me in other ways: Mary Gardner, Toto Miranda, Porochista Khakpour, David Albrecht, Michael McCarthy, Lorna Brett, Chris Dempsey, Gareb Shamus, Randy Sarf, Gary Delgado, Janine Henkel, Andy Arons, Oberon Sinclair, Gerard McLean, Nyi Nyi Aung, Alma Kim, Ryan Heil, Trish Law, Michelle Muller, Steve Grillo, Nicky Dawda, and Peter Lenkov.

To those named or unnamed in this story who believed in me enough to help: *thank you for believing in me.*

With all my heart, I love the people who worked at, or were part of, Pure Food and Wine and One Lucky Duck. Thank you to everyone who wrote letters to the judge before I pled guilty, and to all who wrote me letters—or sent books—while I was at Rikers. To those who've lived through similar nightmares, for telling your stories and continuing to speak out, including Mark Vicente, Sarah Edmondson, and Anthony Ames. To James Nelson, David Bahnsen, and most especially Jon Knautz, for making it possible to get the useful and honest version of this story in a *new* docuseries.

Thank you to my family for things I don't know how to articulate, including being there to pick me up at my lowest.

To every person who sent me prayers and messages of encouragement through DMs, emails, and otherwise, thank you. To everyone for whom my story resonated because you've endured something similar, I'm with you. To the kind people who stuck it out in my Patreon group, even when my personal ramblings dwindled, and to everyone who preordered this book, including the very first, Steven Tracy, thank you.

Thank you to Elsie, the woman in Harlem who colored my hair just before I went to Rikers and refused payment. To Scott Wagner, then-CEO of GoDaddy, who recovered the OneLuckyDuck.com URL for me when I thought I'd lost it. Anthony Caruana, for having my back. Seth Godin, for being a mentor in the early days of One Lucky Duck, and more recently, even when the advice was what I didn't want to hear. Thank you to friends, colleagues, and neighbors, past and present. And to Mike Barnes, a most stellar human.

By the time these words go to print, I'll likely think of people I wish I'd added. Borrowing an idea from my friend Steve Grillo, who beat me to publication with his own memoir, if you don't see your name but think you should have (or wish you had), please forgive me, and write it in here: _____. I'm grateful to you too.

Thank you, Nigel, for being my advisor and supporter through the copyediting process, and for helping me navigate life with warmth, wisdom, and humanity.

I'm eternally, wordlessly, grateful to Leon, my companion through it all, whose eyes I stared into when I needed to feel it would all, somehow, be okay. The same eyes I stared into as he passed—willing him to know how much I loved him—on July 4, 2024. Leon, you are the trees, the clouds, the moon, and the sky.

Finally, to *you*. Thank you for buying my book, for reading my words. I love you all.

Note: If my story resonated with you, and you think it might help someone else, sharing it would mean the world to me. Thank you.

www.ingramcontent.com/pod-product-compliance
Lightning Source LLC
Chambersburg PA
CBHW060509080526
44586CB00012B/442